NEW SUNDAY AND HOLY DAY LITURGIES

YEAR C

D0943222

Flor McCarthy is a Salesian priest who has worked as a catechist in second level schools and has extensive parish experience in Ireland and the USA. His other books include *Funeral Liturgies* and *Wedding Liturgies*.

Information about the artists whose work is featured appears on page 6.

New
Sunday and Holy Day
Liturgies

YEAR C

Flor McCarthy

DOMINICAN PUBLICATIONS

First published (2000) by
Dominican Publications
42 Parnell Square
Dublin 1

ISBN 1-871552-73-7

British Library Cataloguing in Publications Data.
A catalogue record for this book is available
from the British Library.

Reprint: September 2002

Cover design by David Cooke

Printed in Ireland by
Betaprint, Dublin.

Contents

Artists Featured

Rachel Wroe Sawko is a painter who also designs windows in stained and fibreglass. Her 'Annunciation' (p. 9) is a painting in acrylic on board. A full-colour reproduction is available from Dominican Publications.

Imogen Stuart is an Irish sculptor. Her 'Madonna and Child' (p. 33) can be seen in the Lady Chapel of Christ Church Cathedral, Dublin.

Benedict Tutty, O.S.B., was a monk of Glenstal and a noted sculptor; his 'Good Samaritan' (p. 175) was commissioned for *Doctrine and Life*, vol. 12, no. 12, December 1962, where it was first published.

Paddy McElroy is a Dublin-sculptor. His 'Resurrection' (p. 105) was commissioned for *Doctrine and Life*, vol. 11, no. 1, January 1961, where it was first published.

Phyllis Burke is a Dublin painter and stained-glass artist. Her 'Eucharistic Symbols' (p. 163) was was first published in *Doctrine and Life*, vol. 12, no. 5, May 1962.

Patrick Pye is a painter, etcher and stained-glass artist. His etching 'Jesus Takes His Cross' is on page 67, and his drawing 'Jesus' Farewell to His Mother' is on page 363.

Introduction

Fifteen years have passed since the original *Sunday & Holy Day Liturgies* came out. Much to my surprise they proved very popular. Since then I have accumulated a lot of new material. The new series gives me the opportunity to share this material with others.

Now there are three homilies for each occasion, and sometimes additional material besides. The vast bulk of this material is new. Wherever old material is retained, I have tried to improve it. In general, the homilies are shorter and more focused. And once again I rely heavily on stories.

The homilies must not be regarded as the complete thing. They are put forward as approximations in the hope that the user will take them up, adapt them, and make them his/her own.

But don't turn to this book just for the homily. Every part of a liturgy should speak. For this reason I have put a lot of work into the Introduction to the Mass, the Key to the Readings, the Prayer of the Faithful, and the Reflection. The main thing here is to be brief and to the point. We must guard against turning the Mass into a series of mini homilies.

I have added a brief Scripture Note which highlights the theme of the readings. If no mention is made of the Second Reading it means that I consider what is said in the Key to the Readings to be sufficient. In compiling these notes I am indebted to the works of Wilfrid Harrington and the late Raymond Brown.

My thanks to Frs Austin Flannery and Bernard Treacy and to all the staff at Dominican Publications for their help.

Presiding at the Eucharist

A brief word about presiding at the Eucharist. Its importance cannot be exaggerated. The genuine and full participation of the people depends to a frightening degree on how the presider does his job. Sadly, many priests do it very badly. To all priests I would say: get hold of a book that tells you how to do it. Then get someone to monitor your performance. Meanwhile, the following few points, if observed, would make a difference.

Remember that you are celebrating the Eucharist *with* the people rather than *for* them. Therefore, try be conscious of the congregation at all times. You are to help the congregation to get an experience of being the Church.

With regard to the prayers that are proper to the celebrant, pray them slowly and clearly. Where the congregation are involved with you (e.g. *Gloria*), set the pace and try to keep the congregation together.

Remember that you are not *saying* prayers, but *praying*. The prayers (especially the Eucharist Prayer) should be prayed with passion, otherwise no one will listen.

Look at the people when addressing them, and wait for them to finish their response before going on to the next thing.

In all the gestures that you make, try to be conscious of what each gesture means and make it fully and deliberately. Avoid minimalism, e.g. washing the finger nails instead of washing the hands at the Offertory.

Try to make each gesture in such a way that all feel included.

Have the sacramentary and the lectionary marked in advance.

Don't usurp the functions of the other ministers.

Vary the introduction to the Mass, to the Lord's Prayer, and so on. It's deadly when the same introduction is used again and again. When variety is introduced an enrichment results.

Don't be afraid to use some of the alternative Eucharistic Prayers.

ADVENT

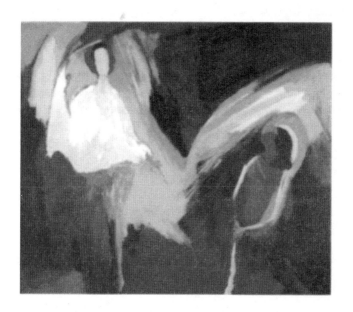

The Annunciation

RACHEL WROE SAWKO

First Sunday of Advent

INTRODUCTION AND CONFITEOR

Advent focuses our attention on the coming of Christ. We live between two comings of Christ – his first coming in humility and weakness at Bethlehem, and his second coming in majesty and power at the end of time. St Paul says that with each passing year 'our salvation is nearer than when we first believed.' Let us reflect for a moment on how much we need the Lord's salvation in our lives and in the world. [Pause]

Lord Jesus, you show your paths to those who stray. Lord, have mercy.
You guide the humble in the right path. Christ, have mercy.
Those who hope in you will not be disappointed. Lord, have mercy.

HEADINGS FOR READINGS

First Reading (Jer 33:14-16). The prophet assures the people that God will send the promised one, the Messiah.

Second Reading (1 Thess 3:12-4:2). Paul prays that the Lord may deepen the love the Thessalonians have for each other, and thus prepare them for the second coming of Christ.

Gospel (Lk 21:25-28,34-36). In language borrowed from the Old Testament, Luke describes the second coming of Christ. Christians should prepare for it with confidence, vigilance and prayer.

SCRIPTURE NOTE

The purpose of Advent is to help us prepare for Christmas. One can't understand the message of Christmas unless we are familiar with at least the broad outlines of the history of salvation.

The Advent liturgy relives in a microcosmic way the history of Israel, viewing it through the eyes of Christian faith. It shows that all of that history was pointing and leading towards Jesus. He was the one who fulfilled the messianic prophecies.

Advent takes us back in time so that we may appreciate the greatness of what we are heirs to. We are the heirs to the promises God made to the prophets. Advent helps us to appreciate the great blessings God has given us in Christ.

Today's First Reading points to the first coming of Christ. It says that the Messiah will be descended from the stock of David, and his reign will be marked by wisdom, justice and integrity.

The Gospel deals with the Second Coming of Christ. The early Christians believed that the Second Coming was near, and would be preceded by cosmic signs. The disciples are urged to await the Lord's coming with confidence, vigilance and prayer.

How to prepare for the Second Coming of Christ is also the topic of the Second Reading.

HOMILY 1   **Setting out again**

This Sunday each year the Church invites us to embark on a great journey – the journey of the Liturgical Year.

When we start the liturgical year, we are setting out to follow in the footsteps of Christ. In the course of the year, the whole of his life and teaching will pass before us. We will re-visit all the mysteries of his time on earth: from his expectation (that is what Advent is about), to his birth, his life, death, resurrection, ascension into heaven, and his sending of the Holy Spirit.

In the course of the year we will relive his whole story. But we have heard the story many times. Hence, there is a danger that we may see it as old and stale. We must try and see it as new and present and alive. It's not like playing an old video. The celebration of each feast brings back the event in its original clarity and vitality, never allowing it to grow cold and lifeless or fade into oblivion.

Besides, we are not spectators but actors in all of this. The mysteries of Christ's life are represented in such a way that we are drawn into them, and become participants in them. That makes it more demanding, but more enriching and exciting too. God is not just a God of the past, but of the present and the future.

Each year we ought to hear the Christ story better, understand it more deeply, and make it more our own. In hearing his story we ought to hear our own stories too. Our stories merge with his and are illuminated by it. His story enables us live our own story more fully and more joyfully.

Even though we've made the journey before, we must try to embark on it today as if for the very first time. This Sunday is a God-given chance to make a new beginning in our following of Christ.

Today the readings concentrate on the second coming of Christ and the end of the world. The reason for this is that before we commit ourselves to a journey we need to know the goal of the journey. So on this day the liturgy directs our eyes towards the goal of our own journey and that of the world, namely, the second coming of Christ.

The early Christians believed that the Second Coming was near, and would be preceded by cosmic signs. We are not so sure about that. All the false prophets speak of the end as a time of gloom and doom. But Jesus spoke of it as a day of liberation and salvation for his followers. The world is not heading for catastrophe or mere ending. God has a goal for the world. That goal is the coming of God's Kingdom in all its glory. Therefore, we should not be afraid of the Lord's coming, but await it with confidence, vigilance and prayer.

However, we should worry more about the end of our own individual world at death, which is certain, than about the end of the whole world, which is out of our hands.

HOMILY 2   **Evergreen followers**

The story is told (by John Shea, *The Legend of the Bells*) that when God was making the trees, he gave a gift to each species. But first he set up a contest to determine which gift would be most useful to whom. He told them, 'I want you to stay awake and keep watch over the earth for seven nights.'

The young trees were so excited to be trusted with such an important task that the first night they would have found it difficult not to stay awake. However, the second night was not so easy, and just before dawn a few fell asleep. On the third night the trees whispered among themselves in an effort to keep from dropping off. Even so, it proved too much for some of them. Still more fell asleep on the fourth night. By the time the seventh night arrived the only trees still awake were the cedar, the pine, the spruce, the fir, the holly, and the laurel.

'What wonderful endurance you have!' God exclaimed. 'You shall be given the gift of remaining green forever. You will be the guardians of the forest. Even in the seeming dead of winter, your brother and sister trees will find life protected in your branches.'

Ever since then all the trees and plants lose their leaves and sleep all winter, while the evergreens stay awake. This story illustrates the two major themes of Advent: wakefulness in the midst of sleepiness, and greenness in the midst of barrenness.

In the evergreen trees we find a note of gentle but resolute defiance. The surrounding world may be asleep or barren, but these continue to bear witness. They are sustained not so much by their own determination but by the power of God. They show us what our role as Christians is. It is to be awake among the sleeping, to be green in the midst of the barren. To bear witness to love in the midst of hate, to peace in the mist of conflict, and to light in the midst of darkness.

There are people in our society who need especially to stay awake. We think of those who do very responsible jobs, people such as pilots, drivers (how many accidents are caused by people falling asleep at the wheel), night nurses, parents with sick children, security people ...

But all of us are called to be wide-awake. Otherwise we will miss so much. Many sleepwalk through life. They have ears but they do not hear, eyes but do not see. All of us need to be awake because life is precious. And Christians most of all. It is not mere 'wakefulness' that is being urged but watchfulness.

The Lord asks us his followers to stay awake. To be watchful, faithful disciples. To be ever-green followers of him. We are his witnesses in the world. It is not too much to claim that we are to watch over the world. We are to witness to life and hope in the midst of disruption, upheaval, and death.

When we witness to truth, justice, love and peace we are witnessing to Jesus. The way to witness to truth is to live truthfully. The way to witness to justice is to act justly in all one's dealings with others. The way to witness to love is to act lovingly towards others. And the way to witness to peace is to live in peace with others.

In short, the most effective way to witness to Jesus is to live a Christian life. We need his strength to remain steadfast and faithful. His help becomes available to us especially through prayer.

HOMILY 3   **Waiting for the Lord**

We are living between two comings of Christ. The first coming is that of his coming two thousand years ago in Bethlehem. The second coming is that which we believe will happen at the end of time when Christ will come in glory. Meanwhile, where can we find Christ?

Once there was a very earnest Jewish student who had a burning desire to see the prophet Elijah, so he pleaded with his father to show him to him. His father replied, 'If you study the Torah with unceasing devotion I promise you that you'll become worthy of seeing Elijah.'

The son applied himself ardently to his studies, pouring over the sacred books by day and by night for several weeks. Then he went to his father and said, 'I've done what you asked me to do, but Elijah has failed to reveal himself to me.'

'Don't be so impatient,' his father replied. 'If you deserve it, he will surely reveal himself to you.'

One night the son was sitting at his desk when a poor man came in. He was dusty from the road and his clothes were torn. He had a rough face, and carried a heavy pack on his bent back. He was about to put the pack down, when the son said to him angrily, 'Don't do that. What do you think this place is – a tavern?'

'I'm very tired,' the wayfarer pleaded. 'Let me rest here awhile, then I'll look for lodgings.'

'No. You can't stay here. My father doesn't allow tramps to come and settle themselves here with their dusty packs.'

So the stranger sighed, lifted his pack to his shoulders, and went away. About an hour later the father came in. 'Well, have you seen the Prophet Elijah yet?' he asked.

'No, not yet,' the son replied.

'Did nobody come by here today?' the father asked.

'Yes,' the son answered. 'A tramp carrying a heavy pack was here a short while ago.'

'And did you make him welcome?'

'No, I didn't.'

'Why didn't you? Didn't you know it was Elijah? Now I'm afraid it's too late.'

From that day on the son took upon himself the sacred obligation to welcome the stranger, no matter how he looked, or what his station in life might be. And in doing so, he believed that he was in fact welcoming the prophet Elijah.

We can find Christ and serve him in our neighbour, especially in the neighbour who is poor and in need. But we have another task, namely, to make Christ 'visible' to doubters and non-believers. We are Christ's witnesses in the world.

The witness which the world finds most appealing is that of concern for people and of charity towards the poor, the weak, and those who suffer. The generosity underlying this attitude and these actions stands in marked contrast to human selfishness. It raises precise questions which lead to God and to the Gospel. A commitment to peace, to justice, to human rights, is a witness to the Gospel.

While each one has a part to play, what is most needed is the witness of the Christian community. Christians as a body must show forth Christ to the world by their love for one another, and by the hope and joy they radiate. (See Second Reading).

PRAYER OF THE FAITHFUL

President: Let us turn to the Lord in our needs, confident that he will give us his saving help.

Response: Lord, hear our prayer.

Reader(s): For the Church: that it may continue to work and pray for the coming of the Kingdom of God. [Pause] Let us pray to the Lord.

For political leaders: that they may work to create a world where justice and peace may reign. [Pause] Let us pray to the Lord.

For all those who live without faith and have nothing to hope for. [Pause] Let us pray to the Lord.

For all gathered here: that we who recognise Christ as our Saviour, may follow him in our lives. [Pause] Let us pray to the Lord.

For all our dead: that God may keep them in his care – those we have loved and those no one remembers. [Pause] Let us pray to the Lord.

For our own special needs. [Longer pause] Let us pray to the Lord.

President: Heavenly Father, in your mercy keep us free from sin and protect us from anxiety as we wait in joyful hope for the coming of our Saviour, Jesus Christ. We ask this through the same Christ our Lord.

REFLECTION **Life is fleeting**

The hill flowers fade,
but will bloom again next year.
But we never get back our youth.
Life is a fragile gift which we enjoy only briefly;
our life is like the warming of oneself in the sun.
We live in a flash of light; before we know it,
evening comes and night falls.
But the very fleetingness of life
makes it all the more precious.
Lord, may your gentle and sure light
guide us on the unfolding road,
so that we may walk with confidence
towards the light that never fades
and the life that never ends.

Second Sunday of Advent
PREPARING A WAY FOR THE LORD

INTRODUCTION AND CONFITEOR

In today's liturgy we hear the lonely but insistent voice of John the Baptist urging us to 'prepare a way for the Lord'. The Lord comes to us in the Eucharist. Let us pause to prepare ourselves to receive him. [Pause]

Lord Jesus, you take the blindness from our eyes, and the deafness from our ears. Lord, have mercy.

You take the darkness from our minds, and the weakness from our wills. Christ, have mercy.

You take the hardness from our hearts, and the lethargy from our souls. Lord, have mercy.

HEADINGS FOR READINGS

First Reading (Bar 5:1-9). Jerusalem is told to forget the sufferings of the past because God is going to bring back her exiled children to her.

Second Reading (Phil 1:3-6.8-11). Paul urges his fellow Christians to prepare for the second coming of Christ by pure and blameless lives.

Gospel (Lk 3:1-6). John the Baptist urges the people to prepare a way for the Lord through repentance.

SCRIPTURE NOTE

The prophet Baruch delivers a comforting message to Sion (First Reading). Her sorrows are ended and her children will be restored to her from exile. God will level a highway to facilitate their return, and bring about a great restoration. Even though the actual return from exile fell far short of the picture painted here, it did point the way to the messianic era.

This leads into the Gospel where Luke introduces us to the Messiah and his herald, John the Baptist. To underline the universality of salvation, Luke sets the event within the framework of world history. In the manner of an Old Testament prophet, John undertakes to prepare the people for the coming of the Saviour by calling them to repentance.

The Second Reading deals with the final coming of Christ. In his love for his fellow Christians, Paul urges them to prepare for the Second Coming by pure and blameless lives.

HOMILY 1   **God has not forgotten his people**

None of us like to be forgotten. Yet all of us have had some experience of what it's like, even if it was only on an occasion. It may be that we weren't invited to some event, or our contribution to some work wasn't recognised, or our birthday was forgotten. Here we're talking just about being omitted or passed over. But even that can be very painful, for it means to be ignored, to be treated as if you were of no significance.

There is another kind of forgetting. When people forget all about us, this is a far deeper and more painful thing. We feel that we don't matter any more. That no one cares about us. It's as if we didn't exist. We feel we've been not just forgotten but abandoned. It's worse if we are victims of false promises: 'I'll be in touch, I'll write, I'll call again,' and so on.

Once there was a wonderful priest who was admired and loved by his fellow priests and by the parishioners of the parishes he had served. However, this fine priest developed a serious medical condition which forced him to retired from active ministry and enter a nursing home. He spent the rest of his life there, confined to a wheelchair.

At first he had a stream of visitors. But as the years went by, the stream was reduced to a trickle, and in time even that dried up. Now he was on his own. Not a card, letter, or phone-call. Absolutely nothing. Just a great silence, and a great emptiness. He found it very painful, especially in view of the fact that he had given so much to others.

Then one day he received a visit from a priest who had been a classmate of his. He was delighted to see him, and they talked for a long time. But then at a certain point, he turned to his visitor and said, 'Do you think anyone remembers me?' I don't know what reply the visitor gave him. What reply could he give?

No, it's not nice to be forgotten. It is extremely painful. We may feel like that about God too. Something bad may have happened to us, so we think, 'God has forgotten me.' This leads to the feeling that God doesn't care about us, that he doesn't love us any more.

That's how God's people felt at the time the prophet Baruch was writing (second century BC). Their kingdom had fallen. The holy city, Jerusalem, had been destroyed. The beautiful temple had been reduced to rubble. Their sons and daughters had been taken into exile. So they asked themselves: 'Where is God? What has become of his promises?' And they concluded that God had forgotten them.

But the prophet assured them that God had not forgotten them. He told them that their sorrows would soon end. God would bring their sons and daughters back from exile. He would level out a highway to facilitate their return. And there would be a great restoration. So the people took heart. The exiles did indeed come back. However, God's promise was not completely fulfilled until the coming of Jesus.

And we too can take heart. Even though we may forget God, God does not forget us. Advent reminds us of the wonderful promises God made to us, and shows how they are fulfilled in Jesus. The great sign we have that God loves us is the fact that he sent his Son to us. John the Baptist was the one who announced the good news of his coming.

No, God has not forgotten us. God remembers us. Even if everyone else were to forget us, God will not forget us. It's lovely to be remembered, even if only in a small way. It's a sign that someone cares about us. God cares about us. We matter to him, because we are his precious daughters and sons.

Since we like to be remembered by others, we have a duty also to remember others, especially those who have been good to us, and who have sacrificed themselves for us. Christmas is a great time for remembering people. One small way we can do it is through a simple card with a few words that come from the heart.

HOMILY 2   **Prepare a way for the Lord**

There was a famous preacher who Sunday after Sunday faced a large, attentive congregation. One Sunday as he approached the pulpit the words of the Gospel were ringing in his ears: 'Prepare a way for the Lord, make his paths straight.' A thought suddenly struck him: It's not the Lord's paths that need to be straightened out but ours.

From the pulpit he looked into the expectant faces of the men and women before him, and wondered what these words might mean for them. What were the things that needed to be straightened out in their lives? He realised that only they could answer that. Nevertheless, there was one area he felt qualified to speak about - their often twisted and tangled relationships.

He had known these people for a long time. They had come to him for help and guidance with their problems. He knew the petty spites that embittered their hearts, the animosities that set neighbour against neighbour, the silly quarrels that were kept alive, the jealousies and misunderstandings, the stubborn pride.

He decided to address a message to those bitter, unbending ones who refused to forgive and forget. He would impress on them that life was too short to harbour grudges and resentments. He would plead with them for mutual tolerance and understanding. He would speak to them from the heart as though he was speaking to each separately. So, he began:

'My dear brothers and sisters, let me repeat to you the words of the Gospel: "Prepare a way for the Lord, make his paths straight." It's not the Lord's paths that need to be straightened out but ours.

'We let misunderstandings run on from year to year, meaning to clear them up some day. We keep quarrels alive because we cannot quite make up our minds to sacrifice our pride and end them.

'We pass people sullenly, not speaking to them out of some silly spite, and yet knowing that it would fill us with shame and remorse if we heard that one of them were dead tomorrow.

'We let our neighbour starve, till we hear that he is dying of starvation; or let our friend's heart ache for a word of appreciation, which we mean to give him some day.

'If only we could realise that "the time is short", how it would break the spell. How we would go instantly and do the thing which we might never have another chance to do.

'I repeat: It's not Lord's paths that need to be straightened out but ours. So, if there is some crooked attitude, or some crooked way of behaving, or some crooked relationship that needs to be straighten out, let us straighten it out. Then we will truly be preparing a way for the Lord to come to us.'

He ended his sermon there. His words are worth pondering on. How difficult things are for the one who walks a crooked path. But how easy things are for the one who walks the straight path - the path of truth, honesty and goodness. But to walk a straight path one needs strength, wisdom, and single-mindedness.

God doesn't abandon us when we stray from the straight path. He keeps calling us back from our crooked ways to the straight path. Advent is an excellent time to aim ourselves in the right direction, and to commit ourselves to the right path. We must ask the Lord to take the blindness from our eyes, the weakness from our wills, and the hardness from our hearts, so that our lives may be flooded by the grace of his coming

HOMILY 3   **Opening ourselves to salvation**

Salvation is one of the great themes of Advent. Today a great cry goes forth from the liturgy: 'Prepare a way for the Lord, make his paths straight.

Let every valley be filled in, every mountain and hill be levelled, winding ways be straightened and rough roads made smooth, and all humanity will see the salvation of God.'

These are wonderful words. They are a declaration of God's love for us. But a problem can arise here. Some people think that in order for God to love them they must be perfect. They say: 'God would never want me with my imperfections and sins.' So they try to be perfect in order to win God's love. Which effectively means they try to manage on their own. It's hard for God to save people like that.

Once there was a monk by the name of Ambrose. An expert on the spiritual life, Ambrose was in great demand for talks and retreats. He was a highly intelligent man, and an extremely hard worker. An out-and-out perfectionist, he always liked to be organised and in control of things. He dazzled people with his competence and knowledge.

But at the height of his fame, he was struck down with a terminal illness. It seemed as if his ministry was over. However, things didn't turn out like that. Paradoxically it was when he became weak, and things were totally out of his control, that he became most fruitful.

How did this happen? He decided to use his illness to reach out to other sufferers. And so successful was he that his final illness turned out to be the most fruitful period of his life. Before he died he said: 'I had been travelling in one direction, when all of a sudden I was forced to go in another. But in the process I learned more about myself and about the goodness of other people than I had learned in all my previous years of living.'

And on a personal level, Ambrose underwent a wonderful transformation. It was as if some protective shell cracked open, and there emerged a truly charming person. Before this he had been somewhat of a loner within the community. Now he placed himself at the heart of the community, drinking in the support of his fellow monks, but also contributing handsomely to community spirit by the gentleness and peace he radiated. It was the work of grace. And it proves the truth of the little verse:

> Ring the bells that still can ring,
> Forget your perfect offering.
> There is a crack in everything,
> That's how the light gets in.

How strange are the circumstances that open us to what God wants to give us. When we approach God from a position of self-sufficiency and power, we put God off. But when we approach God from weakness and need, we invite God in. It is through our imperfections that our souls become open to God's grace. Our imperfections are the wound that catches God's eye, and qualify us for his mercy and healing.

If there is some crooked attitude, or some crooked way of behaving that needs to be straightened out in our lives, let us try to do so. But we mustn't think that the Lord won't come to us unless we are perfect. If we were perfect, God wouldn't need to come at all. God comes because we are sinners in need of redemption. He comes because we are his wounded children in need of healing. What we need is the humility and trust to show him our sins and wounds.

There are those who say we shouldn't display weakness because it doesn't create respect, and that therefore it is better to bear our burden in secret. But an understanding of our own pain, makes it possible for us to offer our own experience as a source of healing to others. Those who don't disguise their struggles, but who live through them with the help of God, give hope to others.

PRAYER OF THE FAITHFUL

President: The Lord works marvels for those who trust in him. With confidence, let us pray to him for our many needs.

Response: Lord, graciously hear us.

Reader(s): For the Church: that it may be a place where people can experience the loving presence and tender mercy of God. [Pause] Lord, hear us.

For the leaders of governments: that God may inspire them to work for a just and peaceful world. [Pause] Lord, hear us.

For doctors, nurses and all whose task it is to care for the sick and the wounded: that God may give them sensitive hands and compassionate hearts. [Pause] Lord, hear us.

For those who are finding life a burden too heavy to bear. [Pause] Lord, hear us.

For this community: that we may remain steadfast in faith and untiring in love. [Pause] Lord, hear us.

For the dead: that God may bring them into the light no darkness can overpower. [Pause] Lord, hear us.

For our own special needs. [Longer Pause] Lord, hear us.

President: Lord God, you have prepared fitting remedies for our weakness; grant that we may reach out gladly for your healing grace, and thereby live in accordance with your will. We ask this through Christ our Lord.

REFLECTION   **A lesson from the trees**

Not long ago the trees were loaded with golden leaves.
Though pretty to look at, they robbed me of the world beyond.
But now that the leaves have fallen

I am able to look through the skeletal branches
to the deep blue sky beyond.
Teach us, Good Lord,
how to take care of our material needs
without neglecting our spiritual needs;
how to take care of ourselves
without neglecting others;
and how to live joyfully in this world
without losing sight of the world to come.

Third Sunday of Advent
THE LORD IS NEAR

INTRODUCTION AND CONFITEOR

There is a clear note of rejoicing in today's liturgy. (This is known as *Gaudete* Sunday. The word *Gaudete* means rejoice.) The basis for this rejoicing is the nearness of the Lord. As we gather to celebrate the Eucharist, the Lord is very near us. Indeed, he is in our midst. [Pause]

Lord, by your presence you turn our sorrow into joy. Lord have mercy.

You turn our fear into trust. Christ, have mercy.

You turn our indifference into love. Lord, have mercy.

HEADINGS FOR READINGS

First Reading (Zeph 3:14-18). Jerusalem is urged to rejoice because God stands in her midst. We too can take heart from this message of hope.

Second Reading (Phil 4:4-7). Paul urges us to rejoice in the Lord, and to let go of anxiety by living in a spirit of prayer and thanksgiving.

Gospel (Lk 3:10-18). John the Baptist tells the people what they must do to prepare for the Lord's coming and to escape his searching judgement.

SCRIPTURE NOTE

The prophet Zephaniah, writing in the seventh century BC, bids Jerusalem to rejoice because salvation is near (First Reading). God stands in her midst and will deliver her from her enemies. God is portrayed, not only as a king and warrior, but also as a loving bridegroom, who steadfastly loves his unworthy and unfaithful bride.

The theme of joy is even more emphatic in the Second Reading. Paul calls on the Philippians to rejoice because the Lord is near. (Paul was thinking about the Second Coming, which he believed was near.) So there is no need to worry. If they need anything, they are to pray for it, and the peace of God will be with them.

The theme of the nearness of the Lord is also at the heart of the Gospel. John the Baptist tells the people what they must do in order to prepare for the Lord's coming and to escape his searching judgement. At the same time he makes it clear that he is subordinate to Jesus.

HOMILY 1   **Practical Christianity**

It's obvious from today's Gospel that John the Baptist was a very practical man. Christianity is a very practical and social religion. It is not just a matter of God and me, but of God, me, and others.

There is a story about a cobbler by the name of Martin who lived and worked in a basement room. Its one window enabled him to see just the feet of the passers-by on the street above. But since there was hardly a pair of boots or shoes that had not passed through his hands, he was able to identify the passers-by by their shoes.

Life had been hard on him. His wife died, leaving him with a young son. However, the son had barely reached the age when he could be of help to his father when he fell ill and died. Martin was devastated. After burying his son, he gave way to despair. At the same time he gave up the practice of his religion and took to the bottle.

One day an old friend dropped in. Martin poured out his soul to him. His friend advised him to read a little from the Gospels each day, promising him that if he did so, light and hope would come back into his life.

Martin took his friend's advice. At the end of each day he would take down the Gospels from the shelf and read a little. At first he meant to read only on Sundays, but he found it so interesting that he soon read every day. Slowly things began to change. Hope crept back into his life.

One night as he sat reading he thought he heard someone calling him: 'Martin, look out into the street tomorrow, for I will come to visit you.' Since there was no one else in the room, he reckoned it must have been the Lord himself who had spoken to him.

When he sat down to his work next day he was very excited. As he worked he kept a close eye on the window. He scrutinised every pair of shoes or boots that passed above him. He was looking for someone special. But all he saw was the usual people passing by.

In the early afternoon he saw a pair of familiar boots. They belonged to an old soldier called Stephen. Going to the window he looked up and saw the old man hitting his hands together for it was bitterly cold outside. Martin wished that he would move on, because he was afraid he might obstruct his view, and that he would not see the Lord when he passed.

But old Stephen just stood there by the railing. Finally it occurred to Martin that maybe Stephen had nothing to eat all day. So he tapped on the window and beckoned him to come in. He sat him by the fire and gave him tea and bread. Stephen was most grateful. He said he hadn't eaten for two days. As he left, Martin gave him his second overcoat as a shield against the biting cold. All the time Martin was entertaining Stephen he had not forgotten the window. Every time a shadow fell on it he looked up but nobody special passed.

Night fell. Martin finished his work and very reluctantly closed the window shutters. After supper he took down the Gospels and, as was his custom, opened the book at random. There his eyes fell on these words: 'The people came to John and asked: "What must we do?" And he said: "If anyone has two coats he must share with the man who has none, and the one with something to eat must do the same."'

Martin put down the book and reflected. He understood then that the Lord had indeed come to him that day in the person of Stephen, and that he had made him welcome. And his heart was flooded with joy, a joy the likes of which he had never before experienced.

Martin had already received Christ into his life through a prayerful reading of the Gospels. So the second step followed naturally: to make room for him in the person of a needy neighbour.

We are preparing for the Lord's coming at Christmas. And we have no doubt but that he will come and bring gifts to us. But he doesn't come to us only at Christmas. He comes to us always, and at the oddest times and places, and wearing different disguises. He comes in the person in need.

Advent urges us to prepare a way for the Lord. There is no better way to prepare than to be welcoming towards those in need. The way to find peace and happiness and goodness is to forget oneself and love others.

HOMILY 2   **The greatness of John the Baptist**

Once upon a time there lived an extraordinary lamp lighter by the name of Mr T. He was utterly reliable and as punctual as a clock. Each evening, at the onset of darkness, the gas lamps unfailingly came on. How he judged the time nobody knew because he had no watch.

The people often watched from their front windows as he went up and down the street, leaving a trail of light in his wake. It was obvious to all that he loved his job. He lived for one thing only – to light the lamps. His life was not an easy one but it glowed with meaning.

He was loved by everybody, but especially by the children. When darkness threatened to put an end to their street games, Mr T would come along, light the lamps, and they would continue to play.

What was it that made Mr T so extraordinary? After all, there are many people who love their work and who do it faithfully. Mr T's greatness lay in the fact that he was blind. The man who was so faithful in bringing the light to others never saw it himself.

Eventually electricity arrived, and Mr T, now advanced in years, was made redundant. His life suddenly lost meaning. He felt useless and unwanted. Sadly, the people who once loved him, now forgot about him. The new light was so superior to the old that no one regretted its passing. He spent his days and nights alone in the darkness of his basement flat.

Mr T reminds us of John the Baptist. Like Mr T, John worked diligently to bring his own light to the people. For a while he dominated the scene, and enjoyed great popularity. But he was always conscious of the fact that a greater light was coming, a light he himself was not destined to walk in. When that light appeared in the person of Jesus, he moved aside to make way for Jesus. That took greatness.

No man ever came to prominence or achieved fame on his own. You will always find that in the background there has been a facilitator whose task it was to help, guide, and encourage him – in other words, to prepare the way for him. When the person has achieved fame, the facilitator drops out of sight and frequently is forgotten.

To make way, or even just to make room, for another person calls for humility and generosity of spirit. Indeed, it calls for a kind of dying to self. To retire from high office is to die a little, even more than a little. Some people spoil things by holding on too long to the reins of power.

Parents spend the best years of their lives preparing the way for their children, in the sense of opening them to life. But there comes a time when they have to withdraw so that their children can come into their own. Having given life to their children, parents must allow them to live that life.

All of us are tempted to hug the limelight. We often, inadvertently perhaps, dominate others and relegate them to the shadows. We must try to shine to the best of our ability, while being careful not to block the path for others. And we must be conscious of the debt we owe to others who prepared the way for us.

HOMILY 3   **The secret of happiness**

One of the themes of today's readings is that of happiness. All of us want is to be happy. But what is the secret of happiness?

Once a shepherd sent his son to a wise man to learn the secret of happiness. When he arrived at the beautiful castle where the wise man lived, the boy told him he wished to know the secret of happiness. However, instead of explaining the secret to him, the wise man handed him a spoon filled with oil, saying, 'Take a look around the palace. As you go around, carry this spoon with you without allowing the oil to spill.'

The boy began to move around the palace. As he did so he kept his eyes fixed on the spoon. After two hours, he returned to the room where the wise man was.

'Well,' asked the wise man, 'what have you seen?

The boy was embarrassed, and confessed that he had seen nothing. His only concern had been not to spill the oil that the wise man had entrusted to him. 'Well then,' said the wise man, 'go back and observe the marvels of my world. You cannot trust a man if you don't know his house.'

Relieved, the boy picked up the spoon and returned to his exploration of the palace, this time observing all the beautiful furniture and works of art that adorned the rooms of the castle. Then he visited the garden, with its magnificent fountain and beautiful flowers and shrubs, admiring the taste with which everything was laid out. On returning to the wise man, he related in detail everything he had seen.

'But where are the drops of oil I entrusted to you?' asked the wise man. Looking down at the spoon, the boy saw that the oil was gone.

'Well, there is only one piece of advice I can give you,' said the wise man. 'The secret of happiness lies in the ability to see all the marvels of the world, and never to forget the drops of oil in the spoon.'

The boy understood immediately what the wise man was saying. A shepherd may like to travel, but he should never forget his sheep. The secret of happiness consists in being faithful to one's commitments and responsibilities while at the same time enjoying life. It's easy to be happy when we are doing what we want. But to find happiness in what we have to do, not simply in what we want to do, this is a blessing from God.

Happiness is not a shallow self-satisfaction. There can be no happiness for us as long as the things we do are different from the things we believe. And there can be no happiness without love. A sadness falls upon us when we say 'no' to love.

And we mustn't equate joy with pleasure. Pleasure is of the body; joy is of the spirit. You can quickly become tired of pleasures, but you never grow tired of joys.

In the end, only God can fulfil our dreams, and happiness is the best sign of his presence. The presence of God is the cause of our joy. Isaiah said to the people, 'Shout for joy.' What is the cause of that joy? Because 'God is in your midst.' And Paul said to the Philippians, 'I want you to be happy.' Why? Because 'the Lord is very near.' The joy that this world cannot give is the joy that comes from a sense of God and his love for us.

PRAYER OF THE FAITHFUL

President: Paul said to the Philippians, 'If there is anything you need, pray for it.' In obedience to these words, let us bring our needs to the Lord in prayer.

Response: Lord, hear our prayer.

Reader(s): For all Christians: that they may put the Lord at the centre of their lives, and seek to imitate him in their concern for others. [Pause] Let us pray to the Lord.

For political leaders: that they may strive to rid the world of hatred and fear. [Pause] Let us pray to the Lord.

For members of the army and police force: that they may never abuse their power, but may be true keepers of the peace. [Pause] Let us pray to the Lord.

For all those who are suffering from depression, or who are grieving the loss of a loved one: that the Lord may turn their sorrow into joy. [Pause] Let us pray to the Lord.

For all gathered here: that we may realise that the Lord is always close to us, in good times and in bad. [Pause] Let us pray to the Lord.

For our own special needs. [Longer Pause] Let us pray to the Lord.

President: Lord, may the coming of your only Son dispel the darkness of our hearts and help us to walk in the light of truth and goodness. We ask this through the same Christ our Lord.

REFLECTION   **Joy**

There is a clear note of joy in today's liturgy.
Joy is a blend of laughter and tears.
It consists in having a love affair with life.
It is having a heart aglow with warmth
for all one's companions on the road of life.
It is looking for the happiness that comes in small packages,
knowing that big packages are few and far between.
It is making the most of the present,
enjoying what is at hand right now.
Joy is love bubbling over into life.
And it can coexist with pain.
Joy is the flag we fly when Christ, the Prince of Peace,
has taken up residence in our hearts.

FINAL BLESSING AND DISMISSAL

Ordinary Time II, no. 11 in the Missal

Fourth Sunday of Advent

INTRODUCTION AND CONFITEOR

In a few days we celebrate the birthday of Christ. Christ comes most readily to those who realise their need of him. Let us draw near to him now, bringing with us our spiritual poverty, wounds and sins. [Pause]

Lord Jesus, you rouse up your might and come to our help. Lord, have mercy.

You let your face shine on us so we might be saved. Christ, have mercy.

You bring us back, never to forsake you again. Lord, have mercy.

HEADINGS FOR READINGS

First Reading (Mic 5:1-4). The prophet Micah announces to the beleaguered inhabitants of Jerusalem that a Ruler will come from Bethlehem who will bring them peace.

Second Reading (Heb 10:5-10). Jesus came, not to offer the sacrifices of the old law, but to do the will of God. His one perfect sacrifice replaced all the former sacrifices.

Gospel (Lk 1:39-45). Elizabeth praises Mary, and, enlightened by the Holy Spirit, hints at the uniqueness of the child she has conceived.

SCRIPTURE NOTE

When Micah was writing (late eighth-century BC) Jerusalem was under siege and David's dynasty was in jeopardy. But salvation would come from a comparatively insignificant place – Bethlehem. From there a new leader would come to gather together the scattered exiles and unite the nation once more. Christians see this promise as foreshadowing the coming of Jesus, the Prince of Peace, who was born in Bethlehem and descended from the line of David.

The Gospel tells the story of Mary's visit to Elizabeth. Both are pregnant. Enlightened by the Holy Spirit, Elizabeth praises Mary and hints at the uniqueness of the child she has conceived.

The Second Reading states that Jesus didn't come to offer the sacrifices of the old law, but to do the will of God. His sacrifice was essentially one of obedience (an obedience which meant accepting death on a cross). His one perfect sacrifice transcended and replaced all the former sacrifices. His sacrifice did what the sacrifices of the Mosaic Law were unable to do; it brought about reconciliation between God and his people.

HOMILY 1   **The spirit of Christmas**

In his book, *Christmas* (Mercier Press), the Kerry writer, John B. Keane, talks about 'the urging' of Christmas. He tells about a man who in normal circumstances wouldn't give you the crumbs from his table, but who, when imbued with the spirit of Christmas, phoned his estranged daughter in England and begged her to come home for Christmas. The daughter accepted the invitation, and on both sides all was forgiven. John B. says that he wasn't half as mean afterwards and concludes: 'So, my friends, take Christmas by the horns – it can work wonders.'

He goes on to say that we shouldn't be ashamed to be weepy or senti-mental about Christmas, because we might not get the chance during the year ahead to show our humanity to the world. That, after all, is what Christmas is for – taking stock of our humanity and dispensing it where it is most needed.

So, if we feel the impulse to be forgiving and charitable and loving, we shouldn't think twice about it or we'll miss the boat. 'The milk of human kindness doesn't come from cows and goats. It comes from that great repository of compassion and hope, namely, the human heart.'

The spirit of Christmas cannot be killed. It has survived Stalin, Hitler, Mussolini, and many other tyrants. It has survived human greed and human jealousy, and every human failing one cares to mention. Nothing lasts like Christmas. Not all the inhumanity, nor all the greed, nor all the violence will reduce its message by a whit. It's here to stay and there's nothing that evil men can do about it – and that's one great consolation.

Of course, there are things that can damage Christmas. Chief among these is alcohol. It can lead to death on the roads and stupid rows. To take one's drink at the end rather than the start of one's journey, and to take it in moderation, may be one's best Christmas gift to one's fellow human beings.

Christmas is a time of opportunity. It creates a climate which encour-ages us to reveal our better natures. Just as the spring assures the growth of crops, so Christmas assures the growth of love.

It is not possible for us, because of our fallen nature, to be charitable and compassionate all the year round. Let us, therefore, make the most of Christmas. It's not true that Charles Dickens invented Christmas as we know it. Christmas was born out of love and carries on out of love. It springs from God's gratuitous love for us.

How bleak the world would be if there was no Christmas. There is nothing else with the power to move the human heart to its utmost capa-bility. We mustn't take it for granted. If we haven't done anything about it yet, then for pity's sake let us do it now or we'll be guilty of the awful crime of undermining Christmas.

Christmas is a feast of the heart. It reveals to us what the heart of God is like. It was God who started it all when he gave us the gift of his Son. At the same time it reveals to us what the human heart is capable of. Christ-mas causes us to open our hearts. And the extent to which we open our hearts to God and to one another, will be the extent to which we experi-ence the 'great joy' the angels announced to the shepherds, because joy is the fruit of love.

HOMILY 2   **The grace of visitation**

In the old days life was simpler and people visited one another a lot. Today visitation is not so frequent. It has been replaced by the telephone. A phone-call is good but it can't take the place of a visit.

A woman who lives in New York City has had the same neighbour living next-door for some thirty years. She has never had a row of any kind with her, and they always exchange the time of day when they meet. But in all that time she has never set foot in her neighbour's house. It is kind of sad. And there is a loss.

When we pay a visit to someone, we see ourselves as doing good to that person. And that is true. But we too benefit. We too are enriched. If only to see how others cope with difficult or near impossible situations. Even among the sick you can find a shining soul. You may have come to give, only to find that you are receiving. You go away buoyed up. To some extent that happens in every visitation. One is blessed by receiving. The other is blessed by giving.

A priest in parish ministry tells how he went to visit a young woman who was dying of cancer. He went in the hope of bringing her a little comfort. At the end of the visit he came away feeling that he was the one who was comforted. He marvelled at her faith, and at the serenity she had found in the face of death. His own faith was deepened and strengthened by contact with hers.

In the Gospel we see Mary visiting Elizabeth. She herself had just been visited by the angel Gabriel, who had brought her the good news that she was to become the mother of Jesus. However, instead of going off and concentrating on herself, she went with haste to visit Elizabeth, who was also expecting a child.

Elizabeth was her cousin. Our first and holiest duty is kindness towards our own kin. However, this doesn't mean it's easy. One's kin can be very demanding.

Mary's visit meant a great deal to Elizabeth. But Mary too benefited from it. Elizabeth spoke some lovely words of affirmation and confirmation to her: 'Blessed is she who believed that the promise made to her by the Lord would be fulfilled.' As the elder and more experienced of the two women, Elizabeth was able to help Mary. Essentially what we have here is two women in the same condition helping one another.

We can receive by giving. And one of the ways we can give is by visitation. Christmas is a great time for visiting people we may have neglected all year long.

HOMILY 3   **The blessedness of those who believe**

In the Gospel we have the story of Mary's visitation of her cousin, Elizabeth. During that visitation Elizabeth spoke those lovely words to her: 'Blessed is she who believed that the promise made to her by the Lord would be fulfilled.'

The theme of the blessedness of those who believe runs right through the Gospel. Wonderful things happen for those who believe. To take a few examples.

Jesus said to the centurion, 'Go; be it done for you as you have believed,' and his servant was cured (Mt 8:13). To the woman with the haemorrhage he said, 'Take heart, daughter; you faith has made you well,' and her bleeding stopped (Mt 9:22). To the two blind men he said, 'According to your faith, be it done to you,' and they got their sight back (Mt 9:29).

You could say that the central theme of the Gospel is the blessedness of those who believe. All of Jesus' preaching had as its aim to elicit faith in people's hearts. However, it is not simply a matter of believing, but of believing and acting on that belief. It is a question of hearing the word and doing it – taking risks on it, and making sacrifices because of it. 'Don't bother proclaiming that you believe unless you act accordingly.' (Catherine de Hueck Doherty)

You sometimes hear people say, 'It's easy for you; you've great faith.' But it's not like that. Faith doesn't always make things easy. In fact, the opposite is more likely to be the case. It's because we have faith that we refuse to give up. Faith impels us to persevere, to struggle on, often with no guarantee of a happy outcome. A person with faith never gives up.

Mary is blessed because she not only believed but also acted on her belief. Immediately after the visit from the angel Gabriel, she went with haste to visit Elizabeth. From this we see that her religion was not a matter of mere sentimentality. It was something she converted into deeds.

Mary was the first and most perfect disciple of Jesus. This is why the Church proposes her as a model for us. We too will be blessed if, like Mary, we hear the word of God and act on it.

Christmas can be a great help to our faith. Somehow we find it easier to trust God at Christmas than at any other time, because we feel that God is very close to us and very loving towards us at this time.

The essence of the Good News is that God made himself present to us in the life of One who walked on this earth, indeed so truly present that this One, Jesus, was God's Son. At the first Christmas there were those who believed and those who did not believe. The Gospel stresses the blessedness of those who believed the Good News.

Christmas makes it possible for us to enter into an intimate relationship with God. And Christmas also calls us to open our hearts to one another. And in opening our hearts to one another, we are opening ourselves to receive the 'great joy' announced to the shepherds by the angel.

ANOTHER APPROACH   **Celebrating Christmas**

There is a tendency for preachers to stress the absence of Christ in Christmas, and to deplore its commercialisation. There is little to be gained by this. Far better to stress the presence of Christ in Christmas, and help people to find him in it.

Our celebration of Christmas has many layers. In an article in *The Tablet* (December 1998) Anthony Philpot identifies some of these layers.

The top layer is the consumer Christmas from which there is no escape these days – insistent Christmas carols, reindeer and Santa Claus, and the aggressive merchandising of all kinds of goods. It encourages acquisitiveness among children, and creates anxiety about overspending and fatigue among adults. It is a Christmas with a hollow core.

Next comes the Charles Dickens layer – cards depicting snowy scenes, roaring fires, turkey, ham, plum pudding, mince pies … It is the Christmas of the family get-together, of goodwill to all men, of philanthropy and expansiveness. These values have a lot to be said for them. Most people have a shot at this version of Christmas. But in the absence of faith what does it amount to? A little uplift. A few pious phrases. A few gifts given and received. And then everything goes on as before.

The third level is that of the crib, which depicts for us what Christmas is about. This is the layer of the school Nativity play, which re-enacts the Christmas story, and which for all its simplicity can be deeply moving.

The fourth and deepest layer is the spiritual one. It is the story of how in Israel 2000 years ago a baby was born. In the person of this baby God's Son took our nature upon himself and entered our world in weakness and in love. He came to remind us that we are God's children and have an eternal destiny.

There is a tendency to dismiss, or even condemn, the first three layers, and to see the spiritual layer as the only true one. This is based on the supposition that the spiritual and the material are opposed to one another. But this is not so. Christianity includes matter and spirit. There can be no such thing as a purely spiritual Christmas.

What we have to do is find a connection between the secular marketplace and the spiritual content of the feast. Much of the buying and selling that occurs at Christmas fosters gift-giving, good works, joy, and the affirmation of family ties – resulting in giving and receiving.

This approach helps us to see the close kinship between the spiritual and the material, between heavenly and earthly things. We must learn how to integrate the two. The core religious problem is: how to reconcile spirituality and materiality, flesh and spirit, the inward and the outward, the surface and the substance.

There are those who insist on a clear division between the divine and the human, the sacred and the secular, the soul and the body. But we won't find that in Christmas. At Christmas these are so interwoven that they seem to be one and the same thing.

PRAYER OF THE FAITHFUL

President: Let us pray to our heavenly Father, who so loved the world that he sent his only Son, not to condemn us, but to save us.

Response: Come, Lord Jesus.

Reader(s): For all the followers of Jesus: that the light of Christ may shine in their hearts this Christmas. [Pause] Let us pray.

For all government leaders: that Christ, the Prince of Peace, may turn their minds and hearts to thoughts of peace. [Pause] Let us pray.

For families: that scattered families may be reunited, and that those in distress may experience relief. [Pause] Let us pray.

For those who, for whatever reason, are not looking forward to Christmas. [Pause] Let us pray.

For all gathered here: that under the urging of Christmas we may reach out to anyone from whom we are estranged. [Pause] Let us pray.

For the dead, whose absence is felt intensely at Christmas: that Christ may lead them into the joyful vision of his presence. [Pause] Let us pray.

For our own special needs. [Longer pause] Let us pray.

President: Father, fill our hearts with love through the coming of your Son. Give us the grace to overcome our fears and anxieties, and keep us joyful in your service. We ask this through Christ our Lord.

PRAYER/REFLECTION   **Come, Lord Jesus**

Lord Jesus, come into our weakness.
Come into our fears.
Come into our anxieties.
Come into our failures.
Come into our divisions.
Come into our grieving.
Come into our loneliness.
Come into our darkness.
Come into our doubting.
Come into our despair.
Come into our poverty of heart.
Come into our searching.
Come into our joys and hopes.
Come into our dying.
Come, Lord Jesus, come.

CHRISTMASTIDE

Madonna and Child

IMOGEN STUART

Christmas

'Do not be afraid. Behold, I bring you news of great joy … Today a Saviour has been born to you.' As we gather here this night (morning/day) our Saviour is present among us, not as a little helpless baby, but as our risen Lord. Let us cast aside fear, and open our hearts to receive the joy only he can give. [Pause]

Lord Jesus, your light shines in the dark. Lord, have mercy.

You give us power to become children of God. Christ, have mercy.

You are the fullness of grace and truth. Lord, have mercy.

HEADINGS FOR READINGS

Midnight Mass

First Reading (Is 9:1-7). This prophecy about the coming of a Saviour-child who will rescue his people from oppression, is fulfilled in Jesus.

Second Reading (Tit 2:11-14). St Paul reminds us of what is expected of us if we are to enjoy the salvation won for us by Jesus.

Gospel (Lk 2:1-14). We hear about the birth of Jesus, and how the news of his birth was brought by angels to shepherds.

Dawn Mass

First Reading (Is 62:11-12). The joy of the exiles returning from Babylon is a foretaste of the joy Christians experience at the birth of Jesus.

Second Reading (Tit 3:4-7)). We did nothing to merit the birth of Jesus; rather, God sent his Son out of compassion for us.

Gospel (Lk 2:15-20). With Mary we are invited to ponder on the deeper meaning of the birth of Jesus so that, with the shepherds, we may be moved to glorify and praise God.

Day Mass

First Reading (Is 52:7-10). This great hymn of exultation at the return of the exiles from Babylon is also a poem of joy at our redemption.

Second Reading (Heb 1:1-6). The whole history of God's dealings with his people in the past was a preparation for the coming of his Son at a particular moment in history.

Gospel (Jn 1:1-18). This is a great hymn to the Word of God, the source of all life, whose coming among us makes us children of God.

SCRIPTURE NOTE

Luke's account of the birth of Jesus forms the Gospel for the first two Masses today. The story reflects the faith of the post-resurrection Church. The same titles that Peter attributes to the risen Jesus – Lord and Messiah

(Acts 2:36) – are now applied to the new-born Child by the angels. Luke's chief concern is theological. Every detail in the story serves this purpose. This is not to say that there is no historical basis for what he recounts.

Luke gives the birth of Jesus a solemn setting. He is also hinting at the cosmic significance of his birth. Unwittingly Augustus becomes an instrument of the Lord by ensuring that Jesus (the Messiah) was born in the town of David. Jesus' rejection at the inn anticipates his rejection by the Jewish people as a whole. Mary is shown to be a caring mother, wrapping the child in swaddling clothes and laying him in a manger-cradle. Her loving care reflects God's care.

Since Jesus was born in poverty, it is fitting that the news of his birth was first announced to simple shepherds. This also reflects Luke's concern for the poor and the lowly. The faith of the shepherds serves as a model for future believers, and their joy anticipates the blessings that will come to those who accept Jesus as the Saviour sent by God.

For the third Mass of Christmas the prologue of John's Gospel is read. This brings out the fullest meaning of what the feast reveals. John reaches back even before creation and identifies the new-born Child as the Word of God, who brings life and light to the world. To those who accept him he gives the power to become children of God. (For a note on John's prologue, see Second Sunday after Christmas, pp. 49-50 *infra*.)

HOMILY 1 **Connecting with God**

Each year when the time comes around to send out our Christmas cards, we get out our address book. There we may come across a name, and exclaim, 'Gosh! I haven't heard from him for ages.' We can't even remember if we got a card from him last Christmas. So we are faced with a decision: will we or won't we send him a card?

Most of us have someone like that in our lives, someone with whom we communicate perhaps only once a year. At one time we may have been very close. But now it's come to this. For one reason or another, the distance grew between us. We got disconnected. And now we have reached the sorry stage where we are communicating only through a card at Christmas. It shows that a relationship suffers from neglect just as surely as a garden does. And a relationship such as that is hardly a nourishing one. In truth, it has no real impact on our life.

We can get disconnected from God too. It's not necessarily that we stop believing in God. It's just that we get disconnected from him. We may have been very connected as children, but over the years we got disconnected. When people allowed themselves to get disconnect from God an enormous loss occurs, and a huge vacuum results. Life is unintelligible and unbearable without God.

'We don't die the day we cease to believe in a personal deity; but we die the day our lives cease to be illuminated by the steady radiance, re-newed daily, of a wonder, the source of which is beyond all reason.' (Dag Hammarskjold)

A six-year-old child, whose parents were non-believers, one day asked his teacher to take him to visit a nearby church. During the visit he said to the teacher: 'This is God's house, so Grandma says. She says that God is love. She says she prays to him, which means she talks to him. I have never prayed. But I would like to talk to God. I would like to hear what he has to say. There's a boy in my class who believes in God. He's a Catho-lic. But Papa and Mama are not God-believing people, and so I am not. It makes me feel lonely not knowing God.'

'It makes me feel lonely not knowing God' – the words of a six-year-old child. It is lonely not knowing God. If we experience this loneliness we shouldn't be alarmed. It can be an opportunity and a grace. Our hearts are always longing for something more, or rather, for Someone else. In every human heart there is an empty chamber waiting for a guest. That guest is God.

It's easier to trust in God at Christmas than at any other time, because we feel that God is very close to us and very loving towards us at this time. This is the special gift of Christmas. It proclaims that we are not alone in the universe. It gives us an opportunity to reconnect ourselves with God if we feel we have become disconnected from him, trusting that we will receive nothing but love. If we open our souls, we will feel our-selves touched by the divine presence.

An inner peace springs from being connected with God, who is love. We are not specks of dust or grains of sand. We are God's precious sons and daughters. We are heirs to the kingdom of heaven.

Christmas also provides us with an opportunity to reconnect ourselves with other people, especially our families – if we have become discon-nected from them. That too will bring us peace and joy.

The shepherds returned to their flocks 'glorifying and praising God for all they had seen and heard'. Nothing had changed, yet everything had changed. Now their hearts were filled with wonder. They had a new vision, a new hope, a new sense of the love of God for them and of his presence with them. Their lives glowed with meaning. The old world had become like a new country where everything glistened with marvel. To discover God results in a re-enchanted world.

HOMILY 2   **Peace on earth**

One of the things we always associate with Christmas is peace. At the birth of Jesus the angels sang: 'Glory to God in the highest, and peace to his people on earth.' These are some of the loveliest words in the Gospel. You could say that they sum up the Gospel.

On Christmas Eve 1914, the Germans and the English faced each other from trenches filled with mud and rats. In the English trenches letters and cards arrived from home and the soldiers cheered up a little. By midnight some of them even began to sing. Then suddenly a sentry shouted excitedly: 'Listen!' They listened and heard that the Germans were singing too. A short while later two brave soldiers, one from each side, met out in the open. More joined them. From a military point of view it made no sense. As soldiers they were supposed to fight each other. To stop suddenly and to be friends just didn't make sense. But there was a greater force than armies at the front that night.

When Christmas Day dawned soldiers with smiling faces were strolling around No-man's Land. There wasn't a trace of hatred to be seen. They exchanged food, souvenirs and cigarettes. About mid-day as the friendship was growing, a football match between the two sides started up. But it didn't last long. The news had reached the generals, and sharp orders arrived to put an end to the whole thing. The officers herded the men back into the trenches. It was all over. On Christmas night the war had started up again.

If this proves nothing else, it proves the power of Christmas. But peace is not merely the absence of war or dissension. It is something deeper and richer. The Hebrew word for peace – *shalom* – conveys a much richer meaning than the English word *peace*. It conveys a sense of completeness, a state of perfect well-being.

An essential component of peace is righteousness. So, where there is no righteousness, there is no genuine peace. Hence, there can be no peace for the wicked. Peace is not simple harmony. It is the fullness of well-being. It can exist in the midst of a troubled world, and even in the midst of unresolved problems. It is something so deep that it is independent of outer circumstances.

Peace is a state of inner calm and designates right relations with God and with other people. Peace in this complete sense, cannot be created by human effort alone. It is a gift of God. It is the gift of Christmas. God reaches out to us in peace, and wants us to reach out to one another. Peace is God's gift to us; our gift to God is to make peace with one another.

Peace is communion with God. At Christmas God seems to be very close to us and very loving towards us. May he help us to taste the peace that only he can give. The peace which passes all understanding, which this world cannot give. The peace no one can take away from us.

HOMILY 3   **The kingdom of God becomes tangible**

Often in life the day of greatest expectation turns out to be the day of greatest disappointment. This can happen with Christmas too.

Sometimes we can have unreal expectations about Christmas. It is as if we expect something extraordinary to happen, something that will change our humdrum lives for ever. Thanks to an ever-lengthening build-up, as the great day approaches, our hopes soar. However, the substance of these hopes is often dictated by the market place – a glut of things to eat and drink, a glut of TV programmes to entertain us.

But when Christmas Day dawns, what's the first thing we notice about it? It's just like any other day. There are no angels to be seen, or heavenly voices to be heard. Everything goes on as normal. And when the sun goes down on this day, many people feel empty and depressed, and say with a touch of bitterness, 'Christmas is only for the children.'

But this day can be different. Even though there are no signs in the sky, there are signs about – at least for those who know where to look. On this day there is more light, more warmth, more hope in the world. People are friendlier on Christmas Day. No one passes without a greeting. On this day one feels part of the human family, or at least the desire to be part of it. To walk alone this morning seems strange, even wrong.

Indeed, the Kingdom of God becomes tangible on Christmas Day. On this day, if we open our souls, we will feel ourselves touched by the divine presence. The Irish playwright, Hugh Leonard, put it like this: 'I may not know who God is, but I know where he lives. He surrounds me all year, but at Christmas he comes up and digs me in the ribs.' That isn't mere sentiment.

At Christmas we get a sense of the closeness, the warmth, and the goodness of God. We get a feeling that we are not alone, that our life has a meaning, that someone is watching over us and guiding our way. That is the heart of Christmas. We shouldn't be afraid to bask in this warmth, just as we bask happily in a burst of warm sunshine on a cold day.

We also get a feeling of our own goodness and the goodness of others. We get a feeling that life is good and that it has meaning. We are not specks of dust or grains of sand. We are God's precious sons and daughters. We have a divine dignity and a glorious destiny. An inner peace springs from being connected with God who is love.

If Christmas leaves us disappointed it means we have pinned our hopes on the wrong things. Those who pin their hopes on what the merchants offer will always be disappointed, not because they promise too little, but too much – of the wrong things. What our hearts long for is a taste of the 'great joy' which the angels announced to the shepherds. That is the real hope of Christmas.

What do we have to do to tap in to this? Only one thing: open our hearts to receive it. Today a Saviour is born to us; he is Christ the Lord.

HOMILY 4   **The light of Jesus**

We celebrate Christmas at the darkest time of the year (in the northern hemisphere). It's a time when we appreciate the value of light. The Christmas liturgy is filled with references to light. Jesus fulfils the prophecy of Isaiah: 'The people that walked in darkness have seen a great light; on those who live in land of deep shadow a light has shone.'

Mother Teresa told how one day in Melbourne, Australia, she visited a poor man nobody knew existed. He was living in a basement room which was in a terrible state of neglect. There was no light in the room, and he rarely opened the blinds. He didn't seem to have a friend in the world.

She started to clean and tidy the room. At first he protested: 'Leave it alone. It's all right as it is.' But she went ahead anyway. As she cleaned, she chatted with him. Under a pile of rubbish she found an oil lamp covered with dust. She cleaned it and discovered that it was beautiful. And she said to him, 'You've got a beautiful lamp here. How come you never light it?'

'Why should I light it?' he replied. 'No one ever comes to see me.'

'Will you promise to light it if one of my sisters comes to see you?'

'Yes,' he replied. 'If I hear a human voice I'll light the lamp.'

Two of Mother Teresa's nuns began to visit him regularly. Things gradually improved for him. Every time the sisters came to visit him he had the lamp lighting. Then one day he said to them, 'Sisters, I'll be able to manage on my own from now on. But do me a favour. Tell that first sister who came to see me that the light she lit in my life is still burning.'

You could say that the lamp saved him. But of course it wasn't the lamp itself, but the kindness and goodness it symbolised, first in Mother Teresa, then in her Sisters.

We live in a world darkened by war, violence, and suffering of different kinds. And all of us have experienced darkness in our personal lives and in our families – sorrow, disappointment, illness, pain, sin, guilt, loneliness, and so on.

Fortunately the lamp Jesus lit in our world continues to burn. His light was not lit in Bethlehem once and then extinguished. It shines in the midst of devastation, disaster and upheaval. It is a persistent and defiant light, which no darkness can overpower. It shines for all who believe in him and follow him.

History is littered with examples of teachers who brought darkness into the world. Not so Jesus. For two thousand years the teaching of Jesus has exercised an influence over people in a way unequalled by anyone else. But it was above all through his deeds and encounters with people that his luminous goodness manifested itself. Countless people came to him in darkness and went away bathed in light.

The glowing goodness of Jesus continues to illuminate the world. In Jesus and in his Gospel we have a sure source of light which, for two millennia, has shone upon humankind. The light that shone on the shepherds of Bethlehem that first Christmas night, shines on us this Christmas. The light of Jesus does not come to judge us, but to save us. It comes to show us how to live, and to guide us towards the God's eternal kingdom.

Each of us can be sources of light to a darkened world. But unless our own lamp is lighting, we won't be able to enlighten anyone else. There is great joy in being in the light. But there is an even greater joy in being a source of light to others. God has called us out of darkness into the wonderful light of his Son. We must try to live as children of the light. The effects of the light are seen in goodness, right living and truth.

May the Lord in his goodness give us a taste of that joy which the shepherds experienced when the light of God's glory shone around them on that first Christmas night. And may we hear his gentle words echoing in our hearts: 'Anyone who follows me, will never walk in darkness, but will always have the light of life.'

HOMILY 5   **The Gift of God**

The scene: a shanty town in a third-world country. In spite of the bright sunshine, a gloom hung over the rows of shacks. But Christmas was coming. Things would be different, at least for a while.

However, a few days before Christmas, an incident occurred which deepened the gloom of the slum-dwellers. The father of three young children committed suicide. No one will ever know the full story behind his action. But he did give people a glimpse into the darkness which had invaded his heart. Shortly before he died he told a friend that he was very depressed because he had no gifts to give his children for Christmas.

Giving gifts is an important part of our celebration of Christmas. Charles Dickens summed it up: 'Christmas is the one time in the long calendar of the year when people open their shut-in hearts to one another.'

Christmas could be said to be the season of gifts, even though some of our giving may be trivial and routine. A gift points beyond itself. Gifts are a way of telling others that we love them. They have little to do with justice, and everything to do with love.

The giving of gifts takes us back to the origins of the feast itself. Christmas was created by a gift. It was God who started it all. 'God so loved the world that he gave us his only Son, so that everyone who believes in him may not perish but may have eternal life.'

While we give presents to one another, let us make sure that we also give of ourselves to one another. Christmas is not just about giving presents. It's more about *being present* – which means giving of ourselves. And the quality of our presence is everything.

There is a presence which is remote, watery, lukewarm – like that of the sun on a winter's day, which comes and goes without even defrosting the ground. And there is a presence which is close, warm, affirmative – like that of the sun on a summer's day, which brings life to everything it touches.

The giving of gifts is important, but the receiving of them is just as important. Christmas is also a time for receiving – receiving the gifts others give us, and especially the gift God offers us. God didn't give us a present of a thing; he gave us a present of a person. Jesus is God's gift to the poor and the lowly, to assure them that love has not passed them by.

When we give presents we cover them in fancy wrapping, even though we know the wrapping adds nothing to the worth of the gift, and will be torn off and thrown into the trash bag. When God made us the gift of his Son, his gift didn't come in fancy wrapping. He came wrapped in the cloak of our weak, fragile, mortal humanity. In this we see the depth of his love.

Though Christ came among us weak and empty-handed, he brought us priceless and everlasting gifts. He came to teach us that we are not specks of dust, but sons and daughters of the heavenly Father destined for eternal glory.

What kind of disposition do we need to be able to receive the gift of God? We need some sense of our own poverty before God. After that, all we have to do is open our hearts to receive the gift of God. Those who receive the gift of God will always have something to share with others.

> A present that cannot be priced
> Given two thousand years ago.
> Yet if God had not given so
> He still would be a distant stranger
> And not the Baby in the manger.　　　　　*(John Betjeman).*

HOMILY 6　　　　　　　　　　　　　　　　**The longest journey**

In July, 1969, Neil Armstrong and his two fellow astronauts set off on the longest journey ever undertaken by man. Their target was a quarter of a million miles away. The eyes of the whole world were upon them as they took off for our nearest neighbour in space – the moon. They landed on the part of the moon known as the Sea of Tranquillity. They found it lifeless and barren; they brought back a handful of rocks and dust. Yet Armstrong described their mission as 'a giant leap for mankind.'

It made great news at the time. Now it seems rather hazy. We've almost forgotten that it ever happened. People are asking what, if anything, it achieved? And the men whose names were then on the lips of everybody are now seldom mentioned.

Today we Christians celebrate the mystery of the incarnation – the coming into our world of Jesus, the Son of God. He was born of a humble maid, at a time when communication was slow, and in a small country that was no sea of tranquillity but the scene of constant strife. Only a handful of people knew about his coming.

Yet we still talk about it and celebrate it. The Incarnation is the greatest moment in the history of the world. As a result of it, things have never been the same. The importance of the Incarnation has been recognised by artists, poets, and writers down the ages.

In the Incarnation we recognise God's love for us. Though Christ came among us weak and empty-handed, he brought us priceless and ever-lasting gifts. He came to teach us that we are not specks of dust, but sons and daughters of the heavenly Father destined for eternal glory.

There was a teacher who was very fond of giving instructions, direc-tions, criticisms, and corrections. Just after he got married he taught his wife how to wash dishes, because he didn't think she did it the right way. And his way of teaching her was to have her re-wash every dish that she had already washed, under his supervision. Instead of giving her an ex-ample by doing it himself, he gave her advice and instructions. This is not how Jesus did it.

As Son of God, Jesus shares the same divine nature as the Father and the Holy Spirit. But in the Incarnation he took on himself our nature which is weak, fragile, and subject to sin and death. In it he overcame sin, evil, and death. Because the battle was fought and won in our nature, we are able to profit from it. And he doesn't demand anything of us that he hasn't done himself.

There you have the Incarnation. That's the pattern of redemption. God entered our world on our terms. He wanted to feel the grief of our hu-manity and to show us the greatness of it. Now we have a God who un-derstands us when we speak to him about our pain. But he is a God who will not allow us to wallow it in. He will not be satisfied until he has demanded the best of us.

The Son of God came on earth to share in our humanity so that we might share in his divinity. 'They wrapped the baby in swaddling clothes, and laid him in a manger.' From these lowly origins Jesus grew up to show us the greatness of our humanity.

The joy of this day fills our hearts and the whole world. Christ leads us on a far more daring journey than that of the moon-men – the journey to the kingdom of eternal life.

PRAYER OF THE FAITHFUL

President: God dispelled the darkness of this world when Christ, the true light, dawned on us. Let us pray to God with unlimited confidence on this joyful (night) day.

Response: Save us through your birth.

Reader(s): For all who believe in Christ: that the light of hope and love may shine through all they say and do. [Pause] Let us pray to the Lord.

For rulers: that Christ, the Prince of Peace, may direct their minds and hearts to work for justice and peace on earth. [Pause] Let us pray to the Lord.

For those whose lives are troubled: that through his coming among us, Christ may give faith to those in doubt, courage to those in fear, and hope to those in despair. [Pause] Let us pray to the Lord.

For ourselves: that we may welcome Christ into our lives with the faith and love of Mary, Joseph and the shepherds. [Pause] Let us pray to the Lord.

For our own special needs. [Longer pause] Let us pray to the Lord.

President: Father, when your Son came on earth he filled the world with your glory. Help us to live as children of the light, so that when our earthly journey is over, we may come to the kingdom of everlasting day. We ask this through Christ our Lord.

SIGN OF PEACE

Lord Jesus, at your birth the angels sang: 'Glory to God in the highest, and peace to his people on earth.' Grant that we who have heard the message of the angels may enjoy the peace and unity of your kingdom where you live for ever and ever.

REFLECTION   **Journey to Bethlehem**

Joseph and Mary set out for Bethlehem.
When they arrived there,
the time came for Mary to have her baby,
and she gave birth to a son.
All of us are journeying to Bethlehem,
where we hope to be born.
I know we were born once.
Nevertheless, we are still unborn,
in the sense that our true and full self
hasn't yet seen the light of day.
When our second birth occurs,
then all the gifts of grace and nature,
which God gave us as seeds,
will blossom and bear fruit.
Our ultimate goal is the heavenly Bethlehem
where we shall see God face to face.

Feast of the Holy Family
THE FINDING IN THE TEMPLE

INTRODUCTION AND CONFITEOR

As we assemble to celebrate the Eucharist on the feast of the Holy Family, we should remember that we form part of the family of the People of God. Let us pause to reflect on our call to unity, and ask God to remove the things that divide us. [Pause]

Lord Jesus, you came to unite us to one another and to the Father. Lord, have mercy.

You heal the wounds of sin and division. Christ, have mercy.

You intercede for us at the right hand of the Father. Lord, have mercy.

HEADINGS FOR READINGS

First Reading (1 Sam 1:20-22. 24-28). This deals with the birth of Samuel and his consecration to God.

Second Reading (1 Jn 3:1-2. 21-24). We are God's children and should live a life in keeping with this great dignity.

(*Note:* The First and Second Readings from Year A may be used as alternatives).

Gospel (Lk 2:41-52). The story of how the twelve-year-old Jesus got lost in Jerusalem shows that misunderstandings can occur even in the best of families, and gives us a glimpse of the true identity of Jesus.

HOMILY 1   **Reflecting on the readings**

This is a brief commentary on the readings for this feast.

First Reading: Samuel was a very special child. Hannah saw him as a gift from God, a sign of God's favour to her. It's not surprising then that she dedicated him to the Lord. In due time Samuel made his own that dedication, and went on to play a major role in the history of Israel.

In truth, every child is a gift from God. All parents have hopes and dreams for their children. But parents can't determine the future for their children. The children have to find their own way. Besides, God may have other plans for them that conflict with those of their parents.

Gospel: This tells the story of how the twelve-year-old Jesus got lost in Jerusalem. It shows that misunderstandings can occur even in the best of families. We are inclined to say that Jesus got lost in the Temple. But Jesus did not get lost in the Temple. Rather, he was at home there. It was there he began to find himself, and to discover his true identity. He was not just the son of Mary, but the unique Son of God.

Many lost, lonely, homeless souls have come to the house of God, or have wandered into it almost by accident, and felt at home there, and found peace there, and found themselves there. In God's house we discover who we are. Whatever the world may think of us, in God's house we know we are God's precious daughters and sons.

Second Reading: Jesus had a double identity. He was the son of Mary, and also the Son of God. We too have a double identity. We are not just children of our parents but also children of God. St John makes this very clear. We belong to God's family.

It was God who first loved us. There is nothing that we have to do to earn God's love. It is enough that we are, for God to love us. The very fact that we are, is a sign of God's love for us. Children respond to the love of their parents by obeying them. The way we respond to God's love for us is by obeying his commandments, especially his commandment of love.

In the incident of the losing and finding in the Temple, we see the love that Mary and Joseph had for Jesus. Afterwards he went down to Nazareth with them and obeyed them.

Home is a place where we are accepted as we are, with our strengths and weaknesses. This kind of acceptance enables us to grow as human beings and children of God.

In Luke's infancy narrative Mary is the only adult who will last into the public ministry and even into the beginnings of the Church. She is presented to us as a model Christian believer.

HOMILY 2   **Jesus begins to find himself**

Jesus was twelve years old – time for him to take on the obligations of the Law. So Mary and Joseph took him with them to Jerusalem to celebrate the feast of the Passover. It is the task of parents gradually to insert the child into the larger community and to teach him/her its traditions. Children also need to be shown a path to a spiritual well; otherwise they will always be thirsty.

But as Mary and Joseph set out on the return journey Jesus got left behind, and it wasn't until the end of the first day that he was missed. It was no joke – a small boy lost in a large city. It was deadly serious. Yet no one was to blame. It was the result of a misunderstanding. Misunderstandings occur even in the best families.

They began a frantic search for him. Failing to find him among their fellow pilgrims, they returned to the city to look for him. They could not understand why he would cause them such anxiety. But a child doesn't stop being your child when he/she causes you worry. Nor do you stop being a parent. It's easy to love children as infants, when all they need is attention and smiles. It's not so easy to love them when they begin to assert their own will.

When a child is hovering around his parents, it's a bad sign. It means he's insecure. When a child is sure of its parent's love, he forgets his parents, and goes out to explore the world. This is how it was with Jesus. He wasn't really lost. He was having an adventure. He knew where he was. He was in the house of God.

When at last they found him, their first question was very understandable: 'Why did you do this to us?' And he replied: 'I did it because I must be about my Father's business.' Though they didn't understand his explanation they didn't scold him. Had they done so they might have robbed him of the fruits of a marvellous experience. Sometimes parents don't know how to encourage their children even when they are interested in worthwhile things.

But Mary remembered his words and pondered them in her heart. Listening is a very important part of being a parent. We have to listen to what a child is saying with words and without them. Listening means searching for the real reasons behind the problem as opposed to seeking causes for condemnation.

Even though the incident was a painful one it had the effect of bringing them closer together. Jesus appreciated how much Mary and Joseph cared about him, so he gladly obeyed them. And Mary and Joseph realised what a special child Jesus was. And they began to give him scope to grow, even though it meant that he was growing away from them.

The lesson Mary and Joseph learned is a lesson which all parents need to learn. Every day children are less ours and more their own. Birth was simply the beginning of a great separation. Parents, having given life to their children, must not take it back. If they are possessive of their child, they will never know the real love of their child.

When we say that a child is a 'good' child, we seldom mean that the child is generous or morally sensitive. What we mean is that the child is docile and obedient. But obedience is not the highest virtue.

Jesus did not get lost in the Temple. Rather, he began to find himself there and to discover his true identity as the Son of God. Happy are we too if we find our true selves, as human beings and children of God. The Christian family can be a great help to us in this regard.

HOMILY 3   **Mary's pondering**

At the end of today's Gospel there is a very telling sentence. It goes: 'Mary stored up all these things in her heart.' And after the visit of the shepherds to the manger, we find a similar comment. Luke says that 'Mary treasured all these things and pondered them in her heart.' (2:19) Mary kept the memory of these events in her heart with a view to discerning the hidden meaning behind the marvellous happenings.

It's clear that Mary didn't immediately understand the meaning of what was happening to her and what God was asking of her. But that's how it always is. Profound lived experience always begins with perplexity. We never know at the time what is happening to us. It's only afterwards, perhaps long afterwards, that our eyes are opened and we begin to understand. Hence, the importance of reflection.

More than once we read in the Gospels that Mary was perplexed. So what did she do? She pondered, reflected and prayed, seeking to understand what was happening to her and her child. This pondering was not free from uncertainty and anxiety.

Mary comes across as a silent, reflective person. All her life she pondered and prayed over how God dealt with her. When she doesn't understand, she ponders in her heart until she insight comes. And she pondered the painful events even more to discern the purpose of God in them. In this way she acquired insight and wisdom.

Emerson says: 'Life lies behind us like a quarry from whence we get the tiles and copestones for the masonry of today.' Only by reflecting can we come to understand our experiences. We could have the experience but miss the meaning of it because we don't reflect on it. But with reflection, we can derive precious insights from our experiences.

It's easy to recall pleasant experiences, but not so easy to recall painful ones. We are tempted to suppress our painful memories. Even so, they can still influence us. They can distil a poison into us. We need to recall the painful experiences too: it's how we recall them that matters. They can provide the raw-material from which we derive understanding, compassion, and wisdom. The incident in which Jesus got lost in Jerusalem was a painful one for Mary. Yet she stored it in her heart, and, by so doing, learned from it.

Sadly, there are people who seem to learn nothing from experience. But for others experience is the real school. No one has become wise in a day or even in a year. Wisdom is the fruit of much pondering.

Parents need a lot of wisdom. What Mary learned from her praying and pondering she passed on to her child, who St Luke tells us, 'increased in wisdom, in stature, and in favour with God and men.' Jesus was taught, nourished, and formed by a wise woman who loved God with all her heart and soul.

ANOTHER STORY

There is a saying: 'One mother can take care of ten children, but ten children can't take care of one mother.' Of course, it's not always that simple, as the following story illustrates.

Once upon a time there was a mother bird who had a young fledgling which she loved very much. Then the time came to migrate. Knowing that her fledgling was too young to fly so far, she took it on her back.

And so they began the journey south. At first, the flight was relatively easy. But as time went by, the fledgling began to feel heavier, and the mother began to feel very tired. Nevertheless, she kept on going. One day while they were resting the mother turned to her fledgling and said, 'My child, tell me the truth. When I get old and won't have the strength to fly south over the great ocean, will you take me on your back and fly me across?'

'Mother, I can't promise you that,' her fledgling answered.

'And why not?' asked the mother.

'Because I may be busy flying my own children on my back just as you are doing for me now.'

While the mother's request was understandable, is was a little selfish. One must do what one can to care for one's elderly parents. Our first and holiest duty is kindness towards our own kin. But maybe caring for one's own children is the best way of repaying our parents for caring for us.

PRAYER OF THE FAITHFUL

President: The Son of God became part of a human family. Let us pray to him for the well-being of all families.

Response: Lord, in your mercy, hear our prayer.

Reader(s): For all Christians: that they may set an example of unity and peace for a fragmented and troubled world. [Pause] We pray to the Lord.

For world leaders: that they may co-operate with one another for the good of the entire human family. [Pause] Let us pray.

For families: that Christ, who knew what it was to be part of a human family, may turn the hearts of parents towards their children, and the hearts of children towards their parents. [Pause] Let us pray.

For those families that have been orphaned, or widowed, or which are experiencing problems of any kind. [Pause] Let us pray.

For ourselves: that, like the Child Jesus, we may grow in wisdom and in favour with God and other people. [Pause] Let us pray.

For the needs of our own family. [Longer pause] Let us pray.

President: O God, Father of every family, against whom no door can be shut, convert our hearts and our homes into fit dwelling places for your Son, who lives and reigns with you and the Holy Spirit one God, for ever and ever.

PRAYER/REFLECTION   **A prayer for parents**

Lord, grant us children,
who will be strong enough to know when they are weak;
who will be unbending in defeat, yet humble and gentle in victory.
Grant us children, whose wishes will not take the place of their deeds;
children who will know you and know themselves.

Lead them, we pray you, not in the path of ease and comfort,
but rather in the path of difficulties and challenges.
Grant us children,
whose hearts will be clear, and whose goals will be high;
children who will master themselves before seeking to master others.
And after all these things, add, we pray,
a sense of humour, so that they can be serious,
yet never take themselves too seriously.
Then we, their parents, will dare whisper, we have not lived in vain.

(From a prayer by General MacArthur)

Second Sunday after Christmas
HE DWELT AMONG US

INTRODUCTION AND CONFITEOR

St John says: 'The Word [God's Son] became flesh and dwelt among us.'
Our religion is founded on this great mystery. As we gather to celebrate
the Eucharist, Christ is present among us. Let us draw close to him in
confidence, and bring our burdens to him. [Pause]

Lord Jesus, you are the true light that enlightens all people. Lord, have
mercy.

To all who accept you, you give power to become children of God.
Christ, have mercy.

You are full of grace and truth. Lord, have mercy.

HEADINGS FOR READINGS

First Reading (Eccles 24:1-2.8-12). This is a poem in praise of wisdom, a
wisdom that has pitched her tent among God's people.

Second Reading (Eph 1:3-6.15-18). We hear of God's plan of salvation, a
plan which is centred in Christ and realised through him.

Gospel (Jn 1:!-18). This is a great hymn to the Word of God, the source
of all life, whose coming among us makes us children of God.

SCRIPTURE NOTE

The Gospel consists of the prologue to John's Gospel. Here John introduces the main themes that will be developed in his Gospel – life, light,
darkness, truth, witness, glory, the world. It cannot be fully understood
until the whole Gospel has been read.

Through a summary of history, the prologue shows that from the dawn
of creation God has been with humans, and in spite of darkness and ig-

norance, has invited them to knowledge of and intimacy with himself. But in Jesus something infinitely better is offered to us.

In the theology of John's gospel, the Son descends from heaven to our level, and ascends back to heaven bringing us up with him to the divine level. The prologue describes the Son in heaven and the descent; the Gospel describes the Son walking among us and his final elevation and return to the Father.

The first part (vv. 1-11) presents the Son as the Word. Eternally present with God, the Word brings life and light to the world. Sadly, the world, and even his own people, rejected him. This negative response is something that recurs throughout John's Gospel.

The second part (vv. 12-18) notes a more positive response. The Word becomes one of us and lives among us. To those who accept him he gives the power to become children of God.

HOMILY 1   **Love story**

In the incarnation, Jesus, the Son of God, came to share our human lives in order that we might share his divine life. The Incarnation is a mystery of love, God's love for us in Christ. The following parable may shed a little light on this great mystery.

Once upon a time there was a prince who fell in love with a humble maiden. As heir to the throne, he knew that if he married the girl, she would become queen and this would make her happy. But then he realised that something would be missing in her happiness. She would always admire him and thank him. But she would not be able to love him, for the inequality between them would be too great.

So he decided on another way. He decided to renounce his kingship, become an ordinary man, and offer her love as an equal. In doing so he realised that he was taking a great risk. However, he thought it better to risk everything in order to make real love possible.

So he put aside the robes of a prince, donned the clothes of an ordinary man, and left the royal palace. Gradually he befriended the maiden and offered her his love. His love was absolutely pure. He was not seeking anything for himself. The girl, however, found this hard to believe because she didn't think such love existed among humans.

Besides, she had such a poor image of herself that she didn't think she was worthy of anyone's love. She couldn't understand that anyone would love her for herself. However, one day in a sudden burst of faith and trust, she opened her heart to him. And all at once her empty heart was flooded with love.

Once she accepted his love, she began to believe in her own goodness. Then she was able to love in return. And they both were very happy for real love existed between them.

If Jesus had come on earth in all the glory of his divinity, people would have trembled before him. They would not only have accepted him, but would have fallen down to worship him. But he did not want this. He knew that this kind of submission would never bring us happiness.

So he came in humility and weakness. He wanted to gain our love so that we would follow him of our own free will. He wanted our freely given love rather than the servile rapture of slaves.

But this involved a risk. People might not accept him. And this is exactly what happened. St John says sadly, 'He came to his own and his own people did not accept him.' But some did accept him. To these he gave a share in his divine life. He made them children of God.

When we accept God's love we experience our own goodness, and we are able to love God in return. Real love becomes possible between us. In his love for us God made all of this possible through the gift of his Son. In Jesus we have a Brother who loves us to the extent that he came among us and shared our lives to the full. Not only did he share our lives, but he also shared our death.

From his fullness, as from a limitless fountain, all of us have received, and will continue to receive. We should be willing to share with others the love we have received so generously.

HOMILY 2   **He lived among us**

If you want to really understand and be in touch with ordinary people, you have to go where nobody recognises you. You have to see what they see, hear what they hear, live what they live. Understanding it in an abstract way is different from feeling it with your whole being.

This is why God's Son became man. 'It was essential that he should in this way be made completely like his brothers [and sisters].' (Heb 2:14-18) Some try to make themselves different from others, keep part, adopt superior attitudes, as if they weren't quite human. Jesus, on the other hand, became like us in everything except sin.

In the immortal words of St John's Gospel: 'The Word was made flesh, and lived among us.' Jesus didn't come to live among the rich, the powerful and the famous. No, he voluntarily separated himself from the society that 'counts', and lost himself in an obscure village. Nazareth was the place of the poor, of the mass of ordinary people. His was a life made up of obscure human activities, simple things shared by all people. Here we see what the incarnation was really about. There is little we can say about our lives that God's Son could not say when he became man and lived among us.

The Gospels show us Jesus as a healer, teacher and wonder-worker. But these activities lasted only three years. For the rest of his life on earth he worked as a village carpenter. There was nothing spectacular about his work. For the most part it was routine, and no doubt often left him tired and frustrated. He didn't make benches and tables by means of miracles, but by the hammer and the saw. And, as far as we know, nothing he made ever set fashion trends or became collectors' items. Yet he did this work faithfully until the day he heard another call.

For one point of view those years at Nazareth might seen to be a waste of precious time. But nothing could be further from the truth. Those years had immense significance for Jesus. During them he was growing in wisdom and grace. He began by doing. He lived his message before he preached it to others.

There is a great lesson for us in all of this. We must not write off any part of our lives as useless, or any experience as a waste. Everything gives us an opportunity to grow. Life calls for a lot of patient waiting. But we must not wait for something great to happen. We must live the present moment to the full. The future is contained in the present. The future will be the blossoming of the present.

Often our daily tasks may seem to be dull and insignificant. But we must not underestimate their importance. Though nothing great may ever happen, a kind of greatness is still open to us. To perform one's ordinary work well, day in and day out, presents no small challenge. In fact, it calls for a kind of heroism.

We must try to appreciate the value of our daily tasks. If we do them faithfully, like Jesus at Nazareth, we will grow, and mature, and ripen as human beings and children of God.

HOMILY 3   **Loving at close quarters**

The following is a true story. It concerns a young man named Mark. Severely physically handicapped and apparently unable to speak, Mark was locked into a lonely, silent world. The door wasn't actually locked. He was free to leave if he so wished. But it seemed he had no wish to do so. He had retreated from the world, if indeed he ever belonged to it. He had cut himself off from life and from other people. So there he remained, joyless and forlorn.

Why had he done this? Because he felt useless and hopeless. He had nothing to live for – no goal, no aim, no purpose. His self-worth was nil. It is sad and tragic when a human being is locked up in himself and unable to communicate. It results in the death of the heart and a paralysis of the spirit.

From time to time the professionals had made attempts to reach him. But instead of offering him the one thing he desperately needed, and was secretly crying for, namely, human warmth and intimacy, they offered him words. But words proved ineffective, because wounds like his can't be cured by words alone.

Yet only a few years later Mark had come out of his shell. He had become an expert ham radio operator, and was in touch with other radio operators from over thirty countries scattered around the world.

How was the miracle achieved? One day a woman went to see him. Entering his dark, lonely world she said simply, 'Hello, Mark! I'm Claire.' Then she sat down beside him. She did not go away. Now at long last he had a friend, someone who believed in him and cared about him. A spark was lit in his dim life. Gradually this spark turned into a bright gleam. Eventually he followed the gleam. It led him out of his prison.

Love is the only medicine that will heal a wounded heart. Jean Vanier says, 'It's an extraordinary thing for a person with a handicap to discover that he or she is loved.' Vanier knows what he is talking about because he has spent most of his adult life working with the handicapped.

What Claire did helps us to understand today's Gospel, where St John calls Jesus the Word of God. In his love for us, God spoke many words to us through creation, through the prophets, and so on. But finally the Word became flesh, in the person of his Son. This is the ultimate proof of his love. Jesus placed himself beside us. Before starting his public ministry he proved his love by simple presence with people. He didn't drop in, say 'hello', and disappear again. He came and lived among the people.

This was no loving 'from a distance'. This was loving at close quarters. Jesus was not passing through like a tourist. He joined the human family and lived among us. He knows what it is like to be human, what makes us weep, what makes us fall and stumble and somehow rise and go on again. He assumed our fragile, perishable humanity, in order to show us what our humanity is capable of.

Because of the incarnation God is present to us in a way that we can relate to, for Jesus is like us in all things but sin. He is a brother to us. He has made us children of God. From his fullness we have all received. And we should be willing to share with others the love that God has so generously shared with us.

PRAYER OF THE FAITHFUL

President: God's Son was made flesh and lived among us. Let us now bring our needs before him, knowing that he will understand them.

Response: Lord, save us through your presence.

Reader(s): That the followers of Jesus may grow in wisdom and grace. [Pause] We pray to the Lord.

That through his coming as man, the Lord may establish peace among the nations and peoples of the world. [Pause] We pray to the Lord.

That Christ, who shared our human frailties, may give hope to the poor, the sick, the lonely, and the dispirited. [Pause] Let us pray to the Lord.

That workers may find dignity through their work; that the unemployed may not lose hope. [Pause] We pray to the Lord.

That we may have time for one another and share ourselves with one another. [Pause] We pray the Lord.

That God may grant our own special needs. [Longer pause] We pray to the Lord.

President: Lord God, through the coming of your Son a light has been lit in our world, a light that no darkness can overpower. May we walk in that light and so come to your kingdom of everlasting life. We ask this through the same Christ our Lord.

REFLECTION   **A prayer for the new year**

Lord, in this new year which we have begun,
  may we have enough happiness to keep us agreeable,
  enough trials to keep us strong,
  enough sorrow to keep us human,
  enough freedom to keep us happy,
  enough failure to keep us humble,
  enough success to keep us eager,
  enough wealth to meet our needs,
  enough faith to banish depression,
  enough hope to look forward,
  enough love to give us comfort,
  and enough determination to keep going.   *(Anon.)*

The Epiphany of the Lord

INTRODUCTION AND CONFITEOR

The Magi were searching for Christ. When they found him, they worshipped him and offered him gifts. Millions of people have followed in the footsteps of the Magi and come to Christ. We count ourselves among those fortunate millions. Let us open our hearts and minds to encounter Christ in this Eucharist. [Pause]

Lord Jesus, you came to gather the nations into the peace of God's kingdom. Lord, have mercy.

You come in word and sacrament to strengthen us in holiness. Christ, have mercy.

You will come in glory with salvation for your people. Lord, have mercy.

HEADINGS FOR READINGS

First Reading (Is 60:1-6). The prophet cheers the exiles who returned from Babylon with a vision of a restored city. The prophecy is fulfilled in Christ and in the new Israel, the Church.

Second Reading (Eph 3:2-3.5-6). This reading expresses the theological meaning of today's feast: God invites Jews and Gentiles to share in the salvation brought by Christ.

Gospel (Mt 2:1-12). Three Gentiles came from a far country to pay homage to the Christ-child, while the Jewish leaders rejected him.

SCRIPTURE NOTE

For Matthew, the story of the Magi becomes an anticipation of the fate of the Good News of salvation, a fate that he knew in the aftermath of the resurrection. God revealed himself to the Jews through the Scriptures, and to the Gentiles through nature. Hence, Matthew shows the Magi (who were Gentiles) receiving a revelation through astrology. The story highlights the paradox: the Jews who have the Scriptures reject Jesus, while Gentiles come, and with the help of the Scriptures, find and adore him.

There is nothing to be gained by speculating where the Magi came from and what exactly the star was. The star was only the means by which a great mystery was revealed – the revelation of Christ as the Saviour of the Gentiles too.

The Second Reading expresses the theological meaning of today's feast: God invites Jew and Gentile to share on an equal footing the benefits of the salvation brought by Christ.

HOMILY 1   **A light for all peoples**

Rosaleen grew up in a lovely walled garden in the company of thousands of other roses, all red like herself. She was told that it was a great privilege to have been born into the Red Rose Clan. High standards were expected of her, and she had to obey a lot of rules. One of those rules forbade her ever to attempt to climb over the garden wall.

But as she got older she began to ask herself what lay on the other side of the wall. One day, overcome by curiosity, she climbed the wall and took a peep over. What did she see? She saw another walled garden similar to her own. And in it grew lots of other roses, like herself in everything but colour – some were pink, some white, and some yellow.

She was shocked. After all, she had been told that there was only one rose – a red rose. But then an elder of the clan told her, 'Forget those flowers on the other side of the wall. They don't belong to our clan. Remember this: The only true rose is a red rose.'

But try as she might she couldn't forget them. So, another day, she climbed the wall again and began to chat with a pink rose from the other side. Her example caught on. More and more roses from both sides began to meet and talk across the wall.

Slowly a great transformation took place. Having come to acknowledge each other's existence, the roses gradually came to accept their differences. And even though the wall continued to stand between them, they learned to communicate with one another in spite of it. And in time they came to see themselves as members of one large family – the rose family – a family of great variety and beauty.

The feast of the Epiphany is a revolutionary feast. Christ is revealed as the Saviour, not of a select group of people, but of all peoples. Jesus broke down the great barrier that existed between Jews and Gentiles. In fact, all the barriers of tribe, of kinship, are transcended by the message of Jesus, the Universal Brother.

The Epiphany is a beautiful feast because it brings everybody together. 'All now share the same inheritance, they are part of the same body.' But that doesn't mean these barriers have magically disappeared. Wherever we go today we see divisions among people, in families, communities, cities, countries. Today's barriers are racial, ethnic, social and religious ones. All these divisions are reflections of our separation from God.

God sent Jesus into the world to reconcile people with him and with one another. As people reconciled with God through Jesus we have been given the ministry of reconciliation. Talking across the fences is important. Christians are called to be agents of love that can bridge all divisions and heal all wounds. The Church ought to be a place where all barriers fall down, a tent in which there is room for everyone.

HOMILY 2   **They opened their treasures**

One of Aesop's fables goes like this. A child was sitting by a wall when suddenly a toad emerged from a hole. The child quickly spread out her silk scarf in front of the toad, the kind which toads love to walk on. As soon as the toad saw the scarf, it went back into the hole and soon returned carrying a little gold crown which it laid on the scarf, and went back into the hole again.

The girl immediately picked up the crown and put it into her pocket. Before long the toad came out again, but when it did not see the crown on the scarf, it crept to the wall and from sorrow beat its little head against the wall until it finally collapsed and died. Had the girl let the crown lie where it was, the toad would surely have brought out more of its treasures from the cave.

The purpose of this little story is to show that everybody has a treasure to share. The question is: how to get them to share that treasure. A lot of patience is called for. The secret lies in getting them to share it voluntarily. There's no point in forcing people to make sacrifices. If you take things from people, they are impoverished; but if you can get them to give them up, they are enriched. People are essentially good, but this goodness has to be awakened and called forth, if they are to enter the kingdom of love.

Here, Christmas comes to our aid. If God's Son had come in wealth, he would have made us aware of our own poverty. Thus he would have evoked a feeling of envy in us, and done serious damage to our hearts. But he came in weakness, thereby making us aware of our own riches. His poverty evoked in us a feeling of compassion, thereby bringing our hearts to life. To look at the poverty of the infant King of the Universe causes us to open our hearts.

It was the poverty of Jesus that caused the Magi to open their treasures of gold, frankincense, and myrrh, and lay them before him. And instead of being impoverished, the Magi were enriched. It is through giving that we are enriched, because through giving we discover our own riches.

The lovely feast of the Epiphany challenges us to open our hearts. To open one's heart is to begin to live. Jesus no longer needs our gifts. But other people may. He wants us to share ourselves with one another. And we too will find ourselves enriched, if as a result of knowing Jesus, we are able to open the treasures of our hearts and share them with others.

HOMILY 3   **Finding the Lord**

Alan was recovering in hospital from a motorcycle accident. It was coming up to Christmas. One night as he lay in bed he looked out the window and noticed that the sky was full of stars. Suddenly he began to think about the Magi and their journey to Bethlehem in search of Christ.

Then he began to think about himself, something which up to then he had never really done. And he said to himself: 'Here I am, 23 years old, and what have I done with my life? Where have I gone?' The answer was 'nowhere'. He was still living for thrills and excitement. He had wasted the best years of his life, the years a poet called 'the splendid years'.

Next he thought about his relationship with the Lord. The Magi didn't have the Lord at the start. But they set out to look for him, and persevered until they found him. For him it was the opposite. He didn't have to go looking for the Lord. He had him from the very start. He was baptised and brought up a Catholic. He went to church regularly until he was fifteen. But then he gave it all up. He lost the Lord. And instead of looking for him, he deliberately turned his back on him. He was in full flight from him. More, he was in rebellion against him.

That was a very dark night for him when all this came crowding in on him. But when the darkness was at its thickest a beautiful thing happened. It was as if the Lord's star rose before him. He realised that the Lord's light hadn't been extinguished. It had continued to shine all those

[57]

years, except it was hidden by clouds. And a wonderful truth dawned on him: Even though he had abandoned the Lord, the Lord had not abandoned him. All those years the Lord had been searching for him.

He was overcome with joy. He never thought that he mattered to anyone, least of all to the Lord. And he said to himself: 'From now on I have a star that will not play me false, I have a compass that will not lie to me.'

When the Magi found the Lord they offered him wonderful gifts – gold, frankincense, and myrrh. Now that Alan had found the Lord, what could he offer him? For a while he was at a complete loss. But then he realised there was something he could offer the Lord. He could offer the Lord *himself*. But, of course, he would first of all have to find himself before he could offer himself as a gift to anyone else. However, he could at least make a start, and that he was determined to do rightaway.

Christmas came, and Alan remained in hospital. But people saw an amazing change in him. Up to this he had been full of bitterness about life in general, and about his accident in particular. Now he had a smile and a cheerful word for everyone. People were puzzled as to what had produced this change in him. But Alan himself knew what it was. It was the fact that he had found the Lord. No one can truly find the Lord without being changed.

Years later he said: 'That was the first real Christmas in my life. No, I didn't hear angels singing in the sky. But I did experience some of the peace they sang about on that first Christmas night.'

Everybody needs a star to follow, just as ships at sea need a lighthouse beacon to guide them safely to port. Truly blessed are we if the star of the Lord has risen before us, and twice blessed are we if we follow that star steadfastly all our lives. It means we have hitched our wagon to a star, a star of hope, the star of Bethlehem. Many spend their lives searching for what we have and do not find it.

And we mustn't fear if we find our lives changed as a result – the change will be for the better. It will be such that it will bring us a joy this world cannot bring.

ANOTHER APPROACH   **Parting of the veil**

The word *epiphany* means a revelation. Here is a small and simple example. Sometimes on a dull, cold winter's day, a break appears in the thick layer of cloud, and through it we catch a glimpse of a radiant sun. All too soon, however, the break is covered up, and the sun disappears once more. But that short glimpse of a brighter and warmer world can do wonders for us. The mere memory of it can work its magic on our spirit.

Daily life is full of little epiphanies for those who have eyes to see and minds to reflect. They slip in through the cracks in our busy armour – a moment of peace, or of beauty, or of goodness.

On this day, feast of the Epiphany, there was a mysterious parting of the veil which enabled the Magi to catch a glimpse of the radiance of the Child of Bethlehem. Some people looked at the Christ-child and saw just another child. Others, such as Herod, saw the Child as a threat. But the Magi recognised the Christ-child as their Saviour. All those people had the same eyes, yet they did not see the same things with those eyes. It was faith which enabled the Magi to penetrate the veil and 'see' the reality beyond.

Yet for them too the veil closed again, the star disappeared, and they had to return home. What difference did the experience make to them? In one sense, it made no difference. They had to go back to their old lives, their old occupations, and so on. However, in another sense, one would like to think that it made the world of difference to them. They now had a new vision, and a new hope.

For them the epiphany had been one of those moments which takes a short-cut to truth. It was a flash of light that illuminated their lives, and invested every moment with significance. No doubt it took time and reflection for them to understand the meaning of what they had found at the end of their journey to Bethlehem. But on cloudy days they drew courage and hope from the epiphany that had been granted to them.

Like the Magi, on this feast we have come to worship the Christ-child. And, again like the Magi, we have to go back to our homes and get on with our ordinary lives. But hopefully we will see those lives differently, because we see ourselves differently. In the divine Child, we see our own divinity.

People sometimes travel long distances in search of spiritual experiences which they could have in their home place. We don't have to travel anywhere. His star rises up before us here. Because of the coming of Christ, we need no longer fear the darkness. A light has come into the world, a light that shines in the dark, a light that no darkness can overpower.

PRAYER OF THE FAITHFUL

President: God has sent his Son into the world as the light of the world. Let us pray to him in faith for all our needs.

Response: Lord, hear us in your love.

Reader(s): For the shepherds of the Church: that they may be selfless ministers of the Gospel. [Pause] We pray in faith

For all of humankind: that Christ may be a beacon of faith and hope for all the peoples of the world. [Pause] We pray in faith.

For all those who are lost and who have no star to guide them. [Pause] We pray in faith.

For us who have found Christ: that we may live according to his teachings. [Pause] We pray in faith.

For our deceased relatives and friends: that the light of God's glory may shine on them. [Pause] We pray in faith.

For our own special needs. [Longer pause] We pray in faith.

President: Lord our God, lead us from the faith by which we know you now to the radiant vision of your glory, where we shall see you face to face. We ask this through the same Christ our Lord.

REFLECTION   **The light of Christ**

Christ's light was not lit once in Bethlehem and then extinguished.
For two thousand years his light has shone upon the world.
And it will continue to shine
or all who believe in him and follow him.
The light of Christ is a persistent light,
and has the power to draw people to its shining.
It shines in the midst of disasters and upheavals.
It is a defiant light, which no darkness can overpower.
Its purpose is not to judge us,
but to show us the way to the Father's kingdom.
God has called us out of darkness
into the wonderful light of his Son.
We must live as children of the light.
So, let us imitate the Magi,
and walk in the light of the Lord.

The Baptism of the Lord

INTRODUCTION AND CONFITEOR

Even though Jesus was without sin, nevertheless, he joined sinners and was baptised by John the Baptist. Jesus joins us now as we meet to celebrate the Eucharist in his name. Let us draw near to him who is the messenger of the Father's love and mercy. [Pause]

Lord Jesus, you open our ears so that we can hear your word. Lord, have mercy.

You touch our tongues so that we can profess our faith. Christ, have mercy.

You touch our hearts so that we can love you and love one another. Lord, have mercy.

First Reading (Is 40:1-5.9-11). The people are urged to prepare a way for the Lord who is coming to save them.

Second Reading (Tit 2:11-14.3:4-7). God's grace and love are manifested in Jesus Christ.

(*Note:* the First and Second Readings from Year A may be used as alternatives).

Gospel (Lk 3:15-16.21-22). We hear a small sample of the preaching of John the Baptist, and are given a brief account of the baptism of Jesus.

SCRIPTURE NOTE

In the First Reading (Isaiah), the prophet assures the exiles in Babylon that God is coming to save them. The prophecy was fulfilled in the return from exile, but more especially in the coming of Jesus.

John the Baptist was clearly a prophet. Since the spirit of prophecy had long been absent from Israel, John's appearance raised expectations. The question arose: Could he be the Messiah? John denied that he was the Messiah, but declared that the Messiah was at hand. Thus he prepared the way for Jesus.

Baptism was a defining moment in the life of Jesus – it marked the beginning of his public mission. Luke always presents Jesus as praying before making major decisions. It's no surprise then that we find him praying during his baptism. In response to his prayer, the Holy Spirit descends on him in bodily form at the beginning of his mission, just as it will come in visible form on the apostles at Pentecost at the beginning of their mission. The Father puts his seal of approval on Jesus and on the mission he is about to begin.

HOMILY 1   **The greatness of baptism**

The baptism of Jesus reminds us of our own baptism. There are many offices that people can hold in the Church. But all of these pale when compared to the basic gift to all: baptism. When we stand before the throne of God, these other offices will be of no importance. Our dignity will depend on one thing only – the extent to which we have lived out our baptismal calling.

The ceremony of baptism is a beautiful one. In it we were formally given a name and welcomed into the family of God's people. Lovely prayers were said over us. Our body was signed with the sign of the cross, the mark of Christ's love for us. Water was poured over us. Water is a symbol of cleansing, and in baptism we are cleansed of sin. But it is more especially a symbol of life. In baptism we are given a share in the undying life of God.

Not once but twice our bodies were anointed with holy oil. Just as the bodies of athletes were smeared with oil to give them strength to compete, so we were anointed with holy oil to give us strength for the inevitable struggle against evil. And just as kings, prophets and priests were anointed with oil and thus marked out as God's ministers to the community, so we are anointed with the oil of chrism that we may be envoys of Christ in the world.

Our body was covered with a white garment, the outward sign of our Christian dignity. We were given a candle lighted from the Easter candle to signify the precious light of faith. God called us out of darkness into the wonderful light of his Son.

What happened at the baptism of Jesus happened at our baptism too. God called us by name. He said to each of us, 'You are my beloved son,' or 'You are my beloved daughter.' And the Spirit descended on us, in order to help us to live the life of a Christian and to participate in the mission of Jesus.

From a spiritual point of view, baptism is the greatest thing that can happen to us. To be baptised is to be *christened*, that is, to be made like Christ. But this doesn't happen automatically as a result of being baptised. One has to learn what it means to be a Christian, and to grow into it. This is the task of a lifetime. Towards the end of his life a saint was asked if he was a Christian, and he replied, 'not yet.'

There are many vocations in the Church. But the most important vocation of all is common to all the baptised. It is the vocation we received at baptism – the vocation to be disciples of Jesus. This is the core vocation. Every other vocation in the Church must be seen in relation to this one.

We celebrate birthdays lavishly. So we should celebrate our baptismal day, because this was the day we were born as children of God. Every time we enter a church and sign ourselves with holy water we are reminding ourselves of our baptism, and committing ourselves to live up to it. To live one's baptism is to live as a disciple of Jesus.

If this homily was followed by a renewal of baptismal promises, it would help to drive home the message. But the best way to get across the greatness of baptism would be to celebrate an actual baptism during Mass. The ceremony should be integrated into the Eucharist. In this way the members of the congregation will be involved in it, and given the opportunity to relive their own baptisms.

HOMILY 2   **The Christian vocation**

At present the Church is very preoccupied with vocations. But vocation here is understood in a very limited sense. Basically what we are talking about is a vocation to the priesthood. While this is important, it is by no means the most important vocation in the Church.

The first and most important vocation is that which is common to all the baptised, namely, the Christian vocation, or the vocation to be a disciple of Jesus. This is the core vocation. Every other vocation in the Church must be seen in relation to this one. At our baptism we answered Jesus' call: 'Come, follow me.' In other words, we received the call to be disciples of Jesus.

Yet the sad fact is that many of the baptised live no differently from the non-baptised. Their faith, if they practise it at all, is an immature faith, based on non-decision and routine practice. The need is to believe with understanding; and to follow Christ out of personal conviction.

Cardinal Newman once asked his congregation: 'What difference does being a Christian make in the way we live our daily lives?' The conclusion he came to was: 'I fear that most of us would go on almost as we do, if we believed Christianity to be nothing more than a fable.'

What does the Christian vocation consist in? The Christian vocation is, in the words of the Gospel, a call to be 'the salt of the earth, and the light of the world'. Christianity is about how to live, not just about what to believe. There should be no distinction between religious activity and the acts of every day. Faith has to be translated into action. 'Don't bother proclaiming that you believe unless you act accordingly.' (Catherine de Hueck Doherty)

As Christians we have a very positive role to play in the world. We have something to offer, something the world desperately needs, even though it may not always welcome it. We should not be shy or apologetic about our role. A certain boldness and courage are called for.

What does the following of Christ mean for the ordinary person? It means to be a Christian where you are and in your chosen profession. There are many ways of serving Christ and his Gospel. The call in the first instance is not to an apostolate but to discipleship.

No doubt if we had never heard the call of Jesus we would have an easier life. But would we have a happier life, and would we have as much life? Jesus said, 'I came that you may have life, and have it to the full.' The Gospel offers us a deeper and more authentic way of living our lives. And it implants in us the seeds of eternal life.

The Christian vocation causes the vision of a higher and a purer life to rise up before us. At the same time it inspires sacrifice and service of others. It expands the possibilities of human love and courage. The task is not one for the individual Christian only but for the Christian community as a whole. It is easier to witness to Christ as a member of a supportive community. At our baptism we are welcomed into a believing community.

The feast of the baptism of Jesus reminds us of our own baptism, and provides us with an opportunity to commit ourselves once again to the Christian life. In fact, every time we enter a church and sign ourselves with holy water we are reminding ourselves of our baptism, and committing ourselves to live up to it.

HOMILY 3   **Christian on trial**

In a certain country it is a crime to be a Christian. Mr and Mrs. Moran are accused of being Christians. Far from denying the charge, they both openly admit it, and are prepared to face the consequences. They are brought to court to be tried before a jury. Their relatives, all of whom have abandoned the faith, desire to save them from prison or worse. So they hire a lawyer to defend them against the charge. Briefly his defence goes as follows:

'My clients are charged with being Christians. I aim to show that in fact they are no such thing, no matter how courageously they may insist on calling themselves Christians. The facts are against them. And, need I say, this case will have to be judged on facts.

'To being with let me say this: The Morans are a good-living, hard-working couple. As far as I can ascertain, they have never been involved in anything illegal. By any standards they are respectable people.

'There are many things in their lives one can admire. They are sincere people. And one can admire their fidelity to the external observances of their religion, such as attendance at Mass and the sacraments. In fact, I'm willing to concede that they are Christians of sorts. They are Sunday morning Christians, and a very good ones at that. But this is not enough.

'Christ said in the Gospel, and I quote: "By their fruits you shall know them." (Mt 7:15) It's clear from the context that by "fruits" he meant "good deeds". I'm afraid that in the case of the Morans the fruits are simply not there.

'I find no evidence in their lives, or in their attitudes, that they take the teachings of Christ seriously. For instance, can anyone seriously charge my clients with any special concern for the poor, the sick, the unfortunate, or the despised? I suggest that there isn't a shred of evidence to support such a charge. They have done no more than any of us have done. In fact, they have done even less than some people who would never dream of calling themselves Christians.

'Yet these are exactly the kind of people Christ himself went out of his way to befriend when he was on earth. And he stated categorically that his followers would be judged, not on the number of prayers they said or acts of worship they participated in, but on their response to the needs of such people.

'The first disciples of Jesus were fiery apostles whom he sent forth to convert the world. They wouldn't recognise the Morans as belonging to their company.'

(At this point Mr Moran jumped up and shouted: 'But we are Christians.')

'Words are not enough, Mr Moran. I submit to this court that my clients are not Christians in the real sense – in the sense of people to whom their neighbour is as dear as themselves. All they are guilty of is self-deception, and that is no crime. Therefore, I ask that the charge against my clients be dropped because of lack of evidence.'

The judge then said: 'The jury will retire to consider the verdict.'

The feast of the Baptism of Jesus reminds us of our own baptism. At our baptism we received the call to be disciples of Jesus. Hence, the question each of us might ask is: If it was a crime to be a Christian, would there be enough evidence in my life to secure a conviction?

(The homilist might give the congregation an opportunity to reflect on this.)

PRAYER OF THE FAITHFUL

President: The baptism of Jesus helps us to understand the meaning of our own baptism. Let us pray for the grace to live up to it.

Response: Lord, hear our prayer.

Reader(s): For all Christians: that they may strive to live up to the dignity conferred on them in baptism. [Pause] Let us pray to the Lord.

For all political leaders and scientists: that they may obey their conscience, and seek to promote truth and justice in the world. [Pause] Let us pray to the Lord.

For all those who are suffering persecution in the cause of right. [Pause] Let us pray to the Lord.

For each other and for ourselves: that we may believe with our hearts, and practise with our lives the faith we profess with our lips. [Pause] Let us pray to the Lord.

For our own special needs. [Longer pause] Let us pray to the Lord.

President: Almighty God, send us your Spirit to open our eyes blinded by selfishness, and to set us free from the prison of our fears and doubts, so that we can grow to maturity as your sons and daughters. We ask this through Christ our Lord.

PRAYER/REFLECTION   **Sharing in the Lord's ministry**

Lord Jesus, touch our eyes
so that we may see the signs of your presence
in our lives and in the world.
Touch our ears so that we may hear your word.
Touch our tongues so that we may profess our faith.
Touch our hands so that we may give and receive.

Touch our feet so that we may walk in your paths.
Touch our minds so that we may understand your ways.
Touch our wills so that they may be in tune with your will.
Touch our hearts so that we may bring your love
to our brothers and sisters,
to the praise and glory of God.
Amen.

LENT & PASSION (PALM) SUNDAY

Jesus Takes His Cross

PATRICK PYE

First Sunday of Lent

INTRODUCTION AND CONFITEOR

Last Wednesday the Church invited us to embark on a journey, the journey of Lent, which is a journey towards Easter. We are a baptised people but haven't yet lived fully the life of a Christian. Lent calls us to a change of heart and a fuller living of the Gospel. In today's Gospel we see Jesus struggling against temptation. He will help us in our struggles against temptation. [Pause].

Lord Jesus, you were sent to heal the contrite. Lord, have mercy.

You came to call sinners to repentance. Christ, have mercy.

You plead for us at the right hand of the Father. Lord, have mercy.

HEADINGS FOR READINGS

First Reading (Deut 26:4-10). Through the ceremony of offering the first fruits, the Israelites recognised all that God had done for them in the past, especially in the Exodus. Our worship of God is also a recognition of his favours to us.

Second Reading (Rom 10:8-13). The core of the Christian *credo* is that Jesus is our risen Saviour. Anyone who can say that and live by it, will be saved.

Gospel (Lk 4:1-13). Jesus was tempted like we are, but did not sin. Through his grace we too can resist temptation and overcome sin.

SCRIPTURE NOTE

All three readings are concerned with faithfulness to God. The First Reading describes the ceremony of the offering to God of the first fruits of the harvest. It was an occasion for the people to thank God, not only for the blessings of the harvest, but for all he had done for them in the past, and especially in the Exodus. The creed which the offerer recited is a summary of Israel's early history and humble origins. The readings of the following Sundays will focus on significant moments of that history.

The Second Reading contains in its simplest form the Christian credo: Jesus is Lord; he died for our sins and was raised up for our justification. Obviously for this faith to be genuine, it must be professed not just with one's lips but also with one's life.

Luke's account of the temptations follows closely that of Matthew, except that he deliberately changes the order of the last two temptations so that the series ends in Jerusalem. This is in keeping with his theological interest in the holy city. The three scenes serve to correct a false understanding of Jesus' mission. Jesus repels the tempter by quoting from the book of Deuteronomy, which stresses God's will for Israel.

HOMILY 1   **Self-knowledge**

Once a famous rabbi wished to have a glimpse of peoples' hearts and test their opinions of themselves. He called three passers-by into his house. Turning to the first man he said, 'Suppose you found a purse full of gold coins, what would you do with it?'

'I would give it to the owner right away provided, of course, I knew who the owner was,' the man replied.

'Fool!' the rabbi exclaimed. Then he put the same question to the second man.

'I wouldn't give it back to the owner. I'd put it in my pocket. I am not so stupid as to let a windfall like that slip through my hands,' and man replied.

'Scoundrel!' exclaimed the rabbi. Then he put the question to the third man.0

'How can I possibly know, rabbi, what I would do in a case like that?' the man replied. 'Would I be able to conquer the evil inclination? Or would the evil urge overcome me and make me take what belongs to another? I do not know. But if the Holy One, blessed be He, strengthened me against the evil inclination, I would give back the money to its owner.'

'Your words are beautiful,' the rabbi exclaimed. 'You are wise indeed.'

The rabbi called the first man a fool. Why? Because he was completely lacking in self-knowledge. He presumed he would be strong enough to resist the temptation to keep the money. No one is so secure that he can't fall. People don't fall because they are weak; they fall because they think they are strong.

The rabbi called the second man a scoundrel. Because, without the slightest qualm of conscience, he was prepared to keep what didn't belong to him. For a man like this, temptation is an opportunity to enrich himself at someone else's expense.

The rabbi praised the third man. He was a good man, and also a wise man. What made him wise was the fact that he knew he was weak like everybody else. He hoped that when faced with the temptation to keep the money he would be strong to do the right thing. But he knew that to do so he needed help from God, and was prepared to seek that help.

All of us are weak and prone to evil. This may be a disturbing truth, but it is one we ignore at our own peril. The great problem of our time is our failure to know ourselves, to recognise evil and deal with it within ourselves. Yet there is a kind of comfort and freedom in knowing and accepting this humbling truth.

We have to struggle against the evil that is in others, and in society. But our hardest struggle is against the evil that originates inside us. We are born with conflicting impulses, so that doing good is always possible but never easy. The hardest victory of all is over oneself.

Jesus' temptation was no play-acting. It was real. The temptations of Jesus are the temptations of Christians in all ages: to live for material things alone; to seek one's own glory rather than God's glory; and to abandon the worship of God for the worship of worldly power and fame.

Jesus' victory over Satan was no once-and-for all victory. He had won a battle, not the war. There would be other attacks which would need to be repelled. The same is true for us. Some people think that they should reach a stage when they will be beyond temptation. Jesus never reached that stage. Nor did the saints.

God is with us in our struggles, helping us to overcome them.

'It is through temptation that we come to know ourselves. We cannot win our crown unless we overcome, and we cannot overcome unless we enter the contest, and there is no contest unless we have an enemy and the temptations he brings.' (St Augustine)

HOMILY 2 **The temptations of Jesus**

Some people find it hard to believe that Jesus could be tempted. But as well as a divine nature, he also had a human nature. Besides, temptation in itself is not a sin. Did the devil actually appear to him? We don't know. The main thing is that his temptations were real, just as ours are, even though Old Nick doesn't appear to us in person. But what did his temptations consist in?

The first temptation was to turn stones into bread. Besides the obvious meaning, the word 'bread' can mean material things in general. The devil was telling Jesus to use his special powers to give the people all the material things they could possibly want. But Jesus knew that material things by themselves will never satisfy people. His chief task was to nourish their minds and hearts with the word of God.

This was the temptation to give people what they want rather than what they need. The temptation to please the crowd by giving them what will satisfy their immediate wants, when they don't know what they really need.

We have deeper hungers and greater needs. What does the heart really hunger for? It's certainly not bread. Bread is what the body hungers for. After the miracle of the loaves and fishes the people came back the next day looking for more bread. But Jesus refused to give it to them. He said, 'Do not work for food that cannot last, but work for the food that endures to eternal life.'

For a spiritual teacher the food of the spirit has to take priority over the food of the body. To give priority to man's physical needs would mean to diminish man, to treat him as no higher than a beast. We too are tempted to live for material things alone. It's not that we deny the spiritual, but that we neglect it.

The second temptation was to set up a political kingdom, to resort to power rather than love. Power offers an easy substitute for the hard work love can call for. It's easier to control people than to love them, easier to dominate people than to become their servant. Jesus didn't come to rule but to serve. He didn't cling to his divine power, but emptied himself and became the loving servant of all. We are always tempted to replace love by power.

The third temptation consisted in doing something spectacular (throwing himself off the Temple) in order to elicit faith – much as a magician might elicit belief in his arts by doing some showy stunts. The idea was attractive. A stunt like that would have made him the talk of Jerusalem. But sensationalism redounds to one's own glory, rather than to the glory of God. Jesus refused to jump. He didn't want screaming fans. He wanted followers, that is, people who would imitate his way of living.

Throughout his public ministry, Jesus refused to give the people these kind of signs, even when pressed to do so. These kind of things are not helpful. They do not demand the best of us. They cheapen faith. Faith is not magic. Holiness consists, not in trying to get God to do our will, but in trying to get ourselves to do God's will.

The temptations were attacks on all that was fundamental to the mission of Jesus. Yes, he had come to set up a kingdom, but not the kind of kingdom Satan was proposing. And he rejected the temptation to achieve the kingdom by worldly means.

All three temptations come down to the same thing in the end: to put material things and his own glory first, and spiritual things and God second, if at all. These are the major temptations of his Church as a whole, and of each of us who are its members. We have to keep our eyes on the One who refused to turn stones into bread, to jump from great heights, and to rule with great power.

The experience helped Jesus to clarify in his own mind what his mission was and how to achieve it. And once he knew what his mission was, he resolved to make a complete gift of himself to it.

The temptations were no once-off affair. Temptations are never over. They return at opportune times. Temptations continued through Jesus' life as the tempter sought in vain to undermine his mission. Even as he hung on the cross we hear an echo of the second temptation: 'If he is the Messiah, let him come down from the cross, and we will believe in him.'

All those who are struggling to live a good life can take heart. Resisting temptation was not easy for Jesus; nor will it be for us. But in Jesus we have a brother who knows what we are up against. He forgives us and raises us up when we fall. He enables us to obey God's word, to trust him, and to worship him alone.

HOMILY 3   **Not on bread alone**

A human being doesn't live on bread alone. Bread is only one of the basic staples of life – life for the body. To nourish a human person is not the same as to fatten cattle. Our bodies need food. But so do our souls. Our souls are craving for nourishment. The story of Elvis Presley powerfully illustrates the truth of this.

Elvis became very rich. He owned eight cars, six motorbikes, two planes, sixteen television sets, a vast mansion, and several bulging bank accounts. On top of all of that, he was idolised by legions of fans. Yet he wasn't happy. In the midst of all his wealth and success he experienced a spiritual malaise, and complained of loneliness and boredom.

'Money brings a lot of headaches,' he confided to an interviewer.

His mother was worried about him. She never wanted all this for him. She simply wanted him to come home, buy a furniture store, get married and have children.

He grew fearful and depressed. At the age of twenty-two he found that there were no more worlds to conquer. This malaise could have been an opportunity. It was a stark reminder that 'man doesn't live on bread alone', that is, on material things alone.

This message rings out loud and clear in today's Gospel. It is a vital message, and is perhaps more relevant today than ever before. Though we can see its truth, in practice it is not easy to take it on board. We don't live on bread alone – at least not if we want to be fully alive, and fully nourished as human beings and children of God. What else do we need? We need the word of God.

Imagine parents who fed their child but never spoke a word to that child. No guidance, no encouragement, no affirmation, no consolation. Never a word to communicate peace and welcome, or love and joy. The child's body would be nourished, but its heart and soul would be empty. We are God's children. We need to hear God's word.

Bread alone won't always guarantee even physical survival. The poet Irina Ratushinkaya spent some time in prison (as a political prisoner) in communist Russia. She said, 'Many women had more bread than I had, yet they died.' What was it that kept her alive? She has no doubt what it was. It was her Christian faith.

It's not just the human body that gets hungry. The human heart and the human spirit get hungry too. Until we acknowledge and address the hunger of the heart and the spirit, we will always be undernourished.

Jesus challenges us to address our deeper hungers and greater needs. What does the heart really hunger for? It's certainly not bread. It hungers for the food that doesn't perish – the word of God. The word of God has the power to nourish us. It nourishes us with the bread of meaning, the bread of hope, and above all the bread of love.

Time for reflection

Jesus spent forty days in the desert, reflecting and praying. The desert may be a harsh place, but it's an ideal place for reflection and prayer.

This desert experience came at a crucial moment in the life of Jesus, a time of great awakening. It would be impossible to exaggerate its importance for him. As a result he grew to love solitude, and made a habit of seeking it at difficult moments in his life. When people and events threatened to engulf him, he would steal off to lonely place to recover and rededicate himself to the Father. What he was doing was deepening this first desert experience.

We too need a lonely place for reflection. Often we live foolishly and unspiritually, driven on by stupid desires and imprisoned by selfish habits. We are surrounded by noise and constant activity. We get our priorities wrong. We are unable or unwilling to be alone, to be silent, to be still. And we wonder why we aren't happy, why we don't find it easy to get on with others, and why we can't pray.

We need solitude. In solitude we begin to stand on our own feet before God and the world, and accept full responsibility for our own lives. The hermit goes into the desert, not to lose himself, but to find himself. In solitude we meet our demons, our addictions, our lust, our anger, and our need for recognition and approval.

And we don't go into the wilderness to escape from others, but to find them in God. 'Only in solitude and silence can I find the gentleness with which I can love my brothers and sisters.' (Thomas Merton)

PRAYER OF THE FAITHFUL

President: Because Jesus was tempted, he understands our temptations. Let us turn to him for the help we need to be victorious over evil.

Response: Lord, hear our prayer.

Reader(s): For the Church: that it may lead its members to a deeper and more authentic living of the Christian life. [Pause] Let us pray to the Lord.

For government leaders: that they may resist the temptation to seek their own glory, and seek instead to serve their brothers and sisters. [Pause] Let us pray to the Lord.

For those who have fallen to temptation: that they may have the strength to rise again. [Pause] Let us pray to the Lord.

For each other and for ourselves: that Lent may teach us a spirit of self-denial, and move us to show more love and compassion to others. [Pause] Let us pray to the Lord.

For our own special needs. [Longer pause] Let us pray to the Lord.

President: God of power and love, you have shown us that prayer, fasting and alms-giving are remedies for sin. Accept our humble admission of guilt, and when our conscience weighs us down, let your unfailing mercy raise us up. We ask this through Christ our Lord.

REFLECTION   **Repentance alone is not enough**

Repentance of itself is not enough –
grace must be available.
But if grace is offered and not accepted,
then nothing comes of that either.
There is no point in putting up a sail
if there is no wind.
There is no point in planting a seed
if the ground is frozen.
There is no point in pruning the tree
if spring does not come.
It is not enough to cut into people's hearts
in order to save them –
they must be touched by grace.
Lord, touch our hearts with your grace,
so that we may produce the fruits of repentance.

Second Sunday of Lent

THE TRANSFIGURATION

INTRODUCTION AND CONFITEOR

On Mount Tabor Peter, James and John got a glimpse of the glory that was hidden in Jesus. Through faith we too glimpse the glory of the risen Jesus who lives on in the Church and in each of us. Let us reflect for a moment on this. [Pause]

Our sins disfigure our lives and tarnish the image of God within us. Let us ask pardon for them and seek the grace to overcome them.

I confess to almighty God …

HEADINGS FOR READINGS

First Reading (Gen 15:5-12.17-18). We learn of the solemn covenant God made with Abraham which was the foundation of God's relationship with the people of Israel. Through Christ we are the heirs to this covenant.

Second Reading (Phil 3:17–4:1). Paul urges his converts to remain faithful to Christ, and promises them that one day they will share in his glory.

Gospel (Lk 9:28-36). We hear Luke's version of the transfiguration of Jesus on Mount Tabor.

SCRIPTURE NOTE

The First Reading tells of God's promise to Abraham that he would have numerous descendants, and that those descendants would possess the land of Canaan. As a pledge of his fidelity God made a solemn covenant with him.

Our passage describes an ancient rite of covenant or treaty making. To ratify a covenant the contracting parties cut an animal (or animals) in two and walked between the divided parts, invoking the fate of the animals on themselves should they fail to observe the terms of the contract. Since God's covenant with Abraham is unilateral, only God (symbolised by the furnace and the torch) passes between the pieces. The birds of prey symbolise the forces hostile to Israel.

This covenant led to the covenant at Sinai, and culminated in the new and eternal covenant which Jesus sealed in his own blood on Calvary.

The chief significance of the Tabor experience was for Jesus himself, and this is what Luke emphasises. The incident was meant to confirm him in the course he had taken. It comforted him to know that the road he was travelling was marked by the feet of prophets such as Moses and Elijah. The transfiguration also benefited the apostles. It prepared them for the passion, death and resurrection of Jesus, the Messiah.

HOMILY 1   **The human face**

The human face is very important. To remember someone is to remember the face. When we can't picture the face, the person becomes a shadow.

It's amazing the different expressions that can be seen on the human face. That's why faces are such an interesting study. The face always reveals who we are and what life has done to us. This explains why we use the word 'face' so much in talking about others.

We say: 'You should have seen her face when I said this!' In other words, on the face we can read what people are feeling inside, how they really are - whether they are sad or happy, shocked or indifferent. When Matt Busby (famed manager of Manchester United FC) died, Denis Law was asked, 'What's your greatest memory of Matt Busby?' And he replied, 'His face the night we had won the European Cup.'

We talk about 'losing face' and 'saving face'. Here what's at stake is a person's reputation. We may say that a person is 'two-faced'. This is a very serious thing to say about anyone. It implies that someone is deceitful. And we may say that people are 'faceless'. This implies that they are hiding behind others or behind the system, and are too cowardly to come out from the shadows and take responsibility for their actions.

Each of us has many faces. At different times we wear the face of happiness or sadness, courage or fear, peace or unrest, hope or despair, weariness or relaxation, joy or pain, friendship or hostility ... There is nothing to be ashamed of in all of this. It is part of being human. The only thing we should be ashamed of is a false face. These other faces are all real. They tell the truth, whereas a false face tells a lie.

Why is it that people are reluctant to let their real face (that is, their real self) be seen? Why do they often insist on putting on a mask? Is it that they are afraid to be seen in their weakness? Hence the need always to wear a smile, even when they are crying inside.

We are told that on the mountain Jesus' face shone like the sun. It's a mistake to think that was the *real* face of Jesus. What the apostles saw was real. It did reveal something of his inner glory that at other times was hidden from them. But to say that it was the real face of Jesus implies that all the other faces he wore were not real, which means they were false.

The face Jesus showed on Tabor was a very special one, but it was not his only face. He had all the faces that we have, except the false ones. At various times his face showed weariness, disappointment, anger, gentleness, compassion, sadness, fear, anguish, pain, and it was pale and frozen in death. All of these faces were real. Behind all of them lay the person of Jesus, human like us (sin excepted) but also carrying within him the splendour of divinity: 'This is my beloved Son.'

Even though the face is called the window of the soul, every face conceals more than it reveal. What is essential about another person remains invisible. Each person remains a mystery. Our own divine greatness as well as that of others is hidden from us.

Like Abraham, we have to live by faith. The faith that assures us that behind the most ordinary human face lies a son or a daughter of God, a brother or a sister of Jesus, bound for eternal glory.

HOMILY 2   **Glimpses of glory**

On Mount Tabor God's light burst forth from the body of Jesus, and he was transfigured. The three apostles were overcome with the beauty and brilliance of it. It was not a surface thing, but something inside shining through. In short: God was in Jesus.

We too have the splendour of divinity in us because we are made in the image of God. Therefore, we too can have moments of transfiguration. Van Gogh said, 'The poorest woodcutter or miner can have moments of emotion and inspiration which give him a feeling of an eternal home to which he is near.'

A poor man living in a Dublin hostel for the homeless told the following story. One day he was walking along a street in Dublin. At a certain point he found himself outside a church. Before he realised it, he was inside. He couldn't recall whether or not he said any prayers. But his soul was flooded with light. His depression lifted, and a great peace descended on him. He felt that he belonged on this earth after all. He felt close to God and loved by God.

The experience seemed to last for a long time, yet he had a feeling it may have lasted only a few minutes. But he said he'd gladly give the whole of his life for those few moments. What made the experience so wonderful was the realisation that he had done absolutely nothing to deserve it. It was a pure gift from God to him. For one short moment he tasted glory.

However, when it was over he found himself out in the streets once more, going along aimlessly as before. The effects of the experience faded. Though he went back to that church many times afterwards he was never able to recapture that moment.

That homeless man wanted to hold onto that experience. He wanted to go backwards instead of forwards. He might have used the experience to illuminate the darkness in his life, and to go forward more hopefully and courageously.

Peter made the same mistake. He wanted to stay on the mountain top. He wanted to hug and hold onto the blessedness of the experience. He did not want to go back down to the everyday and common things again, but to remain for ever in the enchanted land. But Jesus summoned him to go back down the mountain and to face the future. That experience was not meant to provide an escape from the struggle that lay ahead, but to help him face it. The hour of light was meant to help him face the hour of darkness.

Yet it's clear that something of the wonder of that day remained with Peter and illuminated his life, because many years later he wrote: 'We were eye-witnesses of his glory on the mountain ... A voice came to him saying, "This is my beloved son in whom I am well pleased".' (2 Pet 1:17-18).

We too can experience rare moments of light and joy. We get glimpses of the promised land towards which we are travelling in faith. In his love for us, God allows us to taste on earth the joys of the world to come. But these moments of transfiguration are given to us to strengthen us for our everyday tasks, and to enable us to face the cross which in some shape or form comes to everyone. The moment of glory does not exist for its own sake. It exists to clothe the common things with a radiance they never had before.

Prayer and religion are not escapism. They are meant to help us face life with all its difficulties and challenges, to embrace the high and low moments of life, the hilltop and the pit.

HOMILY 3   **The Covenant**

There is a big difference between a covenant and a contract. A covenant is based on love and friendship, whereas a contract is a strictly business arrangement. Our society hasn't much room for covenants. It mostly goes in for contracts. Contracts fall apart and lose their binding power when one or both of the partners fail to fulfil their part of the bargain. God didn't make a contract with us; God made a covenant with us.

God is a God of power. But he is also a God of love and mercy. In dealing with us God chose to follow the way of love rather than the way of power. God wants to be loved by us, not feared. If you love someone you give him the room and the right to be himself. If you want power over someone you try to control him, and make him do your will whether he wants to or not. But you cannot do both at the same time. Love and power are incompatible.

In order to love and be loved, God has to give us room to choose. He cannot have all the power and leave none for us. The covenant between God and humanity has to be more than a matter of an almighty God laying down the law. It has to be an agreement freely entered into between two free parties.

If we obey God because we are afraid of him, because we are so overwhelmed by his might that we do not dare to challenge him, then he has our obedience but he does not have our love.

The First Reading tells of the solemn covenant God made with Abraham. After the story of creation, this is a key moment in the Old Testament. The story of our redemption could be said to begin here. God did not abandon his fallen people, but through Abraham entered into a special relationship with them. This relationship was not like that which exists between trading partners. It was more like that which exists between a husband and wife. It is summed up in a formula which is repeated many times in the Old Testament: 'You will be my people, and I will be your God.'

It was not Abraham but God who took the initiative in this relationship. God promised him a numerous and unbroken line of descendants. He also promised his descendants that they would have a land of their own, and said that through him all the nations of the earth would be blessed, because the Messiah would come from his line.

Even though the people broke God's covenant, God did not abandon them. Instead, through his Son, Jesus Christ, he bound himself even more closely to the human family by a bond that can never be broken.

God's promise to Abraham was fulfilled in Jesus. It is through him, the Messiah, that all the nations of the earth are blessed. Jesus sealed the covenant anew in his own blood. Through him we have a closer bond than ever with God. We are not just his people; we are his sons and daughters; we are his family.

Jesus is the head of the new People of God. The land to which he is leading us is not some piece of earthly land, but the land of eternal life.

ANOTHER APPROACH   **Mount Tabor and Mount Calvary**

That the transfiguration happened on a mountain top comes as no surprise. There is something about a mountain. A mountain gives us a wider view and an over-all view. It helps us to see the pattern in things and puts things into perspective. It also raises the spirits. We are in the presence of great majesty and beauty. We feel close to God. Indeed, we feel we are in the presence of God.

On Mount Tabor the sky was bright. Jesus was praying. As he prayed his face shone and his clothes became white as snow. On one side of him stood Moses – the great law-giver. On the other side was Elijah – the greatest of the prophets. A luminous cloud overshadowed them, symbolising the presence of God. Out of the cloud, the voice of the Father was hear uttering the lovely words: 'This is my Son, the Chosen One. Listen to him.' Peter exclaimed, 'It is wonderful for us to be here! If you wish, I will make three tents here, one for you, one for Moses and one for Elijah.'

Peter wanted to stay on the mountain. He wanted to build a safe haven there, away from all trouble and danger. But the purpose of this experience was not to encourage escape. The purpose was to comfort and strengthen Jesus and the apostles so that they would be able to go back and face the mess and danger they left behind.

And how much they needed that strength! For there would come another day and another hill. This time the sky would be dark. The face of Jesus would be covered with sweat and blood. His clothes would not dazzle – they would be taken from him. For companions he would have two criminals. There would be no voice from heaven, only the voice of scoffers and mockers. The disciples would be shattered and would want no part of what was happening.

The only thing in common would be that Jesus would once again be praying. From this it's clear that what sustained him in bright and dark moments alike was his special relationship with the Father.

Hopefully, all of us have some experience of Mount Tabor, the hill of joy and exaltation. But we are probably more familiar with Mount Calvary. What happens is that we tend to go from one to the other. On 'Tabor' we have glimpsed the beauty of heaven: encouraged, elated, we have thought, 'It is good for us to be here.' Then we have been plunged into the sorrow of Calvary. On 'Calvary' by the grace of God we can learn to say, 'Thy will be done.'

This would be an excellent approach for a shared homily. We could begin by asking people such questions as: What was the happiest day or experience in your life? What was the saddest or darkest day in your life?

PRAYER OF THE FAITHFUL

President: Let us pray to the Lord who in his mercy hears us when we call to him in good times and in bad.

Response: Lord, hear our prayer.

Reader(s): For the pope and the bishops: that they may sustain the people of God in faith, hope and love. [Pause] Let us pray to the Lord.

For our civil and political leaders: that the Lord may help them to fulfil their responsibilities. [Pause] Let us pray to the Lord.

For the sick and the handicapped: that they may have the strength they need to bear their cross with dignity. [Pause] Let us pray to the Lord.

For those who are going through the dark valley of suffering: that they may not feel that God has abandoned them. [Pause] Let us pray to the Lord.

For all gathered here: that as followers of Jesus we may listen to him and live out his teaching in our lives. [Pause] Let us pray to the Lord.

For our own special needs. [Longer pause] Let us pray to the Lord.

President: God of love and mercy, give us the grace to rise above our human weaknesses so that we may be faithful to your Son and to the Gospel. Grant this through the same Christ our Lord.

REFLECTION   **An unquenchable longing**

All of us can experience moments of great joy
because in his goodness God allows us to taste on earth
the joys of the world to come.
However, moments of joy, no matter how wonderful,
will never satisfy the human heart.
What we long for is a permanent state of happiness.
But that is unattainable here.
So what must we do? Like desert travellers,
we must go forward from one oasis to another,
with the conviction that God has a homeland
prepared for us at the end of our journey.
This conviction will make it possible for us
to travel onwards with an ache in our heart
and an unquenchable longing in our soul.

DISMISSAL

The apostles wanted to stay on the mountain-top. We might want to linger here, because here we feel close to God and at peace. But we have to go from here, to take up our burdens once more.

Go then in the peace of Christ.

Third Sunday of Lent
UNLESS YOU REPENT

INTRODUCTION AND CONFITEOR

'Unless you repent, you will all likewise perish.' These words were addressed by Jesus to his contemporaries, and are addressed to us in today's liturgy. We always begin our celebration of the Eucharist with a call to repentance. Let us listen to that call now. [Pause]

Lord Jesus, you are slow to anger and rich in mercy. Lord, have mercy.

You forgive all our guilt and heal every one of our ills. Christ have mercy.

As the heavens are high above the earth, so strong is your love for those who fear you. Lord, have mercy.

HEADINGS FOR READINGS

First Reading (Ex 3:1-8.13-15). We are shown God's concern for his oppressed people.

Second Reading (1 Cor 10:1-6.10-12). What happened to the Israelites in the desert is a warning for us Christians.

Gospel (Lk 13:1-9). Jesus stresses the necessity of repentance and tells the people that time is running out.

SCRIPTURE NOTE

The First Reading tells how God appeared to Moses in the burning bush and revealed his name as *Yahweh* ('I am the Existing One'). God has heard the cries of his oppressed people, and sends Moses to liberate them. It is a turning point in the Old Testament. It leads to the Exodus and beyond.

In the Gospel we see how Jesus rejected the popular belief that accidents which befall people are inflicted by God as punishment for sin. Still, sin calls for repentance. And Jesus tells the Jews that they will lose the promises unless they repent. The barren fig tree symbolises the barren state of Israel. But God is patient. There is still time to repent, though that time is getting short.

The role of Moses prefigures the role of Jesus. Through Moses God saved his people, Israel, from slavery in Egypt. We are the new people of God, saved through the waters of baptism from the slavery of sin, and now *en route* under the leadership of Jesus to the promised land of eternal life. We too are fed with food 'from heaven', namely, the Eucharist.

In the Letter to the Romans Paul says that in spite of all God had done for them, most of the Israelites were not pleasing to God. Christians must not think that just because they have received the sacraments they are automatically saved.

HOMILY 1   **On holy ground**

In the story of the burning bush God appears to Moses, not in a temple, but in the wilderness. And he appears, not while Moses was praying, but while he was minding his sheep. It was in this secular place, and while he was engaged in a secular task, that God made his presence known to him.

Today the world has become a very secular place. It is difficult to retain a sense of the sacred in such a world. Yet without the sacred, without a sense of the transcendent, life is bleak and one-dimensional.

Moses' encounter with God seems to be dominated by fear. However, this is not so. When the Bible talks about fear of God it doesn't mean being afraid of God. It really means a sense of awe and reverence before the mystery of God. Fear is a negative thing; it constricts us and makes us want to run away. Awe, on the other hand, is a positive and expansive feeling; it draws us to the awe-inspiring object, and makes us want to linger. We stand in admiration of something greater than ourselves. We are at once humbled and elevated.

Religion begins with a sense of reverence, the recognition of God's greatness and our limitations. Awe and reverence precede faith. They are the root of faith. Awe is the beginning and gateway of faith.

Awareness of the divine begins with wonder. Moses was filled with wonder at the sight of a bush on fire which wasn't consumed by that fire. However, it's easy to wonder at something unusual such as that. Even a fool wonders at the unusual. It takes a wise person to wonder at the usual. This is our problem. We long for visions but seldom watch a sunset.

Most of us find it difficult to recognise the greatness and wonder of things familiar to us, the 'miracles' which are daily with us. The root of worship lies in a sense of these miracles. Awe and wonder can be caused by small things. A grain of sand, or a leaf, or a snowflake can suffice.

It's a poor faith that needs miracles to sustain it. Those who are attuned to God do not need to see miracles. They are conscious of living in a world which is sustained by his power, and every part of which speaks of him. Elizabeth Barrett Browning put it like this:

> Earth crammed with heaven,
> and every bush afire with God.
> But only he who sees takes off his shoes;
> the rest of us sit around and pluck blackberries.

Those who are able to nourish their faith from the daily miracles that surround them are like people sitting at a banquet table. Those whose faith must be nourished by 'wonders' are like people depending on the odd snack here and there.

God told Moses that he was standing on holy ground. What was it that made that particular piece of scrubland holy? It was the presence of God. Here in church we are standing on holy ground, because here we are in the presence of God. Moses was told to take off his shoes. This is why Moslems remove their shoes before entering a mosque. We Christians don't take off our shoes before entering a church. But there is something we ought to put on before entering, namely, a sense of reverence.

Here we experience the presence of God. But let us not forget that God is everywhere. Which means that all places are holy, the whole earth is holy. God can be encounter anywhere. The distinction between the secular and the sacred is ours, not God's.

HOMILY 2   **A second chance**

The Pharisees had no time for sinners. They believed they should just be written off. Jesus didn't agree, and told them so in a story.

A vineyard is a very special place, normally reserved for vines only. Yet in his parable Jesus talks about a fig tree which was planted in a vineyard. At that time this was not unusual. Soil was so scarce that trees were planted wherever there was soil. We are dealing then with a tree planted in a very privileged place.

In the normal course of events it takes three years for a fig tree to reach maturity. If by that time it is not fruiting it is not likely to fruit at all. Such was the case with the tree Jesus was talking about. For three years the owner had been coming to it and finding it barren. He came to the conclusion that the tree was useless. It was drawing nourishment from the ground but giving nothing back. It had to go. It was taking up valuable space. So he told his gardener to get rid of it.

But the gardener, who had a great knowledge of fig trees, and was a very patient man, replied, 'Sir, give it one more year. I'll dig the earth around it, and put on plenty of dung. Then, if there are no figs on it this time next year, we'll cut it down.'

The owner of the vineyard agreed. We are not told what happened to the fig tree, but it doesn't matter. Jesus had made his point. Just as that gardener was patient with the fig tree, so God is patient with sinners.

This Gospel has been called the Gospel of the second chance. God is patient. The history of the Church is full of examples of barren fig trees that in time became fruitful; in other words, sinners who repented and became saints.

Moses, who is at the centre of today's First Reading, is a good example. As a young man he had killed another man. Yet God didn't write him off. True, he had a fiery temper. But there was good in him. He was that rare being – the kind of man who couldn't stand idly by when he saw an injustice or a crime happening. It was because of this quality that God chose him to lead his people from slavery to freedom.

Einstein was arguably the greatest mind of the twentieth century. Yet he didn't learn to talk until he was two years old. His parents were so worried about him that they consulted a doctor. Later, one of his teachers was so disappointed in him that he said, 'You'll never amount to anything.' As yet there were no signs of his future greatness. But his parents and teacher had judged him too soon. Some people develop slowly and late, but are all the better for that.

What such people need is someone to believe in them, someone to have patience with them. Otherwise a lot of talent will go down the drain. We tend to be harsh on others until we need a second chance ourselves. We must extend to others the kind of patience and leniency we would like for ourselves.

But the parable also makes it clear that there is such a thing as a last chance. If people refuse chance after chance, the day finally comes, not when God has shut them out, but when they have by deliberate choice shut themselves out. But which of us would want to be barren when we might be fruitful?

HOMILY 3   **Call to repentance**

The fig tree in Jesus' story was a very privileged tree because it was planted in a very special place – a vineyard. Yet in spite of this the tree was barren. Nevertheless, it was given another chance. The fig tree stands for Israel planted in the Lord's vineyard. Its barren state symbolised the barren state of Israel before God.

Jesus began his mission with a call to repentance: 'Repent, for the Kingdom of Heaven is at hand.' Today, through the voice of the Church, the same call is addressed to us. The call to repentance is at the heart of the Gospel. Jesus addressed it, not just to sinners, but also to good people. In fact, to all without exception. But you may ask: how can this be – that good people should need to repent?

In the case of so-called good people, for them their failing consists in the good they fail to do. This is the main thrust of the parable about the barren fig tree. The fig tree is found wanting, not because it produced poisonous figs, but because it failed to produce any figs at all. What is a fig tree for if not to produce figs?

Christians rarely ask themselves the question: What have I failed to do? The call to repentance is not merely a call to turn away from evil, but a call to 'produce the fruits' of good living. That is why it is relevant for everybody.

Jesus' call to repentance disturbs us, and we don't like to be disturbed. We want our quiet life, a life which may contain a lot of selfishness. We may not be guilty of great evil, yet we could be very selfish, very demanding, very inconsiderate. But we don't want to know, much less do anything, about this side of our nature. We are being called from being self-centred, to become other-centred and God-centred.

Most likely we won't have any big moment of conversion such as Moses had. One day he was minding sheep. Next day he was leading an oppressed people to freedom. But conversion is a joyful thing. It is good news. It is a call away from the slavery of selfishness and sin, to a life of freedom and grace. It is a call away from a life of barrenness to a life of fruitfulness. It is a call to enter into the joy of the Kingdom. However, it is not something that is achieved once and for all, but involves a process of growth and development. The Christian life is a continuous process of conversion.

Jesus' parable contains a warning and a threat. Its purpose is to show us what we may be missing out on, or lacking, in order that we might have a deeper, richer, and more authentic life. Let those who think they are safe beware lest they fall. No one can take anything for granted. No one is so secure that he can't fall. No one is so fallen that he can't be redeemed.

OTHER APPROACHES

1. What comes across in the incident of the burning bush is God's concern for his people. God has heard the cries of his people in slavery, and sends Moses to liberate them. Fire is a symbol of love. God's love in not diminished in giving.

What was it that God saw in Moses that made him the right man to lead his people from slavery into freedom? The Bible doesn't tell us much about the character of the youthful Moses. It doesn't say whether he was good or pious. But it does tell us about three episodes in his life prior to the revelation in the burning bush. He saw an Egyptian attacking an Israelite, and he intervened. He saw an Israelite attacking an Israelite, and he intervened. He saw Midianite shepherds preventing Jethro's daughters from watering their flocks, and he intervened.

All these incidents lead us to the same conclusion. They show us that Moses was the kind of man who couldn't stand idly by when he saw an injustice or a crime happening. We can understand then why God chose him to lead his people from slavery to freedom.

Private experiences of God can make people selfish. But this didn't happen in the case of Moses. His experience of God launched him on a mission to save his people.

2. 'The ground you stand on is holy ground.' All of the earth that God gave us is holy ground and deserves to be treated with respect. But the

holiest ground of all is within us.

First of all the body is holy. Our body is the work of God. That is reason enough for respecting it and caring for it. But St Paul gives us a further reason for respecting the body. He says, 'Your body is the temple of the Holy Spirit.'

The mind is holy ground. Many people fill their minds every day with all kinds of trash derived from television, radio, newspapers, and so on. In the words of Thoreau: 'How willing people are to lumber their minds with rubbish - to permit idle rumours and trivial incidents to intrude on ground which should be sacred to thought. Shall the mind be a public arena, or shall it be a quarter of heaven itself?' We should strive to follow the advice of St Paul: 'Fill your minds with everything that is true, everything that is noble, everything that is good and pure, everything that we love and honour, everything that can be thought virtuous and worthy of praise.' (Phil 4:8)

But the holiest ground of all is that of the heart. In our times there is a huge preoccupation with outer cleanness. There is a danger of neglecting inner cleanness, or cleanness of heart. Its from the heart that all our thoughts, words, and deeds flow like water from a hidden spring. If the spring is clean, then all that flows from it will be clean. So we must try to keep the heart clean and pure. It is especially on this holy ground that we will see and meet God. In the words of Jesus: 'Blessed are the pure of heart: they will see God.'

PRAYER OF THE FAITHFUL

President: The Lord is compassion and love. Let us now bring our petitions before him.

Response: Lord, hear us in your love.

Reader(s): For all Christians: that they may produce the fruits of a good life. [Pause] We pray in faith.

For all of us, but for world leaders in particular: that we may see the earth as a gift from God, and take good care of its fragile environment. [Pause] We pray in faith.

For those in authority: that they may be compassionate towards those who fail. [Pause] We pray in faith.

For parents and teachers: that they may adopt a patient and encouraging attitude towards the young. [Pause] We pray in faith.

For those whose lives are barren and empty of the deeds of love. [Pause] We pray in faith.

For all gathered here: that during this Lent we may heed Jesus' call to repentance, and show the fruits of repentance by a new way of living. [Pause] We pray in faith.

For our own special needs. [Longer pause] We pray in faith.

President: God of grace, you are that careful and patient gardener who can produce fruit from the most unpromising of trees. Help us to produce in our lives the fruits of true repentance. We ask this through Christ our Lord.

REFLECTION I   **What I fail to do**

It isn't the things you do,
it's the things you leave undone,
which give you a little heartache
at the setting of the sun.
The gentle word forgotten,
the letter you didn't write;
the flowers you might have sent,
are your haunting ghosts tonight.
The stone you might have lifted
out of your brother's way;
the little heart-felt counsel
you were hurried too much to say.
The tender touch of the hand,
the gentle and kindly tone;
which we have no time or thought for,
with troubles enough of our own.   *(Anon)*

REFLECTION II

Days pass and the years vanish,
and we walk sightless among miracles.
Lord, fill our eyes with seeing, and our minds with knowing.
Let there be moments when the radiance of your presence
illuminates the darkness in which we walk.
Help us to see, wherever we gaze, that the bush burns, unconsumed.
And we, clay touched by your hand,
will reach out for holiness and exclaim in wonder,
'How filled with awe is this place, and we did not know it.'   *(Anon)*

Fourth Sunday of Lent
THE PRODIGAL SON

INTRODUCTION AND CONFITEOR

'Father I have sinned against heaven and before you' – so said the prodigal son whose story we hear in today's Gospel. At the start of this Eucharist we are invited to call to mind our sins, which means we are invited to make our own the words and the sentiments of the prodigal son. [Pause] Fortunately God is prodigal with his forgiveness.

Lord Jesus, you reconcile us to one another and to the Father. Lord, have mercy.

You heal the wounds of sin and division. Christ, have mercy.

You intercede for us at the right hand of the Father. Lord, have mercy.

HEADINGS FOR READINGS

First Reading (Josh 5:9-12). The Israelites, free at last from the humiliation they suffered in Egypt, enter the land of promise and partake of its produce.

Second Reading (2 Cor 5:17-21). Christ brought about a reconciliation between God and humanity. The Church's task is to bring the benefits of this to all people.

Gospel (Lk 15:1-3, 11-32). The parable of the prodigal son shows that God delights in showing mercy to repentant sinners.

SCRIPTURE NOTE

A clear theme runs through all three readings: God's mercy to sinners.

In the First Reading we have the beautiful words God spoke to his people: 'I have taken the shame of Egypt away from you.' The shame of sin and the darkness of slavery are behind them. The years of wandering in the desert are over; they have come home to the promised land. A new era was about to begin. They mark their homecoming by celebrating anew the feast of Passover.

This reminds us of the home-coming of the prodigal son (Gospel). His shame also is behind him. His years of wandering are over and he returns home to a warm welcome and a great feast. A new and bright future lies ahead of him. Jesus told the parable in response to the criticism of the Pharisees that he was too lenient towards sinners. They were meant to see themselves in the older son. For Luke the 'Pharisees' are righteous Christians, for whom God's mercy to sinners is unfair and scandalous.

The Second Reading stresses how God has reconciled us to himself through Christ, not holding our faults against us. The task of the Church is to bring the benefits won by Christ to all people.

I recommend Eucharistic Prayer of Reconciliation II. It would underline the message of the Scripture readings.

HOMILY 1   **Loved in our sins**

The parable of the Prodigal Son is probably the best known and best loved of all Jesus' parables. Yet some maintain that it is an unfair story. They feel sorry for the older son, convinced that he got a raw deal. They believe the younger son got away with murder. He should have been punished. He should have been taught a lesson. Let's see if such an attitude is justified.

The younger son was determined to have his fling. He set out for a city where appetites of every kind could be satisfied. But when his money ran out, the bright lights faded, and all doors were closed against him. He felt sorry for himself. His own pain made him realise the pain he had caused to his father. So he said to himself: 'I will go back to my father and tell him I'm sorry.' It was a brave decision, and it took a lot of courage to carry it out. It's not easy to say 'sorry' even over a trivial matter.

The journey back was a sad, lonely, fearful one. It's easy to come back home when you're a hero laden with trophies and glory. But the prodigal son had no trophies to show his father, no achievements with which to earn his praise, his welcome, and his love. He was coming home empty-handed. Worse, he was coming home laden with shame and disgrace.

Everything was out of his hands. Suppose his father didn't accept him back. What would he do then? He deserved to be punished – and he knew it and even asked for it. Yet punishment was the last thing he needed. In any case, he had already been punished. He didn't have a good time. Maybe he had pleasure, but he certainly had no joy. He had suffered a lot – hunger, loneliness, degradation of soul, the pain of remorse, the sense of betrayal. Each sin of his had brought its sure, swift penalty along with it. To sin is to suffer. He didn't need more punishment.

Nor did he need to be taught a lesson. He had already learned a lesson – something which is far more important. He had learnt some very painful truths about himself, about others, and about life. He had eaten forbidden fruit, and far from being satisfied, he was left with a bitter taste in his mouth. If he had met with rejection it would have destroyed him.

What happened? When the father saw his lost son coming towards him, his heart went out to him, and next minute they were in each other's arms. The father didn't just accept him back. He welcomed him back. All was forgiven.

The biggest discovery the younger son made was that he was loved in his sins. The father never stopped loving him. It doesn't do one much good to be loved in one's goodness. But it is an extraordinary experience to be loved in one's sinfulness. Such love is like a breeze to a dying fire, or rain falling on parched ground. This is what grace is about. Those who have experienced this kind of love, know something about the heart of God.

God's forgiveness is not a cold, half-hearted forgiveness, but a warm and generous one. God doesn't just forgive us; he loves us, and lets us know it. The story doesn't give us a licence to sin. But it does show that if, through human weakness or wickedness, we do sin, then we can come back. Our past can be overcome. We can make a fresh start. This is the great lesson of the parable.

> The moment the prodigal fell on his knees and wept, he made his having wasted his substance with harlots, his swine herding and hungering for the husks they ate, beautiful and holy moments in his life. It is difficult for most people to grasp that idea. I dare say one has to go to prison to understand it. If so, it may be worth while going to prison. (Oscar Wilde).

HOMILY 2   **God's attitude to repentant sinners**

Gandhi tells how when he was fifteen he stole a little piece of gold from his brother. However, he felt so bad about it that he made up his mind to confess it to his father. He wrote out his sin on a piece of paper, asking for forgiveness and punishment, while promising never to steal again.

At the time his father was in bed, sick. Gandhi handed him the note and sat by the bedside waiting for his judgement. His father sat up in bed and began to read the note. As he read it, tears came into his eyes. Gandhi himself also cried. Instead of getting angry and punishing him, the father hugged his repentant son, and that was the end of the matter.

The experience of being loved while he was in sin had a profound effect on Gandhi. He said later, 'Only the person who has experienced this kind of love can know what it is.'

This is the kind of love the younger son experienced when he came back home. There is no question but that he behaved badly. Yet when he came back home, what happened? His father didn't merely receive him back; he welcomed him back. And it was no half-hearted or grudging welcome either. It was a warm, whole-hearted, and prodigally generous welcome.

In the welcome the younger son got, Jesus shows us God's attitude to repentant sinners. If we are sinners – and which of us is not a sinner? – then God loves us not less but more. It doesn't do us much good to be loved for being perfect. We need to be accepted and loved precisely as sinners.

The attitude of the older brother towards his younger brother is a mirror-image of the attitude of the Pharisees to sinners. They would rather see a sinner damned than saved. Yet they were very religious people. But what's the use of religion if it doesn't make a person more compassionate towards those who fall? If we find ourselves sympathising with the older brother, it just shows how much of the Pharisee is in us.

All of us, to a greater or lesser extent, are in the shoes of the younger son. For which of us can say that we have always been faithful? Do we not all squander God's grace and misuse his gifts? Which of us would like to be treated by God according to strict justice? Do we not all need more mercy than justice?

It is in and through our sins that we experience the goodness and mercy of Christ. If we never sinned, we'd never know his forgiveness. This is not an excuse for sinning. But it's nice to know that this is how God receives sinners. Saints bear witness to God's grace and fidelity. Sinners bear witness to God's love and mercy.

'When a father laments that his son has taken to evil ways, what should he do? Love him all the more.' (Baal Shem Tov)

HOMILY 3   **The revelation of hearts**

Let us look at Jesus' parable from the point of view of the heart.

A man had two sons. Though the older son was obedient and dutiful, he was rather formal and distant. He was a cold-hearted person. The younger son, on the other hand, was warm-hearted and affectionate. However, he had a wild and irresponsible streak in him. He was determined to do his own thing, no matter what anyone else might think. One day he selfishly demanded his share of the inheritance, and having got it, left for foreign parts.

There he gave full rein to the most base desires of his heart, living foolishly and recklessly. But when his money ran out, he found himself without a friend or helper.

Suddenly his heart felt very empty. Then, when he realised what he had done, it filled up with bitterness and self-disgust. However, his own pain helped him to see the pain he had caused to others. He had broken the hearts of his parents.

So he decided to go back home. He set out empty-handed. The only thing he brought back was a humble, repentant heart. And his father was waiting for him. As far as the father was concerned, he had never left home because he still carried him in his heart. So, when the father saw him coming, his heart went out to him. And they ended up in each other's arms.

But then a surprising thing happened. He went towards his older brother, only to discover that he didn't want to know him. There was no room for him in his older brother's heart. Instead of his heart filling up with joy at his brother's safe return, it filled up with bitterness and resentment. He had sought the way to his father's heart through duty rather than love. Sadly, it seems that he had never entered it. Because if he had, his own heart would have been enlarged. Instead it was small, narrow, cold and unwelcoming.

The story of the Prodigal Son is a story about hearts: selfish hearts and generous hearts, closed hearts and open hearts, cold hearts and warm hearts, broken hearts and joyful hearts, unrepentant hearts and repentant hearts, unforgiving hearts and forgiving hearts, resentful hearts and grateful hearts .

It reveals so much about the vagaries of the human heart. When all is said and done it is the heart that matters. But how can one sum up the heart? The heart is what I am deep down. It is the real me. Darkness of heart is the blackest night of all. Emptiness of heart is the greatest poverty of all. A heavy heart is the most wearisome burden of all. A broken heart is the deepest wound of all.

But the parable reveals how steadfast is the heart of God. God's heart doesn't blow hot and cold. God never closes his heart to any of his children. No matter how far from home they may wander, no matter what they do, if they come home, the one thing they can be sure of is a warm and generous welcome.

PRAYER OF THE FAITHFUL

President: The father in Christ's story is God the Father. Therefore, let us turn to him with confidence and place our needs before him.

Response: Lord, hear our prayer.

Reader(s): For the Church: that through its ministry people may experience the love and mercy of God. [Pause] Let us pray to the Lord.

For parents: that they may love their children in good times and in bad. [Pause] Let us pray to the Lord.

For young people who have emigrated in search of work and opportunity. [Pause] Let us pray to the Lord.

For runaway children: that they may find friends and shelter. [Pause] Let us pray to the Lord.

For all gathered here: that we may extend to others the compassion we would like to experience ourselves. [Pause] Let us pray to the Lord.

For our own special needs. [Pause] Let us pray to the Lord:

President: Lord God, you reveal your power most of all in your forgiveness and compassion. Fill us with your grace so that we may walk with joy in the way of your commandments. We make this prayer through Christ our Lord.

REFLECTION I   **The prodigal girl**

Great poets have sung of the beauties of home,
its comfort, its love and its joys;
how back to the place of its sheltering dome
I welcome the prodigal boy.
They picture his father with pardoning smile
and glittering robes to unfurl;

but none of the poets thought it worthwhile
to sing of the prodigal girl.
The prodigal son can resume his old place
as leader of fashion's mad whirl,
with never a hint of his former disgrace
– not so for the prodigal girl!
The girl may come back to the home she had left,
but nothing is ever the same:
the shadow still lingers o'er the dear ones bereft,
society scoffs at her name.
Perhaps that is why when the prodigal girl
gets lost on life's devious track;
she thinks of the lips that will scornfully curl,
and hasn't the heart to come back.
Yes, welcome, the prodigal son to his place,
kill the calf, fill the free-flowing bowl;
but shut not the door on his frail sister's face,
remember, she too has a soul.   *(Anon.)*

REFLECTION II   **Loved in our sins**

The prodigal son came home empty-handed.
He had no trophies to show his father,
no achievements with which to earn
his praise, his welcome, and his love.
He was a failure. Worse – he was a sinner.
He deserved to be punished – and he knew it.
Yet punishment was the last thing he needed.
To punish him would be like pouring water on a dying fire.
What happened?
When the father saw his lost son coming towards him,
his heart went out to him,
and next minute they were in each other's arms.
It is an extraordinary experience to be loved in one's sinfulness.
Such love is like a breeze to a dying fire,
or rain falling on parched ground.
Those who have experienced this kind of love,
know something about the heart of God.

Fifth Sunday of Lent
THE WOMAN CAUGHT IN ADULTERY

INTRODUCTION AND CONFITEOR

In today's Gospel we hear again the immortal words of Jesus in relation to the woman caught in adultery: 'Let the one who is without sin cast the first stone.' Even though we are sinners ourselves, we may have cast the stone of judgement at others. As we call to mind our sins, we might remember especially the harsh and unfair judgements we sometimes pass on others. [Pause]

I confess to almighty God ...

HEADINGS FOR READINGS

First Reading (Is 43:16-21). The prophet assures the Jews exiled in Babylon that there will be a new Exodus. This message of hope should inspire us also.

Second Reading (Phil 3:8-14). Paul has willingly sacrificed everything for the privilege of knowing Christ. He hasn't yet arrived but is still running the race of salvation.

Gospel (Jn 8:1-11). Jesus refuses to condemn a woman caught in adultery.

SCRIPTURE NOTE

The First Reading contains a message of hope addressed to the Jewish exiles in Babylon. There will be a new exodus, so glorious that it will put the great events of the first exodus in the shade. And all of this will happen because God is faithful to his people.

This prepares us for the Gospel. Christians see the radically new thing that God has done for us in and through Jesus. Specifically we see God's love and compassion in Jesus' treatment of a sinful woman. The story is taken from John, but it resembles the style of Luke. It's an 'entrapment' story which sought to show Jesus' wisdom in besting his adversaries.

The aim of the Scribes and Pharisees was to set a snare for Jesus. If he pardoned the woman, he could be accused of encouraging people to break the law of Moses. If he agreed that she should be stoned, he would lose his name for mercy. But Jesus turned the tables on her accusers by suggesting that they look at their own sins.

Paul has willingly sacrificed everything for the justification that comes from faith in Christ, and for the hope of resurrection (Second Reading). Like a runner at the final stage of a race, he doesn't look back but keeps his eye on the winning tape.

Fifth Sunday of Lent

HOMILY 1   The compassion of Jesus

As we go on in life we tend to set a higher value on the virtue of kindness – plain, ordinary, everyday kindness. When we look back on our lives we remember with regret acts of unkindness. But we recall fondly times when we acted kindly. Kindness is essential to true justice. Jesus was especially kind to individuals whom he was called to judge. The classic example is the woman caught in adultery.

The story warns us against being too quick to take the high moral ground. Which of us is without sin? We must learn from the example of Jesus. He condemned the woman's sin, but refused to condemn her. It's not that sin didn't matter to him. It did. But he distinguished between the sin and the sinner. He condemned the sin but pardoned the sinner.

And his over-riding motive in all of this was compassion. It wasn't a question of being liberal (anything goes), but of being compassionate. The holier a person is the less he/she is inclined to judge others. In every human being there is a dimension which escapes the powers of judgement of any other human being.

Jesus refused to condemn her. But he did say to her, 'Go and sin no more.' In other words, he didn't deny her sin. He got her to own it and take responsibility for it. It's much easier to deny it, to excuse it, or blame it on others. When one faces it and deals with it, there is no more blame, or regret, or remorse, or despair.

The compassion and forgiveness of Jesus give life. The woman went away free – free to change her behaviour, and to regain her self-respect. Jesus reminds us that people are capable of changing if given the chance.

The mission of the Church is to be a place of forgiveness so that those who fail (all of us in different ways and degrees) may experience the love and compassion of the One who refused to condemn. The Church ought to be a community of grace, a community free from legalism, a community which will not condemn but which will love, a community which is more concerned about mercy than justice.

One day a mother came to plead with Napoleon for her son's life. The young man had committed a serious offence. The law was clear. Justice demanded his death. The emperor was determined to ensure that justice would be done. But the mother insisted, 'Your Excellency, I have come to ask for mercy not for justice.'

'But he does not deserve mercy,' Napoleon answered.

'Your Excellency,' said the mother, 'it would not be mercy if he deserved it.'

'So be it,' said Napoleon. 'I will have mercy on him.' And he set her son free.

Mercy, of its nature, is pure gift. It is something we all stand in need of, and hence it is something we must be ready to extend to others. The Lord said, 'Blessed are the merciful; they will obtain mercy.'

HOMILY 2   **No one is without sin**

Once upon a time a man was caught stealing and was brought before the king, who immediately gave orders that he be hanged. However, as he was being led to the gallows, the man told the prison governor that he knew a wonderful secret, which was taught him by his father. He claimed that using this secret he could plant the seed of a pomegranate and make it grow and bear fruit overnight. He said that it would be a pity if the secret died with him, and that he was willing to reveal it to the king.

The governor was so impressed that he halted the execution, and brought the man back before the king. There the man dug a hole in the ground, and taking a pomegranate seed said, 'Your Majesty, the seed must be planted by a person who has never taken anything that didn't belong to him. I being a thief cannot do it.' Then turning to one of the king's officials he said, 'Maybe you would like to plant it.'

But the official refused, saying, 'In my younger days I kept something that didn't belong to me.' Then the man turned to the king's treasurer and said, 'Well then, maybe you would like to plant it.' But the treasurer too refused, saying, 'Over the years I've handled a lot of money. Now and again I might have kept a little for myself.'

And so it went on. Finally there was only the king left. Turning to him the man said, 'Perhaps your Majesty would do the honour of planting the seed.' But the king said, 'I'm ashamed to say it, but once I kept a watch that belonged to my father.'

Then the thief said, 'All of you are great and powerful people and want for nothing. Yet none of you can plant the seed, whilst I who have stolen a little because I was starving am about to be hanged.'

The king pardoned him. That story would have ended very differently if the king had not been prepared to listen. Instead, thanks to his patience and to the imagination of the condemned man, no one died and they all learned a salutary lesson.

The Gospel scene could have ended in a very ugly manner. If Jesus had gone along with the script of the Scribes and Pharisees, the woman would have died a horrible death. Who would have benefited from that? Instead, thanks to the understanding and compassion he showed her, she was able to put it behind her and make a new start.

The fact that he didn't condemn her does not mean that he thought lightly of adultery. He realised that she had already been condemned. What she needed now was compassion. He treated her in such a way that it made her want to reform her life.

What God wants is not the death of the sinner but that he/she be converted and live. In his wisdom God understands our weakness, and in his mercy he forgives our sins. He not only helps us to put our sins behind us, but to draw good from them. And surely the fact that we have all sinned, and therefore stand continually in need of God's mercy, will make us refrain from casting stones at others.

HOMILY 3   **Christ's way**

There is no more judgmental and condemnatory person than the self-righteous phoney. Where others are concerned, he has such high standards, makes such exacting demands, accepts no excuses, makes no exceptions, tolerates no slip-ups. But when it comes to himself he can be so blind and all-forgiving.

The opposite is also true. There is no more compassionate and understanding person towards those who fall than the genuinely holy person. This is exemplified in the lives of the saints, and especially in the life of Jesus. We have a marvellous example of it in the way he dealt with the woman caught in adultery.

On the surface there appears to be only one sin involved – the sin of adultery. But there are other sins there, and very serious ones at that.

There is the horrible sin involved in the way the Scribes and Pharisees treated the woman. They exposed her to the most humiliating kind of shaming – a public shaming. People have been known to commit suicide rather than face a public shaming. They showed not the slightest regard for her feelings, not the tiniest shred of concern for her as a person. She was someone they could use to entrap Jesus. She was to them what bait is to fishermen. The bait is gladly sacrificed in the hope of catching a fish. To use another person in this way is a despicable thing.

Then there is the sin involved in their attitude towards Jesus. Here are men who are pursuing the path of darkness. They have only one aim – to get rid of Jesus. In other words, they have murder on their minds.

Yet in spite of the way the Scribes and Pharisees shamed and humiliated the woman, and the murderous attitudes they harboured towards himself, there is something marvellously gentle and subtle in the way Jesus dealt with them. He did not condemn them. He exposed them, but didn't spell it out in public. He didn't even judge them. He invited them to judge themselves. Instead of answering their question straightaway, he began to write on the ground. He did this in order to give them time to examine their consciences.

And what a contrast there is between the way the Pharisees treated the woman and the way Jesus treated her. He refused to condemn her. He corrected her, but did it ever so gently. His approach was like that of a good surgeon: a combination of courtesy, gentleness and tenderness while using the scalpel. His mission was about mercy and forgiveness, not judgement and condemnation. He did not come to expose the sores of people but to heal them.

Jesus illuminated a dark scene with the radiance of his compassion. There is a marvellous lesson here for us. It's easy to condemn others. We must learn from the example of Jesus not to condemn. The very act of condemning another involves a sin. There surely is a time to correct another. But there is an art is doing so. It consists in being totally kind and totally honest at the same time. Honesty for honesty's sake can be very destructive.

We must look to ourselves. We must be willing to extend to others the same compassion we would like to receive if we were involved in the same situation. There is no more important thing in life than to show compassion for a fellow human being.

'Let him who is without sin cast the first stone. It was worth while living to have said that.' (Oscar Wilde).

ANOTHER STORY

A story is told about King Solomon. We know from the Bible that he was a wise judge. Year in and year out he sat in judgement on people. But it seems that as the years went by he gradually became hard and insensitive. In fact, he became positively harsh and cold towards people.

One day as he sat on his throne before commencing a judging session, the crown he was wearing slid down over his eyes. He straightened it up immediately, only for the same thing to happen again. Eight times this happened. Finally he said to the crown, 'Why do you keep falling down over my eyes?' And the crown replied, 'I have to. When power loses compassion, I have to show what such a condition looks like.' In other words, it is blind.

Solomon grasped the truth at once. And to his credit he knelt down and asked forgiveness from God. The crown immediately centred itself on his head.

When something goes wrong, look first at your own behaviour to see if the cause might not lie with yourself. Even the wisdom of Solomon can go blind.

PRAYER OF THE FAITHFUL

President: Let us pray for our needs to God who is rich in mercy and compassion.

Response: Lord, hear our prayer.

Reader(s): For Christians: that they may imitate the compassion of Christ in their dealings with one another. [Pause] Let us pray to the Lord.

For judges: that they may strive to temper justice with mercy. [Pause]

Let us pray to the Lord.

For those who have been unfairly treated or unjustly condemned. [Pause] Let us pray to the Lord.

For this congregation: that we may extend to others the same compassion we would like to receive if we were in the same situation. [Pause] Let us pray to the Lord.

For all gathered here: that we may never use the sins of others to justify our own. [Pause] Let us pray to the Lord.

For our own special needs. [Pause] Let us pray to the Lord.

President: Father, help us to keep our hearts pure, our minds clean, our words true, and our deeds kind. We ask this through Christ our Lord.

REFLECTION   **Mercy**

The quality of mercy is not strain'd;
it droppeth as the gentle rain from heaven
upon the place beneath.
It is twice blest:
it blesseth him that gives and him that takes.
'Tis mightiest in the mighty;
it becomes the throned monarch better than his crown.
It is enshrined in the hearts of kings.
It is an attribute of God himself.
And earthly power doth then show likest God's
when mercy seasons justice.
Therefore, though justice be thy plea, consider this -
that in the course of justice none of us should see salvation.
We do pray for mercy,
and the same prayer doth teach us all
to render the deeds of mercy.   *(William Shakespeare)*

Passion (Palm) Sunday

SOLEMN PROCESSION

The solemn procession with palms is the traditional start of this, the first liturgy of Holy Week. When the procession reaches the church, Mass begins with the Collect. If there is no procession Mass could begin as below.

SIMPLE INTRODUCTION

Today we begin Holy Week, which commemorates the week in which

Christ died. He died because of sin. Let us pause to call to mind our sins, especially those through which we hurt others. [Pause] Christ forgave those who put him to death. He will forgive us too.

Lord Jesus, you forgave Peter who denied you. Lord, have mercy.
You prayed for those who condemned you. Christ, have mercy.
You received the repentant thief into paradise. Lord, have mercy.

HEADINGS FOR READINGS

Gospel for Procession (Lk 19:28-40). Jesus' entry into Jerusalem as messianic king is a sign that the peace and salvation decreed by God are at hand.

First Reading (Is 50:4-7). The prophet suffers in carrying out his mission, but is confident that God will vindicate him.

Second Reading (Phil 2:6-11). Because Jesus took on himself our human condition and accepted death on a cross, the Father has made him Lord of heaven and earth.

Gospel (Lk 22:14-23:56). Luke's version of the Passion Story. As in the rest of his Gospel, so in his account of the Passion, Luke presents a Christ who is merciful and forgiving, even to his executioners.

SCRIPTURE NOTE

Luke's Passion narrative resembles that of Mark but has its own emphasis. The devil who departed from Jesus after the temptations returns now, entering Judas and demanding to sift Peter. Throughout his Gospel Luke portrays Jesus as the merciful and forgiving Saviour of humankind; in death he forgives his executioners, and on the cross he brings salvation to a criminal.

Typical of Luke is his special attention to women in a society where they were downgraded. His story is that of a disciple who relives the drama of his Master. Personal attachment to Jesus is expressed by the repeated affirmations of his innocence. He develops the personal relationships between Jesus and the various characters in the tragedy, especially Judas and Peter.

To understand the Passion message we have to keep in mind the other half of Luke's two-volume work, the Acts of the Apostles. The Jesus who is accused by the chief priests before the Roman governor prepares the way for Paul being brought before the same cast of adversaries. The innocent Jesus who dies asking forgiveness for his enemies and commending his soul to God the Father prepares the way for the first Christian martyr, Stephen, who will die voicing similar sentiments.

HOMILY 1   **The triumph of love**

Each year on this Sunday the Church reads an account of the Passion of
Jesus. As we listen to it, we are reminded of the cowardice of the followers who abandoned him in his hour of greatest need, of the wickedness of
the religious leaders who plotted his death, and of the cruelty of the soldiers who carried out his execution. And we need to be reminded of these
things, because we have a kinship with them. But that is not the purpose
of the Passion reading. We hear too much bad news as it is.

The emphasis is not there. The emphasis is on Jesus, the central character in the story. What we are remembering is the fidelity, the courage,
and the sheer goodness of Jesus. Against the darkness of Calvary his goodness shines all the more brightly. The day of his death is not called 'Bad
Friday' but 'Good Friday'. What makes it good is the love of Jesus. 'Greater
love no man has than to who lay down his life for his friends.' It is that
love that we are remembering this week.

The early Christians saw in the passion and death of Jesus the triumph
of failure. With the help of the Scriptures, they came to understand that
this was precisely how Jesus triumphed and entered into his glory. His
glory cannot be separated from his passion.

On the surface, it may seem as if it was a defeat for Jesus. It was not a
defeat. It was a victory. It was the triumph of good over evil, of love over
hate, of light over darkness, and of life over death.

The Passion Story shows how Jesus responded to what was done to
him. He absorbed all the violence, transformed it, and returned it as love
and forgiveness. This was the victory of love over all the powers of destruction. There was nothing but love in him. Even when they nailed his
hands and feet, he was loving. It helps to think about that when we are
going through hard times.

It is a consolation for us to know that Jesus suffered. Yet his suffering
would have been wasted if he had not endured it with love. It was not
Jesus' suffering that saved the world but his love. Anyone who pretends
to love suffering is crazy. Suffering is something that you would give
almost anything to avoid. Yet we are glad to suffer for someone we love.
Our love gives a meaning to our suffering. Jesus was the Good Shepherd
dying because he loved his sheep.

Suffering that is merely endured does nothing for our souls, except
perhaps harden them. It is the spirit in which we bear our burden that
matters. All the coal and firewood in the world are no use without a fire.

It is not suffering that redeems the world, but love. It is not our suffering that God wants but our love. However, love inevitably brings pain.
But it also brings great joy. The Christian must not only accept suffering:
he/she must make it holy. Love makes it holy.

HOMILY 2   **Jesus' suffering and ours**

One evening a London commuter was hurrying home. As he neared Westminster Cathedral, he was drawn to enter it. He could not explain why because he had long dismissed religion.

Having entered the building, he was startled by the cross hanging from the dome. He was taken aback at the sight of a man on a cross, tortured, abandoned, dead. He had seen terrible pictures of men, women and children slaughtered in Bosnia, they too abandoned. In other places, he had seen pictures of people starving, emaciated, flies crawling over their faces, eyes staring, no longer appealing for help but waiting – waiting for death.

The man sat and gazed at that cross for some time. Slowly its inner meaning revealed itself to him. He began to see, in the tortured and dying figure on the cross, a mother mourning her dead sons in Bosnia, a starving child in Africa, the grieving parents of loved ones killed in an accident, the suffering of the mentally or physically sick. All human pain seemed to be gathered up and, as it were, made his own by that man on the cross.

Then he looked around him and saw men and women praying quietly. They seemed to possess a precious secret. They looked at ease with themselves and at home in this vast cathedral. Then he saw an elderly woman approach a crucifix that stood near a shrine. After kissing the wounds of Christ, she moved away comforted and consoled by such great love.

As he watched, his mind and heart seemed to be carried upwards into another sphere of reality. For the first time in his life he was at prayer. The cross was not so much speaking about death as celebrating love, life and hope. The cross of horror became the cross of hope, the tortured body became the body of new life, the gaping wounds became the source of forgiveness, healing and reconciliation. When he finally left the cathedral and joined the evening traffic, he felt at peace with himself and the world.

Jesus' passion was no play-acting; it was real. And it was freely chosen. He suffered the pain of being let down by his friends. He suffered the pain of being betrayed by one of them – Judas. He suffered fear and anguish in the garden, and he had no one to support him during his agony.

He was subjected to a barrage of false accusations. He endured insults, blows, taunts, spits; then the lash of the whip and the piercing of the thorns and the nails. He suffered the shame of being condemned to death like a common criminal. As he died he had to endure more taunts, insults and mockery. Who could plumb the depths of what he suffered?

By uniting our suffering to the sufferings of Jesus, we can find peace. There is no loneliness, hunger, oppression, exploitation, torture, imprisonment, violence, or threats that have not been suffered by Jesus. There can be no human beings who are completely alone in their sufferings, since God, in and through Jesus, has become Emmanuel, God with us.

The passion of Jesus gives courage, strength and hope to all who suffer. It means we are not alone.

HOMILY 3   **Witnessing to Christ in public**

On Palm Sunday Jesus' disciples openly acknowledged their belief in him and loyalty to him. What made their display of support all the more praiseworthy was the fact that it was carried out in the teeth of bitter opposition from the Pharisees. When some Pharisees came to Jesus to protest he said, 'If they kept silent, the very stones would cry out.'

There are occasions when a public demonstration is called for. This was one of them. It was the only time that Jesus accepted something akin to hero-worship from the people. He knew that his disciples had a right and a need to express publicly their belief in him. But one has a doubt about the commitment to those disciples. Not that one doubts their sincerity. But it was a mass response, and a mass response is often more loud than deep.

It's easy to witness to Jesus here in church. We are among our own. But it's not so easy to witness to him out in an indifferent and sometimes hostile world.

There are times when we too need to profess our faith in Jesus publicly. And there are times when the occasion cries out for it.

The stones will not speak out. Only humans can do that. Let us not remain silent when a word cries out to be said: a word of support in defence of someone who is being treated unjustly; a word of praise to someone whose contribution is being forgotten; or a word of truth where deliberate lies are being told. But it's not easy to speak out. It's far easier and safer to stay silent.

So let us be careful while we profess our faith in Christ here in church, that we do not ignore him or deny him in the market-place. Christ says to us, 'Anyone who acknowledges me before others, I also will acknowledge before my Father in heaven.'

We can draw inspiration from the first disciples of Jesus. They are revealed in the Gospels as people who were not afraid to admit their doubts, their needs, their lack of faith. Yet on the first Palm Sunday they were strong and bold in their witness to Jesus.

May the Lord take pity on us, his timid and fearful disciples, and give us courage so that our lives may bear witness to the faith we profess with our lips.

PRAYER OF THE FAITHFUL

President: This week we celebrate the love that God has shown us in Christ. Let us now turn to God and bring our many needs before him with confidence.

Response: Lord, hear us in your love.

Reader(s): For Christians: that they may learn from the example of Jesus' disciples on the first Palm Sunday not be afraid to show loyalty to Christ in front of unbelievers and cynics. [Pause] We pray in faith.

For those who administer our justice system: that they may strive to ensure that in all cases the truth is told and justice is done. [Pause] We pray in faith.

For those who are unjustly deprived of liberty and life. [Pause] We pray in faith.

For all gathered here: that we may be aware of those who suffer so that they need not carry their cross alone. [Pause] We pray in faith.

For each other and for ourselves: that meditating on the Passion may help us to bear our own sufferings in a Christlike way. [Pause] We pray in faith.

For our own special needs. [Longer pause] We pray in faith.

President: Lord God, your Son showed his love for us in suffering and dying for us. Help us to return his love by loving one another. We ask this through the same Christ, our Lord.

INTRODUCTION TO THE OUR FATHER

On this day when Jesus said that if the people kept silent, the stones would cry out, let us not be afraid to let our voices be heard as we pray to our heavenly Father.

REFLECTION   **Weep not for me but for yourselves**

This week each year Christians are drawn to Jerusalem,
if not in body, at least in mind.
They stand at the foot of the cross, beating their breasts,
and staring with pity at Jesus of Nazareth.
They listen with reverence as he prays for his killers:
'Father, forgive them, for they know not what they do.'
But when the week is over they return to their homes
to resume their deep-rooted spites
and the burden of things they can't forgive.
Let us not then weep for Jesus.
Let us weep for our own sins.
Then maybe, like Jesus, we will be able
to forgive others who sin against us.

EASTERTIDE

The Resurrection

PATRICK

Easter Sunday

Easter Day is the greatest day in the Church's calendar. Jesus has over-come death, not only for himself, but for all of us. The joy of Easter fills all the earth, the joy that death has been conquered. Let us open our hearts to receive this great joy. [Pause]

Lord Jesus, through the grace of your resurrection you show us that light is stronger than darkness. Lord, have mercy.

You show us that good is stronger than evil. Christ, have mercy.

You show us that life is stronger than death. Lord, have mercy.

HEADINGS FOR READINGS

First Reading (Acts 10:34.37-43). We hear part of an early sermon of Peter.

Second Reading (Col 3:1-4). Through our Baptism we already share in the risen life of Christ, though in a hidden and mysterious way.

Alternative Second Reading (1 Cor 5:6-8). Christians are to celebrate Easter (the new Passover) by getting rid of old attitudes and living in sincerity and truth.

Gospel (Jn 20:1-9). On discovering that Jesus' tomb is empty, the disci-ples begin to grasp what the Scriptures had foretold, namely, that he would rise from the dead.

SCRIPTURE NOTE

The reading from Acts is part of an early sermon of Peter. In it he summa-rises the ministry of Jesus, which culminated in his death. But it didn't end there – God raised him to life, allowing him to be seen by certain witnesses. Peter is one of those witnesses. He goes on to declare that Je-sus is the one all the prophets spoke about, namely, the Messiah. All who believe in him will have their sins forgiven.

The Gospel tells about the discovery of the empty tomb. The empty tomb (with the discarded linen cloths) in itself is not a direct proof of the resurrection. Nevertheless, it was the first step towards establishing the truth that Jesus had escaped the bonds of death, and it prepared the dis-ciples to encounter the risen Lord.

Many of readings of the Easter cycle were meant to instruct the newly baptised on the Christian way of life. Today's Second Reading and its alternative are good examples. Thus the Easter season provides us with an opportunity to reflect on what it means to be baptised members of Christ's Body.

HOMILY 1   **Confirming our faith**

Every year on Easter Sunday tens of thousands of pilgrims gather in St Peter's Square in Rome for the Pope's Easter Blessing. It's a wonderful occasion as the successor of Peter proclaims the Easter message: 'Christ is risen, alleluia.' He is doing what Peter did on the first Easter – he is confirming the faith of his brothers and sisters. And there can be no doubt but that it does confirm the faith of those fortunate enough to be present.

Peter was doing what the Lord had asked of him during the Last Supper when he said: 'Simon, Satan will sift you like wheat; but I have prayed for you, that your faith may not fail, and once you have recovered, you in your turn must strengthen your brothers.' (Lk 22:31-32)

Peter to strengthen the faith of his brothers! He would seem a strange choice when we consider how he performed during the passion. How could someone whose own faith was so fickle, confirm anyone? Let us remind ourselves briefly how he performed the night Jesus was arrested.

We recall his brave words at the Last Supper: 'Even if all the others should lose faith in you, I will never lose faith in you.' He really meant those words. He thought he was brave and strong. A short while later, when Jesus was sorrowful, lonely, and fearful in the garden, he asked Peter to watch with him. But Peter couldn't manage even that – he fell asleep. He left Jesus to drink the cup of sorrow alone. Worse was to come.

Later that night, in the courtyard of the high priest's house, someone turned to Peter and said, 'Aren't you one of his? Weren't you with him in the garden?' And what happened? Not once but three times Peter denied Jesus, denied ever having known him. Then the cook crew. At that moment Jesus looked at Peter, and Peter immediately realised what he had done – he had denied his friend. And he went outside and wept bitterly.

It was the lowest moment in his life. He found out a very painful truth about himself. He wasn't as strong, or as brave, or as generous as he thought he was. But Jesus didn't write him off. He had foreseen all this. He had even predicted it. He continued to believe in him. He knew that there was another and better side to Peter. After the resurrection he restored a wiser and humbler Peter to where he was before, and made him the rock on which he would build his Church.

And Peter came good. He recovered and went on to strengthen the faith of his brothers and sisters in the community. It was he who led the apostles in witnessing to the resurrection. (First Reading). It was he who gathered together the scattered followers of Jesus. It was on the basis of his testimony that the community exclaimed: 'The Lord has risen indeed, and has appeared to Simon.' (Lk 24:34)

Peter has been called a stumbling saint. He is a favourite with many, probably because his human frailty makes us feel kinship with him. Courage fails us all. In the end, all of us are mere mortals who are inconstant in our beliefs. But we must not judge ourselves or others by momentary lapses, but by commitment over a long time to our beliefs.

It was Jesus himself who confirmed the faith of Peter. The same risen Lord confirms us in our faith. We are a community of believers whose common faith strengthens the faith of each individual.

HOMILY 2   **Making the leap of faith**

We sometimes envy the apostles and the first disciples. We are convinced that they had an advantage over all later Christians because they were actually present at the events related in the Gospels. They saw the risen Jesus with their own eyes, and touched him with their hands. Therefore, faith was easy for them. And we are convinced that it would be easy for us too if only we could see Jesus personally, as the apostles did, or if only we could see for ourselves the miracles he performed, as the first disciples did.

Yes, the first disciples had the advantage of seeing Jesus with their own eyes. But did that make faith any easier for them? When they looked at Jesus what did they see? They did not and could not have seen God, for God is not immediately visible and knowable. In Jesus they saw a human being ostensibly like themselves. But to go from there to believe that he was the Son of God required a huge act of faith.

This accounts for the fact that there were many who heard Jesus speak and who saw him act, who did not believe in him. Even the apostles themselves, who had been with him from the beginning, are shown to be slow to believe. Seeing is not necessarily believing.

The shock caused by his passion and death on the cross was so great that the apostles were slow to believe in the news of the Resurrection. When Jesus appeared to them on Easter evening, he rebuked them for their unbelief and hardness of heart, because they had not believed those who saw him after he had risen. (Mk 16:14)

Where does all this leave us? We can't see Jesus the way the apostles saw him. We can't be present in the upper room going over the events of Holy Week when Jesus drops in. We can't put our finger in the wounds of Jesus. We can't look into his face and say, 'My Lord, and my God.' We must live by faith, not by sight. Yet if we would believe in Jesus we must see him somehow. But just how may people like us see Jesus? What must we do in order to believe?

We are disciples at second hand. For the disciple at second hand, things are harder in some ways, but easier in others. Things are harder because twenty centuries have gone by since Jesus walked the earth. A lot of dust has gathered. The light has dimmed. But on the positive side, the notion that the Son of God walked the earth has become 'naturalised' over time, and so in some ways has become easier to believe. But at the end of the day, all disciples are essentially equal - all have to make the leap of faith. We become disciples through faith.

The friends of Jesus saw him and heard him only a few times after that Easter day, but their lives were completely changed. And by sharing their faith our lives will be changed too. We are able to travel in hope because we know that good will triumph over evil, and life will triumph over death, because Jesus is risen.

HOMILY 3 **Visiting the grave**

On Easter morning the women went to the tomb where Jesus had been buried. They had a sad task to perform – to complete the embalming of his body. But that was not the only reason they were going to the tomb. They wanted to be near the one who had filled their lives, and whose death plunged them into an inconsolable grief.

We've often done the same thing ourselves. When someone we love dies, we find it hard to accept that he/she is gone from us forever. We feel a need to maintain a link with the one who has died. One of the ways we meet this need is by visits to the grave. However, far from easing the pain of our loss, this may exacerbate it. It tends to make the dead even more dead, because nowhere do we become so sure that our loved one is dead as at the grave.

If things had gone as expected that first Easter morning, the women would have embalmed the body of Jesus, closed the tomb again, and come away more convinced than ever that what happened on Friday was not a bad dream but a terrible reality. But things did not go according to plan.

At the tomb they met two angels who said to them, 'Why do you look for the living among the dead? He is not here, but has risen.' It was to these faithful women disciples that the Easter message was first given: Jesus is not dead; he is alive. So they must not waste their time looking for him at the tomb.

All of us have stood forlornly in graveyards, where everything speaks of death. Yet it was precisely in such a place that the resurrection was first announced. It was fitting that it was here, where death seems to reign supreme, that the good news of Jesus' resurrection was first announced.

Through the voice of the liturgy, the same message is given to us: Do not look for your loved one in the grave. He/she is not there. Jesus overcame death, not just for himself, but for all of us. He is the first to rise from the dead, but we will follow him. For a Christian, then, there is no such thing as death in the sense of final extinction. Our dead are not dead. They are alive, and live a more real and beautiful life than ours. And they are not far from us. Those who die in grace go no further from us than God, and God is very near.

Let us continue to pray for our dead in case they still need our help.

And let us continue to visit the cemetery if it helps to keep their memory alive. But let us not look for them there. And if sadness persists in our hearts, because of what happened on Easter morning, a quiet hope is mingled with our sadness.

STORIES

1. Viktor Frankl spent three years in Auschwitz. He survived though his wife and family perished. He tells how one day shortly after the liberation of the camp he went for a walk through the country towards the market town a few miles from the camp.

The meadows were full of flowers. Larks rose singing into the sky. There was no one to be seen for miles around. There was nothing but the wide earth and sky, the singing of the larks, and the freedom of space. He stopped, looked around him, and then up into the blue sky. Then he went down on his knees to give thanks to God for his liberation. As he prayed one sentence came to mind that expressed what he was feeling: 'I called on God from my narrow prison and he answered me in the freedom of space.'

How long he knelt there repeating that sentence he could not tell. But he said later: 'On that day and in that hour my new life started. Step by step I progressed, until I again became a human being.'

We cannot separate the joy Frankl felt that day in that flower-filled meadow from the suffering he experienced in the camp. In fact, that joy would have no meaning were it not for the suffering that preceded it. In the same way we can't separate the resurrection of Jesus from his passion and death. His glory cannot be separated from his pain. The early Christians came to understand, albeit slowly, that the passion and death was precisely how Jesus entered into his glory.

And so it must be for us. The resurrection is the main thing, but we must not forget that it was preceded by the passion and death.

We can't have Easter Sunday without Good Friday. But when we are experiencing Good Friday we should remember Easter Sunday.

2. As the women disciples made their way to Jesus' tomb on Easter morning they had one big problem: Who would roll away the great stone that had been placed at the entrance to his tomb?

There was a man who had a row with his father, as a result of which he hadn't spoken to his father for several years, even though they lived only a few miles apart. He was an only child; the mother had deserted the family. So now the father was living alone. His world was getting smaller and darker with each day that passed. He wasn't yet dead, but in a sense he was already in the tomb.

We marvel at the power Jesus had to raise people from the dead, and rightly so. But in a sense we can do the same. For instance, the son in the story had the power to roll away the stone from his father's tomb. With a word or a gesture he could set him free from his tomb of loneliness and despair. And in helping his father he would have helped himself too. It is one of the lovely compensations of life that we cannot raise another without raising ourselves also.

PRAYER OF THE FAITHFUL

President: Christ, the Morning Star, has come back from the dead, and now sheds his peaceful light on the world. Let us pray to him with confidence for all our needs.

Response: Lord, hear our prayer.

Reader(s): That the Lord's light may shine on all his followers, and renew their faith and hope. [Pause] Let us pray to the Lord.

That his light may shine on world leaders, encouraging them in their search for justice and peace. [Pause] Let us pray to the Lord.

That his light may shine on the bereaved. [Pause] Let us pray to the Lord.

That his light may shine on the sad and the lonely. [Pause] Let us pray to the Lord.

That his light may shine on the sick and the troubled. [Pause] Let us pray to the Lord.

That his light may shine on prisoners. [Pause] Let us pray to the Lord.

That his light may shine on our deceased relatives and friends. [Pause] Let us pray to the Lord.

That his light may shine on our own special needs. [Longer pause] Let us pray to the Lord.

President: God our Father, you raised your Son from the darkness of death, and brought him into the glorious light of your kingdom. Grant that we may follow his light faithfully and come to your kingdom where there are no more shattered hopes or broken dreams. We ask this through the same Christ our Lord.

SIGN OF PEACE

Lord Jesus Christ, on Easter Sunday evening you appeared to your frightened and disheartened disciples and said: 'Peace be with you.' Then you showed them your wounded hands and side, and they were filled with joy. Grant that we who have heard the message of Easter may enjoy the peace and unity of your kingdom where you live for ever and ever.

PRAYER/REFLECTION   **A quiet joy and peace**

On Easter Day we still feel pain,

our own pain and the pain of others.
But a new element has been introduced.
It doesn't remove the pain,
but gives it a meaning, and lights it up with hope.
All is different because Jesus is alive
and speaks his words of peace to us.
Therefore, there is a quiet joy among us, and a deep sense of peace.
Jesus has broken the power of death,
and given us the hope of eternal life.
Lord, guard this hope with your grace,
and bring it to fulfilment in the kingdom of heaven.

Second Sunday of Easter

INTRODUCTION AND CONFITEOR

Like the apostle Thomas, from time to time we all doubt. We should not hide our questions. We must do what Thomas did – bring those doubts to the Lord. And our risen Lord will say to us what he said to Thomas: 'Cease doubting and believe.' [Pause]

Lord Jesus, you raise the dead to life in the Spirit. Lord, have mercy.

You bring pardon and peace to the sinner. Christ, have mercy.

You bring light to those in the darkness of doubt and unbelief. Lord have mercy.

HEADINGS FOR READINGS

First Reading (Acts 5:12-16). This tells of the high regard in which the apostles were held by the ordinary people, and of the cures they worked for the sick.

Second Reading (Rev 1:9-13.17-19). John is bidden to write a message – one which has meaning for the Church until the end of time.

Gospel (Jn 20:19-31). By seeing and touching the wounds of his risen Lord, Thomas the doubter is cured of his unbelief.

SCRIPTURE NOTE

In the Gospel we have John's version of Pentecost, birthday of the Church. The risen Jesus appears to his apostles, showing them his wounds and bestowing peace on them. He gives them the gift of the Spirit and inaugurates the mission of the Church, which is the continuance of his own mission (to preach repentance for the forgiveness of sins).

One of the effects of the gift of the Spirit was that the Church had the power to forgive sins. John did not tell us who could exercise this power or how it should be exercised. Though we cannot read back into this text the later Sacrament of Penance, we can confidently say that the Church's use of the Sacrament of Reconciliation is one valid and legitimate way of exercising the power over sin given by the risen Jesus to his disciples.

Thomas' profession of faith, 'My Lord and my God', is the supreme christological statement of John's Gospel. Originally John's Gospel ended where today's passage ends.

For this and the next five Sundays the Second Reading is taken from the Book of Revelation. The book is the revelation of Jesus Christ, made known through an angel to an unidentified prophet, John. It describes the battle between good and evil, and assures believers that good (God) will triumph. It was addressed to the whole Church and was meant to be read at liturgical assemblies to encourage believers to hold fast to the faith in times of persecution.

HOMILY 1   **The wounded healer**

The risen Jesus still bore the wounds of his crucifixion on his glorified body. Why was this? This story may give us a clue to the answer.

It is about a single, working mother, who lives in New York. In a period of six years she saw her three sons shot dead, the youngest of them right in front of her door. It has left a deep wound in her heart. She relives her grief every time a child is killed in the neighbourhood.

Yet she has refused to be trapped by fear and a sense of victimhood. Instead, she has reached out to others. She has become an eloquent advocate for gun control and community responsibility, talking at schools and other places. She started a support group for mothers in similar positions. And when a child dies, she visits the parents to comfort them.

She says that in the beginning she wished her sons had never been born. But now she says, 'In their deaths there is sorrow, but there is also some unbelievable joy. If I had not had my three sons, I would not be the kind of person I am today. They help me to be strong. They help me not to be selfish.'

The frame of her door still bears the marks of the bullets which killed her youngest son. Although she doesn't always notice them, she knows they are there. Why doesn't she have the frame repaired? 'I want those holes to be a constant reminder that a young man lost his life at that spot. When you fix things, people tend to forget.'

When you fix things, people tend to forget. Maybe that is why Jesus kept the marks of his wounds on his risen body. Firstly, those wounds helped the apostles to recognise him. The same Jesus who during his life manifested his power over evil is the one in whom God has manifested

[113]

his power over death. Secondly, those wounds were the proof of his love. Jesus didn't just talk about love; he gave an example of it, and had the wounds to prove it – the mortal wounds the Good Shepherd suffered in defending his flock from the wolf.

Jesus did not hide his wounds. He showed them to Thomas and invited him to touch them. When Thomas touched the wounds of Jesus, his doubts vanished, and his faith was re-born.

The sacred and precious wounds of Jesus are a source of consolation, courage, and hope to us. They help us to come to terms with our own wounds. They help us not to be selfish. By his wounds we are healed of self-pity and the sense of victimhood.

There is a tendency to hide our wounds, because of the belief that displaying weakness does not create respect. However, those who don't disguise their own struggles, and who live through them, give hope to others. An understanding of their own pain enables them to convert their weakness into strength, and to offer their own experience as a source of healing to others.

HOMILY 2   **Learning from Thomas**

It's easy to make the mistake that believing was easier for those who saw Jesus than it is for us. The Gospels show that there were many people who saw Jesus and yet didn't come to have faith in him. Seeing is not necessarily believing. The act of faith involves a decision to believe.

In fact, the Gospel shows that even the apostles had their problems believing. Thomas wasn't the only apostle to doubt the resurrection. All of them did. St Mark tells us that when Jesus appeared to them on Easter evening, 'he upbraided them for their unbelief and hardness of heart, because they had not believed those who saw him after he had risen.' (16:14)

We can sympathise with the apostles. The crucifixion of Jesus dealt them a devastating blow. They had invested an enormous amount in Jesus. They had given up their jobs, and left everything to follow him. And suddenly he was gone. The more the reality of his death came home to them, the greater their loss appeared. The value and meaning of everything was threatened: their comradeship, their faith, their whole lives.

And then the incredible happened—he was once more in their midst. The first thing he did was to show them his wounds. Why this? Firstly, because those wounds helped to identify him as the one who was crucified. And secondly, those wounds were the proof of his love for them. Love is proved by deeds. Then he invited them to 'see and to touch'.

The example of Thomas is particularly enlightening for us. He showed a refreshing honesty. He made no attempt to hide his doubts. Doubt is often looked on as a sign of weakness. We tend to feel guilty about having doubts. But doubt can be a growing point, a stepping stone to a deeper understanding. It certainly was for Thomas, because he went on to give expression to the highest statement of faith in Jesus in the entire Gospel of John: 'My Lord and my God.'

Here on earth, there is no such a thing as absolute certainty about spiritual things. If there was, then faith would not be necessary. Absolute certainty can lead to arrogance, intolerance, and stupidity. 'The man of faith who has never experienced doubt is not a man of faith.' (Thomas Merton)

Every community could do with a character such as Thomas, that is, someone who has the courage to ask the questions no one else dares ask. Such people are truthful, and they help to keep the others truthful too. They upset the believers by demonstrating the fragility of their faith; they upset the sceptics by making them feel the torments of the void.

Having overcome his crisis of faith, Thomas went on to bear courageous witness to Jesus, and became one of the greatest missionaries of the early Church. According to tradition, he brought the Gospel to Persia, Syria and India, where he was martyred. Thomas was the first of the apostles to die for the faith.

Jesus invites us to draw close to him in faith and to look at his wounds. Even though we can't touch him physically, we can draw close to him spiritually. And we too are called to bear witness to others. Our task is to make Christ 'visible' in the world. That's the way it was with the first disciples. Once they had seen Christ, they felt compelled to make him known to others.

The world today is full of doubters and unbelievers. The only way they will be converted to belief is if they can 'see' Jesus and 'touch' him in his followers. But if his followers have no wounds of love to show them, the unbelievers are not likely to be convinced.

May we deserve to be numbered among those whom Jesus declared blessed, namely, 'those who have not seen and yet have believed.'

HOMILY 3   **Fundamentalism**

'Unless I see the holes that the nails made in his hands … and put my hand into his side, I refuse to believe.' Thomas was looking for absolute certainty. We could call him a fundamentalist. For the fundamentalist, issues are either black or white. If something isn't literally true, then it isn't true at all.

Today there is an increase in fundamentalism. Frightened by the absence of certainties, many people have retreated into fundamentalism. Fundamentalism can be very attractive. For a fundamentalist the path is straight. The answer is simple. But fundamentalism is an impoverished way of seeing reality. It means that life is one-dimensional. It deprives faith of its richness. It results in a rigid, simplistic, moralistic, authoritarian religion. This makes people into a herd following the exact same path, rather than a group of individuals, each with his own story to tell, and his own particular path to follow.

A parable. Two travellers found themselves confronted by a great forest. Since there was no way around it, they had no choice but to go through it. Naturally they felt apprehensive, fearing that they might lose their way in the forest. But they had the good fortune to meet a gatekeeper who gave them a map showing the various trails through the forest.

The first traveller studied the map, found the trail that seemed to be the most direct, and followed it unswervingly. In doing so, he saved himself a lot of time, trouble and danger. But he also cut himself off from the riches of the forest.

The second traveller studied the map every bit as carefully. He noted not only the main trails through the forest, but also the many lesser trails. For him the map was not something to be followed rigidly. Its main purpose was to give him bearings, so that no matter where he was in the forest he wouldn't be lost. Using the map in this way opened up the whole forest to him, and made all its riches available to him.

The forest represents the world of truth. The map represents the Christian faith. The various trails represent the doctrines of the faith.

The first traveller represents the fundamentalist. He understands the doctrines of the faith in a narrow and literalist way and as unrelated to the rest of life. The second traveller uses those same truths to give him bearings. In that way they open up everything for him. They enable him to plunge himself into life with all its complexities and wonders. They give him a key to unlock the mystery of life.

A fundamentalist faith offers a safe way. It protects one from the hard work of finding one's own meaning and values. It spares one the anxiety of dealing with choice, responsibility, and a continually changing sense of self. Fundamentalism is a faith which is born out of insecurity.

For the fundamentalist, religion is just a part of life. For the non-fundamentalist religion is life seen and lived from a religious perspective. Every fact receives a two-fold, if not a three-fold significance, and is therefore richer and more mysterious. Faith fills our life to the brim with things without which our lives would have no meaning and our souls would wither and die.

Jesus didn't encourage fundamentalism. He didn't want blind followers. Quite the opposite. He tried to open people's eyes. He didn't threaten or coerce. He invited. He wanted people to follow him freely, and with both eyes open. And he came that we might have life, not just in the hereafter – but here on earth too – and have it to the full.

ANOTHER APPROACH   **Crisis of faith**

Thomas underwent a crisis of faith. Many people undergo a crisis of faith. Tolstoy is a good example, except his was a crisis of meaning too.

In 1879 he was fifty-one years of age. He had every reason to be satisfied with himself. His two great novels, *War and Peace* and *Anna Karenina*, were written. If he had written nothing else these would have assured him an exalted place in the annals of world literature. The writing of these had enabled him to give expression to his genius and creativity. He should have been happy. Yet he was feeling miserable. He felt that his life was meaningless. One question haunted him: 'Is there any meaning in my life that will not be destroyed by death?'

It was a painful and dangerous time for him – he contemplated suicide. He searched for an answer to his questions in every area of human knowledge. He searched persistently, day and night, like a dying man seeking salvation. But he found nothing.

Then he turned to the beliefs of Christians. He had been brought up in the faith but had long since abandoned it. These beliefs repelled him and seemed meaningless in the mouths of people who led lives in contradiction to them. But these same beliefs attracted him and seemed sensible as he saw people who lived by them.

So it was that he was drawn back into them and found them full of meaning. He said:

I thought that there was no sure truth in life. But then I found a sure source of light. I found it in the Gospel, and was dazzled by its splendour. In the teachings of Jesus, I found the purest and most complete doctrine of life. For two thousand years the lofty and precious teaching of Jesus has exercised an influence over men in a way unequalled by anyone else. A light shone within me and around me, and this light has not abandoned me since.

Some people are born into a religious faith, and with the passage of the years find this faith increasingly strong and sustaining. To possess a faith like that is a tremendous blessing. But for others faith is a constant struggle. Indeed, some people may have to undergo a crisis in order to arrive at a deep and personal faith.

Only faith can answer the most important and profound questions of life. But we mustn't expect faith to clear everything up. Just because we believe doesn't mean we know all the answers. But we don't need to know all the answers. Faith is trust, not certainty.

The story of Doubting Thomas brings home to us just how frail is the human container in which the gift of faith is carried. And it also shows us that Christian faith is essentially faith in a person who loves us – and has the wounds to prove it. At the heart of biblical faith is not only the faith we have in God, but the faith God has in us.

A STORY

Walter Ciszek, a Polish Jesuit priest, spent fifteen years in forced-labour camps in Siberia. Through all those years he belonged to the lowest brigades, forced to do the dirtiest work – digging foundations by hand, loading and unloading heavy construction materials, crawling in damp, dark mines, where death was only one careless step away.

What kept him going? 'Men died in the camps,' he says, 'especially when they gave up hope. But I trusted in God, and so I never felt without hope. It was not I who kept the faith; it was the faith that kept me.'

Happy the one who possesses a faith like that.

PRAYER OF THE FAITHFUL

President: As people who have not seen yet believe, we bring our needs to the God who conquers death.

Response: Lord, hear our prayer.

Reader(s): For the Church: that the Holy Spirit may deepen the faith of its members. [Pause] Let us pray to the Lord.

For all those in high positions: that they may show special concern for the poorer and more disadvantaged members of our society. [Pause] Let us pray to the Lord.

For those whose faith is weak or non-existent: that the Lord may touch their minds and hearts through the lives of committed Christians. [Pause] Let us pray to the Lord.

For all gathered here: that our faith in Christ and in his love for us may continue to grow in spite of doubts and difficulties. [Pause] Let us pray to the Lord.

For our own special needs. [Pause] Let us pray to the Lord.

President: Lord, give us the certainty that beyond death there is a life where broken things are mended and lost things are found; where there is rest for the weary and joy for the sad; where all that we have loved and willed of good exists, and where we will meet again our loved ones. We ask this through Christ our Lord.

REFLECTION   **Cease doubting and believe**

While Jesus was alive Thomas was as strong as an oak.
But when Jesus was put to death,
he became a reed shaking in the winds of doubt.
The truth was, though he didn't realise it at the time,
that it was the Master who was the oak.
He was a mere sapling growing in his shade.

When the oak fell he was defenceless.
All of are shaken by the winds of doubt.
We need to look at the Lord's wounds,
and hear his gentle voice saying to us:
'Cease doubting and believe.'
Then with Thomas we shall make bold to say:
'My Lord and my God.'

Third Sunday of Easter
THE RESTORATION OF PETER

INTRODUCTION AND CONFITEOR

In spite of the fact that he denied him, Jesus did not write off Peter, but confirmed him as chief shepherd of his flock. Jesus doesn't write us off when we fail. He gives us a chance to cancel out our failures by love. [Pause]

Lord Jesus, you restore life to all who sink into the grave of remorse and despair. Lord, have mercy.

Your favour lasts all life long. Christ, have mercy.

You have changed our mourning into dancing by your loving forgiveness. Lord, have mercy.

HEADINGS FOR READINGS

First Reading (Acts 5:27-32.40-41). We see the apostles courageously witnessing to the resurrection of Jesus and gladly suffering for it.

Second Reading (Rev 5:11-14). We hear a hymn in praise of the crucified and risen Christ.

Gospel (Jn 21:1-19). This relates an appearance of the risen Jesus to seven of his apostles on the shore of the lake of Gennesareth. The incident is built around Peter.

SCRIPTURE NOTE

The First Reading tells of the opposition the apostles encountered from the Jewish authorities. Persecution did not come as a surprise: Jesus had predicted it. (Lk 21:12-13) It became an opportunity for the apostles to bear witness to him. They refused to be silenced. Always the central point of their witness is the resurrection of Jesus. Far from being demoralised, they were glad to suffer for the sake of Jesus.

The Gospel shows that a constant feature of the resurrection stories is that Jesus is not recognised at once; it takes some word or familiar gesture for him to be known. This is an effective way of making the point that the resurrection is not a return to earthly life – Jesus has risen to a new life beyond death. He is the same Jesus, yet transformed. He is not as he was; but he is still who he was.

The miraculous catch of fish symbolises the mission of the apostles to be 'fishers of men'. The large catch shows how successful the disciples can be with Jesus' help. The meal symbolises the eucharistic meal in which Jesus is present among them and feeds them. Peter, who three times denied his Master, is now given three chances to profess his love, and then is given a mandate to care for the Lord's flock. In giving authority to the man who denied him, Jesus wanted to show that he was establishing his Church not on human strength, but on his own love and faithfulness.

HOMILY 1   **Not writing people off**

It was said of Stalin that if you made one mistake it was like mishandling a detonator – it was the last one you made. We too sometimes write people off because of one bad experience. But which of us would like to be judged on a single moment of our lives?

After what happened on Holy Thursday night, we would have expected Jesus to write Peter off as being weak, cowardly, and unreliable. Had he done so, most people would have said that he had no other option. After all, Peter was the leader of the apostolic team. He had set a terrible example for the others.

Yet Jesus did not write him off. He didn't even demote him. And there were no recriminations either. Judas' betrayal was a planned thing, and was carried out in a cold, calculating manner. Peter's denial was not a planned thing, and was the result of weakness rather than malice. Jesus, the reader of hearts, knew this.

After breakfast he turned to Peter and said, 'Peter, do you love me more than the others love me?' What a strange question to ask: 'Do you love me?' Hadn't he proved beyond any shadow of doubt that he didn't love him? Yet this is the question Jesus asked Peter. And Peter said, 'Lord, you know that I love you.' He sincerely meant those words. What's more – they were true. He really did love Jesus.

Jesus knew that there was another and better side to Peter. Strength and weakness can co-exist in the same person. Jesus called Peter forward. He asked him to declare his love in public, since his denial had also been in public.

Jesus kept no record of Peter's sins. But he did ask him to do something for him – to feed the sheep and lambs of his flock, that is, to love and serve his brothers and sisters in the community. That, if you like, was his penance. That is the best way to make atonement for sin. As Peter himself later wrote: 'Love covers a multitude of sins.' (1 Pet 4:8)

I'm sure that Peter never forgot the fact that he denied Jesus. Yet I doubt if it haunted him the way some people are haunted by their sins. He learned a great lesson from his fall. He learned that he wasn't as brave as he thought he was. It's a far better and more salutary thing to learn a lesson than to be taught a lesson. When we learn from a fall, the recalling of it is more likely to evoke gratitude than self-recrimination.

And he also learned a wonderful truth about Jesus. He learned that in spite of his denials, Jesus still loved him. It was that love that brought Peter back to life. It's an amazing experience to be loved in one's weakness and sinfulness. To be loved in one's goodness is no big deal. But to be loved in one's badness – that's tremendous. That's what grace is about.

Peter had the guts to get up again after his fall. We can imagine that he made a very good leader. A leader has to be aware of his own weakness. The experience rid him of pride and blind reliance on his own resources. At the same time it enabled him to understand the weakness of others.

And Peter came good. In the reading from Acts we see how he stood up before the Sanhedrin and bore witness for Jesus. Peter is a great consolation to us. Courage fails us all. In the end, all of us are mere mortals who are inconstant in our beliefs. We must learn to forgive ourselves momentary weaknesses and failures. We must not judge ourselves or others by momentary lapses, but by commitment over a long time to our beliefs.

HOMILY 2 **Suffering for the Lord**

The reading from Acts tells of the opposition the apostles encountered from the Jewish authorities. They came out of it with great credit, especially Peter. It's hard to believe that this is the same man who a short time before this denied Jesus three times. Now he stood his ground and courageously bore witness for Jesus. And suffered for that stand: he and his fellow apostles were flogged. But they were glad to suffer for the sake of Jesus. From where did Peter get his new-found courage? He got it from the Holy Spirit, and from the support of his fellow apostles.

Fortunately, ever since the time of the apostles there have been Christians who, by the grace of God, have been able to overcome fear and witness to the Gospel, even in the most difficult circumstances.

In March 1983 the Russian poet, Irina Ratushinskaya, was sentenced to seven years hard labour and five years internal exile. Her crime – writing poetry which the communist authorities didn't approve of. In prison she suffered beatings, forced feeding and solitary confinement in freezing conditions. She developed heart, liver and kidney trouble, as well as chronic bronchitis. Even in such conditions she continued to write, smuggling the poems out on scraps of paper given to sympathetic warders, soldiers and visitors. She was released in October 1986.

Her Christian faith was vital to her survival. She says: 'When you are in trouble, under pressure, God always seems closer. God was like a hand on our shoulder in the camp.'

Another key to Irina's survival in the camp was the incredibly strong relationships she had with the dozen other women prisoners of conscience in the camp. Danger binds people together and makes them feel responsible for one another. With the pace and pressures of modern life we are so self-absorbed that it takes an accident or an illness to teach us how much we depend on one another.

Irina and her companions regularly went on hunger strike if one of their number was ill-treated. She says: 'I feel happy that all of us survived. During the time I was there, one-third of the population of the male camp died. All the women who were in the camp are Christian now, even if they weren't at the beginning. One of them has become a Catholic nun.

'My faith also taught me how to prevent my psychological life being damaged by hatred and bitterness. The experience has taught me a lot about the enormous capacity of the human spirit to be happy in spite of any circumstance.'

People like Irina and her companions are an inspiration to us. They expand the possibilities of human love and courage. It's easy to believe in God when you are on your knees with your eyes closed, just as it is easy to be a Christian far away from the clamour and the trials of the world of people. But it's a poor religion that believes God is to be found only in places far removed from the world. God can't be confined in this way.

We are disciples of Jesus. He depends on us to bear witness to him in the world today. Few of us will be called on to suffer what the apostles or people like Irina and her companions suffered. But we may have to face something which is almost as bad – the deadly indifference of our fellow citizens.

We can't tell in advance where the Christian vocation will take us, or what it may demand from us. If we could see those places, perhaps our hearts would grow faint and courage would fail us. In that respect we are like Peter. When he first responded to the call of Jesus, he had no idea that it would lead him to martyrdom. But whatever the Christian vocation demands of us will be returned with a hundredfold increase.

HOMILY 3   **The second calling**

Once upon a time there was a fire-maker. As he was making his way home one winter's night snow was falling. He was taking a shortcut across a piece of waste ground when he saw the fire. It was hardly a fire at all – just a bunch of smouldering logs. Huddled around it, was a group of people, their threadbare rags pulled closely around them in the vain hope of warding off the biting cold. He stopped, but made his stay as brief as possible. He felt uneasy in the company of these people. Having said a few words about the value of fire, he slunk away.

Yet he had no sooner left them than he felt bad. He thought how he might have kindled that fire if only he had been willing to take the time and the trouble. But then, what if he had caught pneumonia in the process? And most likely they wouldn't appreciate his efforts.

A little further on he came upon another group of people sitting under a roof around a blazing fire. Noticing his famished appearance, they shouted, 'Come in! Come in!' He didn't have to be asked twice. He stayed longer than he intended. When he finally left, a chorus of voices said, 'Thanks for stopping by.'

Once home, he went straight to bed. That night he had a dream in which the Lord appeared to him and said, 'I appointed you as a fire-maker, but you have failed me.' That's all the Lord said. The fire-maker got the message at once. He woke up and was unable to get back to sleep. His mind went back to his early days as a fire-maker. How enthusiastic he was back then. And what a beautiful occupation was his – to bring warmth into the lives of cold people.

But back then he had no idea of the hard sacrifices his calling would demand of him. Nor had he given much thought to how messy fire-making could be, and how unresponsive and unappreciative people could be. But over the years all these things were brought home to him. The result was that the fire of his love grew dim. He grew cold in his vocation.

But on this wretched night in which he plumbed the depths of his weakness, this night in which his selfishness had been so cruelly exposed, this night in which his own need for warmth had been painfully revealed to him, the spark of his vocation was kindled once more in his heart. He made up his mind that next day he would become a fire-maker all over again. And he did.

There are two calls of Peter related in the Gospels. The first occurred at the start of Jesus' ministry. (Mk 1:16-18) The second occurred after the resurrection, and is related in today's Gospel. Three years separated those two calls. During that time a lot of things had happened for Peter. He had found out a lot about the man who called him, about the task to which he called him, and, above all, about himself. When the second call came, Peter was a wiser and humbler man. Therefore, his second 'yes' was far more mature and enlightened than his first 'yes' had been.

Peter's story is one of calling, falling and re-calling. It shows that Christ's call doesn't exclude falls. A vocation is not something one hears once and answers once. The call has to be heard many times, and responded to many times. Each day a part of the chosen path opens up before us, a part we have not trodden before. As one goes on, the call gets deeper, and the response becomes more interior and more personal.

All vocations are vocations to love – love of the Lord, and love of the lambs and sheep of his flock (our brothers and sisters in the community).

PRAYER OF THE FAITHFUL

President: Let us pray to God, who through the resurrection of his Son, strengthens us in hope and love.

Response: Lord, hear us in your love.

Reader(s): That Church leaders may be devoted to the welfare of their brothers and sisters in the community. [Pause] We pray in faith.

That the Lord may direct and bless the work of his disciples today just as, under the direction of Jesus, the disciples made a great catch of fish. [Pause] We pray in faith.

That the Lord may direct and bless the work of our political and civil leaders. [Pause] We pray in faith.

That we may find joy in serving others, remembering that the Lord prepared food for his apostles. [Pause] We pray in faith.

That we may be kind and forgiving towards all those who disappoint or fail us, just as the Lord has been kind to us. [Pause] We pray in faith.

That the Lord may grant our own special needs. [Longer pause] We pray in faith.

President: Father, our source of life, you know our weakness. May we reach out with joy to grasp the hand you extend to us in Christ, so that we may walk more readily in your ways. We ask this through the same Christ our Lord.

REFLECTION   **Believing in people**

It can happen that we lose interest in people,
and even become blind to their strengths,
when we discover their limitations.
During his passion Jesus discovered the limitations of Peter.
Yet he didn't write him off.
He continued to believe in him,
and in time he came good.
Like Peter, we are weak human beings,
who are inconstant in our beliefs.
We need someone who understands our weaknesses,
who realises that it may take time for us to overcome them,
and who doesn't write us off because
we don't produce the goods at once.

Fourth Sunday of Easter
THE GOOD SHEPHERD

INTRODUCTION AND CONFITEOR

In today's Gospel Jesus, the Good Shepherd, says to us, 'I know my sheep. They listen to my voice and follow me.' Let us reflect for a moment on our failure to respond to the love and care of Jesus, the Good Shepherd. [Pause]

Lord Jesus, you call us to be your people, the sheep of your flock. Lord, have mercy.

You help us to listen to your voice and to follow you. Christ, have mercy.

You lead us to the green pastures of eternal life. Lord, have mercy.

HEADINGS FOR READINGS

First Reading (Acts 13:14.43-52). Paul and Barnabas preach the Gospel firstly to the Jews but they reject it; then they preach it to the Gentiles who receive it with joy.

Second Reading (Rev 7:9.14-17). This contains a vision of those who will come through times of persecution to share in Christ's glory in heaven.

Gospel (Jn 10:27-30). Jesus, the Good Shepherd, will not allow anyone to snatch from his care the sheep the Father has given him.

SCRIPTURE NOTE

The reading from Acts shows that Paul's policy was to preach to the Jews first, because they were the chosen people. But when they reject his message, he turns to the Gentiles. In this way the prophecy that the light of salvation would reach the ends of the earth was fulfilled. (Is 49:6)

Jesus is the True Shepherd, and will not allow anyone to snatch from his care the sheep that belong to him. (Gospel) He will give them eternal life. What does belonging to him entail? It entails listening to his voice and following him.

HOMILY 1   **Belonging to his flock**

The image of Jesus as the Shepherd of the Father's flock is one of the most beautiful images we have of him. And we owe it to Jesus himself. This is how he described himself and his mission.

Jesus is no hireling. The hireling doesn't own the sheep, and runs away as soon as he sees a wolf approaching. Jesus is the Good shepherd. The sheep belong to him, and he is ready to die for them.

Jesus made the most wonderful promises to those who belong to him. He said that none of them would ever be lost. No one would succeed in snatching from his care the sheep the Father has entrusted to him. The sheep that belong to him will be safe with him because the Father's power is in him. (He and the Father are one.) And he will lead them to the pastures of eternal life.

The feeling of belonging to Jesus, and of being known and loved by him, is enormously comforting and reassuring. Who would not want to belong to his flock? But how can we tell if we truly belong to his flock? What does belonging entail? Essentially three things.

The first and basic requirement is to believe in him. We enter the flock by becoming believers. But belief is only the beginning. The second requirement is to listen to his voice: 'My sheep listen to my voice.' To listen to his voice is to heed his teachings. And the third requirement is follow him: 'My sheep follow me.' To follow him is to do his word. There we have it in a nutshell. It's really very simple.

Obviously the relationship has to be a two-way thing. The sheep have to choose to belong. Jesus won't or can't save people against their will. But it is wonderfully consoling to realise that if we do sincerely want and try to belong to him (following him and doing what he says), then he will take care of us in life and death. He promises to give us eternal life. We can pin our hopes on his word: 'I give them eternal life ... they will never be lost [eternally].'

It doesn't mean that belonging to Jesus will guarantee us an easy life here on earth. The opposite is more likely to be the case. Those who belong to him are likely to be persecuted, but those who remain faithful through their trials, will share in his glory in heaven. (Second Reading) Trials and sufferings are an opportunity to prove one's faith and obedience to the Lord.

The flock is an image of community. Even on a human level we have a deep need for community. Jesus knew this. That's why he wanted his followers to live as a community. In community we find mutual support, encouragement, and companionship. We can't belong to Jesus without belonging also to his flock. The privilege of belonging is not something that is offered to a chosen few, but to everyone, Jews and Gentiles. (First Reading)

HOMILY 2   **The Good Shepherd knows his sheep**

About the middle of the nineteenth century St John Bosco began to work for poor and endangered youth in the Italian city of Turin. The young people soon realised that in him they had a true friend. They so loved him that once when he got seriously ill, they stormed heaven with their prayers, and some went so far as to offer their lives to God in his place. As it happened, John Bosco recovered. This kind of bond cannot exist unless there is closeness, and closeness involves knowing and being known.

Jesus, the Good Shepherd, says, 'I know my sheep.' He knows his sheep precisely because he is a good shepherd. There are various levels of knowing. We know some people just as a face or a name. Others we know as acquaintances. And others we know as friends.

There is a sadness in not knowing people. The Jewish writer, Elie Wiesel, was very attached to his father, who died in Auschwitz in 1944. Yet when he came to write his autobiography he declared:

I never really knew my father. It hurts to admit that. I knew little of the man I loved most in the world, the man whose merest glance could stir me. I wonder if other sons have the same problem. Do they know their fathers as someone other than the authoritarian figure who leaves in the morning and returns in the evening, bringing bread to the table?

I fear that it is a common cry. Children don't know their parents; parents don't know their children. To know takes time and effort, but bears great fruit. When this knowledge is absent a great loss results. Life passes by so quickly. We barely know each other. You can't love someone you don't know.

Knowing is particularly important for carers. Carers need to know those for whom they care. To know their names is a good start. But to really know them is to know their life stories. Unless the carers know something about the world from which their clients come, and to which they return, those clients will be little better than shadows to them.

The kind of knowing that we are talking about demands time, patience and sacrifice. But it is immensely rewarding. No matter how we might dislike an individual, once we know the person's story, our attitude towards him/her will soften.

However, this knowing has to be a two-way affair. Jesus, the Good Shepherd, knows his sheep intimately. But they also know him: 'My own know me.' Jesus wasn't afraid to let himself be known. But we sometimes are. We refuse to let others into our lives. No one will know what our true feelings, needs, hurts and hopes are.

Perhaps it is fear of rejection that holds us back. We fear that if people really knew us for the imperfect people we are, they would reject us. The result is that we will be known for the image we project rather than for the persons we are. It would be sad to live and die and never to have been deeply known, never to have told our story.

How can we form a bond with people if we keep our distance from them, thus preventing them from getting to know us? Can we blame them if they too keep their distance from us, and if as a result they distrust or fear us?

Jesus is a Good Shepherd to us. He wants us to have life here and eternal life hereafter. But it has to be a two-way affair. We have to respond to his love. The faithful sheep listen to the voice of the shepherd and follow him. We have to get to know the Lord, listen to his word and do it.

If we have the heart of the Good Shepherd, then wherever we are we will find an outlet for our love. Caring means getting close to people, as Jesus, the Good Shepherd, got close to us.

HOMILY 3   **Giving his life for his sheep**

Jesus said, 'No one will ever snatch my sheep from me.' In this way he was emphasising how precious the sheep were to him. Nothing bad would never happen to any of them if he could help it.

The wolves have no trouble in snatching the sheep when the hireling is in charge of the flock. As soon as the hireling sees a wolf approaching he abandons the flock. His only thought is to save his own skin. Not so the good shepherd. He defends his sheep against the attacks of the wolf, even at the risk of losing his own life.

We live in a world where unfortunately the sheep, and especially the lambs, are often snatched away and done to death. But it is a world in which there is more need than ever of the good shepherd. Everything today tends to be big and centralised. It doesn't make knowing and caring easy, for everything is so impersonal. In this kind of system people are hired and promoted for efficiency, not for the love and care they are capable of showing.

Today the good shepherd is unlikely to have to face a pack of wolves. But he or she may have to face something worse – a gang of thugs. Philip Lawrence was the headmaster at St George's Catholic school in London. On a December day in 1995 he was stabbed outside his school while trying to protect one of his pupils who was being attacked by a gang, and died as a result of his wounds. He was voted Personality of the Year by listeners to BBC Radio 4's *Today* programme. He received 23,130 votes, ahead of John Major, then Prime Minister (18,260 votes).

His wife said that her husband 'would probably have been extremely embarrassed by all of this. He was very modest to the point of being self-deprecating.' It's nice to know that people still recognise the greatness of an act like that. And it's nice to know that someone can do such an act, and look on it as something normal and natural.

Philip Lawrence was a good shepherd to his pupils. He tried to create a safe environment in which they could learn and could grow up to be proud of themselves. It was unthinkable for him to allow one of his pupils to be beaten up by a gang of thugs without intervening.

Philip Lawrence is a reminder to us all of what true loving means, and of what it may cost. It is not enough to love the young, they must know they are loved. This applies not just to schools but also to families.

Lawrence drew his strength and inspiration from his Christian faith. He was imitating the love of Jesus, the Good Shepherd, who gave his life for his sheep. Jesus' life wasn't taken from him. Nor did the Father demand it of him. Jesus gave his life, and gave it willingly. He sacrificed himself for his sheep. He did so in order to bring them to the pastures of eternal life.

Every Christian is called to be a loving and caring person. This Sunday is the feast of carers. It gives encouragement and support to all those who are trying to imitate the Good Shepherd, and should prod the consciences of the hirelings.

Those who follow the way of love open themselves to the possibilities of a greater happiness than they have ever known, and of a greater pain too. But, as Carlo Carretto says, 'There is nothing terrible about suffering a bit on earth if it has taught us how to love.'

OTHER STORIES

1. Psalm 23, 'The Lord is my Shepherd', is attributed to King David who was a shepherd before being called to be King of Israel. It is one of the best loved prayers in the Bible.

The story is told that two people were asked to recite it for a congregation. The first was a Shakespearean actor but a non-believer. He did a magnificent job. He used just the right tone of voice, the right inflection, the right emphasis, the right pace, and the right pauses. Every word was clearly and beautifully enunciated. All who heard him were deeply impressed.

Then the second man, a believer, got up. His delivery was poor. So too was his diction. He used mostly the same tone throughout. He went too fast. Some of his emphasis was wrong. He paused in the wrong places. In short, he made just above every mistake an amateur reciter could make. But he had one powerful thing going for him: he spoke from the heart. He meant every word he said. The result was that his hearers were deeply moved.

Later the actor came up to him and said, 'Congratulations. You did a wonderful job.'

'I think I did a terrible job. It's you who did a wonderful job,' he replied.

'Believe me, you did a much better job than I did. One thing came across very clearly: I know Psalm 23, but you know the Shepherd.'

Notice that King David did not say, 'The Lord is *a* shepherd,' though that he is. Nor did he say, 'The Lord is *the* shepherd,' though that he is. What he said was, 'The Lord is *my* shepherd.'

In other words, he was speaking from personal experience, out of a personal faith. That makes all the difference.

2. One day an undertaker phoned the local parish and informed the pastor that one of his parishioners had died. He gave the name. But neither the pastor nor his associate recognised the name, even though the deceased had faithfully attended Mass every Sunday in the parish church. Fortunately they had all the parish records on computer. So to the computer they now went. Sure enough, his name came up on the screen. Below the name was his age, his address, and a number of other facts about him. Now they felt happy. They knew who he was.

But did they? We may know a number of facts about a person, but that doesn't mean we know the person. There is a vast difference between knowing about a person and knowing the person. The computer is a help to a busy pastor, but it is no substitute for the personal touch. When the Good Shepherd says he knows his sheep, he doesn't mean he simply has them on the computer.

PRAYER OF THE FAITHFUL

President: Let us now bring our needs before the Lord, who is faithful from age to age and whose love is eternal.

Response: Lord, graciously hear us.

Reader(s): For the pope and the bishops: that they may faithfully and lovingly watch over the flock of Christ. [Pause] Lord, hear us.

For doctors and nurses and all in the caring professions: that the Lord may fill them with a strong and unselfish love. [Pause] Lord, hear us.

For all those who have no love in their lives, and who are not important or precious to anyone. [Pause] Lord, hear us.

For all gathered here: that each of us, no matter what our state in life, may strive to be people who care. [Pause] Lord, hear us.

For vocations to the priesthood and religious life: that the Lord may inspire men and women to devote their lives to caring for his flock. [Pause] Lord, hear us.

For our own special needs. [Longer pause] Lord, hear us.

President: Heavenly Father, grant that what we have said with our lips, we may believe with our hearts, and practise with our lives. We make our prayer through Christ our Lord.

REFLECTION   **The vocation to love**

The deepest wound of all is that which affects the heart:
the feeling that one has not been loved,
that one is not precious to anyone.
Many people today are wounded at heart.
Each of us can do something to heal their wounds.

We have hands that can make things,
and minds that can understand things.
But above all we have hearts that can give life.
We are not sterile people.
We can give life to people who are inwardly broken.
We can show them that they are important,
and so bring life to them.
Today, Good Shepherd Sunday, is also vocations Sunday.
But all vocations are vocations to love.

Fifth Sunday of Easter
THE COMMANDMENT OF LOVE

INTRODUCTION AND CONFITEOR

'Love one another as I have loved you.' Of all the commandments Christ gave us this is the most important. It includes all the others. The only failure in the life of a Christian is the failure to love. Let us think about the people whom we find difficult to take into our hearts, and ask the Lord to help us to be more loving towards them. [Pause] It is God who sets the example for us to follow.

Lord Jesus, you are kind and full of compassion. Lord, have mercy.

You are slow to anger and abounding in love. Christ, have mercy.

You do not treat us according to our sins, nor repay us according to our faults. Lord, have mercy.

HEADINGS FOR READINGS

First Reading (Acts 14:21-27). Paul and Barnabas retrace their steps, encouraging the little communities of Christians they had founded.

Second Reading (Rev 21:1-5). Taken from the final part of Apocalypse, this opens with the vision of a new world and the new order of things inaugurated by Christ.

Gospel (Jn 13:31-35). During the Last Supper Jesus gives his apostles a new commandment – to love one another as he has loved them.

SCRIPTURE NOTE

The First Reading tells of the conclusion of Paul's first missionary journey. He and Barnabas retrace their steps, encouraging the little communities they have founded, and preparing them for the persecutions which would inevitably come.

In the Gospel the scene is the Last Supper. Judas has departed and

Jesus is alone with his own. Jesus is going forward to the cross. By so doing, he is giving glory to God, who in turn will give glory to him. The apostles can't follow him yet. In the meantime they are to live by a 'new commandment' – the commandment of love. It is new only in the sense that it sets a new standard – 'as I have loved you'. The world will know that they are his disciples by their fidelity to this commandment.

The Second Reading, which comes from the final part of Revelation, is one we frequently hear at funerals. The final part of Revelation opens with a vision of a new heaven, a new earth, and a new Jerusalem. This glorious future to which God is leading us will be fully realised only in the hereafter.

HOMILY 1 **By this all will know ...**

Once upon a time a man planted a fruit tree in a forest. At first the little fruit tree felt lost in the midst of so many great trees. The sight of those mighty trees made it feel insignificant. They were so tall, strong, and useful. It was so small, weak, and useless. So what did it do? It set about gaining a place and a standing for itself in the forest.

How hard it worked and how well it succeeded! In time its head reared up into the sky so that it was able to hobnob with the tallest trees of the forest. Its branches spread outwards like a giant umbrella, claiming more and more space for themselves. Its trunk grew stout and strong so that it was able to laugh at the storms which from time to time roared through the forest.

But then one day the man who planted it made an unexpected appearance in the forest. Looking at the tree, he said, 'How you've grown! Why, you have the most wonderful branches I've ever seen. And your trunk is like the outer wall of a castle.'

'But I still have many faults,' said the tree, feigning humility. 'Just look at all these hollows, clefts, and knots. If only I could rid myself of them I'd look a whole lot better. But I'm working on them.'

'Those faults are of no concern to me. In fact, I don't even see them as faults,' the man replied. On hearing this the tree began to glow with pride. But then the man added, 'However, there is one thing I'm not happy with.'

'Oh, so you're not happy with me,' the tree responded, suddenly becoming defensive. 'I don't understand. You can see for yourself how I've prospered. I can hold my own with the oaks and the elms. I thought you might be proud of me. I've worked so hard to secure the standing I now enjoy amongst the other trees.'

'I don't doubt for one minute that you've worked hard,' said he.

'Well then, what more do you want from me?'

'The one thing I hoped to find in you is missing,' he replied. 'You've neglected the most important thing of all – the one thing necessary.'

'What's that?' asked the tree disconsolately.

'Fruit,' came the reply. 'You are not a pine or an oak or an elm. You are something far rarer and more precious. You are a fruit tree. I was depending on you to provide wholesome fruit for the many famished little creatures who roam the forest. But you have failed to do so because you have forgotten what you are. You have become just another tree in the forest.'

The one thing Jesus has commanded us to do is to love one another. It is a new commandment only in the sense that it sets a new standard – 'as I have loved you'. Often Christians have gone after worldly success, and in many cases have achieved it. But in so doing they have forgotten the one thing Jesus expects from them, namely, love. 'By *this* all will know that you are my disciples.'

Love makes us instruments of God's providence in the lives of others. Our love becomes the channel through which they will experience the love of God. An American journalist, watching Mother Teresa as she cared for a man with gangrene, remarked, 'I wouldn't do that for a million dollars.' Mother Teresa's reply: 'Even I wouldn't do it for that amount. However, I do it out of love for God.'

HOMILY 2   **What love does**

Writing about his experience in Auschwitz, Elie Wiesel said that the Germans tried to get the inmates to forget relatives and friends, to think only of themselves, and to tend only to their own needs, or else they would perish. That is what they kept telling them day and night. But Wiesel says that what happened was the opposite. Those who lived only for themselves, had less chance of surviving, while those who lived for a parent, a brother, a friend, an ideal, had a better chance of getting out alive. It was through what they gave that they survived.

Selfishness keeps us shut in, it confines us. It erects barriers, even walls between us and others. What frees us from this captivity is every deep, serious affection for others. Being friends, being brothers and sisters, love – that is what opens the prison. Love frees us from the prison of selfishness.

Brian Keenan spent four years as a hostage in Lebanon. Later he wrote:

It is only when we reach out beyond ourselves to embrace, to understand, and to finally overcome the suffering of another that we become whole in ourselves. We are enlarged and enriched as another's suffering reveals us to ourselves, and we reach out to touch and embrace.

Love always demands the best of us, and brings out the best in us. Being loved gives one a surprising courage and energy. So also does loving. They say: love and the energy will be given to you. Where there is great love there are always miracles. 'Love is the flame that warms our soul, energises our spirit and supplies passion to our lives. It is our connection to God and to one another.' (Elizabeth Kübler-Ross)

On going into prison Oscar Wilde said, 'At all costs I must keep love in my heart. If I go into prison without love what will become of my soul?'

Without love what are people? Those who do not love have a poor life. But those who love have a more abundant and fruitful life. What's the purpose of life if not to love? 'We are put on earth a little space that we may learn to bear the beams of love.' (William Blake) Freedom from selfishness and the ability to love others – that is what life is about.

A doctor, who has been privileged to share the most profound moments of people's lives, says that people facing death don't think about what degrees they have earned, or what positions they have held, or how much wealth they have accumulated. At the end, what really matters is who you loved and who loved you.

Those who opt for love open themselves to the possibilities of a greater happiness than they have ever known. Love is well-being. It makes us fruitful. To refuse to love is to begin to die. To begin to love is to begin to live. While faith makes all things possible, love makes all things easy. Love heals everyone – both those who receive it and those who give it.

HOMILY 3   **Varieties of love**

Today we understand more than we ever did about the complexity of human nature, and the mixed motives behind everything we do. There are (at least) five kinds of love.

The first is utilitarian love. We love another because he or she is useful to us. But that's more like selfishness than love. I want something from you, but I don't want you.

The second kind is romantic love. This is the kind of affection we bear another because of the pleasure the other person gives us. We are infatuated with the other person. But that's not love. We may think it is the other person we love, but we are in fact loving ourselves. Usually this doesn't last, which is one reason why some marriages fail.

The third kind of love is democratic love, which is based upon equality under the law. We respect others because they are fellow citizens. We recognise their liberties in order that ours, in turn, may be recognised. The reason for contributing to the good of others is the expectation of a return good.

The fourth kind is humanitarian love. This is love for humanity in general. The weakness of this type of love is that it is love in the abstract, rather than in the concrete: 'I love humanity, but can't stick people.'

The fifth kind is Christian love, summed up in the commandment of Jesus: 'Love one another as I have loved you.' Here we are talking about disinterested love, loving even when there is nothing in it for us. This love persists despite hostility and persecution. It is not a spasmodic enthusiasm, but an enduring relationship. It expresses itself in service, affection, and self-sacrifice. This kind of love can be achieved only with the help of the Holy Spirit.

It has been said that if you do a good deed, but have an ulterior motive, it would be better not to do it at all. The only exception is charity. Even though it is not as good as doing it with a pure motive, it is still a good deed, and benefits the other person, no matter what your motive. Besides, the fact that selfishness and generosity coexist in us makes the good that we do all the more praiseworthy. It comes out of struggle.

People tend to see the problem of love as being loved rather than being a loving person. Hence, all their efforts go into making themselves loveable through being successful, or glamorous, or powerful, or rich … And so they end up without love, for they are loved, not for themselves, but for something they possess or that they have achieved. Whereas if they became loving people, they would be loved, and loved for themselves. And in the end, all of us want to be loved for ourselves. Those who are not loved seek to be admired.

There are three states: (1) Not to love and not to be loved – this seems like hell on earth. (2) To love but not to be loved in return – this, though painful, is better than the first. (3) To love and to be loved – this the blessed state Jesus enjoyed: 'As the Father has loved me so I have loved you.'

Love brings out the best in the one who loves. People are at their best and brightest when they love. They are like a glowing lamp. Love is a choice, not a feeling. But to refuse to love is to begin to die. The worst thing of all is a cold indifference.

OTHER STORIES

1. A fifty-year-old Greek was dying in a New York hospice. He had a good life, so he said. He would have it all over again. He would gladly forgo money and health and making it in America, if only he could have the same wife, the same family, the same love again. Love – that was what was important in life. It was love which kept things together and made sense of life.

The day before he died he sent for the members of his family, who were, he said, quarrelsome and at odds with one another. He told them solemnly that they must learn to love one another, they must try harder. It was everything, everything. They must believe this, for it was the word of a dying man.

Jesus spoke similar words to his friends the night before he died. He gave them a simple, clear message: 'Love one another, as I have loved you'.

2. A story is told about a twelve-year-old called Stephen who was lame from polio. He had a brother, Mark, who was ten. Though they fought a lot, as boys will, deep down they were good to each other. At times Stephen envied his brother who had two good legs.

One night he dreamt that he was in a deep and mysterious forest. There he came to a dark cave. At the centre of the cave a bright fire burned. Then out of the shadows came a man wearing a long robe. He told Stephen that he was the warlock of the forest, and that as a reward for finding the cave he could have one wish fulfilled – just one wish, anything he desired.

Stephen didn't need much time to make up his mind. 'I wish that I may have two good legs,' he said. With that the warlock threw his cloak around him and before he knew it Stephen was back in his own bed. His brother was sleeping soundly in the next bed. The warlock lifted the blankets off Mark's legs.

'What are you doing?' asked Stephen.

'I'm beginning the operation?' said the warlock.

'What operation?'

'The transference. When the operation is over you will have Mark's legs and he will have yours. But don't worry. No one will ever know. They will think that it was always like that.'

'I never thought it was going to be like this,' said Stephen.

'You hardly expected me to pluck a pair of good legs out of the air, did you?'

But Stephen was in a state of deep shock. A picture flashed through his mind. He saw himself running freely along, and behind him, dragging his leg came his brother Mark. He couldn't do that to his little brother.

'I don't want it,' he cried out.

On hearing this the old warlock was very angry and went away. Stephen was glad to see the back of him. Next morning he awoke and looked across at his brother. Remembering his dream, he smiled. From that day on he never again felt envious of his little brother and he loved him more than ever.

Stephen wanted to be happy but not at the expense of causing misery to his brother. True happiness is found only in unselfish love. To love is to put the other person first.

PRAYER OF THE FAITHFUL

President: By the love we have for one another, everyone should know that we are followers of Christ. Let us pray for the gift of love.

Response: Lord, teach us to love.

Reader(s): For all the followers of Christ: that their love for one another may be sincere and generous. [Pause] Let us pray to the Lord.

For those who are well-off: that they may share with the less well-off. [Pause] Let us pray to the Lord.

For those who do not know Christ: that they may see him and meet him in Christians. [Pause] Let us pray to the Lord.

For this congregation: that we may be able to rise above the grudges, jealousies and meanness of spirit which prevent us from loving one another. [Pause] Let us pray to the Lord.

For all gathered here: that we may not limit our love to our friends, but may try to be kind to everyone. [Pause] Let us pray to the Lord.

For our own special needs. [Longer pause] Let us pray to the Lord.

President: Heavenly Father, your Son, Jesus gave us a wonderful example of love. Grant that as we receive him in this Eucharist, we may follow his way of love in our daily lives. We ask this through the same Christ our Lord.

SIGN OF PEACE

Lord Jesus Christ, you said to your disciples: 'A new commandment I give you: love one another as I have loved you.' Touch our hearts so that we may be people who are able to love, and thus we will enjoy the peace and unity of your kingdom where you live for ever and ever.

REFLECTION   **Where love begins**

It's easy to love at a distance,
but not so easy to love at close quarters.
It's easier to give a few pounds to relieve famine in Africa
than to relieve the loneliness of someone living next door.
It's easy to love people who are far away,
but not always easy to love those who are close at hand.
Yet, these are the people Christ asks us to love.
We must begin by loving the people near us.
That is where our love must start.
But, of course, it doesn't have to end there.
And it shouldn't.

Sixth Sunday of Easter

THE GIFT OF PEACE

INTRODUCTION AND CONFITEOR

Jesus said to his apostles, 'Peace I leave with you, my own peace I give you.' We can't give peace to others if we don't have it ourselves. Jesus was able to give peace to others because he had it himself. The Lord will give us too his peace. [Pause]

Lord Jesus, you help us to be at peace with God. Lord, have mercy.

You help us to be at peace with ourselves. Christ, have mercy.

You help us to be at peace with others. Lord, have mercy.

HEADINGS FOR READINGS

First Reading (Acts 15:1-2.22-29). A big issue for the early Church was how much of the Law and traditions of Moses should be imposed on Gentile converts. This reading tells us how the problem was solved.

Second Reading (Rev 21:10-14.22-23). We are given a majestic picture of the new Jerusalem, the heavenly Church of the future, when God's Kingdom will come in all its glory.

Gospel (Jn 14:23-29). We hear yet another portion of Jesus' farewell discourse at the Last Supper. It is dominated by the thought of his imminent departure.

SCRIPTURE NOTE

Many Gentiles had accepted Christianity as a result of the preaching of Paul and Barnabas. But then a question arose: how much of the Law and traditions of Moses should be required of these Gentile converts? The answer was: the bare minimum. They must abstain from meat sacrificed to idols, from blood (symbol of life and which belonged to God), from the meat of strangled animals (which still had blood in them), and from marriage within degrees of kindred forbidden to Jews though allowed in other traditions. And so, instead of becoming a Jewish sect, Christianity became a universal religion.

The Gospel reading is taken from Jesus' discourse at the Last Supper, and is dominated by his imminent departure. He is concerned to assure his disciples that he will not leave them orphans. Despite his leaving, he and they will not be apart. If they keep his word they will be drawn into the love of the Father and the Son. The Holy Spirit will remind them of his words. Peace is his final gift to them, a peace the world cannot give.

HOMILY 1   **The gift of peace**

During the Last Supper Jesus said to the apostles, 'Peace I leave with you, my own peace I give you. A peace which the world cannot give, this is my gift to you. So do not let your hearts be troubled or afraid.' These are some of the loveliest words in the Gospel.

The Hebrew word for peace is *shalom*, a word very widely used in the Bible. It is so rich in content that the English word 'peace' conveys only a fraction of what it means. In general it conveys a sense of universal completeness, a condition in which nothing is lacking. The state of perfect well-being which the word signifies belongs only to God. When one possesses peace, one is in perfect communion with God.

The false prophets prophesied peace when there was no peace. Jesus, on the other hand, is sometimes referred to as a 'disturber of the peace'. But the peace he disturbed was a false peace. Peace does not consist in mere prosperity and well-being. An essential component of peace is righteousness. So, where there is no righteousness, there is no genuine peace. Hence, there is no peace for the wicked.

Peace is not just the absence of war or dissension. Nor is it simple harmony. True peace is not the same as tranquillity. Tranquillity is external. Peace is essentially internal. Peace is a state of inner calm, and designates right relations with God and with others. Peace in this complete sense, a peace which surpasses all human thought, cannot be created by human effort alone. It is a gift of God.

God desires the peace of those who serve him. God speaks peace to his people. In biblical times *shalom* was an ordinary greeting. But it was more than that. It was an expression of good wishes. Peace is one of the greatest gifts we can give to one another. But we can't give it if we haven't got it, just as we can't give money to a beggar if our own pocket is empty. And we can't give it to someone who doesn't want it or who is unable to receive it. We can create the conditions where peace is able to take root, but we can't impose peace.

Jesus was able to offer peace to his apostles because he had it himself: 'My own peace I give you.' Peace is communion with God. Since Jesus is in perfect communion with God, he can give us the gift of peace. What other peace can we give but our own? The Christian has a vocation to peace. But often, alas, instead of giving peace to others, we inflict on them our own unrest and unhappiness.

When Jesus appeared to the apostles after the resurrection he didn't blame them or even scold them for failing him. Instead, he broke through the closed doors of fear and doubt and spoke the words they desperately needed to hear. He said, 'Peace be with you.' And by means of those lovely words he turned their despair into hope, and their sadness into joy.

Fortunate are we if we taste the peace of Jesus – the peace which passes all understanding, the peace which this world cannot give, a peace no one can take away from us, a peace which can exist in the midst of a troubled world, and even in the midst of unresolved problems. Peace is God's gift to us, but it can also be our gift to one another.

HOMILY 2   **Peace in the midst of turmoil**

In his book, *Go Down to the Potter's House*, Donagh O'Shea has a story about a king who had two artists in his court who were bitter rivals. One day the king said, 'I want to decide once and for all which of you is the better artist. You must paint the same theme, so that I can judge between you. And let the theme be peace.'

The two artists agreed, and a week later came back with their paintings.

The first presented his painting. It showed a dreamy landscape with rolling hills and a lake with not a ripple on the surface. The whole scene spoke of contentment, peace, stillness. However, as the king looked at the picture, he could barely suppress a yawn. Then turning to the artist he said, 'Your picture is pretty, but it puts me to sleep.'

Then the second man presented his work. It showed a thundering waterfall. It was so realistic that one could almost hear the roar of the water as it crashed onto the rocks, hundreds of feet below.

'But this is not a scene of peace as I ordered,' said the king angrily. The artist made no reply but motioned him to continue looking. Then the king spotted a detail that had hitherto escaped him: among the rocks at the base of the waterfall a small shrub was growing with a bird's nest in its branches. On looking closely at it he noticed that there was a bird in the nest: a sparrow sitting on her eggs, her eyes half-closed. She was waiting for her chicks to be born, a perfect picture of peace.

On seeing this, the king was delighted. Turning to the man who had painted it he said, 'I like your picture very much. You have conveyed a very important thing about peace, namely, that it is possible to be at peace even in the midst of the hurly-burly of life.'

Jesus spoke about peace during the Last Supper. He said to the apostles, 'Peace I leave with you, my own peace I give you. A peace which the world cannot give, this is my gift to you. So do not let your hearts be troubled or afraid.'

It was a strange time to talk about peace, because everything was in turmoil around him. How then was he able to talk about peace? Because peace is communion with God. And Jesus was in perfect communion with God. So he was able to talk about peace even as his enemies were closing in on him and death was just around the corner.

Peace is not the same as tranquillity. Tranquillity is external. Peace is essentially internal. Peace is a state of inner calm, and designates right relations with God and with others. An essential component of peace is righteousness. Hence, there is no peace for the wicked.

Peace results when one trusts in God, and when the desire to please him is the dominant thing in one's life. This is something which we can have even in the midst of turmoil, conflict and unresolved problems.

Jesus offers his peace to us: 'Peace I leave with you.' The peace he offers us is not the peace of escape from reality. It is something so deep it is independent of outer circumstances. It is the peace which passes all understanding, the peace which this world cannot give, a peace no one can take away from us.

HOMILY 3   **Letting go**

During the Last Supper Jesus spoke about leaving. Not surprisingly, the apostles were plunged into gloom at the prospect of losing him. They didn't want him to go. They wanted to hold on to him. It's not easy to let go of someone you love. It's not easy to let go even of an object or a pet.

One day a young boy found a shivering little bird lying on the ground under a nest. Feeling sorry for it, he took it inside and put it by the fire, where it soon revived. However, instead of returning it to its nest, he built a cage for it. In the cage he gave it lots of food, drink, and warmth.

The little bird thrived and began to fly around the cage. Next it began to sing. The boy was thrilled. But one day it started to beat its wings against the sides of the cage. The boy asked his grandfather what this might mean.

'It's not happy,' his grandfather replied.

'I don't understand,' answered the boy. 'Hasn't it got everything it needs in the cage?'

'Everything except the one thing every bird longs for.'

'What's that?' asked the boy.

'Freedom,' came the reply.

'You mean, after all I've done for it, it wants to leave me?'

'It just wants to be free, so that it can be a bird like other birds.'

'But how can I let it go?' the boy persisted. 'It knows nothing about the dangers that lie in wait for little birds out in the world. It might get killed or starve to death.'

'That's a risk you'll have to take.'

'But I love it too much to let it go.'

'If you really loved it, you would let it go.'

The little boy grew silent. He looked at the bird. It continued to beat its wings against the cage. With every beat it seemed to be saying, 'Set me free! Set me free!' Unable to endure it any longer, he decided to let the bird go.

As it flew out the window, it took a piece of his heart with it. He stared at the open window for a long time. Then all of a sudden he heard the bird's singing coming from a nearby tree. That singing seemed more joyous and sweeter than ever before. And for the first time in months the boy felt free, happy, and at peace.

The apostles didn't want to let go of Jesus. But in this they were thinking, not of him, but of themselves. He told them so. He said, 'If you loved me you would have been glad to know that I am going to the Father, for the Father is greater than I.' (Jn 14:28) For Jesus to go back to the Father was the goal of his life. To try to hold him back from this was not to show love for him.

Possessive love is very common. Some parents are very possessive in their love for their children. Having given life to them, they refuse to let them live that life in their own way. The same thing happens in some marriages. There is a reluctance to let one's partner have a life of his or her own.

Possessive love causes a lot of pain and does a lot of harm. Non-possessive love, on the other hand, does wonders for both parties.

Growth, progress, change call for a letting go, a losing of something which we have at present and which we value dearly. But the losing is with a view to gaining something new and better.

In leaving the apostles, Jesus made it clear that he was not abandoning them. He said to them, 'It is for your own good that I am going because unless I go, the Spirit will not come; but if I go, I will send him to you.' (Jn 16:7) And he was as good as his word. When we willingly let go of people, they can leave us without us feeling that they are abandoning us. And we open ourselves to receive something new from them, something they could not give us unless they left.

ANOTHER STORY

Some people have a lot of anger inside them with the result that they lack peace of mind and serenity of soul. But other people have an inner peace, and what a difference it makes to their lives.

Two neighbours, James and John, were ploughing in adjacent fields. The ground was hard and stony, and a hot sun beat down on them. James was in a black mood. He lashed out at the horse with his whip. However, the beatings only had the effect of making the horse more stubborn and uncooperative. James was convinced that his neighbour's wheat would grow taller than his. And every time he looked across at him he got the impression that he was laughing at him.

John, on the other hand, was in a calm mood. He worked quietly and well, in spite of pains and aches. Every now and then he stopped to give his horse a rest. He looked across at his neighbour and saw that he was in a very agitated state. He would have liked to help him, but he knew that when he was like this it was better to leave him alone.

The difference between the two neighbours was not in the outer circumstances of their lives but in their inner states of their minds. We see the world and other people, not as they are, but as we are. John enjoyed inner peace and serenity. James was in a state of inner turmoil. Nothing is a greater obstacle to being on good terms with others than being ill-at-ease with oneself.

Jesus comes to bring us life and to liberate us from ourselves. He calms our fears and heals our anguish and hatreds, thus enabling us to look at the world with a still heart and an open soul.

PRAYER OF THE FAITHFUL

President: Let us pray that God's ways may be known on earth and all people may experience his saving help.

Response: Lord, graciously hear us.

Reader(s): For all Christians: that they may be makers of peace. [Pause] Lord, hear us.

For world leaders: that God may guide their feet into the way of peace. [Pause] Lord, hear us.

For our homes: that peace may reign in them. [Pause] Lord, hear us.

For parents: that having given life to their children, they may know how and when to let them go so that they can live their own lives. [Pause] Lord, hear us.

For those who are anxious or fearful: that they may know the peace that comes from trusting in God. [Pause] Lord, hear us.

For peace with our neighbours, and for the courage to seek to be reconciled with anyone with whom we have fallen out. [Pause] Lord, hear us.

For our loved ones who have died: that they may rest in the peace of God. [Pause] Lord, hear us.

For our own special needs. [Longer pause] Lord, hear us.

President: Lord, grant us the serenity to accept the things we cannot change; the courage to change the things we can; and the wisdom to know the difference. We ask this through Christ our Lord .

SIGN OF PEACE

Lord Jesus Christ, you said to your apostles: 'Peace I leave with you, my own peace I give you. A peace which the world cannot give, this is my gift to you. So do not let your hearts be troubled or afraid.' Lord, take pity on our troubled and fearful hearts, and grant us the peace and unity of your kingdom where you live for ever and ever.

REFLECTION   **Signposts on the footpath of peace**

To be glad of life, because it gives you a chance to love,
to work, to play, and to look up at the stars.
To despise nothing in the world except what is false and mean.
To fear nothing except what is cowardly.
To be guided by what you admire and love,
rather than by what you hate.
To envy nothing that is your neighbour's

except his kindness of heart and gentleness of manner.
To think seldom of your enemies, often of your friends,
and everyday of Christ.
And to spend as much time as you can, with body and with spirit, in
God's out-of-doors.
These are little signposts on the footpath of peace.   *(Henry van Dyke)*

The Ascension of the Lord

INTRODUCTION AND CONFITEOR

On this day we celebrate the glorification of Jesus, our Brother, when the
Father raised him up in glory. Jesus wants us to share in his glory. Let us
reflect for a moment on the glory to which we are called. [Pause]

Lord Jesus, you are Son of God and Prince of Peace. Lord, have mercy.

Lord Jesus, you are Son of God and Son of Mary. Christ, have mercy.

Lord Jesus, you are Word made flesh and splendour of the Father. Lord,
have mercy.

HEADINGS FOR READINGS

First Reading (Acts 1:1-11). We hear of the ascension of Jesus into heaven,
and of his promise to send the Holy Spirit to his disciples.

Second Reading (Eph 1:17-23). Paul sets out the meaning of the ascension: God raised Jesus above all earthly powers, and made him head of
the Church and Lord of creation.

Gospel (Lk 24:46-53). Before ascending into heaven, Jesus promises to
send the Holy Spirit to his disciples.

SCRIPTURE NOTE

The reading from Acts speaks of the ascension of Jesus. It also shows how
Jesus, now in the glorious presence of his Father, continues to act through
the Holy Spirit and through his followers.

The theological meaning of the feast is expressed in the Second Reading: God has glorified Jesus, raising him above all earthly powers, and
making him head of the Church and Lord of creation.

The Gospel Reading consists of the end of Luke's Gospel. It contains
Luke's first account of the Ascension, which is here presented as occuring
on Easter Sunday. The risen Lord shows the apostles how the Scriptures
had foretold that the Christ would suffer and rise again. Jesus also gives
them a mission (the proclamation of repentance and forgiveness of sins)

and promises to send the Holy Spirit to them. They return in joy to Jerusalem to await the Spirit.

In his Gospel Luke has shown that 'the time of Israel' has yielded to 'the time of Christ'. Now, 'the time of Christ' is to yield to 'the time of the Church'. The word of salvation will go forth from Jerusalem to the ends of the earth. He will tell us about that in his second book, Acts of the Apostles. The Ascension is seen as the culmination of Jesus' life and the start of the Church's mission.

HOMILY 1   **A strange path to glory**

On the feast of the Ascension we celebrate the glorification of Jesus. The humble Jesus who suffered and died now reigns in glory at the right hand of the Father. But what a strange path led him to that glory. Frankly, at first the apostles found it incredible that anyone, much less a Messiah, could travel to glory by such a path.

It was their hope and dream that Jesus was the promised Messiah. But when he was put to death, their dream was reduced to rubble. A humiliated, crucified Messiah was unthinkable. They searched the Scriptures for answers but found none.

However, gradually their minds were opened and they realised that there was another way of looking at the Scriptures. They came to see that all the prophets had foretold that the Messiah would suffer and die, and *thus* enter into glory. Yes, he would take a strange path to glory. And yet, was it that strange? How can anyone attain to glory except through sacrifice and suffering?

From a worldly point of view the hour of Jesus' death was an hour of failure. Worse, it was an hour of shame and humiliation. But by raising him from the dead, God turned it into an hour of triumph for Jesus, and an hour of grace for us. His death, far from being the end of the dream, was precisely the way in which it was realised. And so the apostles began to understand the message of Jesus' death and resurrection – glory attained through suffering. First the pain, then the joy.

Jesus has ascended to the right hand of the Father. The foremost place of honour in the Kingdom now belongs to Jesus, and rightly so. That position was his by right of his divine sonship; but he renounced that right, and won it by right of his loving service. It wasn't the suffering as such that earned him that glory. It was the life he led, a life of service and self-sacrifice even to death, a death from which he emerged victorious by his resurrection. He didn't seek his own glory, but the glory of his Father. The path that led Jesus to glory was no easy one. But then if it was, it wouldn't be of much help to us.

After seeing Jesus ascend into heaven, the apostles returned to Jerusalem with joy. Why the joy? Because they were now convinced that their beloved Jesus was alive. So their hearts burned with joy. All this shows the goodness of God, who makes our deepest dreams come true in the most surprising of ways. He makes all things work for the good of those who place their trust in him. He brings good out of evil, life out of death, and glory out of pain and suffering.

There are times in life when we may find ourselves going down a sad and lonely road. We must remember that we are not alone. The risen Lord journeys with us. And he knows all about human suffering. He is so close to us that our stories merge with his. It is only his story – glory achieved through suffering and death – that helps us to make sense of our own story. The resurrection and ascension of Jesus open all our stories to the prospect, not just of a good ending, but of a glorious ending.

This feast is as much about us as about Jesus. His ascension shows us the goal of our earthly journey. It is a goal and a destiny which defies even our imagination. It gives an eternal dimension to our lives.

We live in the hope that the words of Jesus will come true for us: 'Where I am, you too shall be.' Meanwhile we have a task to do: to preach the Good News and to be his witnesses in the world.

HOMILY 2   **Presence and absence**

On Ascension Day Jesus withdrew his physical presence from his disciples. But physical absence does not mean the end of presence. The ascension of Jesus is his liberation from all restrictions of time and space. It does not represent his removal from the earth, but his constant presence everywhere on earth.

Physical presence isn't everything. In fact, it can sometimes actually get in the way of intimate communication. Many of our disappointments in life are caused by the fact that seeing and touching do not always create the closeness we seek. Two people can be physically close, and yet live separate, lonely lives, because there is no meeting of minds and hearts. They are like shells on a shore.

On the other hand, people can be very close to one another even though separated by thousands of miles. For people to grow together there must be periods of absence as well as presence. In absence we see each other in a new way. We are less distracted by each other's idiosyncrasies, and better able to appreciate each other's true worth.

If we are able to be fully present to our friends when we are with them, our absence too will bear fruit. The memory of that presence, the warmth of it, will continue to nourish the other person. Thus, not only our presence but also our absence becomes a gift.

When we think of each other with love a spiritual bond is created between us, and we enter into a new intimacy. For those who love one another there is no such place as 'far away'.

Jesus' ascension was not a journey into outer space, but a journey home. We must not think that he has abandoned us; that he once lived on earth but has now gone back to where he really belongs. If this were so then Christianity would be no more than a remembrance religion. Jesus has gone to God. During his earthly ministry he could only be in one place at a time. But now that he is united with God, he is present wherever God is present; and that is everywhere.

The first Christians understood this very well. They knew that Jesus was still with them, even if not in the same way as before. They believed he still shared their lives, and that death would mean being united with him in glory for ever.

Still, we might look back with envy at the people who were fortunate enough to have seen the risen Lord with their own eyes. But the Gospels show that those who were in that enviable position did not truly know Jesus until the Scriptures were expounded and the bread was broken.

We Christians of the present day have those same means of recognising the Lord – the Scriptures and the breaking of the bread. In the matter of encountering Jesus with faith a past generation is not more privileged than the present one.

Jesus was relying on the apostles (and now on us) to make sure that the Gospel was preached and lived. He needs us to witness to his presence in the world.

HOMILY 3   **Witnesses for Christ**

Before leaving his apostles Jesus commissioned them to preach the Gospel to the whole world. In order to help them carry out that mission he promised to send them the Holy Spirit. On Pentecost day he fulfilled that promise.

The task of preaching the Gospel to the world now depends on us. We are Christ's witnesses. It's a great privilege but a daunting task. However, we also can rely on the help of the Holy Spirit. But how are we to witness?

There is the witness of words. We witness by professing our faith. This could include explaining it and defending it.

There is the witness of deeds. An apple tree that never produced an apple would be a poor witness for the orchard. Even one good apple speaks. 'Never recommend anything unless you can provide a sample of it.' (Thoreau)

Then there is the witness of one's life. Trees witness to life just by being. Tall, straight, motionless, they are silent yet eloquent witnesses to life. Flowers bear witness to beauty simply by being what they are. And Christians bear witness by what they are. The most eloquent sermon is the silent sermon of example. Today people no longer want to listen to sermons on the faith. They want to see the Gospel in action.

The witness of a Christian life is more powerful than any argument. There are those whose lives bear radiant witness to the transforming power of the faith. In their lives the faith is a bright flame, whereas in the lives of others it is a dim glow or an occasional spark. The person who, despite all his/her human limitations and defects, lives a simple life, taking Christ as the model, is a sign of God and of transcendent realities.

The evangelical witness which the world finds most appealing is that of concern for people and of charity towards the poor, the weak, and those who suffer. The generosity underlying this attitude and these actions stands in marked contrast to human selfishness. It raises precise questions which lead to God and to the Gospel. A commitment to peace, to justice, to human rights, is a witness to the Gospel.

There is a fourth degree of witness, namely, to bear witness with one's death. But this is not granted to or asked of everyone. What is asked of each of us is to witness with our lives. This is not a soft, easy way, but a way that calls for a special kind of toughness, strength and courage.

There is a hunger in the world today for the Christ of the Gospels. Jesus said to the apostles, 'Stay in the city, until you are clothed with power from on high.' The power in question was the power of the Holy Spirit. We need that same power if we are to witness to Jesus. Those who witness will share his glory.

A STORY

Once upon a time there was a father who had twelve sons. Though he loved each of them he had a soft spot in his heart for the second youngest of them, Joseph. The others became jealous of Joseph and decided to kill him. However, at the last minute, they changed their minds and instead sold him to some passing merchants. They told their father that he had been killed by a wild animal.

Joseph was taken in chains to Egypt, where he was sold as a slave. He had a wretched life. To make matters worse, he was falsely accused and ended up in the dungeons. Though surrounded by hardened criminals, he continued to trust in God and to live a good life. He even made friends among the criminals. Eventually he cleared his name, and was released.

Then, foreseeing that a terrible famine was coming, he advised the king to get the people to save corn. The king not only took his advice but put him in charge of the operation. Joseph did a splendid job.

The famine duly arrived and the people were able to draw on the corn they had stored away. But things were going badly in the neighbouring countries. People came from all over to Egypt looking for corn. And the king would say to them: 'Go to Joseph.'

One day Joseph's brothers arrived looking for corn. When they recognised him they trembled with fear. But instead of taking revenge, Joseph received them with great kindness, and gave them as much corn as they wanted. He told them to come back and bring their father with them.

The aged father was overcome with joy on hearing that his beloved son was alive. A great treachery had been committed against Joseph by his brothers. But good came out of it all. He was able to save his brothers from the famine, and re-unite the entire family.

The story of Joseph is one of the greatest stories in the Bible. Joseph is a figure of Jesus, the Father's beloved Son, sold by one of his friends, put to death, but now raised up by the Father and placed at his right hand in glory. From his exalted position he saves us, his brothers and sisters, from sin and eternal death. And he seeks to being together all the scattered members of God's family.

This is the day we celebrate the ascension of Jesus to the right hand of his Father. It is a day of joy. But he has given us a task to perform for him. Not to distribute corn, but to preach the Good News to all the world.

PRAYER OF THE FAITHFUL

President: As we bring our needs before God, let us pray in the name of him who now sits at the right hand of the Father in glory and who intercedes for us.

Response: Lord, graciously hear us.

Reader(s): That Christ may enkindle in all his followers an ardent desire for his kingdom. [Pause] Lord, hear us.

That he may strengthen by the power of that Spirit all those who are working for a just and peaceful world. [Pause] Lord, hear us.

That those who have nothing to hope for beyond this life, may be granted the gift of faith. [Pause] Lord, hear us.

That our lives may bear witness to the faith we profess with our lips. [Pause] Lord, hear us.

That God may grant our own special needs. [Longer pause] Lord, hear us.

President: Father, through his ascension your Son has become Lord of the universe, to stand above all that is best in life as its source, and above all that is worst as victor; to stand above all powers and authorities as judge, and above all failures and sin as forgiveness and love. We trust you to pay heed to these and all our prayers through the same Christ our Lord.

REFLECTION   **Lift up your hearts**

The day of the Lord's triumphant return to his Father
is not a day for narrowness or sadness.

Rather, it is a day for openness and joy.
Therefore, let us lift up our hearts.
Let us raise up your minds.
Let our spirits soar and be free.
For sin and evil and death have been overcome.
We know nothing of the mystery of the beyond.
All we have is his word: 'Where I am, you too will be.'
Lord, you have kindled in our hearts the hope of eternal life.
Guard this hope with your grace,
and bring it to fulfilment in the kingdom of heaven.

Seventh Sunday of Easter
WAITING FOR THE SPIRIT

INTRODUCTION AND CONFITEOR

After Jesus left the apostles, they returned to Jerusalem and waited in prayer for the coming of the Holy Spirit. We too need the Spirit. Without the Spirit of Jesus we cannot live the life of a Christian. [Pause]

Lord Jesus, you send the Spirit to give courage to the fearful. Lord, have mercy.

You send the Spirit to give strength to the weak and hope to the fallen. Christ, have mercy.

You send the Spirit to bring pardon and peace to sinners. Lord, have mercy.

HEADINGS FOR READINGS

First Reading (Acts 7:55-60). The most striking feature of the death of Stephen is its similarity to the death of Jesus.

Second Reading (Rev 22:12-14.16-17.20). The last words of the book of Revelation talk about the second coming of Jesus.

Gospel (Jn 17:20-26). We shasre in part of the great prayer which Jesus made on behalf of his present and future disciples during the Last Supper.

SCRIPTURE NOTE

The reading from Acts tells of Stephen's death. We immediatley notice the similarity of that account to Luke's version of the death of Jesus. Jesus was tried before the Sanhedrin and made a decisive statement about the Son of Man at the right hand of God. He was led out of the city to be killed, he forgave his killers and commended his soul to the Father.

Stephen, too, was brought before the council and taken out of the city to be stoned. He forgave his killers, and as he died, committed his spirit, not to the Father, but to Jesus, whom he sees at God's right hand. Luke's intent is clear: the death of the martyr mirrors the death of Jesus.

The Second Reading gives us the closing words of Revelation. The Spirit inspires the Church to respond with eager joy to the Lord's announcement of his coming.

The great prayer Jesus made during the Last Supper (Jn 17) has three parts: Jesus prays for himself (vv. 1-5), for his disciples (vv. 6-19), and for the community of the future who will believe through their preaching (vv. 20-26). Our reading gives the third part of Jesus' prayer. He prays that his disciples may be so united that they share in the unity of the Trinity itself. He prays that his followers will be with him in glory. Meanwhile, he will remain with them in love.

HOMILY 1   **That they may be one**

Chapter 17 of John's Gospel contains the great prayer Jesus made during the Last Supper. In the first part of that prayer Jesus prayed for himself. In the second part he prayed for his disciples. And in the third part (contained in today's Gospel) he prayed for the community of the future who would believe because of the preaching of the apostles. That future community includes us. It is comforting to know that Jesus prayed for us, and still does.

In praying for his future disciples, Jesus' main concern was unity among them. He asked the Father: 'that they may be one as we are one.'

Unity is not the same thing as uniformity. Jesus' choice of followers was sufficiently diverse in temperament, personality, style and social status to suggest that he found diversity a healthy, life-giving force.

True unity cannot be achieved in a community which denies difference. Unity is achieved when each member is different and contributes a different gift, but all are united around the same goal by mutual love. Each of us must be purified of our need to prove that we are best. We must open ourselves to others and welcome their gifts.

We are called from many different backgrounds to form one body in Christ. By rising above our many differences we become witnesses of God who allows his light to shine in a variety of ways.

The story goes that on the third day of creation, having made the trees and the plants, God encountered an unexpected problem. The great cedars of Lebanon seemed too tall, so tall as to make them subject to the temptation of arrogance. And so God decided to create iron.

The trees immediately understood the threat and began to weep, saying, 'Woe to us, for one day we shall all fall before the axe.' But God reassured them by telling them: 'Without a handle, the axe is just a lump of

[151]

iron. Since the handle is made of wood, try to live in peace without betraying one another. Stay united and the axe will be powerless against you.'

Jesus knew that unity was vital for the young community. But it had to be a unity based on love, a unity that resulted from fidelity to the commandment of love: 'Love one another as I have loved you.'

Community is a great challenge. True fraternity is far more than mutual toleration. It involves solidarity, sharing, belonging, compassion, and joy in the well-being of others. Selfishness is a blight on a community: everyone demands that the community be attentive to them, but nobody really wants to be attentive to others.

Sadly, down the ages the unity Jesus wished for his Church was fractured many times. The result is that today we have not one but many Christian Churches. The divisions among Christians are a scandal to outsiders. However, the real scandal is not so much that there are differences in belief and practice between Christians of different denominations, but that there should be enmity between them. We see enmity being taken to the extreme in the reading from Acts which concerns the killing of Stephen. Here we have the adherents of one religion (Judaism) killing those of another religion (Christianity).

So, perhaps what is most needed today is not one Church, but mutual respect and tolerance between the adherents of the various Churches and the various religions. Not that we should settle for that. But it would be great launching pad for a coming together of all Christians.

HOMILY 2 **Learning from Stephen**

St Stephen was the first disciple of Jesus to die for his faith. Stephen was young and generous and brave. He bore witness to Jesus in word and deed, and paid the ultimate price.

The most striking feature of his death is the resemblance it bears to the death of Jesus. Like Jesus, Stephen was innocent. Like Jesus, he was accused of blasphemy, and tried before the supreme council of the Jews, the Sanhedrin. Like Jesus, he died a violent death outside the city. (In this way both were turned into outcasts in death.)

Like Jesus, Stephen prayed for his killers: 'Lord, do not hold this sin against them.' Finally, as Jesus died he surrendered his soul into the hands of God with the prayer, 'Father, into your hands I commend my spirit.' As Stephen died he surrendered his soul into the hands of Jesus, saying, 'Lord Jesus, receive my spirit.' In all of this, Luke's intent is clear: the death of the martyr mirrors the death of Jesus.

The cruelty of his death by stoning hardly bears thinking about. His killers took his clothes away and laid them down like booty at the feet of their leader, Saul. Saul, a fanatical Pharisee, thought he was honouring

God by killing people like Stephen. So do some people today who kill in God's name. The idea that we can honour God by killing anyone is abhorrent.

Paul, as we know, was soon to be converted to the faith and became one of its greatest champions. No doubt he was impressed by the courage and forgiveness Stephen showed as he died. Saul's conversion shows that a person can change, and that God never writes off anyone.

But it was not just in death that Stephen showed these qualities. One doesn't become a hero in death if one has not already been one in life. Stephen had already proved his commitment to Jesus in life. He was one of the first deacons appointed by the apostles to distribute food to widows. But he also preached the word. And it was his fearless preaching about Jesus that aroused the anger of the Jewish religious leaders.

Stephen bore the highest kind of witness to Christ; he witnessed with his death. This degree of witness is not granted to or asked of everyone. What is asked of each of us is to witness with our lives. This is not a soft way. It is a tough way, and calls for great strength and courage. The world today is crying out for the witness of people who are not afraid to be real Christians.

Besides showing us how to witness, Stephen shows us the kind of death to which every Christian should aspire, namely, to die forgiving one's enemies, and surrendering oneself to the goodness and mercy of the Lord.

HOMILY 3   **Learning from Paul**

There in the background, but playing a vital role in the horrible business of the stoning of Stephen was Saul. He held the coats of the stone-throwers, and was a leader in the persecution of the Christians. Yet this is the same man who was soon to be converted to the faith and went on to become one of its greatest champions. Hard to believe that it is the same person.

The fact that Paul took part in the killing of Stephen didn't mean that he was evil through and through. It was more a question of he being blind. He was blinded by religious fanaticism. However, there was another and better side to him. It's quite clear that he was a highly committed person, who was capable of hard work and great sacrifice.

When a person undergoes a conversion we tend to say, 'He/she became a completely new person.' But this is not altogether true. In every conversion there is continuity and discontinuity. Negative elements are overcome, and new goals are set. A person's talents and gifts are not denied, much less lost; rather, they are redirected.

Had we been present at the killing of Stephen and seen Paul's role in it, we would have written him off forever. We have a tendency to 'freeze' people at one particular stage in their lives. We judge them forever on the basis of one bad experience. We tend to divide people into two categories: saints and sinners.

But people are not so easily categorised. Human beings are complex. Some people don't seem to have any understanding of the divided nature of every human being. As soon as they discover a weakness in someone, they write the person off forever. For some the bottle will always smell of the liquor it once held. But is that fair, or even wise? Should we not allow that people can change?

It doesn't help that ours is not a forgiving culture. The attitude to criminals is: lock them up and throw the key away. But a culture that doesn't believe in progress or redemption is a culture without hope. Have we so little faith in ourselves that we can't accept the possibility of change and maturation? It is as if those who kill come from another planet, and don't deserve the chance to be human, to atone, to repair.

We must learn to be patient and lenient, towards ourselves in the first place. We must be hospitable towards all that we are. We must acknowledge that there is a dark side to ourselves, without conceding victory to it. And we must then be lenient towards others. A person will be judged, not on a single act or stage in his life, but on his life as a whole.

The story of Paul shows that a person can change, and God never writes off anyone as beyond redemption. A person may make a great mistake, but by the grace of God be redeemed, as Paul was. That is the great lesson of his life. No doubt one of the factors in Paul's conversion was the example of Stephen. Stephen was a true Christian. Paul was impressed by the courage and forgiveness Stephen showed as he died.

ANOTHER APPROACH   **Fellowship of the weak**

To be a believer in today's world can be a lonely business. Here is where the community comes in. In order to sustain our faith we need the support of the community. During the Last Supper Jesus prayed for unity among his disciples: 'Father, may they be one as we are one.' But is that not an impossible ideal? Would one not need to be perfect to belong to a community like that?

Once there was an idealistic young man who was greatly attracted to a community of monks. It was inevitable that he would want to join them. And join them he did as a novice. At first he was thrilled to be part of a community of holy men. But he wasn't there very long when he got a rude awakening. He discovered that the men whom he had regarded as perfect were full of flaws and imperfections. In fact, they were just as fragile, sinful and selfish as himself. He was so disillusioned that he quit the monastery.

A Christian community is not made up of perfect people. The little community of disciples that Jesus prayed for was made up of people who were timid and weak and fearful. Jean Vanier talks about 'the fellowship of the weak', and says that greater solidarity can result from the sharing of weakness than from the sharing of strength.

This might seem a contradiction. But take a bunch of reeds for example. Individually, reeds are weak and easily broken. But tie a bundle of reeds together, and they are almost unbreakable. So it is with people. Great strength results from togetherness, especially for weak people.

Community seems linked to weakness and vulnerability. When people are enjoying success they look for admiration, but when they are weak they seek communion. If they find it, they know that they are loved not for their achievements, but for who they are. As a result they begin to gain confidence in themselves.

And the heart of a capable, strong person is opened up and touched by the call of love from a weaker person. When someone tells you about his success and prowess, you admire him. But when he shares his failures and weakness with you, he elicits compassion. Humility leads to and creates communion.

Strength is hidden in weakness, and true community consists in the fellowship of the weak. Alcoholics Anonymous is a great example of this. What draws its members together is not shared strength but shared weakness; the honest acknowledgement of their common weakness and vulnerability. No one is a threat to anyone else, and this disposes them to share and receive from one another. One doesn't have to be perfect in order to share community.

The first Christians supported one another by praying and worshipping together, and by a loving service of one another. We can do the same. We can travel together, listening to and learning from one another. We must extend to the other members of the community the same kind of understanding and compassion we ourselves wish to receive from them.

> The redemptive mystery of God's love is to be seen not in a community of spiritual heroes, but of brothers and sisters, who encourage each other on the journey to the Kingdom of hope and mercy. (Timothy Radcliffe)

PRAYER OF THE FAITHFUL

President: Each Pentecost renews the gift of the Holy Spirit in us and in the Church. Let us pray for the coming of the Spirit as the first disciples did.

Response: Come, Holy Spirit.

Reader(s): For all the Church: that the Holy Spirit may renew its life and make it radiant with hope. [Pause] Let us pray.

For unity among all the followers of Christ. [Pause] Let us pray.

For governments leaders: that the Holy Spirit may help them to cooperate in pursuing the twin goals of peace and justice. [Pause] Let us pray.

For all who suffer persecution for the name of Christ: that the Holy Spirit may help them to be strong. [Pause] Let us pray.

For all gathered here: that the Holy Spirit may help us bear witness with our lives to the faith we profess with our lips. [Pause] Let us pray.

For our own special needs. [Longer pause] Let us pray.

President: God of love and mercy, through the coming of the Holy Spirit the apostles received power from heaven. Grant that we also may receive the gifts of the Spirit. We ask this through Christ our Lord.

SIGN OF PEACE

Lord Jesus Christ, at the Last Supper you prayed for your apostles in these words: 'Father, may they be one as we are one.' Heal the divisions among your followers, and make us one in mind and heart, so that we may enjoy the peace and unity of your kingdom where you live for ever and ever.

PRAYER / REFLECTION   **Praying for the Spirit**

Come, Holy Spirit.
Come with strength for the weak,
courage for the fearful,
light for those in darkness,
comfort for the sorrowful,
healing for the sick and injured,
guidance for those who are lost,
faith for those who are in doubt,
hope for those who have no hope,
and love for those who have no love.
Come, Holy Spirit, kindle in us the fire of your love,
and we shall renew the face of the earth.

Pentecost Sunday

INTRODUCTION AND CONFITEOR

Today we celebrate the coming of the Holy Spirit on the apostles. It is a mistake to see this coming as something that happened long ago and can never happen again. Through the prayer of the Church, the Holy Spirit comes to us today. Let us dispose ourselves to receive the Spirit. [Pause]

Lord Jesus, you send the Spirit to lead us into the fullness of your truth. Lord, have mercy.

You send the Spirit to help us to love one another as you have loved us. Christ, have mercy.

You send the Spirit to strengthen us and make us ambassadors of the Good News to the world. Lord, have mercy.

HEADINGS FOR READINGS

First Reading (Acts 2:1-11). Luke describes the descent of the Holy Spirit on the apostles, and the effect it had on them.

Second Reading (1 Cor 12:3-7.12-13). The Holy Spirit gives different gifts to different people, for the good of the Church, the Body of Christ.

Gospel (Jn 20:19-23). The risen Jesus gives the gift of the Holy Spirit to his disciples and inaugurates the mission of the Church.

SCRIPTURE NOTE

Luke has the giving of the Spirit happening on the feast of Pentecost. Jewish tradition saw Pentecost as the feast of the giving of the Law on Mount Sinai. According to a legend a mighty wind turned to fire and a voice proclaimed the Law. In a further refinement, the fire split into seventy tongues corresponding to the seventy nations of the world, to convey that the Law was proclaimed not only to Israel, but to all nations.

Luke exploits this tradition. He, too, has the mighty wind and tongues of fire coming upon the group of disciples. But for Luke the universal proclamation was not that of the Law, but of the Good News, a proclamation that has undone the sentence of Babel and re-united the scattered nations.

In his Gospel John has the giving of the Spirit happening on Easter Day. However, we must avoid any impression of a two-fold initial solemn bestowal of the Spirit. Luke and John are saying the same thing: the risen Lord gives the gift of the Spirit, and inaugurates the mission of the Church. That they differ in their dating is due to theological concerns.

HOMILY 1   **The role of the Spirit**

It's impossible to live the life of a Christian without the help of the Holy Spirit. But to appreciate the role of the Spirit in the life of a Christian we have to start with Jesus himself. Even Jesus needed the Spirit. The Spirit had a big role to play in his life. The Spirit descended on him at his baptism, revealing him as the Father's beloved Son.

At his baptism he also received power from on high for the mission he was about to begin. The Spirit was not just given for a moment; the Spirit remained with him throughout his public ministry. Jesus was continually led, strengthened and guided by the Spirit.

He began his ministry by making his own the lovely words of Isaiah: 'The spirit of the Lord has been given to me, for he has anointed me. He has sent me to bring the good news to the poor, to proclaim liberty to captives and to the blind new sight, to set the downtrodden free, to proclaim the Lord's year of favour.'

What a beautiful mission. And how faithful he was to it. Jesus was filled with the Spirit, and power went out from him through his gracious words and compassionate deeds.

It was the Spirit who raised Jesus from the dead. It was the Spirit who opened the minds of his disciples and helped them to understand the meaning of his death. When he was raised up to glory at the right hand of the Father, Jesus poured out the Spirit on those who were to carry on his mission. The Holy Spirit descended on the apostles, individually and collectively. Filled with the Holy Spirit, they began their mission. And we see the great courage and confidence with which they did so.

And the same Spirit descends on us at our Baptism and Confirmation. The Spirit is not given for a moment but accompanies us on our journey in the footsteps of Jesus. The Spirit gives us power to participate in the work of Jesus. The Holy Spirit is our strength in times of weakness, our guide in times of doubt, our consoler in times of sadness, our advocate who always pleads our cause. We can't take even one step without the Spirit.

The gifts of the Spirit are: wisdom, understanding, counsel, fortitude, knowledge, piety, and fear of the Lord. Wisdom, understanding, and counsel (right judgement) guide our mind and assist our conscience in knowing right from wrong. Fortitude (courage) enables us to do the right thing even when it is difficult or unpopular. Fear of the Lord is really awe and reverence for God.

St Paul talks about the fruits of the Spirit (Gal 5:22). The Spirit brings love, joy, peace, patience, kindness, goodness, faithfulness, gentleness and self-control. These are beautiful things, and make life joyful.

Paul warns us against self-indulgence, which is the opposite of the Spirit. Self-indulgence produces bad temper, fighting, jealousy, cruelty, meanness, revenge, fornication, idolatry, and drunkenness. These are ugly things, and make life miserable. The more we renounce ourselves, and 'walk in the Spirit', the more fruitful our lives will become.

The Spirit that we have been given is not a spirit of timidity, but the Spirit of power. Wind and fire (heat) are symbols of power. Wind has the power to move, to uproot. Fire has the power to refine and transform. The power they symbolise here is the power of God. The coming of the Spirit provided the apostles with the energy, the courage, and the love to get on with the task Christ had given them.

HOMILY 2   **The gift of the Spirit**

We want to cling to someone we love and depend on. We can't bear the thought of that person leaving us. When Jesus told the apostles that he was leaving them, they were plunged into gloom. But he said to them, 'It is for your own good that I go away, because unless I go, the Spirit will not come to you; but if I go I will sent him to you.'

It must have been very hard for them to see how his going away could be for their good. The following illustration may throw some light on the subject.

Imagine that you are watching the sun go down. As it goes down, it appears to be taking the whole world with it. Meanwhile, the moon is high in the sky. But it is so weak and pale that you have to look very carefully to see it. It doesn't appear to be contributing anything whatsoever to the earth.

Then you notice a curious and beautiful thing. The lower the sun dips in the sky, the brighter the moon becomes. By the time the sun has finally departed the scene, the moon has undergone a complete transformation. It is now, far and away, the brightest object in the sky. And when you look around you, you notice to your surprise and delight that the old world has not only been completely restored to you, but made new, bright, and exciting. It is only when the sun has withdrawn that you can see what the moon is contributing.

Loving at times means distancing oneself from the person loved. This means that the person is free to develop in his own way. She is made to feel she has a contribution to make, and is free to receive from another.

Often, however, we hug the limelight. We want to be there all the time. We do not know when or how to withdraw. Thus, in a thoughtless and selfish way, we dominate other people. We stifle their development. We make them play second fiddle, and as a result they remain underdeveloped.

This gives us some insight into what Jesus meant when he said it was necessary for the apostles that he should go, otherwise the Spirit would not come. Had he always remained with them in his physical presence, they would never have come of age themselves.

I have nothing to give to another; but I have a duty to open him to his own life, to allow him to be himself. (Michel Quoist)

No one ever showed more confidence in, or more respect for, people than Jesus. He did not dominate them. He gave them a chance to shine. He handed his entire work over to them. He knew that they still needed help. That was why he sent them the Spirit.

What the Spirit did was bring out what was already inside them. His love awakened energies in them that they didn't know were there, so they were able to do things they didn't think they were capable of. After Pentecost their hearts were on fire and there was a wind at their backs.

We too need the Holy Spirit. We need him to help us to realise the power and the gifts we have within us. We need him to harness that power and release those gifts so that we too can become fearless witnesses for Christ.

HOMILY 3   **The miracle of change**

Before the coming of the Spirit, the apostles were virtually living in hiding in the upper room. A great task had been entrusted to them, yet they had neither the strength nor the will to begin it. But after Pentecost they were changed people.

What was it that the Holy Spirit did to them, and how did the miracle of change come about? Even though we are dealing with mystery, that doesn't mean we can't understand anything about it.

We have to realise that the apostles were wounded people. They were wounded by doubt and grief, by fear and failure, and above all by a sense of inadequacy.

Jean Vanier is a man who knows a great deal about what helps wounded people to change. He has set up little communities around the world for (mentally) handicapped people. When the handicapped are locked away in institutions, terrible damage is done to their hearts and spirits. A wounded body will heal naturally, but not a wounded heart. A wounded heart will harden, just to survive, and then fill up with anger and bitterness.

But when the handicapped are taken out of institutions where they are made to feel unwanted, and put into communities where they are loved, Vanier has witnessed, over and over again, the miracle of change.

This helps us to understand something of what happened to the apostles. In saying that the apostles were wounded, one is not suggesting that they were wounded to the same degree as some handicapped people are. Nevertheless, they were wounded. But after the coming of the Spirit they were changed people. They left their hiding place, and set out courageously to preach the Gospel.

We mustn't think that the change was affected in an instant. It had to be a gradual thing, a growth process. And growth can be slow and painful. We do not easily let go of old habits and attitudes.

People change when they are given hope; when someone believes in them, and gives them a task to do. Above all, they change when they are loved. They come out of their shells, and hidden energies are released in them. The miracle of human change is the only real miracle.

All of us have a capacity for goodness. We have hands that can care, eyes that can see, ears that can hear, tongues that can speak, feet that can walk, and above all hearts that can love. But each of us has some handicaps, which keep us from realising our true and full selves. We need someone to awaken us to what is inside us. Someone who will bid us live, and help us grow.

For us followers of Jesus, that someone is the Holy Spirit. The power that changed the apostles is available to us too, the gentle power of the Holy Spirit. The Spirit awakens us to the mysterious power within us, bids us live, and helps us grow. The poet Pablo Neruda said: 'I want to do with you what spring does with the cherry trees.' That's what the Spirit does.

PRAYER OF THE FAITHFUL

President: Let us pray for the coming of the Holy Spirit into our lives, into the Church, and into the world.

Response: Spirit of the living God, fall afresh on us.

Reader(s): For all Christians: that the Holy Spirit may gather all the followers of Jesus into the unity of the Body of Christ. [Pause] Let us pray.

For world leaders: that the Holy Spirit may guide and enlighten them in their work for justice and peace. [Pause] Let us pray.

For all those who mourn: that the Holy Spirit may dry their tears. [Pause] Let us pray.

For all gathered here: that the Holy Spirit may teach us wisdom and simplicity of heart. [Pause] Let us pray.

For our own special needs. [Longer pause] Let us pray.

President: God our Father, grant that the Holy Spirit may enlighten our minds, purify our hearts, and strengthen our wills, so that we may be recognised as true followers of Christ. We ask this through the same Christ our Lord.

SIGN OF PEACE

Lord Jesus Christ, on Pentecost Day you sent your Holy Spirit on your apostles, and with hearts on fire they went forth to preach the Gospel to the world. Send your Spirit into our world, to gather people of every race, language and way of life into the peace and unity of your kingdom where you live for ever and ever.

REFLECTION   **A new language**

On Pentecost day the apostles spoke a new language.
What was this new language?
It was the language of peace rather than of war;
the language of cooperation rather than of competition;
the language of forgiveness rather than of vengeance;

the language of hope rather than of despair;
the language of tolerance rather than of bigotry;
the language of friendship rather than of hostility;
the language of unity rather than of division;
the language of love rather than of hate.
Through the gift of the Spirit,
people of different languages learned to profess one faith,
to the praise and glory of God.
That is the real miracle of Pentecost,
and it is a miracle which, thankfully, still happens.

FEASTS OF THE LORD

Eucharistic Symbols

PHYLLIS BURKE

Trinity Sunday

INTRODUCTION AND CONFITEOR

The feast of the Blessed Trinity, which we celebrate today, brings us face to face with the mystery of God. We can know certain things about God by looking at creation. But it is Jesus who reveals to us the mystery of God. Sometimes we may so obsessed with God's creation that we forget about God himself. Let us reflect on that for a moment. [Pause]

Lord Jesus, you reveal God to us as a Father who cares for his children. Lord, have mercy.

Through the incarnation you have become a Brother to us. Christ, have mercy.

Through your gift of the Spirit, the love of God has been poured into our hearts. Lord, have mercy.

HEADINGS FOR READINGS

First Reading (Prov 8:22-31). This reading in praise of the wisdom of God can be seen as a groping towards the revelation of the mystery of the Trinity.

Second Reading (Rom 5:1-5). Christ made possible for us a relationship of love with God. This gives us the hope and sustains us in time of suffering. The Holy Spirit helps us to recognise the God's love for us.

Gospel (Jn 16:12-15). The Holy Spirit helps the Church to grasp the full meaning of all Jesus said, especially what he said about the Father.

SCRIPTURE NOTE

It biblical times it was common for wisdom to be personified. The reading from Proverbs looks to the role of Lady Wisdom in creation. This speculation about wisdom can be seen as a groping towards the revelation of the mystery of the Trinity. The Second Reading and the Gospel are chosen because they specifically mention the three Persons of the Blessed Trinity, and the role of each Person in our salvation.

Paul stresses the role of Christ in our salvation. Through him hostility and alienation are overcome, and we are able to enter into relationship with the Father. Therefore, we can hope to share God's glory. This sure hope will enable us to persevere in spite of suffering. Through the Holy Spirit God's love is poured into our hearts.

The Gospel stresses the role of the Spirit – carrying on in the Church the work of Jesus after Jesus has departed to the Father. There will be no new revelation. There can't be, because Jesus is *the* revelation of the Father. The role of the Spirit will be to spell out to successive generations the contemporary significance of what Jesus said and did.

HOMILY 1   **Seeing God**

There was a king who at the end of his life was beset by melancholy. He said, 'During my life I have experienced everything mortal man can experience with his senses. But there is still one thing I haven't seen. I haven't seen God. I would die happy if I could get just one glimpse of God.'

He consulted his wise men, and offered them all kinds of rewards if they could make his dream a reality, but they were unable to do so.

Then a shepherd heard of the king's plight. He came to see him and said, 'Perhaps I can help your Majesty.' The king was delighted and followed the shepherd into the hills. When he saw how poor the shepherd was he pitied him. As he went along he rubbed his eyes in anticipation of what he hoped to see. But the shepherd said to him, 'Your Majesty, if you wish to see God, it's not your eyes you have to purify but your heart.'

They stopped on a hilltop. Then, pointing towards the sun, the shepherd said, 'Look up!' The king raised his eyes and tried to look directly at the sun, but the glare dazzled him. 'Do you want to blind me?' he said. And the shepherd answered, 'But, my king, this is only part of creation, only a small reflection of the glory of God. How then can you expect to look at God with your weak and imperfect eyes? You must begin to search for him with eyes other than your physical ones.'

The king liked the idea and said, 'I thank you for having opened the eyes of my mind. Now answer another question: Where does God live?' The shepherd pointed once more to the sky. Above them birds were flying about. 'Look at these birds,' he said. 'See how they live surrounded by the air. In the same way we live surrounded by God. Stop searching. Open your eyes and look. Open your ears and listen. You can't miss him. Heaven is under our feet as well as over our heads.'

The king stopped and looked and listened. As he did so a peaceful expression came over his sad face. Then the shepherd added, 'There is one other thing, your Majesty.' With that he led him to a well. He stood there looking into its calm deep water in silence. 'Who lives down there?' asked the king. 'God does,' the shepherd answered. 'Can I see him?.' 'Sure. Just take a look.'

The king gazed intently down into the well. But all he saw was his own reflection in the water. Then he raised his head and said, 'But all I see is me'. 'Now your Majesty knows where God lives. He lives in you.'

The king realised that this simple shepherd was wiser and richer than he was. He thanked him and returned to his palace. No one knew if he had seen God, but all could tell that something had happened to his heart. This was evident from the kindly way he dealt with even the least of his servants.

God is all around us. But until we discover him within us, he will always be remote from us, and appear unfriendly and uncaring. When we have experienced God within us, loneliness will never be a big problem for us, because we will know that we are never alone. And we will see creation as the work of an Artist who is a friend of ours.

One God in three persons, a God who is within us and yet utterly beyond us. This is a great mystery, but it is a mystery of love.

HOMILY 2   **Images of God**

There is an African story about God which goes like this. One day, as he travelled up and down the vast continent, God noticed that one particular tribe was losing its faith. So he manifested himself in a field where four men were working, one in each corner. The men saw God standing there in the centre of the field, looked closely at him, and then fell to the ground in adoration.

God then vanished but watched what ensued. The four men ran back to their village, assembled all the people, and proclaimed that there could be no doubt: God truly existed, and cared for them, since he had come down to visit them. Hence, they should all start worshipping him in earnest. The people received the news enthusiastically. They could see that these men had had a holy vision. Then one of the villagers asked, 'What was God wearing?'

'He was wearing a red cloak,' the first man answered.

'No, he was wearing a blue cloak,' said the second.

'You're both wrong,' said the third. 'It was a green cloak.'

'You're all crazy,' shouted the fourth. 'He was wearing a yellow cloak.'

And with that they started to argue. The argument turned into a fight. In the end they despised and hated one another, and split up into four factions.

With a little reflection, they might easily have reached agreement. Each had been given a glimpse of God. Instead of insisting that each had the complete vision, they might have admitted that each had only a partial vision. Had they been open to the other person's point of view, they could have ended up with a larger and richer image of God.

God is greater than us all. We can never fully comprehend God. We struggle to understand even earthly things. So how can we grasp heavenly things? Only the gift of wisdom can help us to understand the ways of God. People can know the truths of the faith and yet not know God.

It is very important to have a correct image of God. If we get this wrong, everything else will be out of focus. How can we pray properly, or how can we have a proper relationship with God, if we have a false or inadequate image of him? The Christian sees life as a response to God's love.

To tell what God is like, all we have to do is look at Jesus. In the words of St Paul, 'He is the image of the invisible God.' What is Jesus like? Of all the images we have of Jesus, one of the loveliest is that of the Good Shepherd. It was Jesus himself who used it. Jesus is the Good Shepherd, who gave his life for his sheep. In Jesus we see the Father's love for us. And what of the Holy Spirit? The Holy Spirit is the bond of love between the Father and the Son, and between them and us.

The mystery of the Trinity is not something to argue about or even study. It is more something to pray about and to live. The Christian lives in the world of the Father, the Son, and the Spirit. This world is not somewhere in outer space. It is the same world of every day. As the African story shows us, that is where God manifests himself to us.

HOMILY 3   **A sense of God**

Faith is not some kind of autosuggestion. It is the grace of a mysterious encounter with Someone. It is beyond reasoning and emotion, but these may be present too. We can grasp God with our minds and with our senses. In fact, with our whole being. We are talking not just about an intellectual conviction about God, but a sense of God – a feeling. What a wonderful experience that is.

The Russian writer, Tolstoy, tells how one night he was praying to God in his bedroom, in front of the Greek icon of the Virgin. The vigil lamp was burning. Then he went out onto the balcony. The night was pitch-dark, and the sky was swarming with stars – faint stars, bright stars, a maze of stars. There was a sparkle in the heavens, and on earth dark shadows and the silhouettes of dead trees. He says:

> It was a marvellous night. How can one fail to believe in the immortality of the soul when one feels such immeasurable grandeur in one's own? I could die. And I heard an inner voice say to me: 'He is here. Kneel to him, and be silent.'

Happy those who have a sense of God and of his presence in their lives. It is the only riches worth having. As one person said, 'Lord, I don't need to believe in you. It's not a matter of belief any more. I just know it.'

When people know something, really know it deep down in their hearts, they don't have to argue about it, or prove it. They just know it, and that's enough. Faith is truly a gift of God. One believes with the heart, without knowing why or even seeking to know. The intimate certitude that fills one is enough.

When we have a sense of God's presence in the world, we need no longer feel alone in the world. We can look with admiration and love at creation as the work of an Artist who is a friend of ours.

It is a great blessing to experience God's presence in the world, but it is a still greater blessing to experience God's presence within us. It took the great St Augustine a lifetime to learn this. He wrote:

> Late have I loved you, O beauty ever ancient, ever new, late have I

loved you. You were within me, but I was outside, and it was there that I searched for you. In my unloveliness I plunged into the lovely things you created. You were with me, but I was not with you. Created things kept me from you; yet if they had not been in you, they would have no being at all. Why do I ask you to come to me when, unless you were with me, I would have no being either.

We meet God not just in the world outside us, but in the world within us, and find that he is closer to us than we suspected. He is part of us. In the words of St Paul: 'In him we live and move and have our being.' (Acts 17:28)

God is everywhere present yet nowhere visible. He is like a biographer whose job is to tell the story while staying in the background.

For many the silence of God is a big problem. But 'a loud and evident God would be a bully, an insecure tyrant, instead of, as he is, a bottomless encouragement to our faltering and frightened being. His answers come in the long run, as the large facts of our lives, strung on that thread running through all things.' (John Updike)

God is the only one to whom we can surrender without losing ourselves.

ANOTHER STORY

Isaac Newton was one of the greatest mathematicians and scientists that ever lived. Yet towards the end of his life he said of his achievements:

> I do not know what I appear to the world, but to myself I appear to have been like a little boy playing on the seashore, and diverting myself in now and then finding a smoother pebble or a prettier shell than ordinary, whilst the great ocean of truth lay all undiscovered before me.

Even when we think we understand the mystery of God, we are still only beginning. We are still only children playing on the shore. The mystery grows instead of diminishing with each new discovery.

Some people want to know everything, to explain everything, break everything down to facts. But it is exciting to live with mystery. Albert Einstein said, 'The most beautiful experience we can have is that of the mysterious.' Even with faith, the mystery, the darkness, the unknowable remain. The whole of life is not visible to us. As Van Gogh said, 'Here on earth we see only one hemisphere.'

PRAYER OF THE FAITHFUL

President: As we pray to the Father for our needs, we pray in the name of Jesus, the Son, and confident that the Spirit prays with us.

Response: Lord, graciously hear us.

Reader(s): For all Christians: that they may be united in praising and honouring the Father, the Son, and the Holy Spirit. [Pause] Lord, hear us.

For all peoples: that they may see themselves as one family under God. [Pause] Lord, hear us.

For all those who are searching for God. [Pause] Lord, hear us.

For those who have become disconnected from God. [Pause] Lord, hear us.

For this congregation: that we may see God as a God of love who is always near us, inspiring us to love one another. [Pause] Lord, hear us.

For our own special needs. [Longer pause] Lord, hear us.

President: Father, in your gentle mercy, guide our wayward hearts, for we know that left to ourselves we cannot do your will. We ask this through Christ our Lord.

REFLECTION   **God is watching over us**

Nowadays, thanks to the security camera,
we are often being watched,
watched by a cold, dispassionate eye,
intent only on catching us in wrong-doing.
The feeling that someone is watching us
is not a pleasant feeling.
But the feeling that someone is watching over us
is a lovely feeling.
God is not watching us.
God is watching over us.
The conviction that God is watching over us
gives us comfort in times of sadness,
strength in times of weakness,
and hope in times of despair.

The Body and Blood of Christ

INTRODUCTION AND CONFITEOR

We are the People of God journeying in faith towards the Promised Land of eternal life. We need food for our journey. We receive this food in the Eucharist. Here we are fed with food far more precious than the manna which sustained the Israelites in the desert. Here Christ nourishes us with the word of God and the bread of eternal life. [Pause]

Lord Jesus, you nourish our minds with the bread of faith. Lord, have mercy.

You nourish our spirits with the bread of hope. Christ, have mercy.

You nourish our hearts with the bread of love. Lord, have mercy.

HEADINGS FOR READINGS

First Reading (Gen 14:18-20). Melchizedek, a pagan priest-king, gives gifts of bread and wine to Abraham. In Christian tradition that bread and wine were taken to prefigure the Eucharist.

Second Reading (1 Cor 11:23-26). When we celebrate the Eucharist we do not merely make Christ present, but re-enact the death by which he saved us.

Gospel (Lk 9:11-17). Jesus provides an extraordinary meal for those who followed him into the desert. In the Eucharist the Church continues the mission of Jesus – teaching , healing and nourishing God's People.

SCRIPTURE NOTE

The First Reading tells how Melchizedek, king of Salem (early name for Jerusalem), comes to greet Abraham. Melchizedek is also a priest. As such he brings an offering of bread and wine to Abraham, and pronounces a blessing over him. In Christian tradition that bread and wine were taken to prefigure the bread and wine of the Eucharist.

Paul's account of the institution of the Eucharist is the earliest written account of the origin of the Eucharist (Second Reading). When we celebrate the Eucharist not merely is Christ present, but we re-enact the death by which he saved us. The Eucharist not only looks to the past, but also looks forward to the fulfilment of the Kingdom.

The eucharistic significance of the multiplication of the loaves is brought out by the use of liturgical language. Luke uses the same words here as at the Last Supper and at Emmaus: Jesus 'took … blessed … broke … gave …' In the Eucharist the Church continues the mission of Jesus to teach, to heal, and to nourish the people of God.

HOMILY 1   **The nourishment Jesus gives us**

Jesus had at least two good reasons why he might have sent those people away. Firstly, Herod (who had already murdered his cousin, John) was expressing an interest in him. So it was surely a time for keeping a low profile. And secondly, the apostles needed a break, having just returned from a mission.

But he didn't send them away. He looked at them with compassion, and saw that they were like sheep without a shepherd. So he gathered them around him. Picture Jesus surrounded by over five thousand people. They were drawn by the magnetism of his words and the warmth of his personality. The first thing he did was to teach them about the Kingdom of heaven. Then he healed the sick.

By the time he had finished it was late afternoon and everybody was hungry. The apostles urged him to send the people away. But he wouldn't hear of sending them away. He worked a great miracle to feed them. How happy they must have been as they made their way back to their homes.

The miracle of the multiplication of the loaves, when the Lord said the blessing, broke and distributed the loaves through his disciples to feed the multitude, prefigured the superabundance of the unique bread he gives us in the Eucharist.

On the first day of the week, the day of Jesus' resurrection, the early Christians met 'to break bread'. From that time on down to our own day, the celebration of the Eucharist has been continued so that today we encounter it everywhere in the Church with the same fundamental structure. It remains the centre of the Church's life.

We are the new People of God. Jesus is in our midst. Here, we hear his voice when the Scriptures are read. His words are not dead words. They are living words which console, inspire and challenge us.

Then, here Jesus heals the wounds of sin and division. He forgives our sins and heals the wounds they leave. He also heals us of our isolationism. We are all healed of our selfishness and indifference to others. The Eucharist forms us into a community of love.

Finally, here we are nourished by the food of the Eucharist. 'Unless you eat my flesh and drink my blood you shall not have life in you.' (Jn 6:53) At the end of Mass we are not simply dismissed, but sent forth as bearers of life to others.

Thus from celebration to celebration, as they proclaim the paschal mystery of Jesus 'until he comes', the pilgrim People of God advance towards the heavenly banquet, when all the elect will be seated at the table of the kingdom.

An elderly Peruvian woman, unable to read or write, on being asked, 'What does the Mass mean to you?' replied, 'The Mass tells me that I matter.'

HOMILY 2 **In memory of me**

At one time or another, all of us have been ignored or passed over. This can be very painful. We feel that our work is not recognised, and we ourselves are treated as if we didn't really count.

But something worse can happen to us than to be ignored. We could be forgotten. This is even more painful. It is to be treated not just as of little account, but of no account at all. It is as if we didn't exist.

We all pine to be remembered. It is said that people do not fear death so much as the possibility of being forgotten. To be forgotten is to be treated as if you were of no significance, that you didn't matter to anyone. It's as if you never existed.

Jesus too wanted to be remembered. The night before he died, as he sat at table with his friends, he took bread and said, 'This is my body given for you.' Then he took the cup filled with wine and said, 'This is the cup of my blood ... Do this in memory of me.'

Of course, Jesus was not just thinking of his own need to be remembered. He was thinking also about his disciples. They too needed to remember him. In his love for them he left them a special way of remembering him, namely, the Eucharist.

Every time we celebrate the Eucharist we recall some of the wonderful things he said and did. We reflect on them and try to apply them to our lives. But the Eucharist is more wonderful still.

When we remember him in this way, he becomes present to us. Not physically present, but nevertheless really present.

Through the Eucharist a spiritual bond is forged between us, with the result that we are able to enter into a deeper intimacy with him than if he were physically present. We are not merely in communication with him, but in communion with him, a holy communion.

Memory is a precious faculty. It connects us with people and events that are no longer present to us. If we cherish the memory of our loved ones, they become present to us. They are not just a memory but a real presence, a presence we feel rather than see. By remembering them we continue to reap a harvest from what they sowed while among us.

How much more fruitful it is to remember Jesus, especially in the way he asked to be remembered.

HOMILY 3   **On the night he was betrayed**

The night before he died, Jesus sat down to table with his apostles. The small group gathered around a table suggests closeness, intimacy, warmth, trust, love. But if betrayal enters into a scene such as this it cuts deeper, it hurts more. When rifts occur among people who are very close, they are harder to deal with than with people who are not so close.

Judas was present. Why did he show up at the Last Supper when he had already made up his mind to betray Jesus? He probably wanted to give the impression that everything was normal, and thus Jesus would not suspect anything.

Paul's account of that Last Supper is the oldest we have in the New Testament. He says: 'On the same night that he was betrayed, the Lord Jesus took some bread, thanked God for it and said, "This is my body, which is for you; do this as a memorial of me." '

One phrase jumps out at us. The phrase is: 'On the night he was betrayed'. On that night of all nights. Instead of cutting the apostles off, he gave them a sign of his love: he sat down to an intimate supper with them. Then he said, 'Do this in memory of me.' This is how they were to remember him. On this night when one of their number betrayed him.

We mustn't think that Jesus wasn't hurt by Judas' betrayeal. He was hurt, and hurt deeply by it. St John says that when he began to talk about the traitor, 'he was deeply distressed.' And no wonder. He had personally chosen and trained Judas. Judas had heard his teaching and witnessed his miracles. He was one of the inner circle. Yet now he was about to betray him. The treachery of a friend is much more hurtful and difficult to deal with than the treachery of an enemy.

Betrayal is very hard to deal with. However, those who have been betrayed can take comfort from the fact that Jesus knows how they feel. They do not have to pretend that they are not affected by it. Jesus showed how hurt he was, and talked openly about it. What matters is how we deal with the hurt. It could make us bitter and tempt us to retaliate.

In spite of feeling hurt, Jesus did not hit back at Judas. He refused even to expose him in front of the others. But in giving him a morsel of bread (a gesture of friendship), he let him know he was aware of what he was planning. In refusing to point the finger at him, he left the door open for him to return to the fold.

What Judas did hurt the other apostles too. After all, he was one of themselves. They had trusted him, and shared everything with him. They thought they knew him, and yet he turned out to be a traitor. In betraying Jesus he betrayed them too.

We do not remember this night for Judas' betrayal. We remember it for the gift that Jesus left us despite that betrayal. The Eucharist should help us to recover from any betrayals we have suffered at the hands of others. And it should help us to avoid betraying anyone else.

PRAYER OF THE FAITHFUL

President: In celebrating the Eucharist we are doing what the Lord commanded us to do. Let us now pray for the things we need in order to be worthy disciples of him.

Response: Lord, graciously hear us.

Reader(s): For the Church: that the Eucharist may form its members into a community of love. [Pause] Lord, hear us.

For well-off countries: that they may share with the poor countries, so that none of God's children will go hungry. [Pause] Lord, hear us.

For those who have been let down by others and who are hurt and bitter as a result. [Pause] Lord, hear us.

For all gathered here: that we who share in the one bread of life may be filled with Christlike love. [Pause] Lord, hear us.

For our own special needs. [Longer pause] Lord, hear us.

President: God of power and love, fill our hearts with your love. Give us the grace to rise above our human weakness, and keep us faithful to you and to one another. We ask this through Christ our Lord.

SIGN OF PEACE

Lord Jesus Christ, the night before you died, you said to your disciples: 'I am the vine, you are the branches; separated from me you can do nothing; united with me you will bear much fruit.' Strengthen the bonds that unite us with you and with one another, so that we may enjoy the peace and unity of your kingdom where you live for ever and ever.

REFLECTION   **Remembering**

Jesus said to his apostles: 'Do this in memory of me.'
We all love to be remembered.
This was true even for Jesus.
But if we want to be remembered,
we have a duty also to remember.
Memory is a powerful thing.
Wrongly used it brings death;
rightly used it brings life,
and is a form of immortality.
It keeps the past alive.
Those we remember never die;
they continue to walk and talk with us.
Lord, when we celebrate the Eucharist
we are remembering you.
May that remembering bring us life here and hereafter.

SUNDAYS OF THE YEAR

The Good Samaritan

BENEDICT TUTTY

Second Sunday of the Year
CANA

At a wedding in Cana Jesus changed water into wine. There are many things in our spiritual lives that should be changed. Jesus' power is available to us too. Let us reflect on our need of his power in order to change the things in our lives that need to be changed. [Pause]

Lord Jesus, you change fear into trust. Lord, have mercy.

You change weakness into strength. Christ, have mercy.

You change selfishness into love. Lord, have mercy.

HEADINGS FOR READINGS

First Reading (Is 62:1-5). We hear of a new wedding feast between God and his people.

Second Reading (1 Cor 12:4-11). Though there are many spiritual gifts, they all come from the same Spirit, and should be used for building up the community.

Gospel (Jn 2:1-12). Jesus fulfils the prophecy of Isaiah. The changing of water into wine is a symbol of the old order yielding to the new.

SCRIPTURE NOTE

The First Reading contains a message of hope for God's people at one of the lowest moments in their history. Jerusalem lay in ruins. The city's plight reflected that of the nation as a whole. Israel, once God's bride, was now like a widow bereft of children. However, her husband, God, has not forgotten her. There will be a new wedding feast, and God and his people will be like newlyweds again.

This prophecy was fulfilled in Jesus, who replaced the old order with the new. This is symbolised by the changing of water into wine. (Gospel). The miracle of Cana links this Sunday with the feast of the Epiphany and with Jesus' Baptism – all are epiphanies of his glory.

John depicts Mary as involved at the beginning of Jesus' ministry, and again at the end of it when she is present at the foot of the Cross. Mary is thus associated with the whole of his ministry. But her role must always be seen in relation to that of her Son.

HOMILY 1   **The wedding feast of the Kingdom**

If we take the miracle of Cana literally, we reduce it to a once-off wonder and greatly limit its meaning. It's not really about the power to change water into wine. We already know how to do that – it happens every year in our vineyards and wineries. The miracle has a deeper and broader meaning, and one that is valid for all time. It's about something far more wonderful.

In attempting to describe the relationship between God and his people, the Bible uses the image of a bridegroom and his bride. And in describing the joy God finds among his people, it uses the image of a wedding feast.

The First Reading contains a message of hope for God's people at one of the lowest moments in their history. Jerusalem lay in ruins and many of the people were exiled in Babylon. Israel, once God's bride, is now like a widow bereft of children. However, her husband, God, has not forgotten her. There will be a new wedding feast. God will restore his people.

This promise was fulfilled in the return from exile, but more especially in the coming of Jesus. It's no surprise to find that Jesus started his public ministry at a wedding feast. At that wedding the wine ran out. This was a way of saying that the old religion, the old observances, had been found wanting. The time has come for the promises to be fulfilled. The time has come for a new law and a new spirit.

The prophets had foretold an abundance of wine in messianic days. At Cana Jesus provided just that. And all those who tasted the new agreed that it was better than the old. We note the sheer generosity of the miracle. Those six jars were capable of holding somewhere between twenty and thirty gallons each. We see not only Jesus' power, but also his generosity. We get a glimpse of the warmth of his heart. The new order began with an act of compassion.

What Jesus did at Cana was not a once-off thing. It pointed to what would happen all through his ministry. The changing of water into wine is a symbol for what he was about. Everywhere he went the old was made new. For the widow of Nain he changed tears into joy. For Zacchaeus he changed selfishness into love. For the thief on Calvary he changed despair into hope. And on Easter morning he changed death into life.

His presence could change beyond recognition the lives of those with whom he came into contact. And he continues to do this for those who believe in him and follow him. He transforms our lives into something wonderful. He offers us something that we pine for but can't achieve on our own. He offers us a share in the divine life – nothing less than the ecstasy of communion with God. But all of this will remain at the level of theory unless we experience it in our lives, unless in some way in our own lives Jesus changes water into wine.

Water is a good thing and essential for bodily survival. However, though it gives satisfaction it doesn't give joy. Wine, on the other hand, intoxicates and raises the spirit.

Blessed are those who thirst for the new 'wine' that Jesus provides. The old is the promise; the new is the fulfilment. Material things are not enough. Jesus brings another dimension to life. He brings a joy which the world cannot give.

He asked the servants to draw out the water/wine and take it to the steward. Jesus always used human intermediaries to convey his gifts. He asks us to share with others the gifts he has shared with us.

HOMILY 2   **When the wine runs out**

What happened at Cana happens sooner or later in every marriage – the wine runs out. What do we mean by this?

The typical marriage starts off with a feast of joy and enthusiasm. The couple are surrounded by friends and well-wishers who shower them with gifts. Full of hopes and dreams, they set off on their honeymoon. The wine is flowing freely.

They come back from the honeymoon and the real business begins – setting up a home and learning to live with one another. At first they find great joy in each other's company. They are convinced that their love was preordained in heaven and meant to last for eternity. The wine is still flowing.

But when human beings are very close to one another problems inevitably occur. Tensions arise. They discover that they did not marry an angel after all, but a human being wounded by sin and selfishness. They are surprised at the poverty they discover in one another. The honeymoon is over. The wine has run out. All that is left is the 'water' of their own meagre resources.

Much the same thing happens in careers, professions, and even in vocations such as the priesthood and religious life. The wine runs out there too. The first joy, enthusiasm and idealism ebb. And all that remains is the 'water' of routine, dullness, and possible disillusionment. But let us stay with marriage.

Now that the first wine has run out, what are they to do? Some are tempted to run out with the wine: 'There's nothing in it for me any longer.' While this attitude sounds reasonable, it implies a terrible selfishness. For such people marriage is only a passing alliance of two selfish human beings. So when they have taken all they can from each other, they begin to look elsewhere for more fruit that can be picked and eaten without pain or effort.

But what can a couple do? They must acknowledge that the first wine has run out. For the moment they will have to make do with water. But let them not panic or despair when it happens. They must hold on. They must resist the temptation to abandon the relationship and lose themselves in a career or a hectic social life. What they have to do is work on their relationship through which they can grow as human beings and discover the real meaning of love. The crisis can become an opportunity.

And here is a surprising thing: it is necessary that the first wine should run out. Otherwise the new wine can't come in. First love, however romantically beautiful it is, cannot last. It is bound to wear out. But this is not a bad thing. In fact, it has to wear out if a new and deeper love is to be born. The new love consists in putting the other person before oneself. One has to forget oneself and find joy in loving rather than in being loved, in giving rather than in receiving.

Love is a difficult adventure. To enter marriage is to enter a school of love, a school in which all are slow learners. That is why we need the presence of Christ.

The new wine is meant not just for married couples but for everyone. The new wine cannot be put into old wineskins. This means we have to change. Christ has to touch our hearts and help us to love unselfishly. For those who seek his help, the miracle of Cana still happens – the water of selfishness is changed into the wine of true love. And wonderful as the old wine was, the new wine is still better.

HOMILY 3   **Mary: model of ministry**

St John depicts Mary as involved at the beginning of Jesus' ministry (at Cana), and again at the end of it (on Calvary). Mary is thus associated with the whole of his ministry. A look at the Gospels shows that she was involved at all the key moments in his life.

At the Annunciation she was asked if she would become the mother of the Saviour. She set aside her own plans, and said a generous 'yes' to what God asked. Ministry sometimes means being willing to set our own plans aside, and to answer a call to lend a hand.

At the Visitation she took the initiative. On hearing that her elderly cousin, Elizabeth, was expecting a baby, she visited her, staying until her child was born. Ministry sometimes means taking the initiative – seeing a need, and responding to it.

At Cana we see Mary's sensitivity. She noticed that the wine had run out, threatening to ruin the occasion for the young couple. She wanted to help them, but realised that she couldn't do it herself. So she turned to her Son and asked him to help, which he did with great generosity. Ministry at times means noticing a need, but realising that we can't handle it ourselves. So we have to refer it to others who can. This is not the same as passing the buck.

During his public life Jesus was surrounded by crowds. Mary didn't understand what he was about. She feared that he was being taken over. As a mother, she felt compelled to rescue him. But he declined to be rescued. She had misread the situation. He was in control. He had a job to do, and was capable of handling himself. Ministry can involve making mistakes and experiencing frustration and failure. But this is not due to a lack of concern, but to a lack of understanding.

On Calvary Mary stood at the foot of the cross, watching Jesus die. Though she desperately wanted to save him, she was powerless to do so. Sometimes in ministry there is nothing we can do. So our only ministry is like that of Mary at the foot of the cross – a silent, supportive presence. A reassuring, supportive presence can mean the world to the sufferer. It saves him/her from the awful prospect of dying alone and abandoned.

These are only glimpses. But a picture emerges of Mary – that of a caring person. In many ways, a typical mother. Mary is a model of ministry. But her role must always be seen in relation to that of her Son. Her role now is that of a mother caring for those who would follow him.

All of us are in ministry in one way or another: towards one another, in our families, in the wider community. Even the work that we do can be seen as a ministry, a service. While women seem to have a special gift, all of us have the capability.

Ministry may mean giving things (like at Cana), but more often it is about giving of ourselves. We must be ready for frustration, misunderstanding, failure, powerlessness. But the only thing we have to fear is indifference. No particular skills are needed. At the end of the day, it comes down to love. Ministry is an expression of love.

In ministry what we are doing is what the servants did at Cana. They were just the agents of Jesus. They drew out the water that had turned into wine and gave it to the guests. Ever since, Christ's ministers have been drawing out of the same source. They have been sharing the gifts of Jesus to his Church and to the world. From his fullness we continue to receive and to share.

PRAYER OF THE FAITHFUL

President: Jesus brought joy to the wedding guests at Cana by turning water into wine. Let us bring our needs before him with confidence.

Response: Lord, hear us in your love.

Reader(s): For the Pope, the bishops, and all who exercise any ministry in the Church: that they may see themselves as agents of Christ's love and compassion. [Pause] Let us pray in faith.

For all those who hold public office in our society: that they may be agents of truth, justice and peace. [Pause] Let us pray in faith.

For all married couples: that they may taste the new wine of unselfish love. [Pause] Let us pray in faith.

For couples who are experiencing difficulty in their marriages. [Pause] Let us pray in faith.

For those who have never known the wine of love and joy in their lives. [Pause] Let us pray in faith.

For the faithful departed: that they may be admitted to the wedding feast of eternal life. [Pause] Let us pray in faith.

For our own special needs. [Longer Pause] Let us pray in faith.

President: God of love and mercy, may we experience your Son's presence in our lives, so that when our own efforts are not enough, he may support us with his grace. We ask this through the same Christ our Lord.

REFLECTION   **Water into wine**

Jesus brought the wine of God's love into the world.
Everywhere he went the old was made new.
For the couple at Cana he changed water into wine.
For the widow of Nain he changed tears into joy.
For Zacchaeus he changed selfishness into love.
For the thief on Calvary he changed despair into hope.
And on Easter morning he changed death into life.
Lord, be present with us today and throughout our lives.
And when through human weakness
the wine of love is found wanting,
touch our hearts and strengthen our wills,
so that we may taste the wine of unselfish love.

Third Sunday of the Year
FULFILLED IN YOUR HEARING

INTRODUCTION AND CONFITEOR

Jesus began his ministry by making his own the words of Isaiah: 'He sent me to bring good news to the poor.' The good news is that God's mercy is freely available to all those who seek it. Let us not be afraid then to admit our sinfulness and poverty before God, for Jesus made himself the friend of sinners and the poor. [Pause]

I confess to almighty God ...

HEADINGS FOR READINGS

First Reading (Nehemiah 8:2-6.8-10). After the Jews returned from exile in Babylon, Ezra sought to re-establish the Jewish religion. Here he reads the book of the law of Moses to the people.

Second Reading (I Cor 12:12-30). Just as the human body is one though made up of many parts, so the Church, though composed of different members with different gifts, forms a unity in Christ.

Gospel (Lk 1:1-4; 4:14-21). God's promises are fulfilled in Jesus, the long-awaited Saviour of the poor and the oppressed.

SCRIPTURE NOTE

Today we begin the consecutive reading of Luke's Gospel, which was originally joined to Luke's other work, the Acts of the Apostles. The way the story is told prepares us for what happens in Acts.

When the Jews returned home after the exile in Babylon, the nation had to be rebuilt. The Persians entrusted this task to Ezra. Ezra brought back with him from Babylon the book of the law of Moses which he solemnly read to the people (First Reading). Thus he called upon them to rededicate themselves to God.

The Gospel shows Jesus too proclaiming the word of God. In the synagogue at Nazareth, he makes his own a passage from Isaiah, and uses it to announce a programme for his ministry. He is sent, not to the wealthy or the powerful, but to the poor and the lowly, the oppressed and the suffering. Here we see Luke's concern for the poor and the afflicted.

Who are the poor? The poor are all the dispossessed of this world, all those who are waiting for liberation. The good news must not be limited to spiritual blessings only. But the poor are also those who live on bread alone and who never hear the Word of God.

HOMILY 1 **A day of the Lord's favour**

When prime ministers are taking office they make a solemn speech in which they outline their policies. Jesus did something similar at the start of his ministry. In the synagogue at Nazareth he read a passage from Isaiah which summed up his mission. He announced that the long-awaited 'Day of the Lord' had come at last, and that it would be a day of favour for everyone, but especially for the poor and the oppressed. The following story tries to show just how wonderful that announcement was.

Once there was a landlord whose tenants fell into arrears with the rent. Pretty soon they found themselves entangled in a web of squalor and debt. They saw no way out of their predicament. Now the landlord was a kind and patient man. Even so, the tenants wondered how much time he would give them to pay up. The awful thing was that even if he gave them till doomsday, they would not be able to do so.

Then a new chief bailiff appeared on the scene and began to make his rounds. During his rounds, the bailiff asked each one how much he owed. But, surprisingly, he didn't leave it at that. He visited their homes. He enquired about what they ate. He asked about the old, the sick and the disabled. He acquainted himself with their problems and worries.

Then one day he called them all together, saying that he had a very important message from the landlord for them. The tenants assembled in fear and trepidation, convinced that the dreaded day of reckoning had finally arrived. The tenants knew, or thought they did, the speech he was about to deliver.

He was going to say: 'In the course of my rounds I have discovered that every single one of you is up to his eyes in debt. You have no one to blame but yourselves. You're a bunch of lazy, good-for-nothings. The landlord is fed up with you. He has given you umpteen chances, and still you have failed to come up with the goods. You have left him with no option but to take the land away from you and give it to others who will pay their rent.'

This is what they were expecting him to say, though in their heart of hearts they were longing for something else. Then he began to speak:

'The landlord knows that all of you have run into serious debt. He asked me to deliver the following message to you.' He paused. They waited for the blow to fall, and braced themselves against it. 'Well,' he resumed, 'I've got good news for you.' Again he paused.

Good news! They couldn't believe what they were hearing. 'The landlord has asked me to tell you that you can forget about your debts. He is wiping the slate clean. From this day you can start all over again.'

Shouts of joy went up. The tenants embraced one another. Some began to sing and dance, things they hadn't done for a long time. As they made their way home with light hearts, they noticed for the first time in years that the sun was shining, birds were singing, and fragrant flowers were blooming in the fields.

Such was the good news announced by Jesus in the synagogue at Nazareth. He was the new bailiff sent by God to his debt-ridden people. According to the Pharisees, the Day of the Lord would be a day of judgement. And here was Jesus declaring that it was a day of the Lord's favour, not just for the deserving, but for everyone.

The Lord's favour is not limited to a particular day. It can fall upon us any day. Yes, even this very day it can be fulfilled for us.

The Good News is that salvation is not achieved through our own merits, but through the goodness of God. This is the heart of the Good News. The only thing to be done is to open our hearts to the Saviour who has come to bring us salvation and joy.

Jesus didn't merely announce the Good News and leave it at that. He began to make it a reality. At the root of innumerable wrongs in our world is the discrepancy between word and deed. It is the weakness of Churches, parties and persons. This was the chief fault Jesus found with the Pharisees: 'They do not practise what they preach.' 'My life is my message,' said Gandhi. And so it was with Jesus. And so it could be with us.

HOMILY 2   **The book**

When the Jews returned home after a half-century of exile in Babylon, the nation had to be rebuilt. Ezra called on the people to to rededicate themselves to God. He began by reading to them the book of the law of Moses.

From his time on, the life and religion of Jews was based on strict adherence to the Law. As Christians we too are a people of 'the book', except in our case the book is the book of the Gospels.

There is a story about a people who had never heard of the Gospel. One day a stranger arrived and announced, 'I came to bring you the good news.' Unfortunately he contracted a disease and died before he could tell them what he meant. They found a small book in his rucksack. The title read: *The Good News of Our Lord Jesus Christ*. They concluded that this is what the stranger was talking about. They began to read it.

Though the book was old, its message sounded brand-new. The central character leaped out at them from its musty pages – a man full of vitality, yet possessing great gentleness and compassion. They read accounts of miracles he performed on behalf of sick and needy people. They read how he went out of his way to associate with outcasts. The beauty and authority of his words made a deep impression on them. What a strange and fascinating book!

'What a pity the carrier of the book died,' someone said. 'Obviously he was a follower of this Christ.'

'But there must be more where he came from,' another said. 'Could we not send someone there to see how the people live this new teaching? Then he could come back, make a report, and perhaps we could try it ourselves?'

They chose Francis, a young man of deep integrity. He travelled widely and observed keenly. He went out of his way to meet as wide a cross-section of people as possible. He didn't jump to conclusions or rush to judgement. Finally the day came when he felt he had seen enough, so he headed for home. No sooner had he arrived back than he was bombarded with questions:

'Do the adherents of The Book love one another?'

'Do they live in peace with one another?'

'Do they live simply?'

'Are they happy?'

But all the questions could be reduced to one: 'Do the followers of Christ live according to The Book?' Here, in summary, is the account he gave them of his findings.

'Basically I found five kinds of Christians. Firstly, I found some who are Christian in name only. Even though they were baptised, they adhere to none of the observances of Christianity, and have no commitment to it.

'Secondly, I found some who are Christian by habit only. Even though they are committed to the outward observances, it doesn't affect the way they live. As far as I could see, they live according to principles that have nothing to do with the teachings of The Book, and in many cases are contrary to it.

'Thirdly, I found some who are clearly devoted to the Christian faith. They are engaged in good works. Yet a vital element seems to be missing. They seem to possess few, if any, of the qualities which made their Master so appealing.

'Fourthly, I found some whom you might call practical Christians. It seemed to me that these have grasped the heart of what The Book is about. They are clearly concerned about other people, and are not ashamed to be seen to be Christians. In some places I saw them being persecuted. In other places I saw them meeting something which is probably worse – the deadly indifference of their fellow citizens.

'Lastly, I met some, admittedly not many, whom I would have no hesitation in calling the genuine article. They are deeply spiritual people. In meeting them I felt I was meeting Christ himself.'

The story doesn't tell us whether or not those people accepted the Gospel. Today the task of preaching the Gospel to the world depends on us. It's a great privilege but a daunting task. But like Jesus, we are given the help of the Holy Spirit. The best way to preach the Gospel is by living a Christian life. The only book some people will ever read about the Gospel is the book of our lives.

HOMILY 3   **The Church is the Body of Christ**

Today in medicine there is so much specialisation that the body tends to be broken up into parts. Some doctors specialise in the heart, others in the brain, others in the eye, others in the ear, and so on. Specialisation is good but it can have a downside. Specialists may be concerned only with organs, not with human beings. They may know scarcely anything about the person whose eye or heart or hip they are treating.

The human body forms a unity even though it is composed of many members. Those members are very different from one another and have very different functions. Some undoubtedly are more important than others. Yet to be complete the body needs all of them, and the members need each other.

So it is with the Church. We though many form one body in Christ (Second Reading). By means of our baptism we have become members of the Body of Christ, the Church. Some might wish to go it alone, independent of the community. But there can be no such thing as an isolated Christian. Those who deliberately cut themselves off wound the community. We are part of one another and must not try to go it alone.

Community makes demands on us. For this reason, the temptation to go it alone, to seek salvation independent of others, is strong. But this cannot be. We need each other, just as the parts of the body need each other. And the Church needs all of us. We need to have a sense of belonging to one another and to Christ. We have to get involved even when we would rather just look after ourselves.

Belonging to a community has obvious benefits. Take reeds for an example. Individually they are weak and easily broken. But tie a bundle of them together, and they are virtually unbreakable. So it is with people. Great strength results from togetherness. People take courage from knowing each other, encouraging each other, and from standing together. Great things can be done when people work together.

The emphasis on community comes from Jesus himself, only he used a different image to describe it. He used the image of a vine and its branches: 'I am the vine, you are the branches.' It is a simple but profound illustration of unity and interdependence.

It's obvious that the branches need the vine. But the vine also needs the branches, because it is the branches that produce the fruit.

This is how Jesus wanted it to be between him and his disciples. This is the way he wants it to be between him and us. He is the vine, we are the branches. Or to use Paul's language: 'Jesus is the head of the body, we are the limbs of the body.' Without a sense of belonging together, of caring for one another and being responsible for one another, one is not really a Christian.

The fruit which Jesus desires from us is primarily that of unity among ourselves. By this all will know that we belong to him – by the bond that exists between us and the care we show for one another.

PRAYER OF THE FAITHFUL

President: Let us pray to Christ our Saviour, who through the power of the Holy Spirit, is still present and active among us.

Response: Lord, hear our prayer.

Reader(s): For the Church: that through its voice, the Good News may be preached throughout the world. [Pause] Let us pray to the Lord.

For all temporal leaders: that they may be committed to freedom, justice and peace. [Pause] Let us pray to the Lord.

For the poor and the oppressed. [Pause] Let us pray to the Lord.

For the sick and the handicapped. [Pause] Let us pray to the Lord.

For prisoners. [Pause] Let us pray to the Lord.

For carers. (Pause). Let us pray to the Lord.

For own our special needs. [Longer pause] Let us pray to the Lord.

President: Almighty and ever-loving God, grant that we may share generously with others the blessings we have received from you. We ask this through the same Christ our Lord.

REFLECTION   **Grace is unlimited**

Human beings are frail and foolish.
We have been told that grace is to be found in the universe.

But in our human foolishness and short-sightedness
we imagine divine grace to be finite, and for this reason we tremble.
But the moment comes when our eyes are opened,
and we see that grace is infinite.
Grace demands nothing from us
but that we await it with confidence
and acknowledge it with gratitude.
Grace makes no conditions and singles out none of us in particular.
Grace takes us all to its bosom
and proclaims a general amnesty. *(Isak Dinesen).*

Fourth Sunday of the Year
REJECTING THE PROPHET

INTRODUCTION AND CONFITEOR

Like so many prophets before and after him, Jesus was rejected by his
own people. They couldn't take the truth he was telling them. Let us reflect for a moment on the fact that we too have no great appetite for the
truth, and often reject the messengers God sends to us. [Pause] Let us
turn to Christ, the messenger of God's truth, love and mercy.

Lord Jesus, you came to heal the brokenhearted. Lord, have mercy.
Lord, you came to call sinners to repentance. Christ, have mercy.
Lord, you plead for us at the right hand of the Father, Lord, have mercy.

HEADINGS FOR READINGS

First Reading (Jer 1:4-5.17-19). This reading tells of the call and commission of the prophet Jeremiah.

Second Reading (1 Cor 12:31–13:13). Paul stresses the primacy of love in
the life of a Christian.

Gospel (Lk 4:21-30). Jesus shared the fate of every true prophet: rejection by his own people.

SCRIPTURE NOTE

The First Reading tells of the call and commissioning of the prophet Jeremiah. Jeremiah never wanted to be a prophet and was overwhelmed by
the sheer burden of it. He stands out as a lonely figure whose mission
seemed to have failed. He is the supreme example, until Jesus, of the triumph of failure.

The Gospel is a continuation of last Sunday's reading. We see the reaction to the homily Jesus gave in the synagogue at Nazareth. The people

can't believe that the words of Isaiah could apply to him, the humble son of Joseph. On hearing that the benefits they have rejected will be offered to the Gentiles, the people rise up in fury and attempt to do away with Jesus. This foreshadows the ultimate fate of Jesus; but his hour has not yet come.

St Paul has been speaking of gifts and charisms. But here (Second Reading) he stresses the supreme importance of love. Without love all these gifts are useless.

HOMILY 1   **Bringing out the best or the worst**

When Jesus went back to his home place, Nazareth, they invited him to preach in the synagogue. Their first reaction to him was extremely favourable. They were astonished at the gracious words he spoke. However, their admiration soon turned into doubt, then into hostility. What went wrong?

They still saw him as just the son of Joseph. And they felt that if he had anything to offer, then they, the people of his own home town, should be the first to benefit from it. Without showing any real faith in him, they demanded that he do in Nazareth some of the wonderful things he had done elsewhere – after all, charity begins at home. They felt they had a divine right to be the first to benefit from his gifts.

But he said that what matters is not who you are, but whether or not you have faith. There is no room in the Kingdom of God for privilege. God's charity begins wherever there is human need, and the faith to receive it. He gave two examples – the cure of the widow of Zarephath and the cure of Naaman, both of whom were Gentiles.

On hearing that the benefits they had rejected (through lack of faith in Jesus) would be offered to the Gentiles, the people were outraged. As Jews, they were the people of God. Those others were outsiders and sinners. How dare he suggest that the Gentiles would be preferred to them. In a burst of nationalist fervour they turned on him. They took him from the synagogue, and tried to do away with him.

Why did they turn on him so angrily? Because of what he said. That was the first reason. But there was a deeper reason. It was because he showed up the ugly things that lay hidden in them. If you stir up a stagnant pond a lot of mud will rise to the surface.

Regrettably, religion sometimes brings out the worst in people. It makes them narrower, more bigoted, and more apt to hate and kill. We see an ugly example of this in the citizens of Nazareth. But this kind of thing still happens. Religion can get distorted and turn into something repulsive such as fanaticism and bigotry. Religion becomes synonymous with narrow-mindedness, small-heartedness and intolerance.

But religion can also bring out the best in people. It makes them more tolerant and more loving. True religion liberates the heart and the mind, and fosters harmonious relationships with others. Religion is beautiful when it is like this. The question each of us must ask is: What does religion bring out in me?

There is an essential link between faith and love. St Paul says, 'There are three things that last: faith, hope and love; and the greatest of these is love.' (Second Reading). What's the use in having faith and hope if we are lacking in love?

HOMILY 2   **Rejected by his own**

Years after leaving his native village in the Transkei, Nelson Mandela returned home for a visit. By now he was a lawyer and lived in Johannesburg. Of that visit he later wrote: 'There is nothing like returning to a place that remains unchanged to find the ways in which you yourself have changed. The old place went on as before, no different from when I had grown up there. But I realised that my own outlook and world views had evolved.' In effect, he was saying that, while it was nice to go back home, he could no longer live there – it had become too small for him.

Jesus went back to Nazareth and to the people among whom he had grown up. He wanted to bring them too the benefit of his gifts. They were the people who knew him best. You would have thought, then, that they would have appreciated him most. Sadly they had no faith in him.

The view you get of a great cathedral from a distance is very different from the view you get from close up. From a distance the cathedral stands resplendent in its setting. You can see its outline, its form, and its beauty. But from close up all you see is the grime and the cracks.

Something similar happens with people. A person is never a hero to his own relations. A genius is not likely to be discovered by his friends. The person near at hand suffers because his faults and limitations are clearly visible. The person far away, on the other hand, is held in esteem because only his virtues are visible.

But what happened to Jesus at Nazareth went deeper than this. It wasn't just a case of they not appreciating him. They rejected him. Why? Because he pointed out their lack of faith, and told them that the Gentiles were more open to God than they were. The benefits of the promises were meant for all.

Jesus suffered the fate of all prophets – rejection by his own people. Prophecy is not about pleasing people. It's about speaking the truth that no one wants to hear, the truth that is often covered up. But Jesus' overriding motive was compassion.

What was he to do? He might have said, 'I'm fed up with them! I'm fed up with everybody!' And then retired to a shack in the woods, and let the weeds grow in the gate.

Or he could have said, 'What do they want?' And having found out what they wanted, he could have proceeded to give it to them. But in that case the special gift he wanted to give them, and which they sorely needed, would be lost.

Finally he could have tried to find even a few who were ready to receive what he wanted to give them. If he found a few, he could give it to them, and in proportion to their ability to receive. This is what he chose to do.

It's very hurtful to be rejected by one's own. Jesus was saddened by what happened to him at Nazareth, but he didn't get embittered and bury his gifts. He did what he could for those who believed in him at Nazareth, and then took his gifts elsewhere.

HOMILY 3   **The primacy of love**

There is an essential link between faith and love. This is illustrated in a story that is told about George Herbert, an English poet, priest and amateur musician. One day on his way to a music session with some of his friends he came upon a poor man whose horse had fallen under his load. Both man and horse were in distress and in urgent need of help.

Herbert took off his clerical robes and helped the man to unload the horse, get him on his feet, and then load him up again. Then he gave the man some money to refresh himself and his horse. That done, he set out again to keep his appointment with his friends.

Normally he kept himself very clean and trim. So when he turned up with his hands dirty and his clothes soiled, his friends were very surprised. When he told them the cause of it, one of them expressed disapproval that he should have got himself involved in such dirty employment.

But he answered: 'The thought of what I have done will be like music to me at midnight. The omission of it would have caused discord in my conscience. For if I am bound to pray for all who are in distress, I am sure that I am bound so far as it is in my power to practise what I pray for.' Then he said, 'And now, let's tune our instruments.'

In today's Second Reading St Paul gives us what is acknowledged to be one of the best descriptions of love ever written. Love is a much-used word today. But what our culture calls love, in its songs and films, frequently is not love at all; it is the opposite to love. It is desire and control and possessiveness.

Today a lot of people are cynical about the existence of real love. They are sceptical about the existence of goodness unsullied by self-interest. One reason is that today we have a better understanding of the complexity of human nature, and the mixed motives behind everything we do.

St Paul was well aware of the mixed motives behind what people do.

He understood how people could make great sacrifices, yet those sacrifices are worthless because they are done from motives of self-interest.

But still he believed in the possibility of love, and that it is central for the Christian. What he proposes in his description of love is clearly an ideal. An ideal is like a star. Though we can never reach it, it still guides us. But the main point Paul is making is the primacy of love in the life of a Christian. We must be willing to try. But we must also be willing to accept our weakness and failures without anger and frustration.

To be possessed with love is to be filled with a power which will not be denied; which will do anything, brave anything, suffer anything, endure anything, for the sake of who or what it loves.

Love, kindness, charity, doing things for others – these are the essential qualities. Love never fails. Other things fade and pass away, but love endures. If a person truly loves, he/she possesses all other virtues as well.

Faith, hope and love are the three great virtues. These remain, and the greatest of these is love. All things pass away, but the kind word, the kind deed, never pass away.

PRAYER OF THE FAITHFUL

President: St Paul says: 'Without love I am nothing at all.' With love in our hearts let us bring our needs before God in prayer.

Response: Lord, hear us in your love.

For all Christians: that they may give an example to the world of true love. [Pause[We pray in faith.

For government leaders: that they may listen to the voice of the prophets in their midst. [Pause] We pray in faith.

For mutual respect and tolerance between the adherents of the various religions. [Pause] We pray in faith.

For all gathered here: that the practice of our religion may make us more loving towards others. [Pause] We pray in faith.

For our own special needs. [Longer pause] We pray in faith.

President: Lord, send your Spirit to make us strong in faith and active in good works, because alone and unaided we cannot hope to please you. We make this prayer through Christ our Lord.

REFLECTION   **A loving person**

Jesus fulfilled the ideal of love Paul speaks about.
He was never in a hurry, and was always kindness itself.
He never envied anybody, and never boasted about himself.
He was never snobbish, or rude, or selfish.
He did not take offence easily,
    nor did he keep on talking about the wrong things other people did.

He preferred to remember the good things and to rejoice in them.
He was tough – he could face anything.
And he never lost trust in God, or in people.
He never lost hope; he never gave in.
He never stopped loving.

Fifth Sunday of the Year
THE CALL OF THE FIRST DISCIPLES

INTRODUCTION AND CONFITEOR

All the saints were conscious of their sinfulness – and this forced them to rely more on the grace of God than on their own strength.

While our sinfulness humbles us, we must not let it get us down, or make us feel that we do not belong in the company of Jesus. He came to help us to overcome our sins. Therefore, let us approach him with confidence and confess them. [Pause]

I confess to almighty God ...

HEADINGS FOR READINGS

First Reading (Is 6:1-8). We hear of the call of Isaiah to the ministry of prophecy.

Second Reading (1 Cor 15:1-11). Paul energetically defends the doctrine of the resurrection from the dead.

Gospel (Lk 5:1-11). This tells the story of a miraculous catch of fish and the call of Peter to share in the work of Christ.

SCRIPTURE NOTE

The First Reading tells of the call of Isaiah to the ministry of prophecy. In a vision in the Temple God reveals himself to Isaiah as the All-holy One. The vision evokes in Isaiah a sense of his own sinfulness. But then, cleansed of his sins, he responds without hesitation to the divine call. This prepares us for the Gospel which deals with the call of the first disciples. Here again we see that it is God who takes the initiative, and also the total response he requires.

The miraculous catch of fish convinces Peter of the holiness of Jesus. This evokes in him a sense of their own sinfulness and unworthiness, so much so that he asks Jesus to depart from him. Peter has not yet grasped the fact that it was to call sinners that Jesus came, to call them away from sin to a new way of life. Nevertheless, at the word of Jesus, Peter and his companions leave everything and follow him. The phrase 'they left everything' shows the importance for Luke of detachment from possessions.

The Second Reading stresses the central belief of Christianity – the resurrection of Jesus. Paul declares that, in spite of his unworthiness, he is a witness to the resurrection.

HOMILY 1   **Coping with failure**

Peter and his companions had done their best. They had fished all night but had caught nothing: all their time and effort had been for nothing. They were now tired and dispirited as they washed their nets.

It's possible to do one's best, yet at the end of the day (or night) to have nothing to show for it, nothing but weariness and wounds. But who has eyes for such things? One might study hard for an exam, yet not get the desired results. One might play one's heart out, yet lose the match. One might do one's best to be a good parent, yet a child goes wrong.

Jesus might have said to the apostles, 'I'm surprised at you. You're supposed to be experienced fishermen. How could you fish all night and catch nothing? How come the men in that boat over there made a catch?'

He might have said this. Had he done so, he would have been saying in effect, 'It's your own fault.' He would have been blaming them. Now when we fail after having done our best, the last thing we need is blame. To fail is painful enough without someone rubbing salt into the wound. It's terrible if one's best isn't good enough.

Most of us experience failure at one time or another. There is no point in being sentimental about it. Failure breeds despair. The person who can draw strength from failure is very rare. What we need is not blame but someone to believe in us, to encourage us, and to challenge us. Failure is not the falling down, but staying down.

Besides, success isn't everything. We can win an argument but lose a friend. Through competition and promotion we may advance in our profession, but in terms of relationships we may be impoverished. Success is sweet at the moment it is achieved. But almost immediately the cup of success begins to drain away and a feeling of emptiness sets in.

Jesus did not blame Peter and his companions. But he didn't encourage them to wallow in self-pity either. Nor did he allow them to rest in failure. He challenged them to try again: 'Launch out into the deep and let down the nets for a catch.'

Emerson says that each of us has a greater possibility. There is in each of us a chamber, or a closet, that has never been opened. If we are to realise this 'greater possibility', we need to be challenged to go beyond ourselves, beyond what we think we are capable of and have settled for. We need someone to say to us, 'Launch out into the deep'.

Jesus knew that Peter was a sinner. But he knew that he was also capable of greatness. Many cults appeal to people's weaknesses. But Jesus appealed, not to Peter's weakness, but his strength. He knew that Peter and his companions were capable of better things. So he threw down a challenge to them – to leave their nets and become fishers of men. And, to their credit, they responded wholeheartedly. They left everything and became his first disciples.

We all need someone who accepts us for what we are, but who believes we are capable of more, and challenges us to realise it.

'From success to failure is one step. From failure to success is a long road.' (Yiddish saying).

HOMILY 2   **At your word, Lord**

Night-time was the time for fishing. If anyone else had said to Peter, 'Launch out into the deep and let down the net for a catch,' he would have said, 'Are you mad? Do you want me to make a fool of myself in front of all these other fishermen? If we didn't catch anything during the night, what chance have we of catching anything in broad daylight?'

But when Jesus said those words to Peter, Peter's spontaneous response was, 'Lord, we fished all night long and caught nothing. But if you say so, I will let down the net.'

For Peter, the word of Jesus was different from the word of anyone else. It carried an authority which no other word carried. Hence, if Jesus called for it, then no matter how hopeless the situation might seem, or how tired he was, or how foolish he might appear, he would try again.

Peter had absolute trust in Jesus. At his word he was prepared to attempt the impossible. We see this again later in the Gospel when he attempted to walk on water at the word of Jesus.

How many people are there whose word we would take seriously? Whose word we would trust absolutely? Whose word we would completely rely on? The answer is, 'Very few.'

Fishing is a worthy calling. However, Jesus saw that Peter was capable of other things. He was the kind of man he wanted to have helping him with his work. What qualities did Jesus see in Peter that made him call him to share in his work? He had the first and most essential one – faith in Jesus. He also had humility.

The Gospel story is not so much a story about fishing, but about trust. Jesus was saying to Peter: 'How far are you prepared to trust me?' It was a turning point in the life of Peter. What started out in failure ended in a new beginning, starting out in a new direction.

Fishing was an important occupation. But Jesus was calling Peter and his companions to an even more important occupation. He was offering them not just a new work, but a cause to which to dedicate their lives. They understood that he was calling them to service of others: 'I will make you fishers of people.' When the leaders of cults call people to follow them, they turn them into their personal slaves. Jesus called the apostles, not to service of himself, but to service of others.

The Lord still calls people, and the need is just as great today. And there still are those who respond. Some people (like the apostles) are called to dedicate themselves totally and in a 'professional' way to the following of Christ. But not all Christians are called to follow Christ in this way.

By our baptism we too are called to follow Christ. But what does the following of Christ mean for the ordinary person? It means to be a Christian where you are and in your chosen profession. There are more ways than one of serving Christ and his Gospel. The call in the first instance is not to an apostolate but to discipleship.

HOMILY 3   **A good beginning**

Isaiah, Paul and Peter are at the centre of today's readings. All three men did great things for God. Yet each of them had an inferiority complex. They had a low opinion of themselves. They had low self-esteem, to use the modern jargon. They did not put themselves forward, but were called by God. They accepted that call reluctantly, convinced that they were unworthy of it.

Isaiah said, 'I am a man of unclean lips.' Paul said, 'Of all the apostles I am the least. I don't even deserve the name apostle.' And Peter declared, 'Leave me, Lord; I am a sinful man.' This was not false humility on their part; it was the plain truth.

Each starts by acknowledging his unworthiness and inadequacy. From a spiritual point of view, such a start is ideal. People who put themselves forward are more likely to do harm than good. Such people rely on their own resources, and are seeking their own glory. Pride and self-sufficiency are but sand, and the spiritual house built on them is sure to fall.

When, on the other hand, we meet someone who is fearful, reluctant, hesitant, we find that person much more believable, and much more human. This element of reluctance is of the essence of the matter, for the saint or martyr who seeks his fate with eagerness never rings true.

There is a great paradox here. Paul said, 'When I am weak, that is when I am strong.' (2 Cor 12:10). The meaning is that when he recognises his own weakness and turns to God, God's power becomes available to him.

When we acknowledge our weakness, God can strengthen us. When we acknowledge our emptiness, God can fill us. When we acknowledge our poverty, God can enrich us. Then we become available to do his work, and he accomplishes in us the things we find impossible.

Humility is the starting point. It's not that we are rotten through and through. Far from it. It's just that we are weak, selfish and cowardly. Without grace we are unable to save ourselves, much less save anyone else.

However, people can use their sins and weaknesses as a cop-out. Isaiah

[195]

asked God to choose someone else, someone with a clean mouth. Peter asked Christ to leave him alone because he was a sinner. When we do this we are giving in to our weakness. We are using it as a ploy to escape from the challenge of goodness.

According to Peter Jesus the holy one should distance himself from sinners. But Jesus refused to do so. It was for sinners that he came. Thereby he changed people's understanding of God. God was not a God who shunned sinners, but a God who wants them to be saved, and who gives them a new start.

Isaiah, Paul and Peter eventually accepted God's invitation, and all three did a splendid job. This is the paradox – strength arising out of weakness. When we answer God's call, he empowers us so that we can do things we never thought possible.

We should ask the Lord to give us the humility to acknowledge our weaknesses, and the strength to rise above them. Then we will have the joy of discovering that it is when we are weak that we are strong, because the Lord's power becomes available to us.

PRAYER OF THE FAITHFUL

President: Let us pray to the Lord who strengthens us in our weakness, and who does not abandon us when we fail.

Response: Lord, hear our prayer.

For all the disciples of Jesus: that they may follow him with humility and generosity. [Pause] Let us pray to the Lord.

For those who hold public office: that they may bring all their talents and energies to their work. [Pause] Let us pray to the Lord.

For those who suffer from an inferiority complex . [Pause] Let us pray to the Lord.

For those whose life is dogged by failure. [Pause] Let us pray to the Lord.

For all those engaged in the difficult and often dangerous work of catching fish. [Pause[Let us pray to the Lord.

For grace to acknowledge our sinfulness, but not be satisfied until we have tried to overcome it. [Pause] Let us pray to the Lord.

For our own special needs. [Longer pause] Let us pray to the Lord.

President: God of mercy, grant us in all our tasks your help, in all our doubts your guidance, in all our weaknesses your strength, in all our dangers your protection, and in all our sorrows your consolation. We ask this through Christ our Lord.

REFLECTION   **Let your light shine**

Our deepest fear is not that we are inadequate,

but that we are powerful beyond measure.
It is our light, not our darkness, that most frightens us.
We ask ourselves, 'Who am I to be brilliant,
gorgeous, talented and fabulous?'
Actually, who are you not to be?
You are a child of God.
Your playing small doesn't serve the world.
There's nothing enlightened about shrinking
so that other people won't feel insecure around you.
We are born to make manifest the Glory of God that is within us.
It's not just in some of us; it's in everyone.
And as we let our own light shine,
we unconsciously give other people permission to do the same.
As we are liberated from our own fear,
our presence automatically liberates others.

(From the inaugural speech of Nelson Mandela).

Sixth Sunday of the Year
THE WORLD OF THE BEATITUDES

INTRODUCTION AND CONFITEOR

A tree that is planted by the riverside grows and bears fruit. In the same way, those who trust in God are truly blessed. As we gather in this house of God, let us ask God to increase our trust in him and reliance on him. [Pause]

Lord Jesus, you give us refuge and you never le tus be put to shame. Lord, have mercy.

You grant that those who hope in you will not be disappointed. Christ, have mercy.

You will receive us and guide us. Lord, have mercy.

HEADINGS FOR READINGS

First Reading (Jer 17:5-8). The prophet contrasts the life of the wicked with the life of the righteous.

Second Reading (1 Cor 15:12.16-20). St Paul stresses the reality of Jesus' bodily resurrection, and the meaning of that resurrection for Christians.

Gospel (Lk 6:17.20-26). We hear Luke's version of the Beatitudes.

SCRIPTURE NOTE

For this and the following two Sundays we will be reading from Luke's

'Sermon on the Plain' which parallels Matthew's 'Sermon on the Mount'.

The First Reading is a little bit of wisdom poetry. It contrasts the wicked who trust in human beings and the righteous who trust in God. The former are compared to a barren desert shrub; the latter to a fruitful tree planted beside a flowing river. This prepares us for the Gospel, where Jesus declares the poor blessed. The poor are the 'little ones' who have no one to trust in but God.

The beatitudes echo the programme Jesus announced in the synagogue at Nazareth. Whereas Matthew has nine Beatitudes, Luke has only four, with, however, four corresponding 'woes'.

HOMILY 1   **The poverty of the rich**

A thing you notice about the houses of the rich: they lack life and laughter. You never see children playing on the lawns. So, while they are beautiful, an air of melancholy seems to surround them. Saul Bellow calls it 'the melancholy of affluence.'

The American writer, Maya Angelu, tells how her aunt was once a live-in housekeeper for a wealthy couple in California. The couple lived in a splendid house that had fourteen bedrooms. The aunt's main job was to do the cooking. Every day she cooked and served a light breakfast, a good lunch, and a full dinner to the couple and their frequent guests.

But the years passed and the couple grew old. As they did so they stopped entertaining. Eventually their evening meal consisted of scrambled egg, toast, and weak tea. They ate it in silence, hardly seeing each other at the table.

On Saturday nights the housekeeper would invite some of her friends into her basement quarters. There they would eat some plain but good food, have a few drinks, play records, dance, and finally settle down to a game of cards. Meanwhile, jokes were told and there was lots of laughter.

One night in the midst of all this hilarity the door opened. It was her employers who beckoned to her to come out. In the hallway the wife said to her: 'We don't mean to disturb you. But you all seem to be having such a good time. We hear you and your friends enjoying yourselves every Saturday night, and we'd just like to watch you. We don't want to bother you. We'll keep quiet and just watch.' Then the husband added, 'If you'll just leave your door ajar, your friends don't need to know. We'll never make a sound.'

Her aunt agreed. But she found it sad that her employers owned a large house, a swimming pool, three cars, and lots of palm trees, but had no joy. Picture the wealthy couple standing in a darkened hallway, peering into a lighted room where black servants were lifting their voices in merriment and camaraderie.

This true story illustrates how in a deep sense the poor can be better off than the rich, if they know how to enjoy themselves. The secret lies in a love of life, and the ability to take great pleasure from small offerings. When things are easy, people expect good things to happen, and so they bring no great joy when they come. But when life is hard, it is also richer. People have fewer expectations, so that the good things of life become unexpected gifts which are accepted with gratitude and joy.

The story also gives us an insight into what Jesus was talking about in the Beatitudes. In the eyes of the world, the rich seem to be blessed by God, while the poor seem cursed. But Jesus spoke about the strange poverty of those who live for the wealth of this world, and the strange wealth of those who trust in God; the strange hunger of those whose only food is the food of this world, and the strange nourishment of those who seek the food that only God can give; the strange sadness of those who laugh, and the strange joy of those who know how to weep; the strange happiness of those who are persecuted in the cause of right; the strange weakness of the strong, and the strange strength of the weak who put their trust in God.

The rich tend to rely on their riches. For them it's this world that matters. God is moreorless redundant, and the other world remote and hazy. The poor, on the other hand, turn to God instinctively. As a poor old lady said to a priest: 'Isn't it great that we have God to lean on.'

It's not that poverty in itself is a good thing. When Jesus says, 'Blessed are the poor and the hungry', he isn't giving a blessing to abject poverty and starvation - these are evil things. Nevertheless, it's a fact that the very hazards of life for the poor make death very close, but make the other world close as well. This is why Jesus says, 'Blessed are the poor, the Kingdom of Heaven is theirs.'

The poverty that is blessed is the poverty of those who put their trust in God rather than in material things. Only God can fill our emptiness; only God can satisfy the hunger of the human heart.

HOMILY 2   **Spiritual awakening**

Christ faced people with a radical choice: to live by the values of the world (pursuit of money, pleasure, popularity, power, prestige,), or to live by the values of the Kingdom (poverty of spirit, cleanness of heart, capacity to show mercy, ability to suffer in the cause of right ...)

In his novel, *The First Circle*, Solzhenitsyn tells the story of a Russian diplomat named Innokenty. It was during Stalin's regime. Innokenty and his wife Dottie lived a pampered life. In each post he was sent to, a lavishly furnished house awaited them. And they lapped it all up. They had everything they wanted, at a time when the world was torn apart by World War II. But not a breath of the sorrow of the world touched them.

However, in the sixth year of their marriage, Innokenty began to experience a sense of revulsion towards all material things. The feeling puzzled and alarmed him. He had everything, yet he lacked something. Even his lovely wife Dottie was becoming a stranger to him. Their smart way of life he found embarrassing, where everybody was the same, and where they would all jump up to drink a toast to Comrade Stalin, whom they feared and secretly despised.

One day he started to go through some letters and books his deceased mother had left him. As he read the letters, he discovered a set of values that were in complete contrast with those of the circle to which he belonged.

The values of his mother began to make sense. In her letters she spoke about such things as compassion, truth, goodness, and so on. Then he came across this extraordinary piece: 'The most precious thing in the whole world is the consciousness of not participating in injustice.'

Suddenly he discovered what was missing from his life. And for days and nights he continued to sit there breathing in the values of his mother's world like a man breathes in fresh air. He was discovering a new way of seeing and judging life. Up to this his philosophy of life had been that we only live once. To put oneself out for another person was sheer folly. Now he was grasping another truth: that we have only one conscience, and that a crippled conscience is as irretrievable as a lost life.

There was an elderly doctor who had treated his mother during her last illness. In a day's time he was going to Paris where he intended to pass on some medical secrets to the West because he believed the world had a right to know them. But a trap had been set for him. Innokenty knew about the trap. He made a phone call to the doctor. But the call was traced and Innokenty was arrested.

Innokenty knew what it was like to be rich. When you are rich you have a name, you are a member of a respected group, and are never really oppressed. A phone call and everything is fixed up. But now that he had lost his job, his prestige, his wealth, and even his wife, he was discovering what it meant to be poor. To be poor is to have no friends, and no security.

Yet Innokenty had gained a treasure, and he knew it. He had experienced a spiritual awakening. And, as Kahlil Gibran says, 'Spiritual awakening is the most important thing in life; it is the sole purpose of our being.'

How many Christians could say that they live by the values of the Beatitudes? In things that affect us directly – jobs, cars, comforts, homes, the future of our children – do we not live as the world lives? Today the disciples of Jesus are frequently in comfort while so many are in misery.

Riches and comforts in the end leave us in a spiritual wilderness. Only in living by the values of the Gospel will our deepest hungers be satisfied. To understand the Beatitudes, we need a spiritual awakening.

HOMILY 3   **Poor but rich in faith and trust**

At the heart of today's readings is the theme of trust in God. The First Reading contrasts the fate of those who trust in human beings with the fate of those who trust in God. Those who trust in human beings are like a barren desert shrub; whereas those who trust in God are like a fruitful tree planted beside a flowing river.

To trust in God is to rely on God as to the one source of life. Those who trust in God are the poor, whom Jesus declares blessed in the Beatitudes (Gospel).

When Jesus says, 'Blessed are the poor,' he is not giving a blessing to starvation and misery. Starvation and misery are evil. What is being blessed is reliance on God. Those who put their trust in human things will be disappointed; those who put their trust in God will not. Only God can fill our emptiness; only God can satisfy the hunger of our hearts. But often God is the last one we turn to rather than the first.

St James says that it is those who are poor according to this world that God makes rich in faith (2:1-5). Anyone who has been in ministry for a few years will be able to confirm the truth of this.

The rich tend to rely on their riches. For them it's this world that matters. God is more or less redundant, and the other world remote and hazy. The poor, on the other hand, tend to turn to God instinctively. For them the very hazards and difficulties of life make God and the other world close and real.

It's not that poverty in itself is a good thing. But it's a fact that as life becomes harder and more threatening, it also becomes richer, because the fewer expectations we have, the more the good things of life become unexpected gifts that we accept with gratitude. This is why Jesus says, 'Blessed are the poor, the Kingdom of Heaven is theirs.'

One day a poor man was walking along a street when he came upon a beggar who asked him for alms. Ashamed, the man answered, 'Sorry, but I'm just as poor as you are.'

On hearing this the beggar said, 'Thank you, my friend, for your gift.'

Not understanding what the beggar meant, the man asked, 'Why are you thanking me? I didn't give you anything.'

'Oh, yes, you did,' the beggar replied. 'You gave me your honesty, your poverty, and your trust.'

God is not poor, but we are. Even so, there is something we can give God. We can give him our honesty, our poverty and our trust.

PRAYER OF THE FAITHFUL

President: Those who trust in God are like a tree planted beside a flowing river. Let us bring our needs before God with great trust.

Response: Lord, hear us in your love.

Reader(s): For the followers of Jesus: that they may live by the values of the Gospel. [Pause] We pray in faith.

For all in positions of authority: that they may work to eliminate poverty and injustice. [Pause] We pray in faith.

For those who are spiritually poor: that they may discover the riches of the Gospel. [Pause] We pray in faith.

For those who suffer in the cause of right. [Pause] We pray in faith.

For grace to hunger for a life of goodness. [Pause] We pray in faith.

For our own special needs. [Longer pause] We pray in faith.

President: Almighty and ever-living God, your love for us surpasses all our hopes and desires. Forgive our failings, keep us in your peace, and lead us in the path of eternal life. We ask this through Christ our Lord.

REFLECTION   **Beatitudes of the heart**

Blessed are the clean of heart; they will see God.

Blessed are the humble of heart; they will find rest for their souls.

Blessed are the warm-hearted; they will radiate goodness.

Blessed are those who work with the heart; they will find joy in their work.

Blessed are those who do not lose heart; they will find the strength to persevere.

And blessed are those who set their hearts on the Kingdom of God; everything else will be given to them.

Seventh Sunday of the Year
THE VALUES OF THE KINGDOM

INTRODUCTION AND CONFITEOR

Jesus says, 'Be compassionate ... Do not judge ... Do not condemn ... Treat others as you would like them to treat you.' These words are taken from today's Gospel. How many of us could say that we treat others in this way? [Pause] The Lord himself shows us the way.

Lord Jesus, you are slow to anger and rich in mercy. Lord, have mercy.

You do not treat us according to our sins. Christ, have mercy.

As far as the east is from the west, so far do you remove our sins. Lord, have mercy.

HEADINGS FOR READINGS

First Reading (1 Sam 26:2.7-9.12-13.22-23). David turns down an opportunity to kill Saul because he believes it would not be right before God.

Second Reading (1 Cor 15:45-49). Paul draws parallels between Adam and Christ: to Adam we owe the life of earth; to Christ the life of heaven.

Gospel (Lk 6:27-38). Jesus stresses the duty of loving one's enemy and the obligations of fraternal charity.

SCRIPTURE NOTE

Because of his great successes on the battlefield, David was very popular with the people. As a result, Saul saw him as a threat and sought to kill him. The First Reading contains the moving story of how David had an opportunity to kill Saul, but refused to do so because in his eyes Saul, as king of Israel, was a sacred person.

This passage prepares us for the Gospel, which contains Jesus' injunction to love our enemies. Jesus goes on to stress the obligations of fraternal charity. The ideal of love to which his followers must aspire is that of God himself. We are to love as God loves.

Jesus' vision of human behaviour is at such variance with the view most people have, that many people regard it as humanly unachievable, and therefore ignore it. From a human point of view it is unachievable. Divine help is needed.

HOMILY 1   **Loving one's enemy**

Jesus says to us, 'Love your enemies ... pray for those who treat you badly.'

There was a Belfast woman whose husband was shot as he drove the family to Mass. Soon after the tragedy she was praying with the children when her young son, Gavin, asked, 'Mummy, will the men who killed Daddy go to heaven?'

Breathing a silent prayer, the mother replied, 'If they are really sorry and ask Jesus to forgive them, then they will go to heaven.'

On hearing this Gavin replied, 'Well, if they are going to be there, I don't want to be in heaven with them.'

The mother thought about this for a while, then replied, 'If Jesus forgives and saves them, setting them free from their terrible sin, he will change them. They will be completely different people.'

Gavin paused, then said, 'Mummy, let's pray for these men and ask Jesus to save them.'

Jesus challenges us to respond to darkness with light. To respond to what is worst in the other with what is best in us. The most important issue today is how to resist evil without doing further evil in the process.

Most of us think we have done our Christian duty if we refrain from doing harm to our enemy. But Jesus asks more of us. He asks us to love our enemies. Even though this is difficult, that wonderful Belfast mother shows that it can be done. So does the youthful David (First Reading).

Even on a human level, the teaching of Jesus makes sense. The escalation of evil can be stopped only by one who humbly absorbs it, without passing it on. Revenge and retaliation only add darkness to darkness. By adopting a vindictive attitude, we become poisoned by hatred. We use up a huge amount of energy in hating. Revenge may satisfy one's rage but it leaves the heart empty. It's vital to keep the heart free of hatred. 'When Jesus says, "Forgive your enemies," it is not for the sake of the enemy, but for one's own sake that he says so, and because love is more beautiful than hate.' (Oscar Wilde)

Love releases extraordinary energies in us. The power of love is greater than the power of evil. Still, one of the most difficult things in the world is to love someone who hates you. Yet true love is love of the difficult and the unlovable. Mercy is stronger and more God-like than vengeance.

It is a struggle to overcome the feelings of bitterness and revenge that well up inside us, and can keep welling up, when we are badly treated by another. Forgiveness is never easy. Each day it must be struggled for, and prayed for and won. Resentments can smoulder for a long time. Prayer is the only answer. Anger cannot continue to develop where there is humble, sincere prayer.

'What you hate for yourself, do not do to your neighbour.' (Hillel)

HOMILY 2   **Do not judge**

How easy it is to be destructively critical, to be over hasty in making judgements, to be intolerant of the faults of others. How terribly arbitrarily and superficially people criticise and judge. By our judgements we convict ourselves. Jesus says to us, 'Do not judge, and you will not be judged yourselves.'

A true story. One morning a priest was saying Mass when he noticed a woman coming in very late. He was so annoyed that when she came up for Communion, he refused to give her Communion. He didn't stop to consider that she might have had a very good reason for being late. No, unfortunately he rushed to judgement. In doing so, he made a terrible mistake and hurt her deeply.

Obviously he didn't know the first thing about the woman or about her home situation. She was a very good mother and a deeply committed Catholic. She was not in the habit of coming late to Mass. But she was trying to cope with a very sick husband and a handicapped daughter. Daily Mass, and Communion in particular, meant the world to her.

Why was she late for Mass that morning? She had to take her handicapped daughter to the bus so that she could get to a day-care centre. But the bus was half an hour late.

Where others are concerned, we seldom see the wider picture, much less the full picture. Even so, it doesn't stop us from jumping to conclusions and rushing to judgement. Even when we do see the full picture, we still should refrain from hasty judgements. Even then we are still only on the surface. In every person there is a dimension which escapes the powers of judgement of any other human being. We can't see into the mind and heart of another. We may see the deed, but we cannot see the motives behind the deed.

We should be very slow to judge other people because we seldom know all the facts. Even when we do, we still have no right to judge them. At some time or other all of us have been the victims of hasty judgements, and we know how unhelpful and hurtful this can be. When it happens, it makes us hate all judgement.

All of us are sinners. Though we deserve God's judgement, which of us wants to receive that judgement? Do we not all long for mercy and forgiveness rather than judgement? As people who are conscious of our own need, not for judgement and condemnation, but for forgiveness and compassion, let us not rush to judgement. If possible, let us refrain from judgement altogether.

HOMILY 3   **Giving without hope of return**

Jesus says to us, 'Give a full measure, pressed down, shaken together, and running over. Because the amount you measure out is the amount you will be given back.'

The image Jesus used was one that would have been very familiar to his listeners. It was taken from the marketplace. In those times they didn't use weighing scales. Instead they used vessels for measuring things. So, if you wanted some wheat, you might say to the merchant, 'I want a panful of wheat.'

But a 'panful' could vary significantly from merchant to merchant. A miserly merchant would take the pan, fill it up loosely, but not quite to the top. A generous merchant would fill it up to the top. Then he would shake it together so that it packed down and created more space. Then he would top it up until it was overflowing.

It's easy to give to a friend or to someone from whom we can expect a return in kind. It doesn't call for virtue. As Jesus says, 'Even sinners do as much.' If we love those who love us, we are not doing anything exceptional, and shouldn't look for a reward for doing so.

The real test is: can we give to an enemy or to someone from whom we have no hope of getting a return? This is the ideal that Jesus puts before us in the Gospel. He says: 'Love your enemies, and do good ... without hope of return.' In fact, we are to imitate the goodness and compassion of

God. But is this not an impossible ideal? Yes, it's difficult but not impossible. In telling of his experiences as a prisoner in Auschwitz, Viktor Frankl gives a beautiful example of it.

On returning from work in the evening, with soup bowl in hand, the prisoners lined up for their meagre ration of food. Frankl was always happy when he was assigned to the line in which prisoner-cook F was giving out the soup.

Why? Because he was the only cook who did not look at the faces of the men whose bowls he was filling. He was the only one who dealt out the soup equally, regardless of who the recipient was. He did not make favourites out of his friends or fellow countrymen, picking out the potatoes for them, while others got watery soup skimmed from the top.

How difficult it is to find someone to do this in normal circumstances. Yet here was a man who did it in the hell that was Auschwitz, where everyday people were faced with decisions of life and death. How did he manage to do it? From where did he get his inspiration?

It can all be summed up in the Golden Rule (which Jesus quotes): 'Treat others as you would like them to treat you.' Sadly, what we tend to do is to treat others as they treat us. But Jesus says, 'Treat others as you would like them to treat you.' There's a world of difference between the two.

The more we open our hearts to others, the more we open our hearts to what God is offering us. The vessel with which we give to others is the vessel with which we receive from God. The Lord in his goodness will see to it that the blessings we have bestowed will be returned to us, a full measure, pressed down, shaken together, and running over.

ANOTHER STORY

During the Second World War there were Russians who fought for the Germans in the hope of getting rid of Stalin. The last thing these wanted was to be captured by the Russians.

In December 1943 an interesting encounter took place. Snow covered the ground so both sides were wearing camouflage – white cloaks that covered their overcoats and caps. As the soldiers dashed back and forth among the forest trees things got very confused.

Two soldiers, one from each side, lay down close to one another, and continued firing at shadowy figures some distance away among the trees. They shared their ammunition, and encouraged one another. The first took out a packet of cigarettes and offered one to the second. The second took out a bar of chocolate and gave half of it to the first.

After a while they decided to take a break from the fighting. They pulled back their white hoods and in the same instant each noticed the other's cap. One had the eagle of Germany on it, the other the star of Russia. In a flash they recognised that they were on opposite sides. They jumped to their feet at once, drawing their pistols as they did so. But these refused to work because of the cold. Then, grabbing them by the barrels and swinging them like clubs, they set upon one mother like two primitive cavemen. This was not politics. Nor was it love of the Motherland. It was just like two crabs, victims of blind mistrust. If I pity my enemy he will kill me.

Solzhenitsyn who told the story, doesn't tell us how it ended. But there is a lesson in it for us. It shows how easily enemies might become friends. There is always something in our enemy that we like, and something in our friend that we dislike.

PRAYER OF THE FAITHFUL

President: Let us pray to God who is kind and compassionate to all his creatures.

Response: Lord, graciously hear us.

Reader(s): For all Christians: that they may be an example of generosity, compassion and forgiveness to the world. [Pause] Lord, hear us.

For countries where there is war: that their leaders may take the path of peace and reconciliation. [Pause] Lord, hear us.

For judges: that they may show wisdom and compassion in the exercise of their office. [Pause] Lord, hear us.

For those who have been the victims of harsh or unfair judgements. [Pause] Lord, hear us.

For those whom we find hard to love. [Pause] Lord, hear us.

For our own special needs. [Longer pause] Lord, hear us.

President: Lord, only with the help of your grace can we love as you love. Give us the strength to overcome anger with love, ugliness with beauty, and evil with good. We ask this through you, Christ our Lord

REFLECTION   **Giving**

There are those who give but only on condition
that they receive something in return, and receive it immediately.
There are those who give on condition
that they receive something in return
later on and with a handsome profit.
And there are those who give
without expecting anything in return now or ever:
they scatter the seeds of the heart without looking for any harvest.
These are imitating the generosity of God,
who bestows his love on good people and bad,
and grants mercy to saints and sinners.

Eighth Sunday of the Year
THE PLANK AND THE SPLINTER

INTRODUCTION AND CONFITEOR

At the start of each Mass we are invited to examine our conscience and to call to mind our sins. This means, of course, calling to mind our own sins, not the sins of anyone else. And we must not blame others for our sins, but accept full responsibility for them ourselves. [Pause] Let us confess our sins to God and to one another.

I confess to almighty God …

HEADINGS FOR READINGS

First Reading (Sir 27:4-7). A person's talk shows the kind of person he or she is.

Second Reading (1 Cor 15:54-58). The resurrection of Christ takes the sting out of death for those who believe in him.

Gospel (Lk 6:39-45). A blind guide cannot lead others. A person's words flow from what fills his heart.

SCRIPTURE NOTE

Just as an orchard is judged by the quality of its fruit, so a person's talk shows what kind of person he is. (First Reading) This links with what Jesus says in the Gospel: 'A tree is known by its fruit … the words of the mouth flow out of what fills the heart.'

In the Gospel it is no longer a question of love of enemies, but of love of one's brothers and sisters in the community. A Christian is his brother's keeper. But one cannot undertake to guide others unless one has found the way oneself. Hence, self-criticism must precede criticism of others. This applied especially to Christian teachers.

But it had even more relevance for prophets. There were many prophets in the early Church. These were people who had received this gift from God and more or less guided the community. But the community had to be careful because there were also false prophets.

Just as we judge a tree by its fruit, so we judge a prophet by his actions. Any prophet who teaches the truth is none the less a false prophet if he does not himself practise what he teaches. The true prophet is one who behaves in the Lord's way.

HOMILY 1   **Attending to our own faults**

It is easy to see another's weaknesses and faults, but a psychological wall prevents us from seeing our own. Each of us has a plank in our eyes which blinds us to our faults. We can be blind to certain facts about ourselves which are perfectly clear to anyone who has ever lived in the same house with us or worked in the same office.

Once there was a young monk who committed a serious fault. Immediately the elder monks assembled in community to pass judgement on him. However, they wouldn't proceed until their abbot joined them. So they sent him a message: 'Come, the community is waiting for you.'

The abbot arose, and taking an old basket which was riddled with holes, he filled it with fine sand. Then he started off, carrying the basket behind him. Naturally, as he went along, he left a trail of sand in his wake.

The elders came out to meet him and asked him what he meant by this. And he replied, 'My sins are running out behind me. Everywhere I go I leave a trail of faults after me, only most of the time I don't see them myself. And today you want me to sit in judgement on my brother.'

On hearing this the elders felt ashamed of themselves. They abandoned the trial and pardoned their brother.

Without realising it, we can become professional fault-finders and critics. But critics are not the ones who reform the world. Jesus tells us to take the beam out of our own eye first, and then we can think about removing the splinter from our neighbour's eye. We must put our own house in order first before daring to try to put someone else's house in order. If we neglect this, we will not judge our brother in care for him, but in hatred, and wishing to expose him. There are few things that give as much satisfaction to the ego as pointing out the mistakes and faults of others.

A leader can lead only if he sees the way himself. The teacher can impart only what he himself has learned. If one is to avoid being a blind guide one must exercise self-criticism.

How anxious we are to correct others. If only we could tell so and so about that fault of his, and get him to see the error of his ways, how fine our community would be. When we think like this we are thinking only of ourselves. But how we hate and dread being corrected ourselves! We find it unbearable especially if it is done by certain people.

An old sailor gave up smoking when his pet parrot developed a persistent cough. He was worried that the pipe smoke which frequently filled the room had damaged the parrot's health. He had a vet examine the bird. After a thorough check-up the vet concluded that the parrot did not have psittacosis or pneumonia. It had merely been imitating the cough of its pipe-smoking master.

Pseudo-religion, which Jesus calls hypocrisy, is forever trying to make other people better. True religion tries to make oneself better.

HOMILY 2   **Plank in the eye**

Nothing so blinds us to our own faults as a preoccupation with the faults of others. We can be blind to certain facts about ourselves which are perfectly clear to anyone who has ever lived in the same house with us or worked in the same office.

Once there was a Rhino named Roddy who suffered from the delusion that he was perfect. Hence, he believed that he had a duty to correct the other animals, and that he did. In his eyes the most serious defect was the wearing of any kind of horn. Those poor animals that had been born with horns never got a moment's peace from him.

Now all this time Roddy had a big horn right on top of his thoroughly ugly nose. It was the first thing the other animals noticed about him. Yet he himself was unaware of it, and none of the other animals had the courage to point it out to him.

One day Roddy was drinking from a stream. A robin was perched on an overhanging branch, singing its morning song. Now old Roddy hadn't a note in his head. Anything at which he didn't excel was anathema to him. In the middle of his drinking he looked up and said, 'Be quiet, you little twit! Can't you see I'm drinking.'

'You're not so handsome yourself,' said the robin. 'Some day you ought to take a good look at yourself in a clear pool, and you'll see what I mean.'

'What are you talking about? Why, everybody knows I'm perfect.'

'Perfect! Take a look at yourself in that pool up there,' said the robin.

Firmly convinced he had nothing to fear, Roddy took a look at himself in the clear water. He was horrified on seeing the horn on top of his nose. He quickly took refuge on the bank. His self-image was in smithereens. How was he going to be able to face the other animals? During the next few days he wandered around, his head held low, talking to himself. 'I'm ruined,' he moaned. 'I can't face them and I can't face myself.'

But slowly and painfully he realised that he had no choice but to accept the truth. Having plucked up the courage to face himself, it was comparatively easy to face the others. And face them he did. And what a different Roddy they discovered! A more charming fellow you could not wish to find.

He became renowned for his acceptance of others, not as he wished them to be, but as they were, warts and horns and all. As far as himself was concerned, he never again pretended to be something he wasn't. Nor was he unduly worried about how others saw him. He would just try to be himself, but to be the best that he could be.

It's easy to see the rotten fruit on another person's tree. But Jesus asks us to look at the kind of fruit our own tree is producing. If there is good fruit there, it doesn't mean we can be complacent. The fact that we do some good things, doesn't make us thoroughly good people. And if we find some bad fruit on our tree, we shouldn't let it get us down. It doesn't mean we are bad through and through. Let us extend to others the same kind of understanding.

While the fruits Jesus is talking about are primarily 'good works', words too can be a great pointer. Some never stop talking about themselves. Others are highly critical of others. Others are very pessimistic. And so on. Words are a revelation of the heart. Jesus said, 'the words of the mouth flow out of what fills the heart.'

We need to listen to ourselves, to look at ourselves, and then correct what needs to be corrected. Because we can't guide others if we are blind ourselves. And we can't correct others effectively if we are riddled with faults ourselves.

HOMILY 3   **Death, where is your sting?**

It's not all that long ago since diabetes was a killer disease for which there was no remedy. But then insulin was discovered, and suddenly suffers were given back hope. Insulin doesn't stop people from getting diabetes, nor does it rid them of the distress it causes. But it does take the sting out of the disease for sufferers because they know it is not fatal. That makes a huge difference. It enables them to live with it.

St Paul says that the victory Christ gained over death has taken the sting out of death for us (Second Reading). How? Because we know death doesn't have the final say. But this doesn't mean all the pain, sadness and anguish have been taken out of it.

In her marvellous little book, *Wouldn't Take Nothing for my Journey Now,* Maya Angelu says:

> I can accept the idea of my own demise, but I am unable to accept the death of anyone else. I find it impossible to let a friend or relative go into that country of no return. Disbelief becomes my close companion, and anger follows in its wake. I answer the heroic question 'Death, where is thy sting?' with 'It is here in my heart and mind and memories.'

Death is an enormous reality. Today there is a tendency to deny it or at least to cover it up. Undertakers do their utmost to pretty it up. Preachers often use soothing phrases and euphemisms when talking about it. The next-of-kin are sometimes given drugs to cope with it. All of this is counterproductive. People must be helped to confront death and to become reconciled with it. Those who do so will find their lives enriched.

What best helps us to confront death is, of course, our Christian faith. Faith enables us to face death with courage and hope, because we know we can conquer it in Christ. We still have to face the pain and anguish of death. But because of Christ's victory over it, the sting has been taken out of it. Or rather, the sting is still there but it's no longer fatal.

However, just because we believe in the resurrection doesn't mean we know all the answers about what happens to us after death. But we don't need to know all the answers. It is enough that we trust in God. In a world where many desperately seek to know all the answers, it is not easy to admit this.

Each night we make a big act of faith. We abandon ourselves, body and soul, into the arms of sleep. We let go of everything, and for all practical purposes become like dead people, in the hope of rising again the following morning. Most people like to say some prayer before abandoning themselves to sleep. Here is an excellent prayer for the end of the day:

Lord, grant that each day before we enter the little death of sleep, we may undergo the little judgement of the past day, so that every wrong deed may be forgiven and every unholy thought set right. Let nothing go down into the depths of our being which has not been forgiven and sanctified. Then we shall be ready for our final birth into eternity, and look forward with love and hope to standing before you, who art both judge and saviour, holy judge and loving saviour. (Bishop Appleton).

ANOTHER STORY

Once there was a monk who was prone to outbursts of anger, so much so that he became a burden to himself and to his fellow monks. He believed he was making no spiritual progress in the monastery. He told the other monks that they were holding him back, constantly doing things that annoyed him and interfered with his prayer.

So he decided to leave the monastery and become a hermit. He thought that if he ceased to have any dealings with others, and lived by himself, his anger would die away because of lack of stimulation. And so he shut himself up in a cell, taking with him a jug of water.

In a careless moment he spilt the water. He went back to the monastery to refill the jug. But when he got back to his cell, he spilt it again. The same thing happened a third time. In a fit of rage he smashed the jug on the ground. Then he sat down, thoroughly disgusted with himself.

When his anger subsided he started to do some hard thinking. He came to realise that the cause of his bad temper lay not with the other monks but with himself. His anger was within him, and therefore would be with him wherever he went. He made up his mind to return to the monastery. There he apologised to his fellow monks, promising to work on his anger, and was taken back.

It's not difficult to see ourselves in this. We blame our problems on others. But the cause of our restlessness and impatience lies in ourselves, and not in others. We must mortify our passions, and in that way we will have peace with others.

PRAYER OF THE FAITHFUL

President: Let us bring our needs before God, confident that he will listen to our prayers.

Response: Lord, hear our prayer.

Reader(s): For the pope and the bishops: that they may guide the flock of Christ by word and example. [Pause] Let us pray to the Lord.

For all our temporal leaders: that they may bring transparency and integrity to their office. [Pause] Let us pray to the Lord.

For grace to be able to accept others as they are. [Pause] Let us pray to the Lord.

For the courage not to accept ourselves until we have tried to be as good as we can be. [Pause] Let us pray to the Lord.

For all gathered here: that faith in Christ's victory over death may take the sting out of death for us. [Pause] Let us pray to the Lord.

For our own special needs. [Longer pause] Let us pray to the Lord.

President: Father, source of all life, be our guide when we stray, our strength when we fall, and our comforter when we grow discouraged. We ask this through Christ our Lord.

REFLECTION   **Where to start**

When I was young and fired with the love of God,
I thought I would convert the whole world.
But soon I discovered that it would be quite enough
to convert the people who lived in my town,
and I tried for a long time to do that, but did not succeed.
Then I realised that my program was still too ambitious,
so I concentrated on those in my own household.
But I found that I could not convert them either.
Finally, it dawned on me: I must work on myself.
When people complain about what's wrong with the world,
they are usually blaming somebody else.
They should look at themselves first.
That way, they will know they are
making a difference in at least one life.
We can't take anyone farther than we've gone ourselves.

Ninth Sunday of the Year
A CENTURION'S FAITH

INTRODUCTION AND CONFITEOR

In the Gospel we see how Jesus praised the faith of a Roman centurion.

[213]

Our faith is the most precious thing we have. However, it may not be as strong or as deep or as active as it might be.

So let us turn to God, and ask him to strengthen our faith and help us to express it in service of others. [Pause]

Lord Jesus, you strengthen our faith when it is weak. Lord, have mercy.

You enliven our faith when it is stagnating. Christ, have mercy.

You make our faith generous when it is selfish. Lord, have mercy.

HEADINGS FOR READINGS

First Reading (I Kgs 8:41-43). Israel was gradually brought to a realisation that she had a mission to bring salvation also to other nations.

Second Reading (Gal 1:1-2.6-10). Paul warns the Galatians against troublemakers, that is, people who preach a different version of the Gospel to that which he originally brought to them.

Gospel (Lk 7:1-10). A story about the extraordinary faith shown in Jesus by a Roman army officer.

SCRIPTURE NOTE

The First Reading is part of a prayer Solomon made at the dedication of the temple he had built. Here he prays that the foreign sojourner might be received and find a hearing in the temple of the Lord. From this we see how Israel was gradually brought to a realisation that she had a mission to bring salvation to other nations.

This leads nicely into the Gospel. Here we see Jesus responding to the prayer of a Gentile, a Roman centurion. Although a healing happens, the emphasis is not on the healing, but on the faith of the centurion. Jesus contrasts the faith response of this Gentile with that of his own people. Luke is preparing us for the rejection of the Gospel by the Jews and its acceptance by the Gentiles.

HOMILY 1   **The centurion's faith**

It's clear that the centurion who came to Jesus was a good man. He had won the respect and gratitude of the local Jewish religious leaders by building a synagogue for them. And it's clear too that in his own way he was a spiritual man.

When his servant fell gravely ill he got some of the elders of the Jewish community to appeal to Jesus on his behalf, and did so with a faith so great that it surprised even Jesus. It caused him to declare, 'Nowhere in Israel have I found faith like this.'

What surprised Jesus was the fact that this great faith was shown by an outsider. Where did the centurion get his faith? It may have something to do with the fact that he was a soldier. As a soldier, he would have faced danger and death many times. People like that have a depth to

[214]

them which others who have lived a quieter life don't have. They have faced the hard issues and have found their own answers.

The centurion not only had faith, but great faith. What was so great about his faith, and what might we learn from it?

His faith was a courageous faith. He was not afraid of what others might think or say. Nor was he afraid to go to someone who belonged to the other camp. Our faith tends to be very timid. We don't dare enough.

His faith was a public faith. A private profession of faith is a good thing. But a public profession of faith is even better. At times we may be afraid to express our faith publicly in case others might ridicule us.

His faith was a strong faith. He had absolute faith in the power of Jesus. Alas, our faith is often weak and half-hearted.

His faith was a humble faith. It can't have been easy for a tough army man to go and ask for help from someone like Jesus. Furthermore, he didn't consider himself worthy that Jesus should come to his house. This was an amazing attitude coming from a man in his position.

Finally, his faith was an unselfish faith – it expressed itself in concern for another. That's a big test. Sometimes faith can be quite a selfish thing, centred entirely on one's own salvation. But there is no salvation for us independent of the salvation of others. True love shows itself in concern for others. So does true faith. A loveless faith is not a Christian faith.

The faith of the centurion shows us what to aim at. We often talk about keeping the faith, or losing the faith, as if faith were a thing. Faith is not a thing but a relationship with God. A relationship can wax and wane. It is not just a question of keeping the faith but of growing in it.

The centurion didn't need signs and wonders. The word of Jesus was enough for him. And he was not disappointed. His servant recovered. At the end of the day, all we have is the word of Jesus. To live by that word, is to live by faith.

HOMILY 2   **Faith expressed in love**

Those who say they believe often deny it in their lives. Whereas those who say they don't believe often affirm it in their lives. Sometimes it seems that outsiders (non-religious people) have more real faith than insiders (religious people). There is a fine example of this in today's Gospel.

The Gospel story is both a healing story and a faith story. But the emphasis is clearly on the latter – on the faith of the centurion. One would not have expected a man like him to have any faith. He was not a Jew but a Gentile. Yet not only had he faith, but he had great faith. Jesus praised his faith. What was so great about it?

First of all we must not mistake religious practice for faith. People might attend religious services, and yet live like pagans. Their deeds are a contradiction of their beliefs. Nothing so turns people off religion as those who give mere lip service to it.

It's clear that in the case of the centurion we are dealing with real faith. He was a good man and in his own way a spiritual man too. He had an excellent relationship with the local people for whom he had built a synagogue. This was very unusual. After all, he was a Gentile. And there was no love lost between Jews and Gentiles.

And then there was his deep concern for one of his servants. This again was unusual. In Roman law a servant had no rights. Yet here we see the centurion treating his servant as if he were his son.

From where did the centurion get his faith? It may have something to do with the fact that he was a soldier. As a soldier, he would have faced danger and death many times. People like that have a depth to them which others who have lived a quieter life don't have. They have faced the hard issues and have found their own answers.

Faith can blossom in the most unlikely places. At the end of the day we really don't know where the centurion got his faith. But that's not important. What matters is the quality of his faith. It shows how some nonbelievers surpass Christians in their purity of outlook and in their concern for their neighbour.

The quality of our faith must be reflected in the way we live – in the goals we pursue, in the values we live by, and especially in our dealings with others. The one essential quality that our faith should have is love. A loveless faith is like a lamp that doesn't give light. It is not Christian faith.

Faith is concerned with the mind, that is, with truths. But it is even more concerned with the heart, that is, with love. Essentially it consists in a relationship of love with God, a relationship which expresses itself in love for others. St John says: 'Whoever does not love does not know God, for God is love.' Faith is important, but love is even more important. The ideal is a faith which expresses itself in love.

HOMILY 3   **Immortal words**

A story is told that in ancient Rome, at the time of the Emperor Tiberius, there lived a good man who had two sons. One son was in the army, and had been sent to a distant region of the empire. The other son was a poet, and delighted all of Rome with his poems.

One night the father had a dream. An angel appeared to him and told him that the words of one of his sons would be known and repeated throughout the world for all generations to come. The father woke from his dream a very proud man.

Shortly after this the father died as he tried to save a child from being crushed by the wheels of a chariot. He went straight to heaven, where he met the angel that had appeared in his dream.

'You were a good man,' the angel said. 'I can grant you any wish you desire.'

And the man said, 'When you appeared in my dream, you said that my son's poems would be read by people for generations to come. I don't want anything for myself. But I would like to see what you said about my son come true.'

With that they were both projected far into the future. They were surrounded by thousands of people speaking a strange language. The man wept with happiness.

'I knew that my son's poems were immortal,' he said through his tears. 'Can you please tell me which of my son's poems these people are repeating?'

'The verses of your son who was the poet were very popular in Rome,' the angel said. 'Everyone enjoyed them. But when the reign of Tiberius ended, his poems were forgotten. The words you are hearing now are those of your son in the army.'

The man looked at the angel in disbelief. The angel continued: 'Your son went to serve in a distant place where he became a centurion. He was a good and just man. One day one of his servants fell ill, and he appeared doomed to die. Your son had heard of a holy man who was able to cure illnesses, and he rode out to meet him. When he met him he told him about the servant. The man made ready to go to his house with him. But your son said these words, words that have never been forgotten. He said, "Lord, I am not worthy that you should come under my roof. Say only the word and my servant will be healed."'

The words of the centurion were recorded in the Gospel, and we repeat them every time we approach Holy Communion. We believe that when we receive Communion, we receive Jesus. Each of us can say: Jesus comes to me as if I were the only person in the world. There is no better way of disposing ourselves to receive the Lord than to echo the words of the centurion: 'Lord, I am not worthy to receive you, but only say the word and I shall be healed.'

But it's not enough to merely echo those words. We must try to have the same sentiments the centurion had – humility, trust, and firm faith. We too need the Lord's healing.

PRAYER OF THE FAITHFUL

President: As we come to God with our needs, let us draw inspiration from the faith of the centurion and encouragement from Jesus' response to that faith.

Response: Lord, hear our prayer.

Reader(s); For Christians: that their lives may bear witness to the faith they profess with their lips. [Pause] Let us pray to the Lord.

For government leaders: that God may create a society in which all people can worship God freely. [Pause] Let us pray to the Lord.

For those with weak faith or no faith. [Pause] Let us pray to the Lord.

For grace to be aware of the needs of our neighbours, and to have the courage to love them as brothers and sisters. [Pause] Let us pray to the Lord.

For our own special needs. [Longer pause] Let us pray to the Lord.

President: Lord, grant that what we have said with our lips, we may believe in our hearts, and practise in our lives. We ask this through Christ, our Lord.

REFLECTION   **Faith for the new millennium**

Talking about faith for the new millennium Pope John Paul says:

May your faith be certain, that is, founded on the Word of God, on the Gospel message, and especially on the life, person, and word of Christ.

May your faith be strong; may it not hesitate or waver before the doubts and uncertainties which philosophical systems or fashionable movements suggest to you.

May your faith be joyful, because it is based on awareness of possessing a divine gift.

Let your faith be active; let it manifest itself in generous charity towards those who are in need; let it be expressed in your availability for initiatives for the building up of the Kingdom of God.

Tenth Sunday of the Year
GOD VISITS HIS PEOPLE

INTRODUCTION AND CONFITEOR

There are many things that cause tears to fall, but without doubt the greatest offender is death. Death brought tears to the eyes of Jesus too. But in Jesus, God visits all who mourn and gives them hope and consolation. Let us draw close him who at Nain dried the tears of a widow crying for her dead son. [Pause]

Lord Jesus, you visit us with forgiveness for our sins. Lord, have mercy.

You visit us with a peace this world cannot give. Christ, have mercy.

You visit us with a hope that brightens our darkest nights. Lord, have mercy.

HEADINGS FOR READINGS

First Reading (1 Kgs 17:17-24). Elijah restores the son of a widow to life.

Second Reading (Gal 1:11-19). Paul stresses that the Gospel he preaches came to him as a revelation from Jesus Christ.

Gospel (Lk 7:11-17). Jesus raised to life the only son of a widow at Nain.

SCRIPTURE NOTE

The First Reading tells the story of how Elijah restored life to the son of the widow of Zarephath. This miracle prepares the way for the parallel Gospel miracle. In both cases the hand of God is seen in the activity of the one who performs the miracle. The widow of Zarephath hails Elijah as a 'man of God', and the people of Nain recognise Jesus as a prophet, and see his deed as a merciful intervention of God in favour of his people.

The Gospel story is not about faith (no faith is required), but about the compassion of Jesus. Luke portrays Jesus as someone who is deeply affected by human suffering and does not pass by. By touching the bier he would have incurred ritual uncleanness, but that didn't worry him. For Luke, the widow is one of the 'little ones' to whom the Good News is brought.

HOMILY 1   **They have gone before us**

Any funeral scene is sad. But the scene which greeted Jesus and his apostles at Nain was a particularly sad one. It involved the funeral of a young boy, the only son of his widowed mother. The loss of a child is surely the heaviest cross any parent could be asked to carry.

They say that when the old die, they take part of our past (our history) with them. And when the young die they take part of our future with them. The sense of loss can be so great that it causes the one who mourns to neglect his/her own life, and perhaps to lose the will to live.

The Bible tells a very moving story about the agony King David went through when his young son fell gravely ill. (2 Sam 12:16-25). He was overcome with anguish, and pleaded with God for the child. He kept a strict fast and spent the night lying on the ground, covered with sacking. The officials of his household stood round him, trying to get him to rise from the ground but he refused. They were terrified as to what would happen if the boy died. On the seventh day the boy did die.

The people were now more afraid than ever that the king would do something desperate. They said, 'Even when the child was alive, we reasoned with him and he wouldn't listen to us.' When David hear them whispering he guessed that his son had died. 'Is the child dead?' he asked. 'Yes,' they replied.

'What will the king do now?' the people wondered. And they watched in fear. But the king surprised them. He got up off the ground, bathed and anointed himself and put on fresh clothes. Then he went into the sanctuary and prostrated himself before God. On returning to his house, he asked to be served with food and ate it.

Greatly puzzled at this behaviour, his retinue said, 'Why are you acting like this? When the child was alive you fasted and wept; now that the child is dead, you get up and take food.'

And King David replied, 'When my son was alive, I would have done anything to save him. But now he's gone. He cannot any more come to me. But I can go towards him.'

Thus David was able to get on with his life. He set an example of how to accept the claims of life in the face of unchangeable loss. We don't forget the deceased, and we have occasions for remembering them. But because life is precious we must go on living it. We grieve because a life is lost. But to spend our lives mourning would be to lose two lives.

At a time of death we may experience an apparent absence of God. But the opposite can also happen. Death can actually bring us close to God. Why is this? Because we realise that in death human things are of no avail. Only God can help us. God alone holds the keys of death. Therefore, we throw ourselves on the love and mercy of God. And just as God visited the people of Nain in the person of Jesus, so he visits us at a time of death with his gifts of comfort, hope and peace.

The dead are not dead. They have merely changed worlds. Our dead are not far from us. They still love us and can help us. But the dead don't come back. We go towards them. They are waiting for us. We go towards our loved ones in the sure hope that we will see them again.

HOMILY 2   **Consolation in grief**

A story is told about a famous rabbi by named Nahman. When Nahman's son died, he was inconsolable. In an effort to console him, some of his disciples visited him with advice.

Rabbi Eliezer said to him. 'Adam had a son and he died. Nonetheless, Adam allowed himself to be comforted. From this we can conclude that he and Eve reconciled themselves to their loss and fulfilled their allotted tasks on earth. So you too, Master, should find comfort in your bereavement.'

'Not enough that I have my own sorrows,' cried Rabbi Nahman, 'must you remind me of the sorrows of Adam?'

Rabbi Joshua said to him, 'Job lost all his sons and daughters in one day. Nonetheless, he found comfort. How do we know that? Because he said, "God gave and God took, blessed be the name of the Lord." Therefore, you too must find comfort.'

'Not enough that I have my own grief, must you remind me of Job's grief?' said Rabbi Nahman.

Next came Rabbi Solomon. He said to Nahman, 'Aaron had two grown sons and both died on the same day. Nonetheless, Aaron allowed himself to be comforted. How do we know that? Because it says in the Torah, "Aaron was silent." This means he ceased to lament. And so, Rabbi, you too must accept solace in your bereavement.'

'Not enough that I have my own sorrows,' said Nahman, 'must you remind me of the sorrows of Aaron?'

Rabbi Solomon was followed by Rabbi Simeon. He said, 'King David had a son and he died. Nonetheless, he permitted himself to be comforted. How do we know that? Because he went on with his life and had another son, whom he named Solomon. Like David you too must find comfort.'

'Not enough that I have my own grief, must you remind me of David's grief?' said Nahman.

Finally in came Rabbi Moses who said, 'Allow me to tell you a story. A king had given one of his servants a valuable object to hold for him. Each day the servant would lament, "Woe is me! When will the king come and take back his possession so that I won't be burdened with such a great responsibility?"

'The same holds true of you, Rabbi. You had a son who was an upright young man. He departed from the world unstained by evil. Therefore, you must find comfort in the thought that you have returned unsullied the possession entrusted to your care by the King of Kings.'

On hearing this Nahman cried, 'You have comforted me.' And he rose and put aside his grief.

This story doesn't mean that grief can be avoided. To live fruitfully after the death of a loved one, people need to go through a period of mourning. Those who do so will emerge enriched as persons. To grieve over the loss of a loved one is a good and necessary thing. Even Jesus grieved.

So, while faith is a wonderful comfort and support at a time of death, it doesn't do away with the necessity of grieving. What it does do is enable us to grieve with hope – the hope that we shall see our loved ones again.

When Jesus entered the town of Nain, he noticed that a boy was being carried to an early grave. Moved with compassion, he restored the boy to life, and gave him back to his widowed mother. On seeing this the people knew that God had visited them in the person of Jesus.

God visits us also. He, the Lord of life and death, has compassion on us in times of loss. And as he awakened the little boy of Nain to life on earth, we are confident that he will use his divine power to awaken us and our loved ones to eternal life in heaven. Let us comfort one another in our losses with this hope. This hope will enable us to get on with our lives as God wants us to.

HOMILY 3 **Getting life back**

In his book, *The Master,* the late Bryan MacMahon looked back on his years as a teacher in Listowel, Co. Kerry. He told the following story. One day a small farmer arrived at the school holding a sturdy boy by the hand. After the preliminary greetings and the child's particulars had been given and taken, looking down at the lad at his side, the man said, 'You see him? The winter morning he was born the doctor, a gruff and rough man, came up out of the room and said, "Your wife is okay, but the child is gone." Then he left without expressing one word of sympathy.

'I went down into the room and looked at the blue infant. He seemed as dead as a doornail. The wife was out for the count, so I took the child up to the kitchen fire. I warmed the little body and rubbed olive oil all over it. There was no kiss of life that time. I massaged him, turning him this way and that. Heat, oil massage for twenty minutes. The child suddenly gave a gurgle. He began to change colour. I worked away. A big belch and a cry – he was back from the dead. Here he is for you now, Master, I leave him in your good hands.'

The story stresses the beauty of life, and the great joy that results in getting life back. You see that joy in recovering alcoholics, and in people who have got their health back after a serious illness or accident. It's as if they were reborn.

Life is such a precious thing. But, alas, we tend to take it for granted. What we must try to do is to receive it daily as a gift from God. Then we will not cease to be amazed at the wonder and mystery of life.

But there is much more at stake in the story of the raising of the widow's son than adding some extra years to one's earthly life. What is really at stake is eternal life. Jesus in the source of eternal life for all who believe in him.

Only God has power to overcome death. It was because Elijah had access to the divine power that he was able to restore the widow's son to life. But it's clear from the miracle at Nain that Jesus had that power in himself. And we see the compassionate way in which he exercised it.

In death, particularly if it is sudden or tragic, people often experience an apparent absence of God. But death can actually bring us close to God. Why is this? Because we realise that in death human things are of no avail. Only God can help us. God alone holds the keys of death. Therefore, we throw ourselves on the love and mercy of God. And just as God visited the people of Nain in the person of Jesus, so God visits us at a time of death with comfort, hope and peace.

ANOTHER STORY

Near the entrance to New York Harbour there is a sunken shoal called Robbins Reef. A small lighthouse stands there, and for many years the keeper was an elderly widow. When they were first married, she and her husband lived on another lighthouse. She was very happy there because the lighthouse was on land, and she had a garden and was able to grow vegetables and flowers.

But then her husband was transferred to Robbins Reef. After one look at their new abode she didn't even want to unpack. She told her husband that she couldn't possibly stay there. It would be too lonesome. And since she wouldn't be able to have a garden, she wouldn't know how to pass the time.

However, she decided to give it a try, and eventually settled in. But she was only there a few years when her husband caught a cold while tending the light. The cold turned into pneumonia. He was taken to a hospital on the mainland. She stayed behind to tend the light. A few days later a boatman brought her the sad news that her husband had died. He was buried on a hillside which was visible from the lighthouse.

When she returned to the lighthouse she had decided to retire. But the first morning back she looked across towards her husband's grave, and it seemed that she received a clear and simple message from her husband. The message was: 'Tend the light!' And she decided to stay on as keeper of the lighthouse.

And whenever she felt like quitting, all she had to do was look across at the grave, and the same message came back to her: 'Tend the light!'

The way to manage a bereavement is to accept the loss. It doesn't mean forgetting it, but moving beyond it by getting on with life. The person who languishes in self-pity is doomed. Only the person who deliberately picks up and starts again triumphs over it.

PRAYER OF THE FAITHFUL

President: Jesus comforted the widow who had lost her only son. Let us pray to him who is the Lord of life and death.

Response: Lord, hear us in your love.

Reader(s): For the Church: that through its deeds the compassion of Christ may be seen and felt in the world. [Pause] We pray in faith.

For those who work for the sick and the dying: that Christ may give them warm hearts and gentle hands. [Pause] We pray in faith.

For parents who mourn the death of a child: that God may visit them with comfort. [Pause] We pray in faith.

For this community: that God may visit us with his grace, and keep us rooted in hope and love. We pray in faith.

For our departed relatives and friends: that God may awaken them to eternal life. [Pause] We pray in faith.

For our own special needs. [Longer pause] We pay in faith.

President: God of mercy and compassion, grant that in this Celebration we may experience your loving presence among us, and know that life is stronger than death. We ask this through the same Christ our Lord.

REFLECTION   **Giving them back to the Lord**

We give them back to you, O Lord, who first gave them to us;
and as you did not lose them in the giving,
so we do not lose them in the return.
Not as the world gives do you give, O Lover of souls.
For what is yours is ours also, if we belong to you.
Life is unending because love is undying,
and the boundaries of this life are but an horizon,
and an horizon is but the limit of our vision.
Lift us up, strong Son of God, that we may see further.
Strengthen our faith that we may see beyond the horizon.
And while you prepare a place for us, as you have promised,
prepare us also for that happy place;
that where you are we may be also,
with those we have loved, forever.   *(Bede Jarrett O.P.)*

Eleventh Sunday of the Year
GATE-CRASHING THE PARTY

INTRODUCTION AND CONFITEOR

People sometimes allow their sins to prevent them from drawing close the Lord. They say: 'I'm a sinner; I'm not worthy.' But in today's Gospel we see a sinful woman drawing close to Jesus in love and trust to hear from him the words: 'Your sins are forgiven, go in peace.' Let us then approach the Lord, sins and all, confident that we will find acceptance and forgiveness. [Pause]

Lord Jesus, you raise the dead to life in the spirit. Lord, have mercy.
You bring pardon and peace to the sinner. Christ, have mercy.
You plead for us at the right hand of the Father. Lord, have mercy.

HEADINGS FOR READINGS

First Reading (2 Sam 12:7-10.13). When challenged about his sin by the prophet Nathan, King David readily admits it and repents.

Second Reading (Gal 2:16.19-21). All Paul's strength comes from his belief in and union with Christ.

Gospel (Lk 7:36-8:3). We hear of a moving encounter in the house of a Pharisee between Christ and a sinful woman.

SCRIPTURE NOTE

David committed adultery with Bathsheba and then engineered the death of her husband, Uriah. It was a despicable move on the part of someone who had been so highly favoured by God. The only redeeming feature is that when the prophet Nathan confronted him with his sin, David immediately acknowledged it and repented. Nathan then assured him that God had forgiven his sin.

In the Gospel story Jesus shows himself to be 'the friend of sinners', which is Luke's favourite way of portraying him. The Pharisees had nothing to do with sinners. As a Pharisee, Simon was shocked at seeing Jesus allow a sinner, not only to approach him, but to actually touch him. He reckoned that Jesus must be unaware of the character of the woman. Otherwise he wouldn't have allowed her to touch him, thereby incurring ritual uncleanness. Hence, he concluded that he could not be the prophet whom many believed him to be.

Luke contrasts the cold reception Simon gave Jesus with the warm reception of the sinful woman. (There are no grounds for identifying the woman with Mary Magdalen.) What Jesus was saying to Simon (in his parable of the debtors) was that this woman, despite her sinful past, was nearer to God than he was.

There is a debate as to whether the woman was forgiven because she loved much, or whether she loved much because she had already been forgiven. Either meaning would fit Luke's stress on God's forgiveness in Christ and the loving response it evokes.

Luke also introduces us to a number of women disciples of Jesus. The same ones were present on Calvary, at the burial of Jesus, and were witnesses of the resurrection. In this way Luke prepares the way for the service of women in the early Church.

HOMILY 1   **A new beginning**

This is a true story about a white man who lived in Cape Town during the days of apartheid. He had just moved into a new neighbourhood. He soon noticed that the new neighbourhood was crawling with loiterers, all of them coloured (of mixed race). They could be seen hanging around, staring into homes and gardens. He immediately assumed they were up to mischief. But in at least one case he was way off the mark.

He should have known better. Their eyes seemed to caress objects, not to covet them. He had forgotten that up until recently this had been a so-called 'coloured area', but the people had been evicted by the government and dispatched to another part of the city.

One evening on arriving home from work he spotted a coloured man looking into his garden. There was hardly anything in the garden apart from an old pear tree. His indignation flared up. In an extremely angry mood, he went out and confronted the stranger. 'What are you doing here?' he demanded.

'I grew up in this house,' the man replied in an apologetic voice. 'I came around to take a look at the pear tree. Some years it used to produce only a few pears, other years it produced a lot. I just wanted to see how many pears were on it this year.'

On hearing this Tony felt deeply ashamed. In a flash all his anger evaporated. In a mumbling, fumbling way he tried to apologise to the man, but he was already making his way down the street. He regretted not having adopted a gentler approach with him. In a thoughtless and selfish way he had driven a dagger into an already deeply-wounded heart.

Contrast this with the way Jesus dealt with the sinful woman. The sinful woman had no right to show up at that party. She came only because Jesus was present. She appeared before him just as she was, and rendered a lovely service to him. And even though he knew what kind of woman she was, he graciously accepted her service. The others looked at the woman and saw the 'mud'. Jesus looked at her and saw the wounds. He saw that she had been sufficiently judged and punished by life. What she needed was healing, not condemnation.

By treating her with kindness, he helped her to believe in her own goodness. Had he treated her with disdain, he would have sent her back to the darkness from which she had come. You never improve people by rejecting them. The sheer goodness of Jesus made her feel that she too was good, and made her want to be like him.

As a result of her encounter with Jesus she began to live a new and better life. And she would travel further down that road than any of those who were now judging her. By welcoming her as he did, and graciously accepting her gift, Jesus put wind in her sails.

'If you want to find the spark, you must look among the ashes.' (Elie Wiesel)

HOMILY 2   **Reclaiming a person**

One night during a blackout a man fetched an old paraffin lamp from the attic. It was in a terrible state. The globe was cracked and almost black. He lit it anyway but it shed very little light. Besides, the wick smoked and gave off a foul smell. It was all too much for the man, who liked things to be perfect. 'This lamp is useless; it should be thrown out,' he said to his wife. And with that he extinguished it, and lit a candle instead.

Three weeks later another blackout occurred. This time it was the wife who provided the light. She produced a beautiful oil lamp and lit it. Its rosy glow cast an enchantment over the house.

'That's a lovely lamp!' said the husband. 'Where did you get it?'

'That's the lamp you wanted to throw out,' she replied.

'I don't believe it!' he exclaimed.

After examining it at close quarters, he said, 'It must have cost a lot of money to get it into this shape?'

'As a matter of fact, it cost very little money,' she replied. 'All I had to buy was a new wick and a tinted globe. But what it did cost me was a lot of time and effort in cleaning and polishing it. I could see that underneath the layers of dirt there was a beautiful lamp. And don't you think I have been proved right?'

'I couldn't agree more,' he replied.

It was much easier to cast the lamp aside than to take the time and the care to clean it up and polish it. It's the same with people. It's much easier to label and pigeonhole them, than to befriend them and help them up out of their misery. To reclaim a person is a delicate and difficult task.

Simon was a Pharisee, one of the 'separated ones' who would have nothing to do with sinners. Consequently, he was scandalised to see that Jesus allowed a sinner, not only to approach him, but to actually touch him.

In Simon's mind the woman was beyond redemption: she was a sinner, and would always be a sinner. Therefore, he didn't want anything to do with her. You might have thought that Jesus too would have been repelled by someone like her. Yet he allowed her to approach him and to touch him. There wasn't a hint of condemnation.

There are many in our society who won't accept the possibility that people can change? They are not willing to give people a second chance. A culture that doesn't believe in redemption is a culture without hope.

Jesus knew well that the woman was a sinner. But he saw that there was another and better side to her. He saw that she was thirsting to be seen as a person and not as an object. By graciously accepting her humble and loving service, he helped her to believe in that side and to let it unfold. It is marvellous to feel that somebody has confidence in us, that we are not judged or condemned, but loved.

We have to learn to see the goodness in one another, and affirm that. People's faults can be cured only by loving them. We cannot change anyone unless we accept them as they are. Condemnation does not liberate; it oppresses. Jesus did not condemn the woman. He saw her sorrow, her humility, her courage and her love. He affirmed this side of her.

The woman had never experienced anything like this before. Jesus was the best person she had ever met. She was not only forgiven, but loved by Jesus. She was so happy that she was almost frightened of her happiness. When she went away, she was, as the Africans say, walking again with the moon and the stars.

HOMILY 3   **Passing judgement on oneself**

In the Bible we read how King David fell in love with the wife of one of his soldiers, Uriah. In order to marry her, he had Uriah posted to the front in the hope that he would be killed, which is what happened. It was a horrible thing to do. The prophet Nathan decided to confront David with his sin. However, instead of confronting him directly, he told him a story which went like this:

'In the same town were two men, one rich, the other poor. The rich man had flocks and herds in great abundance; the poor man had nothing but a ewe lamb, a small one he had bought. This he fed, and it grew up with him and his children, eating his bread, drinking from his cup, sleeping on his breast; it was like a daughter to him.

'One day a traveller arrived to stay at the house of the rich man. The rich man refused to take a sheep from his own flock to provide for the traveller. Instead he took the poor man's lamb, killed it and prepared it for his guest.

'On hearing this David's anger flared up and he said, "As God lives, the man who did this deserves to die!" Then Nathan said to him, "You are that man."'

To his credit David saw what Nathan was getting at. And he said, 'I have sinned against the Lord.' Nathan assured him that God would forgive him.

By the subtle approach he adopted, Nathan enabled David to see the magnitude of his sin and to condemn it himself. The greatest height a trial can attain is where the accused sees the evil he has done, passes judgement on himself, and repents. 'One pang of conscience is worth more than many lashes.' (Talmud).

Now consider the sinful woman in the Gospel story. It took great courage on her part to enter the house of a Pharisee and come before Jesus in her sinfulness. In doing so she became very vulnerable. She exposed herself to the possibility of public condemnation and shaming.

Far from repulsing her, Jesus received her in a kind and gracious manner. He was deeply moved by what she did. He didn't have to confront her with her sins. She was already painfully aware of them, and sorry for them. He assured her that she was forgiven. Not only that. He let her know that she was loved. Thus she was able to make a new start.

One day a friend paid a visit to Michelangelo. He found the great sculptor chipping away at a huge block of marble. The floor was covered with bits of marble and dust. It was not a pretty scene.

'What in heaven's name are you doing?' the friend asked.

'I'm releasing the angel imprisoned in this marble,' Michelangelo replied.

Simon, the Pharisee, looked at the woman and saw a sinner who would always be a sinner. Jesus looked at her and saw a sinner who was capable of becoming a saint.

As a result of her encounter with Jesus the woman began to live a new and better life. And she would travel further down that road than any of those who were now judging her. By welcoming her as he did, and graciously accepting her gift, Jesus put wind in her sails.

PRAYER OF THE FAITHFUL

President: Jesus received the sinful woman with great kindness and respect. We are confident that he will receive us in the same way as we approach him with our needs.

Response: Lord, graciously hear us.

Reader(s): For the Church: that it may be a place where sinners can experience the love and mercy of Christ. [Pause] Lord, hear us.

For Christians: that they may imitate the compassion and forgiveness of Christ. [Pause] Lord, hear us.

For those who make and administer our laws: that they may be both wise and compassionate in their judgements. [Pause] Lord, hear us.

For those who have been the victims of unfair and harsh judgements. [Pause] Lord, hear us.

For grace never to belittle the dignity of another person. [Pause] Lord, hear us.

For our own special needs. [Longer pause] Lord, hear us.

President: God of mercy, help us to keep our hearts pure, our minds clean, our words true, and our deeds kind. We ask this through Christ our Lord.

REFLECTION   **Jesus, the healer**

I had a dream that I came to the Lord
trembling, ashamed, fearful and sad.
And I told him my tale of betrayals.
When I had finished, I continued to kneel there,
waiting for the punishment I felt I richly deserved.
But what did he do?
He rose from his chair, took some ointment, and said,
'Let me dress your wounds.'
'What wounds?' I asked, puzzled.
'I'm the one who has wounded others.'
But then in a flash I saw he was right.
I too was wounded, for to sin is to suffer.
Astonished by his mercy, I let him dress my wounds.
Afterwards I went away airborne with joy.

His sheer goodness made me feel that I too was good,
and made me want to be like him.

Twelfth Sunday of the Year
A SUFFERING MESSIAH

INTRODUCTION AND CONFITEOR

Jesus asked the apostles: 'Who do people say that I am?' The same question is asked of each of us. Who is Jesus for me? And if I believe in him, what difference does that make to the way I live? [Pause] Let us now make our own the words the Scriptures use to describe the identity of Jesus.

Lord Jesus, you are the Christ, the Son of the living God. Lord, have mercy.

You are the Lamb of God who takes away the sins of the world. Christ, have mercy.

You are the light of the world. Lord, have mercy.

HEADINGS FOR READINGS

First Reading (Zech 12:10-11). The prophet looks forward to a time when a new spirit will be poured out on the people (as happened at Pentecost), and they will mourn over the one they put to death (Jesus, the Christ).

Second Reading (Gal 3:26-29). Our unity in Christ has done away with distinctions, and means that Jews and Gentiles alike are heirs to the promises made to Abraham.

Gospel (Lk 9:18-24). Jesus is revealed as the Messiah, but a suffering Messiah. Suffering will be part of the lives of his followers too.

SCRIPTURE NOTE

It's not easy to determine the original application of the First Reading. But the early Christians saw in it a foreshadowing of the outpouring of the Spirit on the disciples at Pentecost, and of the mourning of the disciples over Jesus, the Christ, who had been put to death.

In the Gospel Jesus raises the question as to what people were saying about him. The apostles, having just returned from their missionary tour, had been in closer touch with public opinion than he. Peter's reply, 'The Christ of God,' meant that Jesus was the one whom God had anointed, namely, the Messiah. Jesus tells them not to reveal this to the people at large because, given the false ideas they had concerning the Messiah, it could only lead to trouble.

Jesus says that his messiahship will involve suffering, rejection and death. He will suffer because of the values he espouses and the kind of people he favours. And his disciples too will suffer for standing for the same values, and favouring the same kind of people.

HOMILY 1 **What is a hero?**

Immediately after Peter had declared that Jesus was the Messiah, Jesus said, 'The Son of Man is destined to suffer grievously ... ' The idea of a suffering Messiah made no sense to the apostles. The Messiah would be a great conquering hero, and was destined for glory. The Messiah, was indeed destined for glory, but not worldly glory. And Jesus would turn out to be a hero. But not the kind of hero they had in mind.

The actor, Christopher Reeve, is best remembered for his role as *Superman*. He tells how when the first Superman movie came out, he gave dozens of interviews to promote it. The question he was most frequently asked was: 'What is a hero?' He remembers how easily he'd talk about it, and the glib response he repeated so many times.

For him a hero is someone who performs a courageous action without considering the consequences. A soldier who crawls out of a foxhole to drag an injured comrade back to safety, the prisoner of war who never stops trying to escape even though he knows he may be executed if caught. Also people like Houdini, Charles Lindbergh, John Wayne, John F. Kennedy, and sports figures like baseball legends, Babe Ruth and Joe Di Maggio.

But then something happened to Reeve which completely changed his perspective on what it means to be a hero. In May 1995 he had a fall from a horse, which left him paralysed from the neck down. Now he thinks of a hero as an ordinary individual who finds the strength to go on in spite of overwhelming obstacles. This is real courage. This takes real strength.

For example, the fifteen-year-old who, while wrestling with his brother, landed on his head, leaving him paralysed and barely able to swallow or speak. Or a man, paralysed from the chest down in a car accident at seventeen, completing his education and working on Wall Street at the age of thirty-two. People like these are real heroes, and so are the families and friends who have stood by them.

As Superman, Reeve came across to many as a hero. But that was easy. He was in perfect health. Besides, as he says himself, 'Superman was only play-acting. But this is real life, where everything is a struggle.' The optimism and courage which Reeve has shown in learning to cope with his disability, and the generosity with which he has taken up the cause of other wheelchair people, has won him legions of new admirers.

We may have the impression that everything was different for Jesus. After all, was the Son of God. But St Paul tells us that when Jesus assumed our condition, he put aside the power and the glory which belonged to him as the Son of God. The glory that finally came to him was a glory he won by a life of obedience to his Father, a life that ended in pain, shame, and death. It was his passion and death that brought him to glory. There is no achievement without pain and sacrifice.

Suffering is not something Christians should seek. Jesus did not seek suffering; Gethsemane makes that clear. But suffering will inevitably be part of the life of the Christian as it was part of Jesus' life. His disciples will suffer for standing for the values he stood for, and favouring the kind of people he favoured.

HOMILY 2 **Becoming ourselves**

Some people have a hunger for approval. They may have grown up with a sense of being ignored, unappreciated, and criticised. People who have a real, deep doubt about themselves are always looking for confirmation from others. The more people lack personal identity and success, the more they feel the need to identify themselves with a group or social class which is thriving. Some put on a mask in order to win approval. But what a person is always comes out. What one projects rarely comes off.

When Jesus asked the apostles, 'Who do people say that I am?' he wasn't asking it for his own sake. He was asking it for their sake. He was sure of who he was. He had such extraordinary self-possession that he was able to face both adulation and hostility with utter calmness.

The Gospel talks about renouncing oneself, and even 'dying to self'. The spiritual life does involve self-denial and dying to a side of oneself, but over-all it's rather a question of *becoming oneself,* one's true, full self. This is the most important thing in life. We can't be fully alive and happy otherwise. So, whatever our path in life, what really matters is that we should become ourselves, and not be paralysed by fear of what others think of us.

The emergence of the true self is especially hard in public life. Pontius Pilate knew that Jesus was innocent but was afraid of losing his position, with its honours and privileges which meant everything to him. When we commit an injustice through fear of losing our position, the 'self' is plunged deeper into darkness. But the true self emerges when we follow our conscience, and are brave enough to risk stepping out of line.

The emergence of the true self takes place in humility, through all sorts of setbacks and even mistakes. It is a slow and beautiful growth through all the stages of life. As we travel towards it, we are called to be patient, and allow all the things that happen to us – illnesses, crises, bereavements – to work gently within us. Where we have a real desire to live in truth, everything will work together for our good and for our growth towards human and spiritual maturity.

It may not be possible to see this growth. It is something that happens inside ourselves. It takes place particularly in people who are humble and socially unimportant. It does not necessarily bring honours or financial rewards. But it will result in a deep communion with others.

In the past, spirituality was concerned with putting on another self – often a pious, holy self. True spirituality is not a question of putting on something from outside ourselves, but of drawing out what we have been given. It is the emergence of the spiritual self. The spiritual self is the true self, made of human stuff but bearing the image of God.

Through all the stages of growth, the real aim in life is to become ourselves, to allow the barriers to come down so that the deepest 'I' can emerge? It's not about becoming what others want us to be, or crying out to get attention at any price. It's not about trying to be someone else, but about growing from the seed of life within each of us. We are strange pilgrims, journeying to become who we really are. It is tragic how few people ever 'possess their souls' before they die.

HOMILY 3   **People's perceptions**

Who do people say that I am? or How do I appear to others? These are questions that many people ask, but especially those who are in the public eye.

When Jesus asked the question: 'Who do people say that I am?', he wasn't asking it for his own sake but for the sake of the apostles. Jesus was sure of who he was. He had such extraordinary self-possession that he was able to face both adulation and hostility with utter calmness.

Some people have a hunger for approval. They may have grown up with a sense of being ignored, unappreciated, and criticised. People who have a real, deep doubt about themselves are always looking for confirmation from others.

We need to find our own reality so that we can stand on our own feet. Then we won't need to be propped up by others. There are people who have a steady flame shining from deep inside them. This is not extinguished when others criticise or ignore them, for it is not dependent on what others think of them. It is what they think of themselves with a quiet certainty.

However, sometimes to see ourselves as others see us can be a salutary thing. Alfred Nobel, a Swedish industrialist, was rich and famous. He had invented dynamite. But as he neared the end of his life he was extremely unhappy. He had never married and all his life he had been plagued by ill-health. As a result he had a pessimistic view of life.

Then one morning he read his own obituary in a newspaper. It had been a mistake by a journalist. He was very disturbed by what he read. What hurt him most was the false image people had of him. The world knew him as the 'dynamite king'. That's how he would be remembered. There was no mention in the obituary of his desire to unite people, and to better the quality of human life.

It came as a great shock to him to discover that everything that was essential, everything that made up the kernel of himself, was hidden from other people; and all that was false in him was out in the open. He felt completely misunderstood. He wasn't like that. He made a decision to take immediate action to let the world know what his true ideals and aims were.

He left most of his vast fortune in trust for the betterment of the world. He set up five prizes that would be awarded to men and women who had made outstanding contributions in the areas of physics, chemistry, medicine, literature and peace. He wanted to be remembered, not as the man who had invented something capable of blowing the world asunder, but as the man who had the good of humanity deeply at heart.

What happened to Nobel shows us how wrong people can be in their judgement of a person. It happened to Jesus himself. Today's Gospel shows what crazy ideas people had of him. Some thought he was John the Baptist (already dead). Others thought he was one of the ancient prophets come back to life.

Jesus was the Messiah, as Peter correctly divined. But he was not to be a glorious Messiah as the people expected. He was to be a suffering one. He wouldn't rule, he would serve. Jesus wasn't interested in projecting the kind of image the people wanted. He knew he had a God-given destiny to fulfil, and would not be deflected from it.

We are in trouble if our main concern is to project a good image and to live up to people's expectations. The only thing that we are called to be is to be true to ourselves. We can't be fully alive and happy otherwise. But we should not be content until we are the best that we can be. So, whatever our path in life, what really matters is that we should be ourselves before God, and before others. This is the journey home.

PRAYER OF THE FAITHFUL

President: Jesus, the suffering Messiah, understands our struggles. Therefore, we can be confident that he will listen to our prayers.

Response: Lord, graciously hear us.

Reader(s): For all Christians: that they may not to be afraid to profess publicly their faith in Christ. [Pause] Lord, hear us.

For those who hold public office: that they may speak the truth and act justly. [Pause] Lord, hear us.

For all those who suffer for their belief in Christ: that may be strong. [Pause] Lord, hear us.

For grace always to strive to be ourselves, and not be unduly influenced either by flattery or criticism. [Pause] Lord, hear us.

For our own special needs. [Longer pause] Lord, hear us.

President: Lord, without your grace we falter. Help us to follow Christ and to live according to your will. We ask this through the same Christ our Lord.

PRAYER/REFLECTION   **True glory**

Some people have an excessive need of approval from others.
The great luminaries of stage and screen
glow under the adulation of their fans.
But when the curtain goes down, and the lights fade,
they often feel empty and lonely,
because they realise that they are valued,
not for themselves, but only for their talent.
Lord, grant that I may not get carried away
when people praise me,
or become downcast when people ignore me.
Grant that I may have a little lamp of my own,
a lamp which will enable me to see
the dignity which you have given me,
and which no one can take from me.

Thirteenth Sunday of the Year
ON NOT TURNING BACK

INTRODUCTION AND CONFITEOR

In today's Gospel we see how Jesus headed resolutely for Jerusalem even though he knew that death awaited him there. In this we see how faithful Jesus was to the task the Father had given him. Fidelity can be very costly at times. Let us bring our commitments to Jesus, asking pardon for our failings, and courage for the future. [Pause]

Lord Jesus, you strengthen us when we are weak. Lord, have mercy.

You give us courage when we are afraid. Christ, have mercy.

You help us to be generous when we are tempted to think only of ourselves. Lord, have mercy.

HEADINGS FOR READINGS

First Reading (1 Kgs 19:16.19-21). Elisha is called to succeed the prophet Elijah.

Second Reading (Gal 5:1.13-18). Despite the Galatians' union with Christ and the gift of the Spirit, they still must struggle against the flesh.

Gospel (Lk 9:51-62). Jesus rejects retaliation and expects wholehearted commitment from his disciples.

SCRIPTURE NOTE

The First Reading relates the call of Elisha. By throwing his cloak over him Elijah was symbolising the transfer of power. We see how total was the response of Elisha. In slaughtering the oxen and burning the plough, he was precluding a return to his old way of life. Jesus demanded a similar response from those who would follow him.

In the Gospel we begin a new section of Luke's Gospel (9:51–18:14): Jesus' journey to Jerusalem. Luke portrays Jesus as one who knows his destiny and accepts it from God. But he is not interested in telling us the actual route Jesus followed. Instead, he tells us about incidents that happened along the way.

In the first passage we see the hostility Jesus encountered from the inhabitants of a Samaritan village, and his refusal to retaliate as James and John suggested. This is followed by the stories of three would-be followers of Jesus. Jesus tells them that total commitment is demanded of a disciple. The choices are not between good and evil, but between the good and the best.

HOMILY 1 **On not retaliating**

Jackie Hewitt, chairman of the Shankhill Community Council, was driving back to Belfast from Millisle on the Antrim coast, where he had been at a war memorial ceremony. He was listening to his car radio when the news came in that a bomb had gone off on the Shankhill Road (Loyalist/ Protestant area), and that three people were dead. Blinded by anger, he thought to himself, 'That's it! We need a bomb on the Falls Road (Nationalist/Catholic area).'

As he neared the city, he heard another news flash on the radio – seven people were now believed dead. And he thought to himself, 'We need two bombs on the Falls.' But when he got to the scene, and stood amidst the grief and anger of his community, his own thoughts haunted him. 'When I heard other people saying what I was thinking, then it frightened me.'

At the time of Jesus, the Samaritans and the Jews were mutual enemies. So, when the inhabitants of that Samaritan village heard that Jesus was heading for Jerusalem, they refused to receive him. James and John were indignant. They howled for revenge. They wanted Jesus to hit back – and how! To call down fire from heaven on an entire village.

Here we see an example of tribalism, and how the tribe demands one's highest if not total loyalty. My tribe right or wrong, it's still my tribe.

Firstly, there is the tribalism of the Samaritans. Whatever they might think of Jesus as an individual, he was a member of the other tribe – the Jews. Therefore, they would have nothing to do with him.

Then there is the tribalism of the two apostles. Their idea was outrageous. According to their way of thinking, those who oppose us are not just our enemies but God's too. By this time they ought to have known that this was not Jesus' way of doing things. As far as Jesus was concerned, the question of punishment didn't arise. Jesus didn't go in for tribalism; he rose above it.

It demands more courage and strength not to retaliate than to retaliate. *Solidarity* was a non-violent liberation movement formed among the shipyard workers of Gdansk in Poland during the Communist era. It's leader, Lech Walesa, says, 'The Solidarity movement was successful because at every point it fought for whatever solution was the most humane, the most worthy, and for whatever was an alternative to brutality and hatred. When it needed to be, it was also a movement that was persistent, obstinate, unyielding. And that is why we eventually succeeded.'

To walk away demands great self-control. Jesus is not advocating weakness. If we want to feel loved and respected, we must give up the need to control. Giving up control is often confused with weakness. The weak person feels he must win; the strong person knows he doesn't have to win every argument.

To follow Jesus' teaching of non-violence and non-retaliation requires exceptional strength and a strange kind of love. Evil must be resisted, but not by doing further evil. Evil can be overcome only by good. Religion can fuel conflicts, but it can also help us to go beyond them. The escalation of evil can be stopped only by one who humbly absorbs it, without passing it on.

HOMILY 2   **No turning back**

In his autobiography, *An Only Child,* the Irish writer Frank O'Connor, recalls vividly the night he finally decided to become a writer. He had lost his job with the Great Southern Railway and had no money. His neighbours regarded him as a mad good-for-nothing. Nevertheless, he gave his first public reading of something that he had written.

> What mattered was the act of faith, the hope that somehow, somewhere, I would be able to prove that I was neither mad nor a good-for-nothing; because now I realised that whatever it might cost me, there was no turning back. When as kids we came to an orchard wall that seemed too high to climb, we took off our caps and tossed them over the wall, and then had no choice but to follow them. I had tossed my cap over the wall of life, and I knew I must follow it, wherever it had fallen.

In the Gospel Jesus dealt in a somewhat similar fashion with three would-be followers who came to them. He said, 'No one who puts a hand to the plough and looks back is fit for the kingdom of God.' He was highlighting the need for commitment, and saying that there could be no turning back. If you wish to plough a straight furrow, you must give your undivided attention to what you are doing. If you keep on looking back you won't do a good job. You need dedication and commitment. If you begin such a task, you should give it your all.

All of us have put our hand to some 'plough' or other. Young people to their studies … husbands and wives to their marriage … priests to their ministry … to mention just a few. And in baptism we have put our hands to another plough – the following of Christ, or discipleship.

If we keep on looking back our attention will be divided. So too will our energy. We won't be fully committed. We will be half-hearted. We are likely to lose time, to lose sight of our goal, and be tempted to turn back or even quit altogether. To look back suggests that we are having second thoughts, and perhaps doubts and regrets. Perhaps we are finding the cost too high. Maybe other things that we thought we have given up are still tugging at our hearts?

But if we keep looking forward, we will give our undivided attention to the chosen task. We will be completely committed. We will be wholehearted. That will give us great strength. All our resources will be enlisted and harnessed to the task. We will not be easily sidetracked. And so we have an excellent chance of completing the task. Those who are wholehearted find joy in the task, despite hardship. There is no such joy for the halfhearted. So the message is: Don't turn back; don't even look back.

The First Reading shows how Elisha obeyed the call of Elijah. His response was total, and by killing his oxen and burning the plough he was precluding a return to his old life. In the Gospel we see the best example in Jesus himself. He set has face towards Jerusalem, even though he knew that rejection, betrayal, and death awaited him there. He would not be deflected from that path. He has given an example to his followers of the kind of dedication that is required.

This kind of dedication is a great challenge. It may be easy at the start. But in order to persevere, we need the grace of God. That grace will keep us faithful to God and to one another. God will help us to stay on the chosen road, to persevere at the chosen task. Then we will know the joy of the dedicated, and in due time be found fit for the Kingdom.

HOMILY 3   **Remaining faithful**

Viktor Frankl, who spent three years in Auschwitz and Dachau, tells the following story. As a doctor he spent a lot of his time tending sick and dying camp inmates. Near the end of the war he and a companion devised a way of escaping.

He began to collect up his few possessions: a food bowl, a pair of torn mittens, notes for a book he hoped to write. Then he took a last look in on his patients where they lay on planks of rotten wood on either side of a hut. He came to one man who was very close to death. Frankl did his best to hide from him the fact that he was escaping. But the man wasn't fooled. In a tired sad voice said, 'So you too are getting out.'

Frankl denied it. But the words 'So you too are getting out' cut him and accused him. After finishing his rounds he came back to the man. Again he was greeted with a look of despair which went right through him. He felt he was betraying this man. Suddenly he decided to take his fate into his own hands. He ran out of the hut and told his friend to leave without him. He was staying with his patients. At once the unhappy feeling of betrayal left him. And he says that even though he had no idea what the days ahead would bring him, he gained an inner peace he had never before experienced. And he also survived the camps.

Today's Gospel begins with the announcement that Jesus turned his face resolutely towards Jerusalem. He knew well what awaited him there – rejection, betrayal, and death. But for him there was no turning back. His Father had given him the task of bringing salvation to his brothers and sisters. He would not opt out now.

Karen Blixen (author of *Out of Africa*) says, 'There is probably always one moment in life when there is still the possibility of two courses, and another when only one is possible. At the latter point I have burnt my boats, and afterwards there can be no retreat.' Jesus had reached that point.

To those who wished to become his disciples he said, 'The person who puts his hand to the plough, and who *keeps on looking back*, is not fit for the kingdom of heaven.' What is at stake is commitment and dedication to the chosen task.

This may be easy at the start. But as the years go by, the difficulties increase. The constant grind of day-to-day living takes its toll. We begin to look back. It's easy to renege in difficult times on what we promised in rosier times. A container which heats up quickly loses its heat quickly also. Today we live in the age of the 'drop-out'.

Fidelity is not an easy road. Jesus didn't hide this from his disciples. He who urges us to be faithful, has set us an example himself, and promises to help us.

The Lord still calls people today, and there still are those who respond. What does the following of Christ mean for the ordinary person? It means to be called to be a Christian where you are and in your chosen profession. There are more ways than one of serving Christ and his Gospel. The call is in the first instance to discipleship rather than to apostolate.

ANOTHER STORY

Dostoyevsky tells how as a young boy he was being taken by his father away from the city. Being young, he was naturally full of dreams and hopes for the new life which was opening up before him. Soon, however, he got a harsh lesson in reality.

They stopped at an inn for refreshments. While there, a government official came in and quickly downed a couple of vodkas. Then he rushed out to his troika and, without a word of explanation, fell on the poor unfortunate driver, a peasant lad, beating him with his fists. Then he ordered him to get going. The driver's response was to bring the whip whistling down the backs of the horses with all his might. Beside themselves with fear and pain, the animals set off at full gallop.

Violence breeds violence. But Christ challenges us to respond to darkness with light, to respond to what is worst in the other with what is best in us. The most important issue of our times is how to overcome evil without doing further evil in the process.

PRAYER OF THE FAITHFUL

President: In setting out for Jerusalem Jesus gave us an example of his fidelity to God and to us. Let us pray for the grace that we too may be faithful.

Response: Lord, hear our prayer.

Reader(s): For all the baptised: that they may be faithful to the call they receive in baptism to be disciples of Jesus. [Pause] Let us pray to the Lord.

For political leaders: that they may renounce violence and embrace non-violent means of resolving conflicts. [Pause] Let us pray to the Lord.

For married couples: for the grace to remain faithful to the commitment they made to one another on their wedding day. [Pause] Let us pray to the Lord.

For strength to overcome anger with love, and evil with good. [Pause] Let us pray to the Lord.

For our own special needs. [Longer pause] Let us pray to the Lord.

President: Lord, grant that we who have committed ourselves to follow you, may not keep on looking back, but may go forward in faith, hope and love, and so be found worthy of your kingdom. We ask this through Christ our Lord.

REFLECTION   **Promises to keep**

Whose woods these are I hardly know,
his house is in the village though;
he will not see me stopping here
to watch his woods fill up with snow.

My little horse must think it queer
to stop without a farmhouse near,
between the woods and frozen lake
the darkest evening of the year.
He gives his harness bells a shake
to ask if there is some mistake;
the only other sound is the sweep
of easy wind and downy flake.
The woods are lovely, dark and deep,
but I have promises to keep;
and miles to go before I sleep,
and miles to go before I sleep.

(Robert Frost)

Fourteenth Sunday of the Year
SENDING OUT SEVENTY-TWO DISCIPLES

INTRODUCTION AND CONFITEOR

Jesus sent out his disciples as bearers of peace, healing and the good news of salvation to others. We must first possess these gifts before we can share them with others. Let us turn to the Lord, from whom all good gifts come. [Pause]

Lord Jesus, you give us a peace this world cannot give. Lord, have mercy.

You heal the wounds caused by our sins and the sins of others. Christ, have mercy.

You help us to open our minds and hearts to receive the good news of salvation. Lord, have mercy.

HEADINGS FOR READINGS

First Reading (Is 66:10-14). Written after the return from the Babylonian exile, this poem paints a glowing picture of the blessings God will bestow on Jerusalem and its inhabitants.

Second Reading (Gal 6:14-18). Paul insists that the Christian life means becoming like Christ. He himself bears the marks of Christ's passion on his body.

Gospel (Lk 10:1-12.17-20). The sending out of seventy-two disciples.

SCRIPTURE NOTE

The First Reading is part of a poem written after the return from the Babylonian exile. It paints a glowing picture of the blessings God will bestow on Jerusalem and its inhabitants. It likens Jerusalem to a mother who lovingly nurses her children. It foreshadows the blessings that will result from the coming of the Kingdom of God with Jesus (Gospel).

While all the synoptic Gospels record a sending out of the Twelve, only Luke records the sending out of seventy-two disciples. This second sending out is explained by the size of the harvest, and the fact that time is short, and Jesus can't do it all by himself. It also foreshadows the preaching of the Gospel to the whole world, a favourite theme of Luke.

The mission of the disciples was an extension of Jesus' own mission. In understanding his instructions to them, we must remember that this was only a temporary mission, of short duration and limited to the surrounding Jewish towns and villages.

HOMILY 1   **Bearers of peace**

When Jesus sent out the seventy-two disciples he said that their first words on entering a house were to be: 'Peace to this house.' They were to be ambassadors of peace and goodwill. Without peace nothing is possible.

One Christmas morning in Northern Ireland, in the height of 'the troubles', a Catholic priest went across the road to the local Protestant church, to wish the minister and his congregation a happy Christmas. The minister received him warmly, reciprocated his greeting, and later made a return visit. However, some elders of his Church reacted angrily and took steps to have the minister removed from the parish.

Those two clergymen felt they were only doing what Christ would want them to do – to be an instruments of peace and reconciliation in a troubled and divided society.

Peace is not a negative thing. It is not just the absence of war or enmity. Peace is a positive thing. It implies openness, friendship, tolerance, goodwill, hospitality, reconciliation. It disposes us to reach out to others. It helps to break down barriers of suspicion, fear, prejudice, bigotry.

Working for peace means welcoming people close to us, those who annoy us or disagree with us, those who provoke anguish within us. To take the path of peace is to accept people as they are, with all their limitations and weaknesses. The people we need to make peace with are not our friends but our enemies.

Shortly before Communion the priest says to us, 'The peace of the Lord be with you always.' What a wonderful gift is being offered to us – the peace of Christ, a peace which the world cannot give. Then he invites us to 'offer each other a sign of peace.' The hand we reach out to our neighbours is the same hand with which we receive Jesus in Communion.

We come to Mass to receive blessings from the Lord. If we took nothing else away with us from here but peace, our time would be well spent. We must be prepared to give back something of what we have received. The end of the Mass is not like the end of a football game or film where we simply get up and leave. At the end of the Mass we are *sent out*. Having received the peace of Christ, we are then sent out as ambassadors of that peace to others.

If we wish to be effective messengers of peace three things are necessary. Firstly, we have to have peace ourselves. Secondly, we have to be willing to share that peace with others. And thirdly, the other person has to be willing to receive it from us.

The harvest is great. The opportunities for sharing peace, for making peace, are many. We may not always succeed, because it takes at least two to make peace. The great danger is that we will allow people to take our peace away. This happens whenever we become angry, hostile, bitter, or vengeful when others do not respond favourably to us.

We have to accept that our peace will not always be accepted. It may come back to us like the echo of our own voice. But at least we ought to try. In a world torn apart by rivalry, anger and hatred, we have the challenging vocation to be living signs of love that can bridge divisions and heal wounds.

HOMILY 2   **The harvest is great**

Christianity is a very practical religion. Catherine de Hueck Doherty was an outstanding Christian. A Russian aristocrat by birth, she spent most of her life in America. She said, 'At an early age I learned that the Gospel has to be lived.'

As a young woman she worked as a cocktail waitress in a Manhattan bar. On one occasion she announced to a group of GIs and their girlfriends (whom she knew to be Catholics) that it was closing time (4 a.m.) and that she had to be off.

'Where are you going to, Katie?' they asked.

'It's Sunday, and I'm going to Mass.'

'That means you're a Catholic then?'

'Yes,' she replied.

They couldn't get over the fact that she could be a practising Catholic and work in a place like that. They all trooped off and went to Mass with her. A couple of weeks later a girl from the group returned. She said, 'You've made me think. If you can live a good life while working in a place like this, then maybe I can too.'

Another time Catherine was travelling in the subway in Montreal when she met a lonely old woman who said to her, 'Would you mind talking to me for awhile?' They made two trips from end to end of the subway, talking all the time. They became good friends, and corresponded until the old lady died.

The harvest is indeed great for those who have eyes to see it and a heart to respond to it. It is in our hospitals, homes, schools, prisons, work places, neighbourhoods. Every day is a harvest day.

Christ sent his disciples out to help him reap the harvest. We tend to leave it to the specialists – to priests, nuns, missionaries. The people Christ sent out weren't specialists. Yet they became his instruments. Few things help an individual more than to place responsibility on him, and to let him know that you trust him.

The seventy-two began by being his disciples. Then he steered them to goals beyond themselves by making them his apostles. That's the way it should always be. The Lord asks us to share with others what we have received from him. There are things which will remain undone if we don't do them. We lift ourselves up in proportion as we help to lift others up.

To be an apostle is to be one who is sent. One doesn't have to be some kind of genius or superhuman person to be able to do the work of Jesus. There is a difference between an apostle and a genius. The difference has little to do with talent or intelligence; it has everything to do with purpose and commitment.

Just because people are called doesn't mean that they become more intelligent, or more imaginative than they would otherwise be. No, they still have to rely on their native gifts. But they now have more purpose, more dedication than they would otherwise have. That can make a huge difference.

HOMILY 3   **Witnessing with wounds**

Forty years after leaving Auschwitz, the Italian writer, Primo Levi, still bore the tattoo with the number he got while there. When people asked him why he didn't have it erased he replied, 'Why should I? There are not so many of us left in the world to bear witness.'

Alexander Solzhenitsyn says that he still has the four patches bearing the number he was given in the prison camps. He was not the only one to have brought them out of the camps. Far from being ashamed of these he says, 'In some houses they will be shown to you like holy relics.'

Nor was St Paul ashamed of the marks he carried on his body because of Christ. In fact, he quietly drew attention to them (Second Reading). He said to the Galatians, 'The marks on my body are those of Christ.' By 'marks' he didn't mean the stigmata, such as Padre Pio and others are reputed to have had. He was talking about the scars left on his body by hardship, illness, flogging, stoning, and so on. His service of Christ had been a costly one.

What's more interesting still is the fact that Jesus kept the marks of the nails and the spear on his risen body. One would have expected him to have shed them to show that all that was behind him, and because he didn't want to embarrass the apostles who abandoned him or the people who were directly or indirectly responsible for causing them.

But Jesus did not shed those wounds. He retained them. For him those wounds were not things to be ashamed of or embarrassed about. They were the living proof of his love, the tangible and telling signs of how costly real love can be. They were more like badges of honour, or hard-won medals of distinction. They were still wounds but the poison had gone out of them, and so they no longer hurt. Because the wounds of Jesus are still visible on his risen body they have become a source of hope for all of us, especially for those who have suffered and who still suffer.

So many times we want to hide our wounds. We want to cover up the hurts of the past. Even when they have healed outwardly, often the poison remains, so that they still hurt. If we love, we must be prepared to get wounded. However, it would serve no great purpose if we thereby were poisoned by bitterness and resentment. Bitterness is internal decay. 'People can live through great hardships yet perish from hard feelings.' (Solzhenitsyn).

ANOTHER STORY

Felix Frankfurter was a famous justice of the Supreme Court of the United States. Once when he was hospitalised he came to know a nurse by the name of Lucy. They had long chats during which he found out a lot about her. She was a devout Catholic. He was not a Catholic, and indeed had no time for any other denomination either. Yet he was very struck by Lucy.

Never before had he met generosity or kindness such as she possessed. And he started to ask questions and to reflect, trying to discover the wellspring of her behaviour. What he discovered was this: the wellspring was no mystery. It was simply a practical application of her faith. He was truly amazed because he had never known anyone whose everyday life was based on a religion as much as that nurse's was.

Lucy may never have known the impact her lived faith had, but she made Jesus a palpable presence in that hospital. She supplied the hands Jesus needed there. Jesus needs the witness of people such as Lucy so that he can be the consoler he wants to be.

A real relationship with Jesus will have an impact, even when the person who has that relationship does not mention Jesus. Of course, those who believe in Jesus and love him, will also, when it is appropriate, speak openly of Jesus.

PRAYER OF THE FAITHFUL

President: As people who are called to be witnesses for Christ in an indifferent world, let us pray for courage and commitment.

Response: Lord, graciously hear us.

Reader(s): For the Church: that it may continue the mission Christ gave it to preach the Gospel to the world. [Pause] Lord, hear us.

For all Christians: that they may witness to Christ before others by word and deed. [Pause] Lord, hear us.

For those who hold public office: that they may strive to be instruments of peace and reconciliation. [Pause] Lord, hear us.

For those who are suffering: that the followers of Christ may ensure that they do not suffer alone. [Pause] Lord, hear us.

For our own special needs. [Longer pause] Lord, hear us.

President: God of mercy, help us to make love the foundation of our lives. May our love for you express itself in our eagerness to do good to others. We ask this through the same Christ our Lord.

PRAYER/REFLECTION   **Instruments of the Lord**

Lord, make me an instrument of your peace.
Where there is hatred, let me sow love.
Where there is injury, pardon.
Where there is doubt, faith.
Where there is darkness, light.
Where there is sadness, joy.
O Divine Master, grant that I may not so much
seek to be consoled, as to console;
to be understood as to understand; to be loved as to love.
For it is in giving that we receive;
it is in pardoning that we are pardoned;
it is in dying that we are born to eternal life.   *(St Francis of Assisi)*

DISMISSAL

President: At the end of Mass we are not simply dismissed. We are sent out in the Lord's name, and with the Lord's power, to build up his kingdom in the world.

Fifteenth Sunday of the Year
THE GOOD SAMARITAN

INTRODUCTION AND CONFITEOR

Today we will hear again the great parable of the Good Samaritan. In this parable Jesus tells us that God wants us to care for one another. The priest and the levite stand condemned for a sin, not of commission but of omission – they refused to help the man who got beaten up. Sins of omission may be our worst sins, yet we don't always think of them as sins. [Pause]

Jesus is *the* Good Samaritan. He binds up our wounds.
Lord Jesus, you have compassion for us in our sorrows and sufferings. Lord, have mercy.
You heal in us the wounds of sin and division. Christ, have mercy.
You bring us to the inn of eternal life. Lord, have mercy.

HEADINGS FOR READINGS

First Reading (Deut 30:10-14). Moses urges the people to obey God's law, not as something imposed from outside them, but as something that springs up from inside themselves.
Second Reading (Col 1:15-20). Paul asserts the absolute supremacy of Christ.
Gospel (Lk 10:25-37). The immortal parable of the Good Samaritan.

SCRIPTURE NOTE

The First Reading is part of Moses' farewell speech to the Israelites. He exhorts them to commit themselves to the Lord by observing his commandments. Whereas previously these commandments were considered as being external to them, now they are presented as springing from within themselves. They are written in their hearts, and therefore are not far away from them or beyond their strength. Jesus reduced the commandments to two (Gospel).

The lawyer's question was meant to embarrass Jesus. But Jesus cleverly put the onus back on the lawyer. So the lawyer tries again: he seeks casuistically to know to whom the commandment 'love your neighbour' applies. Basically what Jesus says to him is: our neighbour is anyone, regardless of class, colour, race, or creed, who needs our help.

HOMILY 1   **The road from Jerusalem to Jericho**

'A man was going down the road from ...'
Jesus doesn't attach any religious or social labels to the man, though it's reasonable to assume he was a Jew. Was he a good man or a bad man? Was he an important man or an unimportant man? These questions are irrelevant. He was a human being. That's all that matters.
'He was set upon by bandits ...'
Heartless, violent men, who prey on the weak. Jesus lived in the real world. He knew that such people existed. We know about them too.
'A priest and a levite saw him lying there half dead ... but passed by.'
The priest and the levite were religious people. Yet they didn't even feel compassion for the wounded man. Religion without compassion is a contradiction. Without compassion one can't call oneself a true human being never mind a truly religious person.

'A Samaritan came along ...'

He saw the wounded man, felt compassion for him, and went at once to his aid. He didn't worry about the trouble it caused him. Nor was he put off by the fact that the man was a Jew – Jews and Samaritans were enemies at that time.

At the start of the story we know very little about the priest, the levite, and the Samaritan. At the end of it we still don't know much about them. Yet we know all that matters. We know the kind of people they were. Their characters have been revealed to us.

The priest and levite were self-centred people. When the crunch came, they put themselves first. The Samaritan, on the other hand, was an unselfish person. He put the other person first.

The priest and levite were guilty of the sin of omission. Sins of omission may be our worst sins, yet we think that as long as we don't do harm to anyone, we're okay. But perhaps we have watched someone being hurt, and not intervened on his/her behalf? There are people who stay clean by distancing themselves from anyone in trouble.

The Samaritan was a carer. Carers are very special people. They are the salt of the earth and the light of the world. They don't care out of a sense of duty. They care because their heart will not allow them to do otherwise.

Each of us has the capacity to care. Small opportunities to care come our way every day. It's within our power to say a kind word, to offer a little sympathy, to give a little support. These are the little drops of 'oil and wine' which can take some of the pain out of a wound.

The road from Jerusalem to Jericho represents the road of life. At the end of the story Jesus said to the lawyer, 'Go and act like the Samaritan'. Those words are spoken to us too. And since we are still on that road, we can still carry them out.

HOMILY 2   **Spontaneous goodness**

Alaska is a wild, desolate, lonely, yet stunningly beautiful country. It is a mecca for adventurous tourists. However, it is not the kind of place in which you would want to have a breakdown. Towns are few and far between. Those who live there have to face long periods of isolation. Farmers in particular live very isolated lives.

Once an American was touring Alaska in a motor-home when his worst fear came true: he broke an axle in the motor-home, and found himself stranded in what looked like the middle of nowhere. Leaving his family in the motor-home, he decided to walk on in the hope of finding someone who might be able to help them. (This was before the mobile phone.)

After going a few miles he had a great stroke of luck: he came upon a farm house. He told the farmer about his predicament. The farmer was very sympathetic. Fortunately he had welding equipment. He towed the motor-home to his farmyard with his tractor, and there repaired the broken axle. When the job was finished the tourist reached for his wallet and said, 'How much do I owe you?'

'You don't owe me anything,' the farmer replied.

'But I feel I must repay you for what you have done for me.'

'You have already done so,' said the farmer.

'I don't understand,' said the tourist.

'You have given me the pleasure of your company for a couple of hours.'

The man was stunned but delighted at having encountered such generosity. People like that restore our belief in the essential goodness of human beings. Goodness is as much a mystery as evil. But whereas evil saddens and depresses us, goodness delights and inspires us.

The highest state we can attain is when goodness becomes an easy flow of grace, uncalculating and natural. When it falls from us without our notice, as a leaf from a tree. It's clear that in the case of the farmer we are dealing with an act of spontaneous goodness. So too in the case of the Samaritan. It's obvious that for the Samaritan goodness had become habitual, spontaneous, second nature. The nice thing about people like that is that they don't think they have done anything special. For some, generosity consists in a few sporadic acts; for others, it is a way of life.

How does one arrive at this happy state? It can't be achieved overnight. It has to be learned by long practice. It is not achieved by a few great deeds but by a lot of little ones. Great things are not done by impulse, but are a series of small things put together. The real reward for a good deed is that it makes the next good deed easier. Every little action of the common day makes or unmakes character.

The most disturbing thing in Jesus' story is not the attack made on an innocent man, but the fact that two people who you would expect to help him passed by without even showing compassion for him. A true Christian is not indifferent to the suffering of another.

'Who is my neighbour?' asked the lawyer. The common answers at that time would be: My neighbour comes from my own tribe, or circle, or religion. But the answer Jesus gave was: My neighbour is whoever I choose to be a neighbour to. The real question is not who do I consider to be my neighbour, but who am I willing to treat as a neighbour?

What kind of a neighbour am I? It's a question we ought to ask ourselves every now and then, but it's one we can't answer ourselves.

HOMILY 3   **The testing of character**

According to Tolstoy, a drama does not tell us the whole of a person's life. What it does is place a person in a situation. Then, from the way the person deals with that situation, his or her character is revealed to us.

This is precisely what Jesus does in his story. He places the priest, the levite, and the Samaritan in a situation. They are faced with a decision: To stop and help the wounded man, or to continue on about their own business? There is no escape for them, and no place to hide. They have to commit themselves one way or another. The priest and the levite decide to pass by; the Samaritan decides to stop and help.

Crisis does not create character, it merely reveals it. In times of crisis people reveal what is already inside them – the generous person or the selfish person, the hero or the coward. One moment or event may cause a person to reveal his essential being. The encounter with the wounded man was such a moment for the priest, the levite and the Samaritan.

What did it reveal about the characters of the priest and levite? It revealed a very damning thing, namely, that they were self-centred persons. They would not put themselves out to help another person. When the crunch came, they put themselves first.

And what did it reveal about the character of the Samaritan? A very admirable thing, namely, that he was a caring person. He was the kind of man who could not pass another human being in pain without wanting to relieve that pain.

Life is continually testing us. Every day we are tested in little ways, and now and again in big ways. These tests reveal the kind of people we are – fundamentally unselfish people, or fundamentally selfish people.

Big opportunities are rare, and few could perform them. But we get many small, less spectacular opportunities to show care and concern for another human being in need.

The extent of our virtue is determined, not by what we do in extraordinary circumstances, but by our normal behaviour. It is modest, everyday incidents rather than extraordinary ones that most reveal character. Every little action shapes our character.

ANOTHER STORY

Larry Skutnik, 28, was a shy man who worked in a government office in Washington. On the afternoon of January 13, 1982, a severe snowstorm hit the city. He was on his way home when he ran into a traffic jam on one of the bridges over the Potomac River. He soon realised what the cause of it was – a plane with seventy-nine people on board had crashed into the river. He got out of his car to investigate and saw three people clinging to the tail of the aircraft which was sticking out of the water.

A helicopter brought two of them to the shore but the third, a woman, fell back into the freezing water and started to go under. Without a thought, he took off his shoes and jacket, dived into the freezing water, and brought the woman to the shore. Afterwards he says he just wanted to go home. And after a brief trip to hospital, he was allowed to do so.

His daring act of rescue was captured on television. He woke up next morning to find himself a national hero. But he shied away from the publicity. 'The word "hero" makes me cringe,' he said. 'I reacted instinctively. That's all.'

It's nice to know that people still recognise the greatness of an act like that. And it's nice to know that someone can do such an act, and look on it as something normal and natural.

PRAYER OF THE FAITHFUL

President: Let us pray that we may learn the lesson of the parable of the Good Samaritan and put it into practice in our daily lives.

Response: Lord, hear us in your love.

Reader(s): For all Christians: that they may strive to be neighbours to the needy. [Pause] We pray in faith.

For all in public office: that they may show special care for the weak and vulnerable members of society. [Pause] We pray in faith.

For all those in the caring professions – doctors, nurses, firefighters, ambulance personnel: that they may show to the wounded the compassion of Christ. [Pause] We pray in faith.

For grace to open our hearts to those who suffer and so ensure that they do not suffer alone. [Pause] We pray in faith.

For our own special needs. [Longer pause] We pray in faith.

President: Lord, give us eyes that see the wounds of others; give us a heart that feels compassion for them; and give us the will to respond as best we can. We ask this through Christ our Lord.

REFLECTION   **Beatitudes for carers**

The good Samaritan was someone who cared.
Blessed are those who care:
they will let people know they are loved.
Blessed are those who are gentle: they will help people to grow
as the sun helps the buds to unfold.
Blessed are those who listen: they will lighten many a burden.
Blessed are those who know how to let go:
they will have the joy of seeing people find themselves.
Blessed are those who, when nothing can be done or said,
do not walk away, but remain to provide
a comforting and supportive presence:
they will help the sufferer to bear the unbearable.
Blessed are those who recognise their own need to receive:
they will be able to give all the better.
And blessed are those who give without hope of return:
they will give people an experience of God.

Sixteenth Sunday of the Year
MARTHA AND MARY

INTRODUCTION AND CONFITEOR

Jesus came to the house of Martha and Mary. Martha got completely carried away by the details of hospitality, but Mary sat at his feet and listened to him. During this Mass we have an opportunity to do what Mary did, namely, spend some time in the presence of the Lord. Let us enliven our faith in his presence among us. [Pause]

Lord Jesus, your presence calms our fears. Lord, have mercy.

Your presence eases our anxieties. Christ, have mercy.

Your presence helps us to focus our attention on the one thing necessary – to listen to your word. Lord, have mercy.

HEADINGS FOR READINGS

First Reading (Gen 18:1-10). When Abraham gave hospitality to three strangers he did not know that he was entertaining God himself, who would reward him with good news.

Second Reading (Col 1:24-28). Paul, a minister of the good news of the calling of the Gentiles to salvation, suffers for his converts.

Gospel (Lk 10:38-42). The Gospel contrasts Martha's activity and Mary's quiet devotion to the Lord.

SCRIPTURE NOTE

The First Reading and the Gospel are hospitality stories. Hospitality was an esteemed virtue in the ancient world. It is still a highly regarded and very necessary virtue.

In the First Reading we see how, when three strangers (Yahweh and two heavenly companions) suddenly appeared to Abraham, he reacted with instinctive hospitality, and how Yahweh rewarded his hospitality.

This sets the scene for Martha and Mary who welcome Jesus to their home. We see the contrast between Martha's activity and Mary's quiet devotion to the Lord. It's not that what Martha does is unimportant. It's just that Mary has chosen something even more important. Her priority is to listen to the word of Jesus.

The story of Martha and Mary can be seen as a parable in action. Whereas the parable of the Good Samaritan stressed the importance of action, or practical love, in the life of a disciple, this story stresses the importance of contemplation. Both are necessary, and have to be integrated into the life of a Christian. Martha is the patron saint of waiters and waitresses.

HOMILY 1   **Priorities**

Our sympathy is with Martha. It might seem then that Jesus was unfair to her. After all, the Gospel places great emphasis on deeds. Yet here he praises, not the doer, but the one who sits and listens. It wasn't that Jesus didn't appreciate what Martha was doing. Nor was he scolding her. What comes across is his concern for her.

He was making a point for the benefit of people like Martha, who are essentially generous people but over-anxious about getting things done. It's not simply that she was busy, but that she was too busy. Always anxious and worried, she was the slave of her duties.

Our daily lives are made up of a round of chores and duties which fall into two categories: the urgent, and the essential. Many of the things we do could be said to be urgent, but only a few are truly essential. We have to distinguish between the two. Like Martha, we tend to give priority to the urgent. The essential, the one thing necessary, gets postponed until later, when, if it is done at all, it is done hurriedly and badly.

How can we tell what our priorities are? The best way to recognise our actual priorities is to reflect on our normal behaviour. What do we give most time to? What gets most of our energy? These are our priorities in fact. It may take a tragedy or an emergency to put things into perspective for us, and to remind us of what really matters.

It's the easiest thing in the world to get one's priorities wrong. When Cardinal Joseph Bernardin, late Archbishop of Chicago, learned that he had terminal cancer he said: 'I came to realise how much of what consumes our daily life is trivial and insignificant.'

Mary got her priorities right – she dropped everything and listened to the words of Jesus. Many people would be able to identify more with Martha – busy about many things, yet constantly short of time. They are workaholics. We need to look beyond the daily chores and urgencies. We need to devote time to ourselves. Above all, we need time for reflection. The American psychotherapist and writer, Thomas Moore, says:

> There is no doubt but that some people could spare themselves the expense and trouble of psychotherapy simply by giving themselves a few minutes each day for quiet reflection. This simple act would provide what is missing in their lives – a period of non-doing that is essential nourishment to the soul.

If we could spend some quiet time with God our lives would be calmer, less driven by anxiety and worry, and deeper and richer. In fact, everything would benefit – our spiritual life, our relationships, even our work.

Action and contemplation are not meant to be contrasted. Both are necessary, and have to be integrated into life.

Giving and receiving

I had a dream that the Lord was coming to my house as he came to the house of Martha and Mary. So I scrubbed it from top to bottom, cleaning and polishing everything. Then I set the table with the best tablecloth, best set of delf, best silverware, and put candles and flowers there too. As for food, I spared no expense. When all was ready and my guest was about to arrive, I rolled out the red carpet.

He came and I think I did him proud. I put on a great performance. I waited hand and foot on him. No king ever had such service lavished on him. I made sure that the conversation never flagged. He, for his part, was most gracious. He showed so much appreciation that I was embarrassed. Everything went off like clockwork. When he left I felt good, and yet something was bothering me.

For a while I was at a loss as to what this might be. Then a question arose within me: What did he want from me? Food? Hospitality? I wondered. But then I heard a second question sounding inside me: What was it that he wanted to give me? I felt sure that he wanted to give me something. But, whatever it was, I gave him no opportunity to give it to me. I created the impression that everything was perfect, and that I wanted for nothing.

Some people are very good at giving but extremely poor at receiving. Dr Marie de Hennezel set up a unit for the terminally ill in a Paris hospital. In her book, *Intimate Death,* she tells of a woman who was brought to the unit. The woman had helped everyone but now was unable to help herself. She always wanted to be given lots of love, and now in the hospital unit she was getting it in abundance. But it was so difficult to receive it. She talked about her family's love, and that of her friends and those who took care of her, as 'a fountain from which she didn't know how to drink.' She needed to learn how to become a child again, humble enough to accept a gift. But this was not easy because she was the absolute opposite: she loved to give egoistically.

Self-centred people hate to receive. Why is this? Because it makes them feel inferior to others and puts them in debt to others. On the other hand, they love to give because it inflates their ego, thereby (unconsciously perhaps) making them feel superior to others.

Giving is important. But so too is receiving. None of us is self-sufficient. All of us are incomplete. We need to receive from one another and above all from God. It's nothing less than tragic not to be able to receive. It's not enough to know how to give, we must also know how to receive. Both are graced activities.

The Gospel story shows the essential difference between Martha and Mary. Martha was not able to receive, Mary was. Mary offered the Lord the gift of an open mind and a receptive heart. Martha, on the other hand, while very good at giving was very poor at receiving. Even the Lord couldn't give her anything. There is a short poem which goes like this:

> If thou could'st empty all thyself of self,
> Like to a shell dishabited,
> Then might He find thee on some ocean shelf
> And say to Himself – This is not dead.
> And fill thee with Himself instead.
> But thou art so full of very thou,
> And has such shrewd activity,
> That when He comes he says -
> This is enough unto itself. It is so full.
> There is no room for Me. *(T. Brown, Manx poet)*

HOMILY 3 **In the presence of God**

We do not take the spiritual life seriously if we do not set aside some time to be with, and to listen to God. Most of us say some morning and evening prayers. But, alas, these prayers often consist of over-familiar words, which we mumble in haste while our thoughts race ahead to the tasks that await us. Such prayers are like washing one's hands fully dressed when what is needed is a bath or shower. We need concentrated, dedicated prayer, prayer that is like a hunger that must be satisfied and for which there was no substitute. That kind of prayer always transforms and fortifies us. 'Prayer is not asking. It is a longing of the soul. It is the daily admission of one's weakness.' (Gandhi).

For many people prayer consists of saying prayers rather than praying. In a sense, prayer begins where expression ends. The words that reach our lips are often but waves on the surface of our being. The highest form of worship is silence.

Probably the most beneficial prayer of all is just to be in the presence of God, without saying or doing anything. Just to sit in his presence, as Mary sat in the presence of Jesus. But to some this might seem a waste of time when there are so many things to do.

To be in the presence of God, without saying or doing anything, is no easy thing. Because as soon as we stop, we feel empty, even useless. Most people get their sense of self-worth from doing. They don't know how to cope with idleness and stillness. The result is that their lives can be shallow and superficial.

A lot of people tend to equate love of God with social action. Of course prayer can be a cop-out and an escape. But so too can social action. Our action can be a cop-out from seeking God. And without prayer it can easily become totally self-directed, self-propelled, rather than inspired by God.

Henry David Thoreau lived for two years in a shack in the woods in Maine. What did he do during those years? He planted a vegetable garden, read books, and observed nature. But sometimes he did nothing at all. He says, 'Sometimes on a summer morning I sat in my sunny doorway from sunrise till noon, rapt in a reverie, amidst the pines, in undisturbed solitude and stillness, while the birds sang around me.'

What fruits did he reap from this? He says:

I grew in those seasons like corn in the night. They were not time subtracted from my life, but so much over and above my usual allowance. It is not enough to be industrious; so are the ants. What are you industrious about? Fear not that your life will end; rather fear that it may never have begun.

Some may dismiss Thoreau as an idle dreamer. But we need to spend time in prayer and reflection, if only to sit quietly in the presence of God. This is not time wasted but time well spent. Each day we should try, if only for a short while, to seek the face of God.

At a superficial glance it might seem that Mary's part was the easier – all she had to do was sit there – and Martha's the harder. But on reflection we can see that at least sometimes Mary's part is by far the harder of the two. It's not easy to set aside one's own work and give one's undivided attention to another person. To give that kind of wholehearted attention to God is not easy. But it's tremendously fruitful spiritually.

ANOTHER STORY

Metropolitan Anthony Bloom says that one of the first people who came to him for advice when he was ordained was an old lady who said, 'Father, I have been praying almost unceasingly for fourteen years, and I have never had any sense of God's presence.'

'Did you give God a chance to put in a word?' he asked.

'Oh, well,' she said, 'no, I have been talking to him all this time. Is that not what prayer is?'

'No,' he said. 'I don't think so. Now what I suggest is that you should set apart fifteen minutes a day, and just sit before the face of God.'

And so she did. What was the result? Quite soon she came once again and said, 'It's extraordinary, when I pray to God, in other words when I talk to him, I feel nothing. But when I sit quietly, face to face with him, I feel wrapped in his presence.'

Ultimately prayer is not about words but about communion with God. Prayer is a resting in the presence of God. It's more a question of staying quiet in his presence than of saying prayers.

PRAYER OF THE FAITHFUL

President: Conscious of our need of God's blessings we bring our needs before him.

Response: Lord, hear our prayer.

Reader(s): For the followers of Jesus: that they may listen to him and be guided by his teaching. [Pause] Let pray to the Lord.

For all in positions of responsibility: that they may seek the guidance of God through prayer and reflection. [Pause] Let us pray to the Lord.

For people who are overworked and overburdened. [Pause] Let us pray to the Lord.

For ourselves: that we may grow in intimacy with the Lord through the practice of daily prayer. [Pause] Let pray to the Lord.

For our own special needs. [Longer pause] Let us pray to the Lord.

President: Father, your Son honoured Martha and Mary by coming to their home as a guest. May we serve you in our brothers and sisters, and be welcomed by you into heaven, our true home. We ask this through the same Christ our Lord.

PRAYER/REFLECTION   **In his presence**

Lord, I place myself in your presence.
After the strain and turmoil of the day
I rest quietly here, as a little boat,
which has been tossed by the waves
and buffeted by the wind,
rests secure in a sheltered harbour.
Here my projects lose their power over me.
A healing process begins.
My fragmented self is reassembled,
and I am made whole again.
In your presence, I experience my true worth,
which consists not in doing but in being.
I surrender myself into your hands. I am at peace.

Seventeenth Sunday of the Year
ASK, SEEK, KNOCK

INTRODUCTION AND CONFITEOR

Jesus says to us what he said to his disciples: 'Ask, and you will receive; seek, and you will find; knock, and the door will be opened to you.' In this way he is urging us to have recourse to God with confidence and

persistence in all our needs. [Pause]
  Lord Jesus, you grant us forgiveness for our sins. Lord, have mercy.
  You grant us joy in the hurly burly of life. Christ, have mercy.
  You welcome us at the door to your kingdom. Lord, have mercy.

HEADINGS FOR READINGS

First Reading (Gen 18:20-32). Abraham intercedes with God on behalf of Sodom, a city full of evil.
  Second Reading (Col 2:12-14). Through Baptism a Christian dies to the old sinful way of life, and rises to live a new life.
  Gospel (Lk 11:1-13). Jesus urges the apostles to pray to God with child-like trust for all their spiritual and temporal needs.

SCRIPTURE NOTE

Prayer forms the subject of the First Reading and the Gospel. Prayer is a favourite theme of Luke. In the First Reading we see Abraham interceding with God on behalf of Sodom, a city full of evil. Troubled by the idea of the innocent being punished along with the guilty, he begins to bargain with God. The story highlights the importance of intercessory prayer, and reveals a lot about the mercy of God.

This prepares us for the Gospel which shows Jesus at prayer and contains the Lord's Prayer. Luke's version is shorter than Matthew's, which is believed to be closer to the original version. Jesus urges the disciples to go on asking for what they need with persistence and confidence.

HOMILY 1   **Dialogue with God**

Note: The most effective way of presenting this dialogue is as follows. Choose a stranger, or at least an unfamiliar voice, to play the part of God. Provide him with a microphone, and keep him out of sight. The person praying is at the lectern. The words in italics are to be emphasised.

Our Father, who art in heaven.
Yes.
Did I hear a voice?
You did.
Just as soon as I began to pray somebody interrupts me. I'd better start again. Our Father, who art in heaven.
Yes.
You've interrupted me again.
But you *called* me. You said: 'Our Father, who are in heaven.' So here I am.
Oh my God!
You sound *surprised.*

Frankly, I'm very surprised. I didn't really expect you to answer.

Oh, so *that's* all the faith you have in me.

Anyhow, now that we've made contact, what's on your mind?

To be quite honest, I haven't given it much thought. I say the 'Our Father' every now and then. It makes me feel good.

Oh, so that's what prayer is for – to make you *feel* good.

I see. Go on.

Hallowed be thy name.

Hold it! What do you mean by '*hallowed*'?

It means … Let me see … Hallowed? … Hallowed? … Good heavens, I don't know what it means.

Do you *normally* use words you don't understand when you're talking to people?

No.

Well then, why do you do so when you're talking to me? After all, that's what prayer is – a *conversation* between me and you.

Good point, Lord. By the way, what does the word mean?

It means '*may it be honoured*' or '*may it be seen as holy*'.

So what I'm really praying for is that your name might be honoured by everybody.

That's the general idea.

May I go on now?

By all means.

Thy kingdom come.

What kind of *kingdom* have you in mind?

I'm not sure. All I know is that the world is in a mess.

What kind of *world* would you like to see?

I'd like to see everyone living in peace.

Do *you* live in peace with everyone?

Nearly everyone. However, there are a few people I'd like to strangle. There's one neighbour whom I'd like to see emigrate to the North Pole.

But what about the trouble *you* cause? *You're* no angel, you know.

This is starting to hurt, Lord. Aren't we taking it a bit too seriously?

But you did pray for my kingdom to come. So why not begin with *yourself?* You *do* want to belong to my kingdom, don't you?

I do, but I'm not sure what it involves.

Ordinary people help to spread my kingdom by being *kind, truthful, honest, just*, and so on. In a nutshell, by doing my will.

Your will – that's the next part of the prayer. May I go on then?

Certainly.

Thy will be done on earth, as it is in heaven.

'*On earth*' presumably means in your life too?

Of course.

Well then, what are you going to *do* about it?

How do you mean what am I going to do about it? Haven't I just prayed about it?

So you have. But I repeat: What are you going to *do* about it?

Actually I wasn't planning on doing anything.

Oh, so *that's* how it is. You pray for my will to be done. Then you sit back, fold your arms, and do sweet nothing about it. Let's be practical for a moment. When last did you put yourself out to help another person? And what about that tongue of yours?

Stop, Lord! I'm no worse than anyone else. Still, I would like to be a better person.

Good! Things are beginning to look up.

Praying could be dangerous you know.

What do you mean?

If you took it seriously you could end up a changed person.

Continue, please.

[Looking at his watch] This is taking a lot longer than I expected. Normally I'm finished my prayers in two minutes flat. What's worrying me is this: I'm supposed to meet someone at … [here name some well-known local pub] in five minutes. Couldn't we finish this another time?

Finished in two minutes flat! Sounds like a rushed job to me. So you can't wait. A minute ago you were praying for *my* will to be done. Now it's *your* will that must be done.

Oh well, I suppose I might as well go on.

Give us this day our daily bread.

What are you praying for now?

For bread – at least that's what the prayer says, isn't it?

Yes, but bread for *whom*?

For myself of course.

For *yourself*? You don't look undernourished to me.

So what more do you want?

Don't get me wrong, Lord. I'm not complaining. I'm grateful for the many good things I have in my life. But I feel there is something missing. At times I feel very empty.

What you're experiencing is a *spiritual* hunger.

A spiritual hunger. I'm not sure I know what you mean.

A human being has a soul as well as a body. The soul too needs food.

I see.

Let us get on then with the rest of the prayer.

I'm *very interested* in the next part of it. [Brief pause]

Well, aren't you going on?

I'm afraid of what you'll say.

Why don't you try me and see?

Forgive us our trespasses, as we forgive those who trespass against us.
What about the mother-in-law?
I knew you'd bring her up. Why, Lord, she the greatest b ... b ... bad person I've ever met. If only she'd mind her own business.
But what about your *prayer*: 'As we forgive those who trespass against us'?
Ah, Lord, be reasonable. Forgive her? Sure I can't even bear the sight of her. Boy, have I got plans for her. When I'm finished with her she'll be sorry she ever crossed my path.
Oh, so it's back to the old business of 'an eye for an eye, and a tooth for a tooth'. It's a good thing everyone doesn't think like you, or half the world would be going around blind and toothless.
I take it then that you're not going to forgive her.
Honestly, Lord, I couldn't promise you that.
And yet you expect *me* to forgive *you*.
You're not going to forgive her – is that final?
That's final.
Well then, for goodness sake go off to ... [name same pub as above] and don't be wasting my time.
Don't cut me off, Lord. Wait a minute. Are you still there, Lord? [No reply] Look's as if I've been cut off. I wouldn't mind but I was just going to say that maybe I can forgive her after all ... I can ... I will ... Are you there, Lord?
I am.
Oh good! You had me scared for a minute. I thought you'd cut me off.
I take it that you don't like to be cut off.
You bet I don't.
Well that's *exactly* what you do when you don't forgive. You cut the other person off from you, and you cut yourself off from me. So you are willing to forgive her?
I've already forgiven her.
Good. Let's go on with the prayer.
Lead us not into temptation.
You know, that one always makes me smile.
Why do you say that, Lord?
Tell me something. When did you need me, or anyone else for that matter, to take you by the hand and lead you into temptation? Do you not walk into it of your own accord and with both eyes open? I mean, no one puts an obscene book or magazine into our hand. No one forces you to take that extra drink.
Stop, Lord, I've heard enough. I get your point. Yes, there are times when I bring temptation on myself. But then there are times when it comes to me unbidden.

True. But temptation isn't necessarily a *bad* thing. It's a chance for you to prove your *loyalty* and *maturity*.

So what should I pray for?

Pray for the strength to avoid the temptations you *can avoid*, and to resist the ones you *can't*.

Sounds like good advice.

You may go on now.

Deliver us from evil.

What have you in mind?

I had a friend who was killed in a car accident. And another who died of cancer while still young.

You're not blaming *me*, are you?

No, of course, not.

You know, I don't *want* those kind of things to happen.

Yet when they happen, you hear people say; 'It's the will of God.'

It's *not* my will that tragedies should happen.

But could you not prevent them?

Your question is not one that can be answered in a few words. But let me say just this. I made the things of nature to follow the law of nature. I've got to respect that law. To people I gave the gift of free will. I've got to respect their freedom.

Then you can't guarantee me a life free from pain and struggle?

No. I couldn't do that even for my own Son.

However, there is something I *will* do.

What is that?

I'll help you to cope with whatever evil comes.

Lord, even if I have to walk through the valley of darkness, I will fear no evil as long as you are with me.

Oh, I'll be with you alright. You can count on that.

I will.

Thank you, Lord. I've finished. That's the end of my prayer.

We've had quite a *chat*.

We sure had.

Many people *say* prayers rather than *pray*. Now if in the course of our chat I've pointed out some of your faults, it's because I *care* about you. I want you to be a *better* and a *happier* person.

You can go now. But just remember this: In spite of all I said, I still love you *just as you are*.

Just as I am? Faults and all? Do you really mean that, Lord?

I do. I trust I'll be hearing from you again soon?

You certainly will.

Well then, let's say 'Amen'.

Amen. [Together]

Note: If this dialogue is used, when the time comes to recite The Lord's Prayer, we could ask the congregation to slow it down.

HOMILY 2   **The Lord's Prayer**

The Our Father is the first and greatest of all Christian prayers (I'm thinking of Matthew's version). Its short and simple phrases embrace every relation between us and God. It not only tells us what to pray for, but also how to pray for it.

However, it tends to be said so hurriedly and unthinkingly that much of its meaning is lost. This is a pity. Because, properly understood, the Our Father contains a whole programme for Christian living. If we were to live up to what it contains, we would be perfectly in tune with the mind of Christ, because undoubtedly this is how he himself prayed and lived.

The first part deals with God.

We begin by acknowledging God's existence, and calling him 'Father'. God is a parent to us, and we are his children. Sometimes he acts like a father, and sometimes like a mother.

Then we praise his name. In praising his name we praise him.

We pray for the coming of his kingdom – a kingdom of truth and life, holiness and grace, justice, love, and peace. We have a part to play in making his kingdom a reality.

We pray that his will may be done on earth. 'On earth' means in our lives too. God's will may not always be the easiest thing to do, but it is always the best thing.

The second part deals with us and our needs.

We begin by praying for our daily bread. 'Bread' stands for all our material needs. All we really need, however, is enough for today.

We pray for forgiveness for our own sins, and for the grace to be able to forgive those who sin against us. Inability to forgive others makes it impossible for us to receive God's forgiveness.

We pray not to be led into temptation. God does not put temptation in our path but life does. And we ourselves sometimes walk into temptation of our own accord. We are asking God to help us to cope with the temptations that come to us unbidden, and to avoid those of our own choosing.

Finally, we pray to be delivered from all evil, both physical and moral. We can't expect never to encounter evil. What we are asking God for is the grace to be victorious over all evil, but especially moral evil.

Notice that the whole of the Our Father is couched in plural terms. This shows that we are one family under God, and that there can be no salvation for us independent of others.

HOMILY 3   **On not punishing the innocent**

The picture of Abraham pleading with God to save Sodom and Gomorrah is a fascinating one. The idea that comes across is that God will not punish a multitude of wicked people if it means punishing a handful of just people at the same time. We go to the opposite extreme. We are quite willing to punish a multitude of innocent people as long as few guilty ones get punished as well. To take a few examples.

When governments are fighting guerrillas, they may think nothing of wiping out a whole village of men, women and children, provided they can get rid of a few guerrillas at the same time. It happened in Vietnam, in Argentina (during their so-called 'dirty war'), and in many other places. Guerrillas don't hesitate to use similar tactics.

Something similar can happen in school. The teacher leaves the classroom for a minute. When he returns to the classroom he finds that a chair has been broken. No matter how he pleads or threatens, the culprit won't own up and the others won't give his name. So the teacher punishes the whole class. Detention for all!

The same thing happens at home. Something gets spilt when the mother has her back turned. Nobody owns up. So all the children are punished. No television for the rest of the evening!

It tends to be our first resort, and we regard it as eminently wise and just. But is it? Is it fair to punish ninety nine innocent people so as to ensure that one guilty person gets punished? Of course not. It's unjust. It's terrible to be punished for something you didn't do. It leaves you with a terrible feeling of bitterness.

Though attractive, it is not a Christian solution, or even a humane one. God never resorts to it. This is what the First Reading is telling us. Jesus taught us the same lesson in the parable of the wheat and the weeds. The sower will not pull up a bunch of weeds in case he might uproot even one stalk of wheat while doing so.

The most important issue of our times is how to overcome evil without doing further evil in the process. Evil has to be resisted. But we have to do so in such a way that we not do more evil in the process. Evil cannot be overcome by evil. It can only be overcome by good.

PRAYER OF THE FAITHFUL

President: Let us pray to God in the spirit of the great prayer that Jesus taught us.

Response: Lord, hear our prayer.

Reader(s): That the followers of Jesus may seek to know the will of God and to do it. [Pause] Let us pray to the Lord.

That all those responsible for public order may work for the coming of the values of the Kingdom of God. [Pause] Let us pray to the Lord.

That those who are hungry may be given daily bread. [Pause] Let us pray to the Lord.

That we may be able to forgive those who have sinned against us. [Pause] Let us pray to the Lord.

For the grace to be victorious over temptation and evil. [Pause] Let us pray to the Lord.

For our own special needs. [Longer pause] Let us pray to the Lord.

President: Heavenly Father, teach us to go on confidently asking, to go on joyfully seeking, and to go on hopefully knocking at the door, so that the good things you want to give us may be ours. We make our prayer through Christ our Lord.

RECITATION OF THE OUR FATHER

Note: I would not use this if the dialogue homily has been used. It would be a great help if the congregation had a copy of the script.

Celebrant: Let us take the Our Father a phrase at a time. I will introduce each phrase, then we will all say the phrase together.

When our faith is weak, Lord, teach us to pray:

All: Our Father who are in heaven.

Cel.: When we are inclined to forget about you, Lord, teach us to pray:

All: Hallowed be thy name.

Cel.: When we feel pessimistic about our lives and about the state of the world, Lord, teach us to pray:

All: Thy Kingdom come.

Cel.: When we have difficult decisions to make, and are tempted to take the easy way out, Lord, teach us to pray:

All: Thy will be done on earth as it is in heaven.

Cel.: When we complain about little upsets and forget that millions of people are poor and hungry, Lord, teach us to pray:

All: Give us this day our daily bread.

Cel.: When we are worried about our sins, and find it hard to forgive those who sin against us, Lord, teach us to pray:

All: Forgive us our trespasses as we forgive those who trespass against us.

Cel.: When we are troubled by temptation, Lord, teach us to pray:

All: Lead us not into temptation.

Cel.: When we find it hard to cope, Lord, teach us to pray:

A. *Deliver us from evil.*

Cel.: When we are preoccupied with ourselves and our own glory, Lord, teach us to pray:

All: For the kingdom, the power, and the glory are yours, now and for ever.

REFLECTION 1   **Ask, seek, knock**

Jesus urges us to ask, seek, and knock.
This means our faith has to be an active one.
However, sometimes we are too proud to ask, so we don't receive;
we are too lazy to seek, so we don't find;
and we are too timid to knock, so the door doesn't open to us.
We mustn't wait for things to happen, or to fall into our hands.
We must be humble and trustful, yet bold and energetic,
if we are to receive good things from our Father in heaven.

REFLECTION 2   **Prayer of petition**

I asked for health that I might do great things;
    I was given infirmity that I might do better things.
I asked for riches that I might be happy;
    I was given poverty that I might be wise.
I asked for power that I might have the praise of men;
    I was given weakness that I might feel the need of God.
I asked for all things that I might enjoy life;
    I was given life that I might enjoy all things.
I got nothing that I asked for, but everything I hoped for.
    Almost despite myself my unspoken prayers were answered.
    I am, among all men, most richly blessed.   *(Anon.)*

Eighteenth Sunday of the Year
HOW MUCH IS ENOUGH?

INTRODUCTION AND CONFITEOR

Possessions exercise a big hold on our hearts. The result is that we forget
the more important things in life. Jesus said our main concern should be
to 'make ourselves rich in the sight of God.' In truth, all of us are poor
before God. Let us reflect on that for a moment. [Pause] It is only God
who can truly enrich us.

Lord, we are rich when we place all our trust in you. Lord, have mercy.
We are rich when we place all our hope in you. Christ, have mercy.
We are rich when we love others as you love us. Lord, have mercy.

HEADINGS FOR READINGS

First Reading (Eccles 1:2; 2:21-23). The things that are supposed to satisfy human beings do not satisfy them.

Second Reading (Col 3:1-5. 9-11). Through Baptism we share in the life of Christ. We hear some of the conclusions that follow from this.

Gospel (Lk 12:13-21). Jesus warns against greed, and stresses the foolishness of depending on material things for one's security rather than on God.

SCRIPTURE NOTE

The First Reading casts a cold eye on the vanity of human life. One example of this 'vanity' is all the toil people put into acquiring wealth, only to have to leave it all to their heirs. The author is making the point that the things that are supposed to satisfy human beings do not satisfy them. Only faith in God and in an afterlife can provide a light in the darkness.

The Gospel is part of a longer section which deals with the difficulties that possessions can cause for the disciples of Jesus. Here Jesus refuses to get involved in a family dispute. Instead, he focuses on the cause of the dispute – greed for possessions. His parable stresses the foolishness of depending on material things for one's security rather than on God. In his search for security and happiness in this life, the rich man forgets God, forgets eternal life, and forgets his obligations to the poor. He is truly a 'fool' because he has not known how to use wisely the wealth which he had.

HOMILY 1   **Wealth is not possession but enjoyment**

Once there was a miser who accumulated a large amount of money, and was looking forward to years of happy living. However, before he could make up his mind as to how best to spend his money, the Angel of Death appeared before him to take his life away.

The miser pleaded with the angel to be allowed to live a little longer. 'Give me three days of life and I'll give you half my fortune,' he begged. But the angel wouldn't hear of it and began to tug at his cloak. 'Give me just one day, I beg of you,' said the miser, 'and you can have everything I accumulated through so much sweat and toil.' But the angel refused his request.

The miser managed to wring just one small concession from the angel – a few moments in which to write down this note: 'Oh you, whoever you are that happen to find this note, if you have enough to live on, don't waste your life accumulating fortunes. Live! My fortune couldn't buy me a single hour of life.'

It's not how many possessions we have but how we enjoy the ones we have that matters. Wealth is not in possession but in enjoyment. Many people have lost their capacity for enjoyment, especially those in affluent countries. They have to have more and more expensive gadgets. They can't enjoy the simple things of life, the way a child can.

It's not the amount of money we have but our capacity for enjoyment that makes us rich. To seek wealth while having no capacity for enjoyment is to be like a blind person who collects videos. We can become possessed by things. Many are so busy adding to their possessions that they have no time to enjoy life.

Money and power can imprison and inhibit just as effectively as barred windows and iron chains. 'Set a bird's wings with gold and it will never fly.' (Tagore)

Some people have had to go to prison to discover how little we can get by with, and what extraordinary spiritual freedom and peace that can bring. It frees us to develop the spirit. 'People don't know what they are striving for. They exhaust themselves in the senseless pursuit of material things, and die without realising their spiritual greatness.' (Solzhenitsyn)

'People,' said the Little Prince, 'rush about in express trains, but they do not know what they are looking for. They raise ten thousand roses in the same garden, and they still do not know what they are looking for. Yet what they are looking for could be found in a single rose.' When we distinguish between our needs and our wants, we will be surprised to realise how little is enough.

'Vanity of vanities. All is vanity. What does a man gain for all his toil and strain that he had undergone under the sun?' – the words of Ecclesiastes. They paint a pessimistic view of life, but they are meant to make us ask: What's the purpose of life? Certainly it's not about accumulating possessions – possessions which in any case have to be left behind.

Earthly things can never satisfy the human heart. Only God can give us the kind of happiness our hearts long for. Hence, St Paul says, 'Let your thoughts be on heavenly things, not on the things that are on the earth.' And Jesus urges us not to store up treasures on earth but to make ourselves rich in the sight of God. What makes us rich in the sight of God is not what we own, or even what we've done, but what we are.

HOMILY 2   **The disease of acquisitiveness**

Tolstoy tells a story about a peasant called Pakhom who desperately wanted to own some land. By saving every penny he had, he bought forty acres. He was overjoyed. However, he soon felt cramped, so he sold the forty acres, and bought eighty acres in another region. But this didn't satisfy him for long, so he began to look again.

One evening a stranger arrived. Pakhom talked about his desire for more land. The stranger told him that beyond the mountains there lived a tribe of simple people who had lots of land for sale.

Off he went next day. The chief welcomed him and said, 'For only a thousand roubles you can have as much land as you can walk round in a day. But you must return to the spot from where you started on the same day, otherwise you forfeit the money.'

Pakhom was thrilled. He couldn't sleep all that night, thinking of all the land that would soon be his. As soon as the sun peeped above the horizon a marker was put down on top of a knoll, and he was off. Men followed him on horseback and drove stakes into the ground to mark the path he traced out.

He walked fast and made excellent progress. The farther he went the better the land became. In his eagerness to encompass as much as he could, he lost track of time. Then to his horror he saw the sun beginning to go down. He headed for the knoll as fast as he could. He just made it to the top as the sun vanished. Once there, however, he collapsed face downwards on the ground.

'I congratulate you,' said the chief. 'You have earned more than any man I can remember.' But Pakhom made no reply. They turned him over. He was dead.

A certain amount of money and material possessions are necessary. Jesus' parable is not about need but about greed. The farmer was rich to begin with, but he still wasn't satisfied. Greed is like a fire – the more wood you pile on it, the hungrier it gets. One of the chief problems of our times – people don't know when they are well-off.

Elvis Presley died at forty-two from drug abuse. He owned eight cars, six motorbikes, two planes, sixteen television sets, a vast mansion, and several large bank accounts.

When the crow builds a nest in the forest, it occupies but a single branch. When the deer slakes its thirst at the river, it drinks no more than it needs at that moment. Why do human beings have to hoard?

People have a craving for security. In biblical times, when famine was a recurrent threat, they sought security by stockpiling grain. In our times they seek in by stockpiling money / possessions. People accumulate things and cling to them, because they give the illusion of security. But security cannot be found in possessions. It can be found only in God.

As well as security, people also seek self-worth in possessions. In our society people are estimated by what they have. To have a lot is to be something. To have nothing is to be nothing.

Mahatma Gandhi was one of the greatest men of the twentieth century. Yet he lived in a simple hut made of wood and mud. By way of possessions he had only the bare essentials. Possessions will never give us inner strength. They are the crutches of a spiritual cripple.

Jesus said that rather than storing up treasure we should seek to make ourselves rich in the sight of God. What makes us rich in the sight of God is not what we own, or even what we've done, but what we are.

It is not possessions that are sinful but possessiveness. To be detached doesn't mean being indifferent or uninterested. It means to be non-possessive. Life is a gift to be grateful for, not a possession to cling to. A non-possessive life is a free life.

The only riches that are worth accumulating are the riches of the heart. A generous heart is a treasure. To have a generous heart is to be rich in the sight of God. Fear and greed are the real enemies. The dread of hunger when the granary is full is the hunger which can never be satisfied.

HOMILY 3   **The best inheritance**

No matter how wisely, skilfully and successfully a man has laboured, he can't take his wealth with him when he dies. Others will inherit the fruit of his toil. (First Reading). To make matters worse, what he leaves behind may tear his family apart. An inheritance can be a blessing or a curse. In the Gospel we see two brothers fighting over an inheritance. How sad to see people, driven by greed and envy, quarrelling over plenty.

Once, there was an executive who worked for a thriving company. He lived with his wife and young family in a fine house in a good neighbourhood. However, he wasn't satisfied. He was young and full of energy and ambition. Anything seemed possible. So he said to himself, 'I can do better than this. I'll just have to work harder.'

He worked a lot of overtime and doubled his income. He moved to a larger house in a more fashionable part of the city. Even though he was doing splendidly, he still wasn't satisfied. He had his eye on a dream house but didn't yet have the money to buy it. But a few more years and he would.

He never did get to own that dream house, for he was struck down by a terminal illness. Suddenly he found himself at death's door. Then, to his horror, he discovered that he hardly knew his children, or his wife for that matter. Worse, he realised he hadn't really lived at all. He had been postponing life until the day when all his goals would be achieved.

In the eyes of the company and of his neighbours, he was a great success. But in his own eyes he knew he was a failure. He had missed out on the most important things in life. He felt empty, spiritually and emotionally. It was not the happiest state to be in now that his earthly voyage was coming to an end. Oh, how he wished he could start all over again. How differently he would do things.

And what was he leaving to his children? A lot of money, yes. But what else? Nothing, absolutely nothing. They had virtually grown up without him, and now would surely survive without him.

Today some parents are learning that they have a lot more to pass on to their children than mere possessions. Through a hands-on approach in the upbringing of their children, they are showing them that they really care about them. These children are heirs to the most important kind of inheritance, and the possessors of something no money can buy.

The rich fool discovered too late that material wealth is not a permanent possession. Because he devoted all his energy to amassing property, he had nothing he could call his own, and death revealed his essential poverty. The only possessions worth striving for are those death cannot take away – those that endure to life eternal. 'When your last hour strikes, count only on what you have become.' (Antoine de Saint Exupery).

There was a good man who refused to make a will, instead he said he would leave his children the best thing he had: the pattern of his life. Give away your possessions, your gifts and your love now. Don't wait until someone else does it when you are dead.

ANOTHER STORY

A wealthy American banker was standing on the pier of a coastal village in Mexico when a small boat with one fisherman aboard docked. Inside the boat were a few large tuna fish. The banker complimented the fisherman on his catch, then asked, 'How long were you out?'

'Oh, an hour or two,' the fisherman replied.

'Why didn't you stay out longer and catch more fish?'

'I've enough here to meet the immediate needs of my family.'

'But what do you do with the rest of your time?'

'I sleep late, fish a little, play with my children, take a siesta in the afternoon, and stroll into the village in the evening to sip a little wine, play my guitar and chat with my friends. Believe me, I have a full life,' said the fisherman.

The banker wasn't impressed. 'You should spend more time fishing,' he said. 'Then with the proceeds you could buy a bigger boat. With the proceeds from that you could buy several boats. Eventually you would have a fleet of fishing boats. Then you could open up your own processing factory and cannery. You would need to leave this village and move to Mexico City, then to Los Angeles, and eventually to New York, from where you would run your expanding business.'

'How long would all this take?' the fisherman asked.

'About twenty years,' the banker replied.

'And what then?' asked the fisherman.

'When the time is right you could float your company on the stock market, sell your stock to the public and make millions.'

'Then what?' asked the fisherman.

'Then you could retire and move to a small coastal village, where you could sleep late, fish a little, play with your children, take a siesta in the afternoon, stroll into the village in the evening and have some fun with your friends.'

'What do you think I'm doing right now?' asked the fisherman.

PRAYER OF THE FAITHFUL

President: Let us pray that we may get our priorities in tune with those of the Gospel.

Response: Lord, graciously hear us.

Reader(s): For the followers of Christ: that they may not judge success in life by the standards of the world. [Pause] Lord, hear us.

For our political leaders: that they may strive to see that the wealth of the country is distributed fairly. [Pause] Lord, hear us.

For the poor and the dispossessed. [Pause] Lord, hear us.

For the gift of wisdom so that we may know what is truly important in life. [Pause] Lord, hear us.

For our own special needs. [Longer pause] Lord, hear us.

President: Almighty God, cleanse our hearts of greed for material things and from envy of others, and clothe us in gentleness and humility. We ask this through Christ our Lord.

REFLECTION   **Heavenly glory**

While out for an evening walk I emerged from an area
where the streets were lit by bright lamps,
and came into an open, dark area.
It was only then I discovered that the sky was full of stars.
And I thought to myself:
how easily and how effectively the earthly lights
extinguish the heavenly ones.
Lord, help us to seek the things that make us rich in your sight,
and grant that the glitter of this world
may not dim our hopes of heavenly glory.

Nineteenth Sunday of the Year
WATCHFUL SERVANTS

INTRODUCTION AND CONFITEOR

We are servants of God and of one another. But what kind of servants are we? [Pause] Let us ask forgiveness for our sins of sloth and carelessness in our service of God and of one another.

I confess to almighty God …

HEADINGS FOR READINGS

First Reading (Wis 18:6-9). Just as God came to the rescue of the Jews in Egypt, so he will save those who put their trust in him.

Second Reading (Heb 11:1-2.8-19). We are called to imitate the faith of the patriarchs, especially that of Abraham, 'our father in faith'.

Gospel (Lk 12:32-48). The parable of the waiting servants urges a constant watchfulness and faithfulness.

SCRIPTURE NOTE

The First Reading is an extract from a long section which recounts God's actions on behalf of Israel during the Exodus from Egypt. It points out how the Israelites benefited from the very things by which the Egyptians were punished and thus sets forth a historical basis for trust in God.

This fits in with the theme of the Second Reading, which deals with faith in God's promises. It extols various figures in the history of Israel, but especially Abraham, as examples of faith.

The emphasis in the Gospel is on readiness for the return of the Lord. Even though the disciples are only a 'little flock' in a hostile world, they must not be discouraged, but must look with confidence to the Father who has chosen them for his kingdom. They are like bridesmaids waiting for the bridegroom (Jesus) to return from the wedding feast. Since they do not know the exact hour of his return, they must maintain a constant watchfulness and faithfulness.

Though these words have relevance for all Christians, Luke was thinking especially of leaders in the community, and calling them to a selfless service of their Lord and of their fellow Christians.

HOMILY 1   **Living with uncertainty**

Most people nowadays have been on a plane. Before the flight gets under way one of the attendants says something like this: 'We'd like your attention for a few moments while we show you some of the safety features of this aircraft ... ' The attendant then shows you how to fasten the seat belt, and advises you to keep it fastened during the flight. You are told the number and location of the emergency exits. And how, in the event of a sudden loss of cabin pressure, an individual oxygen mask will be lowered in front of you. You are told that under your seat there is a life-jacket for use in the event of having to ditch into the ocean.

The idea behind all this is to help the passengers to be prepared for the unexpected. But few pay any attention to what the attendant is saying. If anything, it serves only to further unnerve the nervous.

In the Gospel Jesus gives us some instructions regarding the flight of life – a flight in which all of us are involved. He tells us to be prepared for the unexpected. Like faithful servants we should keep ourselves in a state of readiness/preparedness. Not in fear, but in trust and hope.

As life goes on we become increasingly aware of how fleeting it is, and how precarious is the hold we have on it. We are not made of stone but of very fragile material. Life can be taken away from us in the twinkling of an eye. However, the brevity and fragility of life bring home to us how precious is the treasure we carry in earthen vessels.

Jesus was aware of the uncertainty of life. His parable stresses the fact that death can come at any moment. It isn't that God tries to catch us unawares like a thief breaking into a house. That would be unthinkable. Death, not God, is the thief that robs us of life.

The uncertainty of life should not prevent us from enjoying life in the present. All of us would like to be able to end our lives with our plans carried out and our work done. But we don't know if we will have that chance. What we do have is an opportunity to be faithful to our responsibilities and commitments on a daily basis, like the servant Jesus spoke about. Then we can go forward into the unknown like Abraham did, trusting in God's gracious and loving care.

Once upon a time there was a court jester who for many years had helped to amuse the king and the royal court. But then he committed an indiscretion and was sentenced to death. Before the sentence was carried out the king summoned him and said to him, 'In view of the many happy moments you gave me over the years, I will allow you to choose the method by which you are to die.'

The jester thought for a moment and then replied, 'Your Majesty, if it's all right by you, I choose to die by old age.'

The king was so amused at his answer that he granted him his request. Most of us would make the same choice. But we don't know if we'll get it.

We are servants of the Lord and of one another. Blessed are those servants who are faithful and responsible. The faithful servant doesn't fear the master's return. He (she) welcomes it.

Any time is a bad time for the unfaithful servant. Any time is a good time for the faithful servant. 'We are not called to be successful, only to be faithful.' (Mother Teresa)

HOMILY 2   **The faithful servant**

Death is the greatest event of life, yet it catches many people unawares. To some it comes literally like a thief in the night. It may come early on in the night, or in the middle, or towards the end. However, this unexpectedness can be a grace – it keeps us on our toes, it forces us to be prepared at all times.

To be prepared doesn't mean to have accomplished everything one wants to accomplish. It means to be true to one's responsibilities in the present moment. One day a monk was sweeping a floor in the monastery when someone asked him what he would do if he knew he was going to die within the hour. 'I'd go on sweeping the floor,' was his reply. In other words, he would go on attending to the duty of the moment.

Many people believe that happiness lies in having no commitments, no one to answer to, no one whose needs or problems will ever tie them down. But this is not so. In fact, the opposite is the case. A person's happiness and fulfilment lie, not in freedom, but in the acceptance of duty. But it has to be a duty, not grimly accepted, but lovingly accepted.

Whoever performs only his duty is not doing his duty. The more difficult the task to which we devote ourselves out of love, the more it will exalt us. The greatest grace in life, the greatest freedom, is when what we have to do is what we love to do. 'I slept and dreamt that life was joy. I woke and found that life was duty. I acted and behold duty was joy.' (Tagore).

When Dag Hammarskjold was beginning his second term as Secretary General of the UN he made a speech of thanks. In that speech he quoted a verse from a Swedish poet: 'Will the day ever come when joy is great and sorrow small?' And added his own answer: 'On the day we feel we are living with a duty, well fulfilled and worth our while, on that day joy is great and we can look on sorrow as being small.'

It would be nice if when death comes all our work was done, all our tasks were completed and neatly bound together like a sheaf of wheat. But we can't be sure if this will be the case because the moment of death is hidden from us. However, we might remember this: it's not how or when we die that matters, but how we live. We should strive to live fully and intensely, and not wait for illness or disaster to bring home the fleeting nature of human life.

Some years ago in America a Franciscan priest who worked for deprived children was taking part in a sponsored cycle race to raise funds when he was hit by a car and died as a result of his injuries. It wasn't a nice way to die. Yet from a Christian perspective it was a very good way to die. He died while working for the Lord. He was like the faithful servant Jesus speaks about in the Gospel.

Life is very precious, but we do not enjoy this world everlastingly. Happy those who possess a sense of duty. Their greatness lies in their sense of responsibility. Mother Teresa said: 'We are not called to be successful, only to be faithful.'

HOMILY 3   **Journeying in faith**

Writing in *The Tablet* (April 1, 2000) Pastor Ignotus says that there are two ways of approaching life: one is either a planner or a pilgrim. The planner likes to have total control over his life and to be able to plan each stage according to pre-set goals. Planners take their cue from what society considers success, and spend most of their time trying to match the lifestyle and values of others. They become bitterly disappointed if they fail to achieve these objectives.

The pilgrim, on the other hand, is someone who accepts life as a gift that unfolds as we live it, for however hard we may try, we can never have complete control over what happens. He/she is not deterred by failures and disappointments but sees them as opportunities for spiritual growth. Unlike the planner, the pilgrim never feels entirely comfortable or at ease with society's values.

The planner refuses to live by faith. The pilgrim on the other hand lives by faith, knowing that life is full of risk, yet affirming it. He senses the full insecurity of the human situation, yet rejoices. That is the essence of faith. He puts himself in God's hands, and thus opens himself to the full grace of God's protection. He celebrates the present moment, and thus is able to live life to the full.

Abraham is the great Old Testament model of faith (Second Reading). He is the quintessential pilgrim. At the word of God he uprooted himself, leaving his home and people, and set out for a land God promised to show him, where he would become the father of a great nation. It was a journey into the unknown. The only compass he had was faith in God.

We are the spiritual descendants of Abraham. We prove ourselves true children of Abraham by imitating his faith. Life is full of uncertainty. Like Abraham, we are journeying into the unknown. We literally don't know what lies around the next bend on the road of life. Yet, in spite of frustrations and failures, we journey on – pilgrims homesick for a place where our hopes will be realised, and where our true life will begin.

For all his faith, Abraham died without seeing God's promise fulfilled. As Christians we spend our lives journeying towards the promised land of heaven. But we die without reaching it. Like Abraham we travel in faith and die in hope.

It is especially at death that we are called upon to imitate the faith of Abraham. At death we have to leave everything behind, and set out for a strange land, relying only on God's promise. But if we have lived by faith, the last step in the journey will be no harder than any of the ones that preceded it.

As Christians we should be conscious that we are not alone on the pilgrimage of life. We make the pilgrimage of life as members of a believing community. The faith of the community will support us when our own faith does not measure up.

Meanwhile, like the servant Jesus talks about, we must strive to be faithful to God and to one another. The real test of fidelity is to be faithful in spite of setbacks and failures, even when it just means being faithful in small things, believing that our life does matter, and that we can make a difference. We should draw courage and hope from the words of Mother Teresa: 'We are not called to be successful, only to be faithful.'

PRAYER OF THE FAITHFUL

President: God has made us stewards over the earth. Let us pray that we may be good stewards of his creation.

Response: Lord, hear our prayer.

Reader(s): For the pope and the bishops: that they may be faithful servants of the servants of God. [Pause] Let us pray to the Lord.

For Christians: that the faith they proclaim in words may be borne out by their deeds. [Pause] Let us pray to the Lord.

For government leaders: that they may use wisely the earth's resources and take good care of its fragile environment. [Pause] Let us pray to the Lord.

For husbands and wives: that they may be faithful to one another. [Pause] Let us pray to the Lord.

For all gathered here: that our faith in God may give us strength, courage and hope as we journey on through life. [Pause] Let us pray to the Lord.

For all those who have gone before us and who have died in faith. [Pause] Let us pray to the Lord.

For our own special needs. [Longer pause] Let us pray to the Lord.

President: Merciful God, give us a love for what you command and a longing for what you promise, so that amidst the changes and uncertainties of this world, our hearts may be set on the world of lasting joy. We ask this through Christ our Lord.

REFLECTION   **Beatitudes of life**

Blessed are the faithful:
    they are like safe anchors in a world of broken moorings.
Blessed are the just:
    they are to society what leaven is to bread.
Blessed are the generous:
    they keep alive our faith in the essential goodness of people.
Blessed are the caring:
    they shine like beacons in a world darkened by indifference.
Blessed are the genuine:
    they glow like gems in a world of falseness.
Blessed are those who are not afraid of sacrifice:
    on the day of the harvest they will sing for joy.
And blessed are those who refuse to look back:
    they will be found worthy of the Kingdom of Heaven.

Twentieth Sunday of the Year
FIRE UPON THE EARTH

INTRODUCTION AND CONFITEOR

The Gospel is a great comfort to us, especially in times of sorrow and trouble. But it's also a great challenge. It challenges us to shun darkness and to opt for the light, to be with Christ rather than against him. Let us reflect on this to see where we stand – with Christ or against him. [Pause] Let us ask the Lord to help us to be true to his Gospel.

Lord Jesus, you hear us when we cry to you for help. Lord, have mercy.
You strengthen us when we are weak and indecisive. Christ, have mercy.
You shed your light on us when we are in darkness. Lord, have mercy.

HEADINGS FOR READINGS

First Reading (Jer 38:4-6.8-10). This describes the persecution of the prophet Jeremiah, whom Christians see as a figure of Christ.

Second Reading (Heb 12:1-4). The author exhorts his readers to persevere in their faith, drawing strength from the example of Christ and all those who have gone before them.

Gospel (Lk 12:49-53). The coming of Christ marks a time of division in which people will be called on to declare their loyalties.

SCRIPTURE NOTE

The First Reading describes the persecution of the prophet Jeremiah. Having tried in vain to save his people, Jeremiah was now abandoned to his enemies. Christians have always seen him as a figure of Christ. His sufferings remind us of the sufferings of Jesus, and his rescue from the pit reminds us of Jesus' resurrection from the tomb.

The Gospel contains two sayings about the nature of Jesus' mission. His coming marks a time for making decisions. His followers will have to make crucial choices; they will have to choose to be for him or against him. Choosing for him may divide them from family members. In the early Church, conversion was likely to cause a family row. The convert was rejected by the family, and had therefore to make a choice between Christ and the family.

HOMILY 1   **Casting fire on the earth**

'I came to cast fire on the earth ... I came, not to bring peace, but rather division.' Strange words to hear coming from Jesus! We wouldn't expect him to use fire and the sword (division). Nor did he. When James and John wanted him to call down fire and brimstone on a Samaritan village, he told them they didn't know what they were talking about. And when Peter drew his sword in the garden, Jesus told him to put it away.

Jesus did not come to cause trouble or to break-up families. But sometimes this happened. In the early days of the Church conversion to Christianity was likely to lead to rejection by the family, and therefore the convert had to make a choice between Christ and the family.

It's clear that when Jesus talks about bringing fire and division his words are not meant to be taken literally. Yet those words stand for something real in him. Jesus was gentle. But this doesn't mean that he was weak. When the occasion demanded it he could be very assertive – as when he drove the traders out of the Temple.

These words also stand for something very strong in his teaching. His teaching caused division. He taught that the Kingdom of God was open to everyone – saints and sinners, Jews and Gentiles. This brought him into conflict with the religious establishment of his day. He called the Scribes and Pharisees hypocrites and blind guides. They called him a troublemaker and a man possessed.

If Jesus had flattered people and said only 'nice' things to them, he could have made himself popular. But he chose to disturb people, because they needed to be disturbed. His words shocked some and infuriated others. The words he spoke to the poor were different from those he spoke to the rich. The words he spoke to sinners were different from those he spoke to the Pharisees. We betray the Gospel if we reduce it to a bland message to all, which ignores the differences between rich and poor, between the privileged and the dispossessed. Such an insipid Gospel would not be a leaven in the world.

There is a tendency to domesticate the Gospel, to reduce it to pretty words and feel-good experiences. When that happens, the fire has gone out, the leaven has lost its power, the salt has lost its taste, the light has grown dim.

Christians should not be surprised if the Gospel should divide people. Jesus' sense of justice brought him into conflict with those who exploited the weak and the poor. His integrity brought him into conflict with the dishonest. His tolerance brought him into conflict with the narrow-minded and the bigoted. The brighter the light, the darker the shadows it casts.

'When I give bread to the poor, they call me a saint. But when I ask why the poor have no bread, they call me a communist.' So said the late Archbishop Helder Camara, champion of Brazil's poor.

Jesus says he came to kindle a fire upon the earth. It's only an image, a metaphor. But it's a powerful one. It's a symbol of judgement and purification. Fire burns up what is useless, and refines what is impure.

The Gospel message is a fire that purifies; it is the leaven of society and the world. A fire needs not only to be kindled but also to be tended. We, the followers of Jesus, are the tenders of the fire.

HOMILY 2   **The prophet as 'troublemaker'**

Jesus was a transparently good person. We would have expected then that he would have been universally loved. Yet he stirred up so much hatred that he ended up being crucified. How could that happen? It happened because Jesus was a prophet, a religious prophet, and a prophet is always *persona non grata* to the powers-that-be. Most prophets are persecuted and some are killed.

Jeremiah is a good example. He was called to be a prophet from an early age. He lived out his vocation during a time of great turmoil, which saw the defeat of Israel and the destruction of Jerusalem and the Temple. He was the conscience of his country. He loved his people dearly and never lost faith in the power of God to save them. Yet he was accused of being a troublemaker, and lived with constant threats to his life.

Prophets are 'troublemakers' – in the best sense of that term. There is no greater disturber of the peace than the person who preaches justice and truth. Take Martin Luther King in America. He was a man of peace. Yet by calling for an end to discrimination against black people, he created more turmoil in America than anyone else of his generation. And take the Russian scientist, Andrei Sakharov. He too was branded a 'troublemaker' by the communist authorities when he called for an end to the persecution of dissidents and to the proliferation of nuclear weapons.

Sometimes what we call peace is not really peace at all. Any peace that is not founded on justice is a phoney peace. The late Archbishop Helder Camara of Brazil described it as resembling moonlight over a swamp. Jesus came to bring peace, but not that kind of peace. Just as there is a phoney peace, there is also a phoney unity – one which tolerates discrimination and inequality.

When the South African writer Laurens van der Post was released from a Japanese prisoner-of-war camp and returned to freedom, he was shocked almost as much by the brutalities of peace as he had been by those of war. And Solzhenitsyn says that when soldiers came back to civilian life they were appalled by the callous, often totally unscrupulous way in which people treated each other. By providing them with an opportunity to serve a cause greater than any egotistical pursuit of themselves, war had brought out the best in them.

How abnormal is much of what is accepted as normal. For instance, the inequalities in society, the gap between helpless poverty and insolent wealth. We get so used to all this that it ceases to shock us. We accept it as normal. Hence, we need someone to jolt us out of the sleep of lethargy and indifference.

Jesus says he came to kindle a fire upon the earth. It's only an image, a metaphor. But it's a powerful one. Fire is not something one can remain indifferent to. It's not a weak, pale, lifeless thing. Fire warms and comforts. But it also burns up what is useless, and refines what is impure.

The Gospel message is fire, it is the leaven of the world. We, the followers of Jesus, are the tenders of the fire.

HOMILY 3   **Running the race**

In our times we have witnessed a strange but exciting phenomenon – the phenomenon of running. It's quite common to see ten or even twenty thousand people taking part in city marathons around the world. A question: Would you find it easier to run a marathon on your own or with others? The answer is obvious. The phrase, 'The loneliness of the long distance runner' says it all.

An athlete who is running alone before an empty stadium is not likely to give of his best. But in a stadium full of cheering fans, he strains every nerve and employs all his resources beyond even his ordinary capacity.

We derive strength from seeing ourselves surrounded by other runners. This is especially true when we are not interested in being placed among the top finishers, but only in finishing the race. Then we see our fellow runners as companions rather than competitors. We see them as supporters. This enables us to draw strength from their example. They create a flow so that we are carried along as in a powerful current.

What hinders a runner in a race? Any kind of injury or weakness. Also lack of motivation. When people are highly motivated they are willing to make huge sacrifices in giving time, in dieting, in effort, and so on.

Marathon running is not about winning. The race is what counts. Running the marathon is itself the event. Everybody wins. What matters is the participation, the engagement. And by participating we are helping others through our example: we are contributing a little.

It's not just in running that people draw strength from companionship. The author of Hebrews exhorts his readers to persevere in their faith, regardless of the cost. He says they should draw strength from the 'cloud of witnesses' who have gone before them. He is referring to the saints of the Old Testament who have run the race before them.

Christians are conscious of being part of a holy chain of witnesses which stretches back to the apostles. In the struggle to be faithful, they have always turned to the inspiring examples of prophets, witnesses and saints. We draw hope and courage from 'heroes of the faith', who remained faithful in spite of the fact that they did not see the promises fulfilled in their lifetimes. And when we experience weariness and a sense of failure and futility, they are saying to us, 'We are with you. Don't give up.'

As a pioneer pilot said: 'Sometimes the storms and the fog will get you down. But think of all those who have been through it before you, and just tell yourself: "They did it, so it can be done again".'

But it is especially on Jesus that we must keep our eyes. His faithfulness brought him to the cross, and after that to glory. He is an example greater than the entire cloud of Old Testament examples.

The message is clear: like our Master, we Christians must be ready to struggle against all obstacles on the road to God. It's not a solitary struggle, but one we make together. We are running together in the greatest race of all.

PRAYER OF THE FAITHFUL

President: Let us pray that the fire Jesus came to kindle may burn brightly in our lives and in the world.

Response: Lord, hear our prayer.

Reader(s): That all Christians may be courageous witnesses to Christ. [Pause] Let us pray to the Lord.

That world leaders may heed the voice of the prophets in their midst. [Pause] Let us pray to the Lord.

That all those who are working for peace and justice may find that God upholds them when they suffer. [Pause] Let us pray to the Lord.

That we may draw strength from the example of all the saints who have preceded us and who now intercede for us. [Pause] Let us pray to the Lord.

That all who have died in hope may see that hope fulfilled in the kingdom of heaven. [Pause] Let us pray to the Lord.

For our own special needs. [Longer pause] Let us pray to the Lord.

President: Lord, help us to be messengers of hope, instruments of peace, and agents of love to a world that is riddled with injustice and division. We ask this through Christ our Lord.

REFLECTION   **True and false peace**

A swamp may look nice on the surface,
but its depths are full of rotten things.
Peace that is based on injustice is like that.
It is a false peace and Jesus came to disrupt it.
But then there is true peace –
a peace in which all of God's children have their basic rights respected,
and are able to live in freedom and dignity.
This is the peace Jesus came to bring.
But peace like this doesn't happen; it has to be made.
Sometimes the peacemakers will be branded troublemakers.
But Jesus had another name for them: he called them 'children of God'.

Twenty-first Sunday of the Year
THE NARROW GATE

INTRODUCTION AND CONFITEOR

Jesus said, 'People will come from north and south, from east and west, and take their places in the Kingdom.' We have come here from many different directions. But all of these directions have served to bring us to this house of God. We give thanks to God for that, and ask that we may be found worthy of God's kingdom. [Pause]

Lord Jesus, you help us to enter the kingdom of God by the gate of repentance. Lord, have mercy.

You help us to enter the kingdom by the gate of sacrifice. Christ, have mercy.

You help us to enter the kingdom by the gate of goodness of life. Lord, have mercy.

HEADINGS FOR READINGS

First Reading (Is 66:18-21). Gentiles will be converted and receive a share in Israel's blessings.

Second Reading (Heb 12:5-7.11-13). As a father shows his concern for his son by training him in discipline, so God trains his children through suffering.

Gospel (Lk 13:22-30). The Kingdom of God is offered, not just to the Jews, but to people from the four corners of the world.

SCRIPTURE NOTE

The First Reading presents a vision of all peoples coming to Jerusalem to share in the blessings God has conferred on Israel. This prepares us for the universalist note (typical of Luke) which we find in the Gospel.

God wills that all people should be saved. People will come from all over the world to share in the messianic kingdom, and the Jews will have no advantage over the Gentiles. Jesus refuses to get into the numbers game, or to speculate about matters that are best left to the wisdom and mercy of God. The main thing is: the kingdom is present and the door open. But the door is not so wide that people can saunter casually in at their own convenience; it is a narrow opening through which they must thrust themselves with determination. Besides, the door will not be open indefinitely.

The message was originally intended for the Jews, but Luke now intends it as a warning to the disciples of Jesus. There were those who thought they could enter the kingdom simply because they had a superficial acquaintance with the Master, but whose commitment was limited to words. There are those who even did evil, and who still expected to get in. It's a warning against presumption. Salvation depends on the favour of God and the honest struggle to follow his ways.

HOMILY 1   **Entering by the narrow gate**

A man came to Jesus and said, 'Sir, will only a few be saved?' The man was a Jew. As such he would have believed that only Jews would be admitted to the Kingdom of Heaven. Gentiles had no hope at all.

Jesus took the man's question and used it to deliver a warning to his contemporaries. He said, 'Strive to enter by the narrow door; for many, I tell you, will try to enter and will not be able.' He was telling the Jews that they were in danger of being locked out of the Kingdom because they did not heed his call to repentance.

The main gate to a castle is generally wide, and therefore easy to enter – if you have the right credentials. These credentials have nothing to do with goodness of life. They have everything to do with having the right connections. Those who enter by the main gate are apt to puff themselves up with a feeling of self-importance. They feel they have a right to enter because of who they are.

But in all castles you will find a narrow side gate. In order to enter through this gate you have to make yourself small. You have to humble yourself. And you have to rid yourself of anything that is likely to encumber you.

This illustration helps us to understand what Jesus meant when he said, 'Strive to enter the Kingdom by the narrow gate.' It also helps us to understand why on another occasion he said, 'Unless you become like little children, you will not enter the Kingdom.' The little ones have ready access to the Kingdom. Why? Because they find it easy to make themselves small, and are adept at squeezing through narrow spaces.

All of this is important for us. We must not repeat the mistake of Jesus' contemporaries, who thought they had a divine right to enter the Kingdom. We must really want to enter God's Kingdom, and be prepared to work for it. We must be happy to get in at all, even if it means having to squeeze in.

This ought to be our attitude. We mustn't take anything for granted. We mustn't feel that all we have to do is show up, flash the ID card, or simply tell the gatekeeper that we know the Boss, and in we go. The bottom line is goodness of life. As Jesus said, 'Traffic in good and not in evil.'

How many will enter the kingdom of God? Will it be, as the Jews believed, a chosen few? Is the kingdom a club for members only? Certainly not. Anyone who is prepared to enter by the narrow gate will get in.

At the end of the day, we have to remember that salvation is not something we can earn. It is a gift from God. Jesus opened the Kingdom to sinners, and through humility and repentance they proved themselves better candidates than the so-called virtuous. Think of the good thief he brought in at the very last moment of his life.

Truly, salvation is a gift from God. But that doesn't mean we ought not try to make ourselves worthy of the Kingdom. And we must open our hearts to others, and not begrudge God's generosity to them.

HOMILY 2   **The Kingdom is not a private club**

A man came to Jesus and said, 'Sir, will only a few be saved?'

This reminds us of the story about the man who died and went up to heaven. St Peter met him at the gate, brought him inside, and took him on a tour of the place. At a certain point they came to an enclosure surrounded by a high wall. As they were passing it Peter said, 'Keep very quiet as you pass this place.'

'Why?' the man asked.

'In case we might disturb those inside,' Peter answered.

'Who's inside?' he asked.

'Catholics. You see, they think they're the only people in heaven. If they thought there were others in heaven, they'd be very disappointed. In fact, some of them would probably ask for their money back.'

The man who asked Jesus, 'Will only a few be saved?' obviously thought that heaven was a select club to which only members are admitted. The man was a Jew. As such he would have believed that only Jews would be admitted to the Kingdom of Heaven. Gentiles had no hope of getting in. As for sinners – forget it! (The idea of a chosen people is a dangerous idea. If God chooses a people, he doesn't choose them to the exclusion of others, but to the service of others.)

By the time the man had digested Jesus' answer, he was probably sorry he asked the question in the first place. Because Jesus blew his assumptions to smithereens. He turned everything upside down. He said, 'The first will be last, and the last will be first.' It was a revolutionary statement that shocked and outraged the Pharisees. And Jesus didn't leave it there. He befriended sinners and outcasts. The Pharisees saw this as a betrayal of virtuous people like themselves. But Jesus declared that it was to seek out and save people such as these that he had come.

The world is riddled with exclusive clubs, snobbery, privilege, preference, and so on. We wouldn't expect Jesus to go along with this. Nor did he. He announced the good news of the coming of the Kingdom of God. To those Jews who thought they could enter the Kingdom as a matter of course he said: Produce the fruits of repentance, otherwise your privileged position would benefit you nothing.

Jesus said that conversion was a necessary disposition for entry into the Kingdom. And he succeeded in bringing it about in the most unlikely of people. Many sinners heeded his call to conversion, and made their way into the Kingdom. Whereas many religious people stubbornly resisted his call to conversion, and so excluded themselves from the Kingdom.

It's not up to us to decide who gets into heaven. That is better left to the wisdom and mercy of God. We have to allow God to be God. At the end of the day, salvation is not something we can earn. It is a gift of God. But that doesn't mean we ought not try to make ourselves worthy of it. Through our Baptism we are members of the new Chosen People. We are the 'insiders'. But we must not rely on that fact alone. We must endeavour to produce the fruits of the kingdom, namely, goodness, right living and truth.

HOMILY 3   **Suffering is part of our training**

In the old days the methods used in educating the young were based on endurance: the more inhuman tests a child survived, the better the child would be prepared to meet the hazards of adulthood. We see a good example of this is the rites of initiation found among Indian tribes, rites which were designed to help the young take their place in the adult world.

In one such rite, the youth is taken at dusk by his father to a clearing in the forest. He is told that he must spend the night there on his own, armed only with a spear. Then the father withdraws. When the youth comes out of the forest he will no longer be the child he was.

What a daunting challenge the youth faces. There is the impenetrable darkness. There are the innumerable sounds, the most innocuous of which assume a menacing tone. There is the feeling that some animal is lurking nearby, waiting to pounce, a feeling which causes a cold sweat to break out all over his body. If only he had a friend by his side, how different things would be. But he is on his own.

Time goes by ever so slowly. Every minute is like an hour. But somehow the night passes, and finally the dawn begins to brighten the sky. As the shadows retreat, the youth's fears evaporate, and he begins to breathe again. Then from the dense forest a human figure emerges. It is his father.

The youth runs to his father, throws himself into his arms, and exclaims, 'Oh, thank God you've come!' Then it is the father's turn to embrace his son. As he does so he says, 'Son, I'm proud of you. You conducted yourself like a true adult.' What the youth did not know was that the father had been sitting close by all night long, keeping an eye on him. Everybody who wishes to grow up has to face the 'dark forest' in some shape or form.

The author of the Letter to the Hebrews talks about the kind of training God gives us. We are trained in the school of suffering. However, there is no point in being sentimental about suffering. People can get so hurt that they become bitter and will not accept being redeemed.

Yet suffering can be a great opportunity. The value of suffering lies not in the pain of it, but in what the sufferer makes of it. Suffering can purify one's soul and transform one's character. Suffering can bear fruit. It is an indispensable part in our becoming truly human, that is, people of maturity, depth and compassion. As Van Gogh said: 'One must bear hardship in order to ripen.'

Suffering is a necessary ingredient in building up a mature Christian person. We must not see suffering as a punishment from God. God punishes no one. Suffering is part of the human condition. God allows us to suffer, yes, but only because good can come from it. Our pain can bring us closer to him. In it we experience his power and love. There are truths which only sorrow can teach. One of those truths is compassion for fellow sufferers. Compassion is not learned without suffering.

PRAYER OF THE FAITHFUL

President: Let us pray that we may strive to enter the Kingdom through the narrow gate.

Response: Lord, graciously hear us.

Reader(s): For the followers of Jesus: that their lives may bear witness to the faith they profess with their lips. [Pause] Lord, hear us.

For all government leaders: that they may strive to promote the wellbeing of all their people. [Pause] Lord, hear us.

For the Jewish people, who first heard the word of God: that they may continue to grow in love of his name and in faithfulness to his covenant. [Pause] Lord, hear us.

For all those who are suffering: that their pain may bear fruit. [Pause] Lord, hear us.

For our own special needs. [Longer pause] Lord, hear us.

President: Merciful God, fill our hearts with your love, and keep us faithful to you and to the Gospel. Grant this through Christ our Lord.

REFLECTION   **The two roads**

Jesus said that there are two roads we can follow.
The first is wide and easy to travel.
It is downhill most of the way.
It is the way of comfort and ease, pleasure and self-seeking.
Many are fooled and travel down this road.
But in the long run it leads them nowhere. They die in the desert.
The second road is narrow and difficult.
It is uphill a lot of the way. It is the way of struggle and sacrifice.

Few take this road. But they are the lucky ones.
This road leads to the Promised Land.

Twenty-Second Sunday of the Year
PLACES AT TABLE

INTRODUCTION AND CONFITEOR

Once, Jesus was invited to a supper. During the supper he commented on how the guests were fighting for the places of honour. Here Jesus invites us to his supper. He is the host, we are the guests. Here every place is a place of honour. [Pause] Let us begin by humbling ourselves before God and asking pardon for our sins.

I confess to almighty God ...

HEADINGS FOR READINGS

First Reading (Sir 3:17-20.28-29). There is praise for the person who is humble.

Second Reading (Heb 12:18-19.22-24). This contrasts Mount Sinai, where the old covenant was made, and Mount Zion, which stands for the heavenly Jerusalem.

Gospel (Lk 14:1.7-14). Jesus urges his followers not to covet places of honour, and always to act out of unselfish motives.

SCRIPTURE NOTE

The readings stress the importance of humility, especially for those in high places. The First Reading praises the person who is humble. A humble person is conscious of his own weakness, and never rejects wisdom, no matter where it comes from. Such a person will find favour with God and with his friends and neighbours. Pride raises a barrier to God's graciousness and to communion with our fellows.

This ties in with the Gospel where the key phrase is: 'Everyone who exalts himself will be humbled, and the one who humbles himself will be exalted.' Jesus criticises those who thrust themselves forward and who engineer their way to the top. That's not the way to gain honour in the Kingdom. Honour in the Kingdom comes from the host, not from the guest. God confers honour on those who are humble.

If we want to know the quality of our love, all we have to do is look at the kind of people with whom we share our love. Those who act out of motives of self-interest will receive no reward from God. But those who act from motives of disinterested charity will receive a reward at the resurrection. Here we also see Luke's concern for the poor and the afflicted.

HOMILY 1   **Being watched**

Jesus was invited to the house of a leading Pharisee. However, as soon as he walked into the man's house, he sensed a cold, critical attitude towards him. His adversaries were watching him closely, hoping to find grounds for bringing some accusation against him. We can observe another person with friendly eyes, hostile eyes, or indifferent eyes.

When we look at another person with friendly eyes, it means that from the outset we are well disposed towards him. What a difference that makes. We are looking out for the good in him, and are ready to excuse the not so good. We are open to him and disposed to learn from him. To feel the weight of friendly eyes on us is a beautiful feeling. It puts us at ease and makes us feel welcome.

When we look at someone with hostile eyes, it means that from the outset we are ill-disposed towards him. We are looking for faults, and will be disappointed if we don't find them. We don't give him a chance to prove himself. We have already made up our minds about him. Even if we can't find any fault with what he says or does, we can always cast doubt on his motives. We are not disposed to learn anything from him because our minds are closed against him. And our minds are closed because our hearts are closed. To feel the weight of hostile eyes on us is a horrible feeling.

When we look at another with indifferent eyes, it means we don't care about him one way or another. We may see his efforts, his sadness, and even his tears, but they mean nothing to us. We are not interested in him, or concerned about him. Indeed, we hardly see him at all. It's almost as if he wasn't there.

As soon as Jesus entered that house he knew that the Pharisees were watching him with hostile eyes. They had already made up their minds about him. They wanted to get rid of him. All they needed was some hard evidence.

Many people are inquisitive about the faults of others but negligent to correct their own. In fact, nothing so blinds us to our own faults as a preoccupation with the faults of others. So it was that Jesus was able to turn the tables on the Pharisees. He too had been observing them, though out of different motives. And he saw things he didn't like.

Turning first of all to his fellow guests, he commented on their shabby scramble for the places of honour. This indicated that they were there not to honour their host, but to honour themselves.

Then he had a word for his host. In giving the meal he seemed to be doing a very generous thing – until you looked at the kind of people he had invited. He had invited in his cronies, who would invite him to their houses in return. What was so generous about that? That kind of giving was an investment. He would get it back, and with a handsome profit.

Jesus suggested to him that if he wanted to do something really generous, he should invite in the kind of people who would never be able to invite him to their houses. True giving occurs when nothing is expected in return.

There are obvious lessons for us in all of this. With what kind of eyes do we observe others? The Pharisees would have been better employed looking at themselves and their own faults. So would we.

And what is the quality of our good deeds? Religious people can be woefully selfish. Just as weeds ruin a garden, so selfishness ruins one's Christian witness. Giving is at the heart of the Gospel. But it has to have a certain quality. It has to be disinterested giving.

HOMILY 2   **Places of honour**

Jesus was invited to the house of a leading Pharisee for a meal. When he arrived, he felt that he was being spied upon by the Pharisees. So he decided to do a little spying on them in return. The sight that met his eyes was not an edifying one. The Pharisees were very religious people, and set themselves up as models. Yet here they were scrambling for the places of honour, showing just how proud, vain and selfish they really were. They were there not to honour their host, but to honour themselves. There can be no true spirituality without humility. Jesus says, 'Those who humble themselves will be exalted.'

When we enter a great cathedral we are immediately humbled. We feel small and insignificant. We realise how flimsy and false are the things that we depend on. But in a strange way we are also exalted. Because when we humble ourselves, and let go of those things that give us a false sense of importance and superiority, and which separate us from others, we find that we are exalted. We begin to realise our true greatness, which lies, not in ourselves, but in the fact that we are children of God.

Each Sunday we are invited to a banquet – the banquet of the Eucharist. Here Jesus is the host, and we are his guests. Here there are no special places – you can sit where you wish. Here privilege, status, rank have no meaning. Differences don't count. This is because before God all of us are equal.

It's not that we are reduced to the same common denominator. Rather, it is that all of us are raised up. We are like people on a mountain top. On a mountain top, to speak of first and last places, or higher and lower places, would be silly. The same applies to the house of God. Here every place is a place of honour. Entering here makes everyone equal. When we cross this threshold, privilege blows away like smoke, and we are all humbled, yet elevated too. We have first of all to be humbled in order to be elevated. We should carry this spirit out into life with us afterwards.

Once the mayor of a town invited all the people of the town to a banquet. Among those who showed up was a man of great distinction by the name of Daniel. Daniel was a great scholar and a wise man. Yet he was very humble and didn't like being honoured. When he arrived the mayor naturally invited him to sit at the top table. Daniel thanked him but said he would prefer to sit among the poor at the table nearest the door. And that he did.

When other distinguished guests arrived, the mayor invited them to sit wherever they liked. Naturally they chose to sit at the top table. The banquet hall filled up, and eventually the only place left was one at the bottom table. Then at the last minute this distinguished man arrived. The mayor had no option but to take him to the vacant seat.

'But this is the bottom table,' the man protested.

'No, this is the top table,' the mayor replied.

'I don't understand,' the man said.

'Wherever Daniel sits is the top table,' the mayor answered.

The moral of the story: it's not the place that honours the guest, but the guest that honours the place. We don't know in what place Jesus sat during that meal, but wherever it was, that was the place of honour.

The banquet is a symbol of the Kingdom. We shouldn't be concerned about seeking a place of honour in the Kingdom. We should regard it is a privilege to be invited at all. In any case, in the Kingdom every place is a place of honour.

HOMILY 3   **True giving**

Giving is at the heart of the Gospel, and is of the essence of the Christian life. But not all giving is the genuine article.

Nicholas, who had a great reputation for generosity, died and went to heaven. St Peter met him at the gate. There he showed him two piles of gold, one small and one large, made up of nuggets of varying sizes.

'What are these?' Nicholas asked .

'They are the acts of giving you performed on earth – one nugget for each act.'

Nicholas' heart filled with pride. But then Peter said, 'Alas, not all giving is true giving. A lot of it is tainted with self-interest. So we'll have to run a test on your acts of giving. By the way, the nuggets in the larger pile don't count.'

'How come?' Nicholas asked.

'They represent all the gifts you gave to your friends, relatives, cronies, and so on. They don't constitute real gold. Even gangsters are good to their own.'

With that the nuggets in the larger pile turned into dust. Peter took a sieve which had large meshes in it, and placed the nuggets from the smaller pile in it. After he had shaken it, he was left with the biggest nuggets in the sieve.

'What are you doing now?' asked Nicholas.

'I'm removing those gifts you gave only to get something in return. Such giving is a kind of investment. You get it back, sometimes with a handsome profit.'

With that he tossed the nuggets aside, and they turned to dust. He then made the meshes of the sieve smaller, and put the remaining nuggets into it. He shook it and once again tossed aside those that remained in it.

'What was that for?' Nicholas asked.

'That removed the good deeds you did so as to win the praise of others. One can make an idol of oneself through giving.'

Peter made the meshes of the sieve finer, putting the remaining nuggets into it. As he did so he said, 'Now we'll remove the good deeds you did simply because of the good feeling you derived from the exercise.'

Nicholas watched him toss the nuggets that got caught in the sieve into the air where they turned into dust. Again Peter gathered up the remaining ones and put them into the sieve, having made the meshes finer still.

'What now?' asked Nicholas.

'Now we'll extract all those things you gave only out of a sense of duty.'

He shook the sieve. The nuggets that remained in it he tossed aside, and they suffered the same fate as the others.

'Stop!' Nicholas cried. 'If you go on like this, there won't be anything left. Then how will I earn my passport to heaven?'

'We should go on,' said Peter. 'We should look at the cost of your giving. Suppose we removed the things you gave but which you never missed, how much would disappear? And what of the gifts you gave merely because the receiver was someone you felt deserved your gift?'

But poor Nicholas wasn't listening any more. 'It's a terrible feeling to have gold within your reach, and then to have it snatched from you,' he cried.

'Or if it turns out to be not real gold but fool's gold,' Peter added. 'Ah, Nicholas, real giving is very rare, just as real gold is very rare. To give without expecting anything in return, least of all the great prize of heaven, that is what constitutes real giving. But cheer up, I've good news for you.'

'What good news?' asked Nicholas.

'The Lord is the greatest giver of all. His acts of giving are pure gold. But we've talked long enough. It's time to meet the Lord himself.'

'But I'm empty handed,' Nicholas cried.

'That only means you're poor,' Peter replied. 'But never fear. The Lord gives most generously to those who are poor and who are not ashamed to admit it. So let's go.'

PRAYER OF THE FAITHFUL

President: God is the giver of all good gifts. Let us now pray to him for our needs, and for the needs of the Church and the world.

Response: Lord, hear our prayer.

Reader(s): For Christians: that they may be known for their humility and generosity. [Pause] Let us pray to the Lord.

For those who hold public office: that they may not seek their own glory but to serve others. [Pause] Let us pray to the Lord.

For the poor and the disadvantaged, who have to take the last place in society. [Pause] Let us pray to the Lord.

For peace of mind and generosity of heart. [Pause] Let us pray to the Lord.

For all the dead: that they may have a place at the banquet of eternal life. [Pause} Let us pray to the Lord.

For our own special needs. [Longer pause] Let us pray to the Lord.

President: Merciful God, fill our hearts with your love. Give us the grace to rise above our human weakness, and keep us faithful to the Gospel of your Son. We ask this through the same Christ our Lord.

PRAYER/REFLECTION   **Guests at his table**

Lord, we thank you for having us as guests
at the banquet of the Eucharist.
Here we have listened to your word and eaten the food of eternal life.
May we go forth from here nourished,
honoured, blessed, humbled yet exalted.
May we be so sure of our worth before you
that the honours of this world will never ensnare us.
And in your goodness grant us a place at the heavenly banquet. Amen.

Twenty-third Sunday of the Year
COUNTING THE COST AND PAYING THE PRICE

INTRODUCTION AND CONFITEOR

We measure people's commitment to a cause by the sacrifices they are prepared to make for it. We cannot hope to be genuine followers of Christ without making sacrifices. What does it mean for me to be a Christian?

How does it affect my life? What does it cost me? [Pause] Let us ask the Lord's forgiveness for the way we allow fear and selfishness to weaken our commitment to him.

I confess to almighty God …

HEADINGS FOR READINGS

First Reading (Wis 9:13-18). Without the gift of divine wisdom we would be utterly unable to fathom the mysteries of the universe, the meaning of history, and the mind of God.

Second Reading (Philemon 9-10.12-17). Paul urges Philemon to take Onesimus his former slave back as a brother.

Gospel (Lk 14:25-33). Being a disciple of Christ involves self-renunciation – we must be prepared to accept the cost.

SCRIPTURE NOTE

The First Reading is part of Solomon's prayer for wisdom. God, the Creator of the universe, is all-wise. In contrast, human beings are ignorant. However, God does not leave us in our ignorance, but bestows the gift of wisdom on all who humbly seek it.

Jesus was on his way to Jerusalem (Gospel). He knew that suffering, rejection and death awaited him at the end of that journey. But it seems that some Galileans regarded it as a victory march of the Messiah. In no uncertain terms Jesus disillusioned them.

Knowing that his disciples would have to face a similar challenge, Jesus spoke about the cost of discipleship. He didn't literally mean hating one's father and mother. The word 'hate' is a Semitic expression. 'Love less' would be nearer to what Jesus had in mind. He was telling his disciples that they must be ready if needs be to sacrifice the dearest things in life. In certain (rare) circumstances they might have to choose between him and their own relatives.

The two short parables make the point that discipleship is a serious calling. It could mean persecution and even death. In this, as in any other spheres of life (such as business and politics), one shouldn't walk into it blindly. One must calculate the cost before setting out.

HOMILY 1   **Wearing chains**

Dostoyevsky was only in his early twenties when he wrote his first book, which was entitled *Poor Folk*. It proved a big success. He became famous overnight. The adulation might easily have gone to his head but for the fact that soon afterwards he fell foul of the authorities. Wrongly accused of being an anarchist, he was arrested and, together with some others, was sentenced to death. However, the sentence was commuted to imprisonment, and he and his comrades were packed off to Siberia. Dosto-evsky spent four bleak years there. Ten years went by before he got back to writing.

Instead of embittering and destroying him, the experience greatly enriched him. He now had ten years of suffering to draw on, something which gave him great strength and great authority. Whenever someone approached him and said, 'What right have you to speak for the people?' he had only to lift his trouser legs and point to the scars left by the chains. 'Here is my right,' he would say. And his questioners would be silenced.

To his friends who expressed dismay at all the suffering he had endured he said, 'Prison saved me. Because of prison I became a completely new person. Siberia and imprisonment became a great joy for me. Only there was I able to lead a pure and happy life. It was there that I came to see myself clearly, and there that I learned to understand Christ. It was a good school. It strengthened my faith and awakened my love for those who bear their suffering with patience. It also strengthened my love for Russia, and opened my eyes to the great qualities of the Russian people.'

Paul also displayed his credentials as a disciple of Christ. He too was imprisoned and forced to wear chains (Second reading). This gave him authority when he spoke about the following of Christ.

When young people came to Mother Teresa and expressed a desire to join her congregation, she left them in no doubt as to what they were getting themselves into. She said, 'Our work is hard. We are serving the poor and the homeless twenty-four hours a day.'

In the same way Jesus did not hide the difficulties, the hardships, and the sacrifices that would be required of those who would follow him. He told them in no uncertain terms that it wouldn't be easy. So they could not complain later on, 'Oh, we never thought it was going to be like this.'

There is such a thing as the courage of the blind. But Jesus did not advocate this. In fact, he discouraged it. He said in following him there is a place for common sense, for prudence, for counting up the cost, for discernment to see if one has what it takes.

The most important thing when setting out is self-knowledge. We mustn't take on more than we are capable of. Of course, we won't know in advance what we are capable of. We may underestimate or overestimate ourselves. And we may need a challenge to bring the best out of us.

We can draw encouragement from the example of the apostles. The Gospels show that they struggled at every point to follow Jesus. Yet he did not write them off. And it's clear that they learned from their failures. It was only after his death and resurrection that they became his true followers.

By looking at them we discover our own inadequacies. The Gospel offers hope to Christians who fail. Repentance and a second chance are always possible. Jesus is generous with his grace to those who strive to answer his call.

HOMILY 2   **Following the Master**

In the Gospel we see that Jesus didn't hide the reality from his disciples. He pointed out the difficulties, the hardships, and the sacrifices that would be required of those who would follow him. He told them in no uncertain terms that it wouldn't be easy. So they could not complain later on, 'Oh, we never thought it was going to be like this.'

It's possible to be a follower of Christ without being a disciple. One might just be a camp-follower rather than a soldier of the King. One might not be pulling one's weight, or playing one's part. One might just be a hanger-on in a great work. One might be a talker rather than a doer.

Once someone approached a famous professor about a young man and asked, 'So and so tells me that he was one of your students. Is that correct?' To which the professor replied, 'That man did indeed attend my lectures, but believe me he was never a real student of mine.'

It is one of the supreme handicaps of the Church that in it there are many people who follow Christ at a safe distance, but very few real disciples, that is, people who actually do what he said.

Let's face it. It is not easy to be a disciple of Christ. Discipleship has some practical demands that one cannot escape under pain of betraying the Gospel. Yet we have many comfortable church-goers who gave little heed to the misery of the needy and the groaning of the poor. Still today the Christian is called to renounce many things that are taken for granted by others.

Some followers melt away as soon as a demand is made on them, like snow before the sun. Others are destroyed by opposition and criticism, like a fickle flame that is blown out by the first gust of wind.

When the king visited the monasteries of the great Zen master, Lin Chi, he was astonished to learn that there were more than ten thousand monks living there. Wishing to know the exact number of monks the king asked, 'How many disciples do you have?'

'Four or five,' Lin Chi replied.

Jesus said in following him there is a place for common sense, for prudence, and for counting up the cost. We mustn't take on more than we are capable of. Of course, we won't know in advance what we are capable of. We may underestimate or overestimate ourselves. We may need a challenge to bring the best out of us.

We can draw encouragement from the example of the apostles. The Gospels show that they struggled at every point to follow Jesus. Yet he did not write them off.

By looking at them we discover our own inadequacies. The Gospel offers hope to Christians who fail. Repentance and a second chance are always possible. Jesus is generous with his grace to those who strive to answer his call.

HOMILY 3   **Paying the price**

There are people who have great goals in life, but they will never achieve those goals. Why not? Because they are not willing to pay the price.

There is a story about a girl called Antoinette, who was very pretty but very poor. She had only one goal in life: to be rich. Her only hope was to marry a wealthy man. But she eventually had to settle for a civil servant. He tried to make her happy but couldn't afford the things she dreamed of – pretty dresses, jewellery, a well-furnished home, and so on.

She refused to go out to work, and spent her days in misery and despair. She complained that they never went anywhere. Once her husband got an invitation to a state banquet, but then she complained that she had nothing suitable to wear. So he took all his modest savings from the bank. With these Antoinette bought a new dress. Then she borrowed a necklace from an old school friend, Marie, to go with it.

So she went to the banquet. She was the prettiest woman there and lapped up all the attention she got. However, when they arrived home in the early hours of the morning, she discovered, to her horror, that the necklace was missing.

They searched high and low for it but failed to find it. She hadn't the courage to tell Marie the truth, so they bought a one that looked exactly like the one she had lost. It cost 40,000 francs, money they had to borrow at very high rates of interest. When they gave the necklace to Marie, she never noticed the difference. In fact, she stuffed it into a drawer without even looking at it.

Now Antoinette began to know what real poverty was. But she was determined to play her part in paying off their debts. They gave up their flat and moved into a basement room. They got rid of their maid. She did the housework herself and also went out to work. They scrounged and saved every penny. It took them ten years to pay back what they owed. By now Antoinette looked like an old woman. One day she ran into her friend, Marie, in the street.

'Oh, how you've aged!' said Marie.

'I've been through very hard times since we last met, and all because of you,' Antoinette replied.

'Because of me? I don't understand.'

Then she told her about losing the necklace and how they had worked all those years to recover the money. On hearing this Marie said, 'You mean you bought a diamond necklace to replace mine?'.

'Yes,' said Antoinette, 'and you never noticed it.'

'Oh, my poor Antoinette!' Marie exclaimed. 'Why, my necklace was only imitation. At the most it was worth 400 francs.'

If only Antoinette had been able from the very beginning to put even half of that effort into what she wanted from life, it could have been hers, and she would not have wasted all those precious years. Instead, she spent her time looking out the window and dreaming.

Jesus had one great goal in life, namely, to carry out the task his Father had given him. That's what he lived for. And he was willing to pay whatever price was demanded in order to fulfil his goal. The Gospel shows him headed for Jerusalem. He knew what awaited him there. Suffering, rejection and death lay at the end of that journey. Yet he willingly faced all of that.

And he expected nothing less from his disciples. He talked about the cost of discipleship. When he said they should hate father and mother, he didn't mean that literally. He was telling them that they must be ready if needs be to sacrifice the dearest things in life. In certain (rare) circumstances they might have to choose between him and their own relatives.

By means of two short parables he pointed out that discipleship is a serious calling. It could mean persecution and even death. In this, as in any other sphere of life (such as business and politics), one shouldn't walk into it blindly. One must calculate the cost before setting out, and then see if one is ready to face it.

The goal Jesus sets before us is immensely worthwhile – the goal of an authentic way of life here and eternal life hereafter. There is no higher goal than that. That doesn't mean it is easy. No one can be a disciple without carrying the cross. But Jesus knows our frailty. He lavishes his grace on those who strive sincerely to follow him.

PRAYER OF THE FAITHFUL

President: Let us pray that we may become more committed disciples of Christ.

Response: Lord, graciously hear us.

Reader(s): For all Church leaders: that they may preach the Gospel by word and example to all the world. [Pause] Lord, hear us.

For government leaders: that they may promote justice and unity in the world. [Pause] Lord, hear us.

For all those who suffer because of their belief in Christ. [Pause] Lord, hear us.

For grace to keep our eyes fixed on Christ and to follow him with unwavering commitment. [Pause] Lord, hear us.

For our own special needs. [Longer pause] Lord, hear us.

President: God, our source of life, you know our weakness. May we reach out with joy to grasp your hand, and so walk more readily in your ways. We ask this through Christ our Lord.

REFLECTION   **Beatitudes**

Blessed are those who realise that they cannot live on bread alone but need the word of God too: they will be fully nourished.

Blessed are those who, when they have sinned, follow the example of the prodigal son, and come back home to seek reconciliation: they will cause heaven to ring with joy.

Blessed are those who stop to attend to a wounded neighbour, pouring in the oil of compassion and the wine of hope: they are the Good Samaritans of today.

Blessed are those who remove the plank from their own eyes before telling their brother to remove the splinter from his: their efforts at reforming others will bear fruit.

And blessed are those who, having put their hand to the plough, refuse to look back: they will be found worthy of the Kingdom.

Twenty-fourth Sunday of the Year
THE LOST SHEEP, THE LOST COIN, THE LOST SON

INTRODUCTION AND CONFITEOR

To sin is to stray from God. Which of us can say that we have never strayed from God? But Jesus, the Good Shepherd, comes looking for us, and is overjoyed when he finds us. Let us pause for a moment to call to mind our need to be forgiven the things that separate us from God. [Pause]

Lord Jesus, you have mercy on us, and in your compassion blot out our offences. Lord, have mercy.

You wash us more and more from our guilt and cleanse us from our sins. Christ, have mercy.

You create a pure heart for us and you put a steadfast spirit within us. Lord, have mercy.

HEADINGS FOR READINGS

First Reading (Ex 32:7-11.13-14). Moses intercedes with God for the people because they have fallen into idolatry.

Second Reading (1 Tim 1:12-17). In his conversion Paul is a witness to the fact that Christ came into the world to save sinners.

Gospel (Lk 15:1-32). Through telling three parables Jesus justifies his concern for sinners.

SCRIPTURE NOTE

The theme of all three readings is that of God's mercy towards sinners. In the First Reading we see that the people had abandoned God and fallen back into idolatry. God's reaction seems to portray him as an angry, jealous God, who will resort to the most terrible punishments when his law is disobeyed. But that's not the message of the story. The message is that God pardons the sin of his people in response to the prayer of Moses.

The fact that Jesus welcomed sinners and ate with them was a cause of scandal to the Pharisees. They, the 'separated ones', avoided all contact with sinners. They assumed that God has no dealing with sinners either. But Jesus shows them a very different kind of God. By means of three parables he justifies his concern for sinners. All three parables stress God's concern for the lost one, and his joy when a lost one is found.

The parable of the Prodigal Son occurred earlier this year (Fourth Sunday of Lent), and is dealt with there. Here we might concentrate on the other two.

The Second Reading also fits in with the theme. Paul's conversion is proof of the fact that Christ came into the world to save sinners.

HOMILY 1   **The value of the individual**

It's shocking to see how multinational companies sometimes cut the work force, without any consideration for the individuals they are letting go. For them it's all about profits rather than the welfare of the workers.

This is where Jesus' stories of the Lost Sheep and the Lost Coin come in. What is at stake in both is the value of the individual. But one might say: why all the fuss over one wretched sheep or one miserable coin? To a good shepherd each sheep is important and precious. The coin the woman lost was a drachma, worth about 4 pence That doesn't sound much to us. But at that time it was the equivalent of a day's wage. We can understand then why she searched so diligently for it. It meant a lot of her.

Once a group of concerned people got together to plan opening a reformatory for boys. They invited a well-known educator to advise them on how to go about it. He made a passionate plea for humane methods of education at the reformatory, urging the founders to spare no expense in getting the services of kind-hearted and competent teachers. He concluded by saying, 'If the reformatory were to save even one boy from moral depravity, it will have justified all the cost and labour invested in it.'

Afterwards a member of the board approached him and said, 'Didn't you get a little bit carried away there? Would all the cost and labour be justified if we could save only one boy?'

'If it were my boy, yes,' came the reply.

If you were to ask the shepherd, 'Was all the time and effort you spent in looking for that one sheep justified'? he would have given a similar answer: 'Yes, when the sheep is your sheep.' There was nothing exceptional about the shepherd in Jesus' story. Any shepherd worthy of the name would do the same.

Of course Jesus was not talking about sheep but about people, about sinners, to be more precise. The Pharisees were scandalised at seeing him spend so much time in the company of sinners. And he didn't wait for sinners to repent before befriending them. He befriended them in their sinfulness, in their lostness. This is what scandalised the religious authorities: that he associated with sinners while they were still sinners.

Jesus' defence was quite straightforward: he said he went where the need was greatest. The sheep that is lost, and is therefore endangered, has more need of the shepherd than the sheep that is within the fold. And the shepherd doesn't wait for the lost sheep to come back; he goes looking for it. Sinners have more need of him than the virtuous, because they are lost.

In associating with sinners Jesus wasn't condoning their situation. Rather, he was trying to show them a better way. But he could not do this without associating with them and being sympathetic towards them. You never improve people by shunning them. In acting the way he did, Jesus revealed the mercy of God towards sinners.

St Paul never forgot the fact that he was once an enemy of Jesus. But now he regards himself as a witness to the fact that Jesus came to save sinners (Second Reading). Just as a virtuous person is a witness to the grace of God, so a repentant sinner is a witness to the mercy of God.

'I do not agree with the big way of doing things. To us what matters is an individual.' (Mother Teresa)

HOMILY 2   **The lost are more precious**

Somebody might say: why did the shepherd need to make such a fuss over the one sheep that got lost when he still had ninety-nine others? And why did the woman have to make such a fuss over one lost coin?

Anything we lose assumes an exaggerated value. For instance, suppose you lose a key. As soon as you have lost it, it becomes more important than the sum-total of all the things we still possess. We never know the value of what we have until we lose it.

Once there was a young man who aspired to become a photographer. Every year he brought a bundle of his best prints to an old and famous photographer, seeking his advice and judgement. The old man studied the prints, sorting them into two bundles, good and bad. Every year he discovered that the young man submitted the same photo – a landscape – and it always ended up among the rejects. Eventually he turned to the young man and said, 'You obviously have a high regard for this photo.

[301]

Why do you like it so much?'

To which the young man replied, 'Because I had to climb a mountain to get it.'

A thing becomes precious to us because of what we get out of it. But it can also become precious to us because of what we've put into it. The sacrifices we have made to get it or keep it enhance its value in our eyes.

There is a delightful story that one day Jesus came upon a shepherd who was overcome with sorrow. 'Why are you so sad?' he asked. 'Because I have lost one of my sheep,' the man replied, 'and though I have looked all over for it, I have not found it. It may be that the wolves have already devoured it.' On hearing this Jesus said, 'Wait here. I will look for the sheep myself.'

With that he disappeared into the hills. Some hours later he returned with the sheep. Putting it down at the shepherd's feet he said, 'From this day on you must love this sheep more than any other in your flock, for it was lost and now has been found.'

The point Jesus was making in the stories of the lost sheep and the lost coin is this: Every person is important and precious to God. All the more so if that person is lost. God will love that person more – not less.

The Pharisees, who regarded themselves as paragons of virtue, had nothing to do with sinners. They assumed that God has no dealing with sinners either. The central dogma of their religion was: 'God loves the virtuous, and hates the sinner.' But Jesus showed them a very different kind of God.

Jesus was gentle and loving in his approach to sinners. He knew that rejection and judgement never help to change a person. So he provided the kind of presence in which people felt accepted and loved, and in that atmosphere they were able to respond and change.

Even from a human point of view, his approach makes sense. If a child is wet and starving, he doesn't need a lecture; he needs warmth and food. As Jean Vanier says so beautifully: 'The person is misery does not need a look that judges and criticises, but a comforting presence that brings peace and hope and life.'

'When a father laments that his son has taken to evil ways, what should he do? He should love him all the more.' (Baal Shem Tov)

HOMILY 3   **Lost people**

It's not only sheep and coins that get lost. People get lost too. According to *The Tablet* (December, 1996) about 250,000 people vanish in Britain each year. All ages and sorts, from children to the elderly, for every sort of reason and what seems like none, they take off. Behind them they leave incredulous, guilt-ridden, anguished families who live in a mixture of hope and despair, unable to accept what has happened or to grieve as they would over death. A National Missing Persons Line was set up in England in 1992 and is open 24 hours a day, 365 days a year. It is one of the fastest-growing charities in Britain.

The problem is even greater in America. It is estimated that some 50,000 children vanish every year, of whom 5,000 are eventually found dead. Why do they go missing? Some are abducted by a separated parent. Some are victims of violent crimes. Some run away from unhappy homes.

Kevin was a smiling ten-year old. He lived with his parents and two sisters in San Francisco. One day he left his school after basketball practice. He was never seen again.

Most countries have no accurate count of the number of children who go missing each year. Most police forces do not act on a report that a child is missing for at least twenty-four hours. In America the FBI say that if they were to look for every missing child, they would have time for nothing else. Many countries have sophisticated programmes for tracking down stolen cars and credit cards but not for missing children.

People can get lost in many ways. People addicted to alcohol or drugs, people who can't settle down, people who can't hold down a job or finish a course of studies, people who are unable to maintain a stable relationship – all of these can be said to be lost. And it is very difficult to find them. What makes it so frustrating is the fact that usually they are not far away. They are lost in our midst, lost even within the bosom of the family.

Yet no one seems to be able to reach them. In these cases, the task of the shepherd is not so much to find them, as to help them find themselves.

And of course people get lost morally and spiritually. Such people are like a boat without an anchor, or a sailor without a compass. Some of these are lost through their own fault. But others are lost because they have no guides, no one to take an interest in them. Every Christian ought to show an active concern for those who are lost.

Jesus showed his concern for the 'lost sheep' – tax collectors, sinners, and so on – who had been abandoned by the official shepherds. The official shepherds were shocked at what he was doing. But he replied by saying that he was merely doing what any shepherd worthy of the name would do.

A shepherd doesn't wait for the lost sheep to come back; he goes looking for it. So it is with Jesus. He is the messenger sent to us by the Father. He didn't wait for sinners to come looking for him. He went out of his way to look for them. And when he found them, he escorted them back to the Father's house with joy.

To repent is to come back to God, and to come back to God is to come home.

ANOTHER STORY   **Cry for help**

One afternoon a man went for a walk in the Bog of Allen in County Kildare. He had gone about half a mile when over to his left he saw a worker's hut. As he approached the hut he heard the bleat of a sheep. He looked around but failed to see the sheep. Then he heard the bleat again. It was coming from a spot directly behind the hut. On making his way around to the back of the hut he saw a ditch which was about ten feet deep. Dark, muddy, water lay at the bottom of it. And there knee deep in the mud, was a sheep.

Even though he realised that it would be a messy business to rescue the sheep, he knew he could not leave it there to die. And die it surely would unless he saved it. It took him a while to figure out how to get it out. The one thing he had to guard against was ending up in the hole himself. Inside the hut he found a spade. With the spade he was able to cut out steps in the bank of peat, and thus he made my way down the side of the ditch. He took hold of the wool on the sheep's back, and slowly, a step at a time, drew her out of the hole.

As he made my way home he was no longer thinking of the trouble the sheep had caused him, but only of the joy he felt at having saved a life. But the thing that was most vivid in my mind was the cry of the sheep. Without that cry, there would have been no happy ending, because he would never have known of its plight.

It isn't only sheep that fall into holes. People fall into them too. But they aren't as smart as sheep, because often they are ashamed to ask, much less to cry, for help.

PRAYER OF THE FAITHFUL

President: Jesus is the Good Shepherd who came to seek out and to save the lost. With confidence let us pray to him for our needs.

Response: Lord, graciously hear us.

Reader(s): For all leaders in the Church: that they may faithfully watch over the flock of Christ, showing special care for the lost sheep. [Pause] Lord, hear us.

For those in charge of civil affairs: that they may show special care for the excluded and the disadvantaged members of society. [Pause] Lord, hear us.

For parents: that they may create homes where their children will know they are loved. [Pause)] Lord, hear us.

For people who have disappeared and for their grieving families. [Pause] Lord, hear us.

For all gathered here: that each of us may realise that we are always precious to God. [Pause] Lord, hear us.

For our own special needs. [Longer pause] Lord, hear us.

President : God of love and mercy, give us the certainty that beyond death there is a life where broken things are mended and lost things are found; where there is rest for the weary and joy for the sad; where all that we have loved and willed of good exists, and where we will meet again our loved ones. We ask this through Christ our Lord.

PRAYER/REFLECTION   **Prayer for the lost lambs**

Lord Jesus, we pray for all the sheep that are lost,
but our hearts go out especially to the lost lambs.
Have mercy on the human wolves who steal, exploit,
and sometimes kill the lambs of the Father's flock;
help them to see the horror of what they are doing.
Comfort the grieving parents who in many cases
don't even have the consolation of a burial service.
In your merciful love grant that those lambs,
though lost here, may be found hereafter.
Watch over those who are still straying here below.
Guide them along paths that are safe.
Send shepherds to look for them.
And open the eyes of society
so that we may cease to regard property
as more important than people. Amen.

Twenty-fifth Sunday of the Year
CHOOSING BETWEEN GOD AND MONEY

INTRODUCTION AND CONFITEOR

Of all the idols people worship money is probably the most common. Jesus says, 'You cannot be the slave both of God and of money.' We are here because we want to worship God, and not just with our lips but with our hearts. [Pause]

Lord Jesus, you help us to value the Kingdom of God before all other things. Lord, have mercy.

You help us to do God's will in freedom and joy. Christ, have mercy.

You help us to live as children of the light. Lord, have mercy.

HEADINGS FOR READINGS

First Reading (Amos 8:4-7). The prophet Amos condemns the exploitation of the poor.

Second Reading (1 Tim 2:1-8). Since God wants everyone to be saved, we should pray for everyone, but especially for those who bear the responsibility of public office.

Gospel (Lk 16:1-13). Jesus shows how greed for money can ruin a person, and insists that we can't serve both God and money.

SCRIPTURE NOTE

Amos was a great champion of justice. He savagely assailed the oppression of the poor, as well as the judicial system which denied them any hope of obtaining justice. Our short reading is a good example. Here he depicts the greed of the wealthy, who can't wait for the holy days to be over so that they can get back to making money by dishonest practices. He condemns the separation of worship from the proper treatment of other people, especially the poor.

The Bible doesn't always give us examples to be imitated. At times it gives us examples to be learned from painfully. The servant in Jesus' story is one of these, brought forward to teach Christians the wise use of money. Here Jesus stresses the impossibility of any compromise between God and Mammon. For Luke, to use money wisely is to give it to the poor, and thus ensure one's eternal salvation.

HOMILY 1   **The making of character**

The steward in Jesus' story was unreliable and dishonest. It's obvious that he had been so for quite some time. It probably started off in little ways, but eventually become a way of life. He must have known all along that he was living dangerously. But he got away with it for a long time, thus evading public judgement and even self-examination. However, in spite of his craftiness, he was eventually found out, and his master confronted him with his misconduct.

It must have been a very humbling and painful moment for the steward. He was about to lose not only his job but also his reputation. He had brought shame and disgrace on himself and on his family, if he had a family. Yet it was also a moment of truth and revelation, because it showed him the dishonest reality in which he had been living. It provided him with an opportunity to leave behind illusions and lies. Thus it could have been a turning point in his life.

But what happened? He learned nothing from it. Even after being sacked from his job he continued on in his old dishonest ways. There wasn't the slightest change in his character. Not the least dent in his armour. He refused to take responsibility for the kind of person he had become.

It's very difficult to change the habits of a lifetime. Dostoevsky says,

'The second half of a person's life is usually made up of the habits acquired during the first half.' That's a pretty frightening thought.

It seems that there comes a moment in our lives when the precious clay of which we are made hardens and sets, so that from that point on we can assume no new shape. The dishonest person will remain dishonest to the end. The greedy person will remain that way to the end. An illustration.

Once a holy man was instructing his disciples as they walked through a wood. He pointed to a small oak sapling, and asked one of his disciples to pull it up. The disciple did so with one hand. Then the master pointed to another oak, a little bigger than the first, and asked the disciple to pull that one up. He did so but had to use both hands. The master pointed to a third and bigger oak, and asked the disciple to pull it up. He could do so only with the help of one of his companions. Finally he pointed to a still larger oak and asked the disciple to pull that one up. Even with the help of all of his companions he was unable to do so.

And the master concluded, 'That's how it is with passions and habits. In the beginning, before they have sunk deep roots, it is easy to eradicate them. But if we allow them to sink deep roots, it becomes virtually impossible to rid ourselves of them.'

This, presumably, is what happened to the servant in Jesus' story. He had become so used to a dishonest way of life that he couldn't change. However, what is impossible to us can become possible with the aid of God's grace.

While the story shows the danger of bad habits it also shows the importance of forming good habits. Just as dishonesty can become a way of life so can honesty. Honesty can become habitual, spontaneous, second nature.

How does one arrive at this happy state? It cannot be achieved overnight. It has to be learned by long practice. It is not achieved by a few great deeds but by a lot of little ones. The real reward for a good deed is that it makes the next good deed easier. Every little action of the common day makes or unmakes character.

HOMILY 2   **The homing instinct**

Many birds have a powerful homing instinct. The Manx shearwater is a good example. One of these was caught and ringed in Wales. Then it was taken to Boston, three thousand miles away, where it was released. Two weeks later it was back home in Wales at the exact same spot where it was captured.

The homing instinct is found in humans too – and not just in the physical sense. People have been known to return after painful experiences, not only to their old homes, but to their old selves. They return to pick up

[307]

the pieces of their former lives. Their inner selves seem hardly to have been touched. Indeed, some return enriched.

The Italian writer, Primo Levi, spent a year in Auschwitz. He was one of only three out of 123 people in his train to return. Later he said, 'If I had not been in such a place, I would perhaps be happier and more tranquil, but not so rich.' He was not, of course, talking about money.

In general the homing instinct is a positive factor. However, it can also be negative. The urge to return home cuts people off from new opportunities and new possibilities, and makes reform of life difficult and painful. People have been known to return from close brushes with death to lives of superficiality and mediocrity, or even to lives of crime and sin.

We see a good example of this in the steward of Jesus' story. When he was found out, it must been a very humbling and painful moment for him. But it could also have been a moment of salvation. Because it showed him the dishonesty reality in which he was living, it could have been a turning point in his life. But what happened? He continued on in his old dishonest ways. There wasn't the slightest change in his character.

Whether the homing instinct is a help or a hindrance depends on where our true 'home' lies. Those who are accustomed to living in the light will return to the light. But those who are accustomed to living in the dark will, in all probability, return to the dark.

A firmly-rooted, straight tree returns to its old, upright self after the storm passes, whereas a firmly-rooted, crooked tree returns to its twisted self. When we compromise our integrity we don't lose our humanity, but we lose our sense of wholeness, our sense of being the same person all the time.

Jesus wasn't holding up the wicked servant as a model. He was saying that the children of light can learn something from the children of darkness. Evil people are industrious, single-minded, prepared to make sacrifices, in order to achieve their evil ends. Good people, on the other hand, often just sit around doing nothing. And for evil to triumph, all that is necessary is that good people do nothing.

HOMILY 3   **The lure of money**

Greed for money has brought about the downfall of many a person. Almost every day we read in the newspapers about some minister in high office, or some top executive, who has been accused of corruption. One of the most notorious cases in recent times was that of Nicholas Leeson, the man who brought down a banking empire – Barings Bank of London.

The son of a plasterer from the London suburb of Watford, Leeson never went to university. He joined Barings Bank as a simple clerk but rose quickly to where he was in charge of the bank's Signapore operation. He was very hard-working and very ambitious. He had an annual salary of $350,000, with gigantic bonuses besides.

But he wasn't satisfied. He began to buy and sell derivatives. At first he made huge profits for the bank. He got more and more greedy. He hid some of his transactions from his bosses. In the end he took a huge gamble that didn't pay off, and he bust the whole bank.

In such situations people pay for wrong-doing in currencies far more precious than money. They pay with loss of self-respect, dignity, and hope. Of course, there is always the chance of cashing in by selling one's story to the tabloids. But here again there is a price to be paid. Whatever little dignity one had before, one will have even less afterwards.

Leeson reminds us a little of the servant in Jesus' parable. It seems that like Neeson, the servant was corrupted by money. Given the importance of money in the world we live in, it can easily become our god too. We may put it before honesty, before justice, even before family life. People are brainwashed into believing that owning more is good. The average person can get so fogged up that he has no perspective on what's really important any more.

Amos condemned those who paid lip service to God on the Sabbath but exploited the poor for the rest of the week. Jesus says we can't serve both God and money. You can't serve others and serve money too.

Once a very rich but miserly man went to his rabbi and asked for his blessing. The rabbi greeted him in a friendly manner and brought him into his living room. Then he led him to the window which looked out on the street and said, 'Look out there and tell me what you see.'

'I see people walking about,' the rich man answered.

Then the rabbi took his away from the window and having placed a large mirror before him said, 'Look into the mirror and tell what you see.'

'I see myself,' the man replied.

'Now, my friend, let me explain the meaning of this to you. The window is made of glass, as also is the mirror. However, the glass of the mirror has a veneer of silver on it. When you look through plain glass you see people. But when you cover it with silver you stop seeing others and see only yourself. When you are concerned only with money, you stop seeing others and see only yourself.'

We don't get satisfaction or meaning from things. But when we devote ourselves to serving others, that gives us purpose and meaning. Giving to other people is what makes us feel alive.

Money may buy the husks of things but it cannot buy the kernel. It brings you food but not appetite; medicine but not health, acquaintances but not friends, servants but not faithfulness, days of pleasure but not peace and happiness. (Henrik Ibsen)

PRAYER OF THE FAITHFUL

President: Let us now bring our needs before God, whose help is near to those who turn to him with trust and humility.

Response: Lord, graciously hear us.

Reader(s): For Christians: that their weekday lives may bear witness to the faith they profess on Sundays. [Pause] Lord, hear us.

For all those in positions of responsibility: that they may use their power for the good of all. [Pause] Lord, hear us.

For the children of darkness: that they may see the error of their ways. [Pause] Lord, hear us.

For ourselves: that we may live always as children of the light. [Pause] Lord, hear us.

For those who have died: that they may reach the light that never fades. [Pause] Lord, hear us.

For our own special needs. [Longer pause] Lord, hear us.

President: God of power and love, confirm us in your service, and help us to bear witness to you in the society in which we live. We ask this through Christ our Lord.

REFLECTION   **Being with Christ**

Jesus says: 'Whoever is not with me is against me;
and whoever does not gather with me scatters.'
I sometimes feel that my life is like scrubland,
halfway between garden and desert.
I sometimes feel that I live in a world of twilight,
halfway between day and night.
I sometimes feel like lukewarm water, halfway between hot and cold.
I sometimes feel that I am in a state of indifference
halfway between love and hate.
I sometimes feel I am trudging along a safe little path
halfway between good and evil.
Lord, save me from the illusion
that because I am not against you, I am therefore for you.
Above all, save me from being neutral.

Twenty-sixth Sunday of the Year
RICH MAN, POOR MAN

INTRODUCTION AND CONFITEOR

Jesus told a story about a rich man who refused to share even the crumbs from his table with a starving beggar who sat at his gate. One great evil in the world today is the terrible indifference towards one's neighbour which is so widespread. Yet all of us are beggars before God. [Pause] Let us ask God's forgiveness, especially for our refusal to show concern for those who are less fortunate than ourselves.

I confess to almighty God ...

HEADINGS FOR READINGS

First Reading (Amos 6:1.4-7). Amos speaks against the wealthy of both Judah and Israel.

Second Reading (1 Tim 6:11-16). As Jesus was faithful to his call in face of an hostility that led to his death, so Christians facing persecution should be faithful to God's call.

Gospel (Lk 16:19-31). We hear the story of a very rich man who ignored the plight of a beggar sitting at his gate.

SCRIPTURE NOTE

Amos was the prophet of social justice. He spoke to the wealthy of both Judah and Israel, who were unconcerned about what was happening to the country, which was about to be destroyed by the Assyrians. Indeed, by their life-style they were undermining the very fabric of the country. And they hadn't the slightest concern for the plight of the poor. Amos warned them that they would be the first to be led off into exile.

This is precisely the sin of the rich man (Dives) in the Gospel: cushioned by a lavish life-style, he is oblivious to the presence of a poor man at his gate. Dives was a worldling who didn't look beyond the good things of this life. It's a parable about the responsibility of wealth. Some of the harshest words in the Bible are directed at the uncaring rich.

HOMILY 1   **Living in opposite worlds**

It was a July day in America. A man was sitting at his desk in an air-conditioned room. The temperature in the room was a comfortable 68 degrees. He felt full of energy. From his window he saw that the sun was shining brightly outside, and every now and then a slight breeze stirred the tops of the trees. It was such a beautiful day!

He was watching a teenage boy working in the grounds. Judging by the slowness of his movements one would think that he was a prisoner doing forced labour. He rested frequently. 'What's the matter with him? How can a young man be so lazy?' the man asked himself.

But later in the morning the man went outside on some business. As soon as he stepped outside, he was hit by a wave of heat which stopped him in his tracks. It was 90 degrees out there, and the humidity was almost as high. Now he realised what the boy was up against. And, given the kind of day that was in it, he was amazed that the boy hadn't fainted.

Though his world was separated only by the width of a wall from the world of the boy, those two worlds could hardly have been more different. Yet unless he left his own world and entered that of the youth, he would never have known the difference.

We can be within arm's reach of someone, yet be living in a different world from that person. But we'll never know the difference unless we leave our world and enter that of the other person. We will never understand it from the outside.

The rich man and Lazarus lived in opposite worlds, yet those worlds lay side by side. But the rich man never once entered the world of the poor man. He didn't see Lazarus as a human being, much less as a brother with whom he shared a common humanity. He was indifferent to him, and indifference is a great evil.

How could this be? Riches make a person self-preoccupied. They blind a person to the needs of others and harden the heart. That is the real tragedy. An individual or a country loses its soul as it accumulates ever greater riches.

The rich man didn't do anything wrong – he didn't hurt or exploit the poor man. Yet he ends up in 'the torment of Hades.' He was condemned, not because he was rich, but because he didn't show compassion to the poor man. He lived only for himself.

Sin is not only about doing wrong. It is also about not doing good – the sin of inactivity, of doing nothing, and worse still, of indifference. This is a shocking parable. There is no fairy tale ending – at least not for Dives, and he is the central character in the story.

May the Lord, who entered fully into our world, help us to enter the world of those who are in pain or in need. Then, having experienced what life is like for them, we will surely be moved to do what we can to help them.

As people who stand in daily need of God's mercy and goodness, as people who pray with hands held out like a beggar's bowl, we should in turn try to be kind, generous and merciful with others, because the measure we give will be the measure we receive.

HOMILY 2   **Riches and poverty**

Dives and Lazarus lived in different worlds. Dives was dressed in purple robes; Lazarus was dressed in rags. Dives ate splendidly every day; Lazarus didn't eat at all. Dives was healthy; Lazarus was covered with sores. Dives lived in a palace; Lazarus lived in the streets.

In fact, to say that they lived in different worlds is an understatement. They lived in opposite worlds. Dives lived in a garden; Lazarus lived in a desert. Dives was in an earthly paradise; Lazarus in an earthly hell. And yet, though their respective worlds were as different as day and night, they lay side by side.

Lazarus was living on the edge of Dives' world. And because he was at the gate he got daily glimpses of the paradise from which he was excluded. Though he longed to enter the world of Dives, he didn't entertain the hope of sitting at his table. He would have been blissfully happy to fill his belly with the crumbs that fell from his table. But he didn't get them. It wasn't that it couldn't be done. It was just that there was no one willing to do it.

The one who was in the best position to help him was, of course, Dives. He could easily have entered Lazarus' lonely, desperate world, and made contact with him. But he didn't. He shut him out, not only out of his palace, but out of his mind and heart as well.

Lazarus was about as poor as any man could be. Yet, in a sense, Dives was even poorer. How could that be? A little story will show how.

A businessman in San Antonio, Texas, parked his brand-new car on the street and went off to do some business. When he got back to it he found a poor little boy of about eleven examining it with eyes full of wonder and envy.

'Is that your car, mister?' the boy asked:

'Yes,' he replied.

'It's beautiful. How much did you pay for it?'

'To be honest, sonny, I don't know.'

'You mean you bought it and can't remember what you paid for it?'

'Sonny, I didn't buy it. I got a present of it from my brother.'

'You mean your brother gave it to you and it didn't cost you a penny?'

'That's right.'

'I wish that I ... '

The man was sure the boy was going to say, 'I wish that I *had* a brother like that.' But what he said was, 'I wish that I could *be* a brother like that.'

And the man concluded, 'There was I in my fancy suit, with the keys of a brand-new car in my hand. And there was the boy in rags. Yet the boy had more love in his heart than I had. In that sense he was richer than I was. I was so impressed that I took him and his little brother, who was crippled with infantile paralysis, for a drive. The next few hours were the happiest of my life.'

Dives was suffering from the worst kind of poverty of all – poverty of heart. His heart was devoid of compassion and love.

He wouldn't give Lazarus even the scraps from his table. Even the street dogs were kinder to Lazarus than he was.

The rich are wounded by their riches, just as the poor are wounded by their poverty. 'The greatest evil in the world today is lack of love – the terrible indifference towards one's neighbour which is so widespread.' (Mother Teresa).

The gap between Dives and Lazarus is growing into a gigantic abyss. Poor kids in the third world know what their prospects are. A reporter asked one child, 'What do you want to do with your life?' 'I want to live to see the age of twenty,' came the reply.

HOMILY 3   **Where to begin**

One night a wealthy man had a disturbing dream. In the dream he saw a crowd of poor, disease-ridden, starving people crying out to him for help. When he woke up the following morning, remembering his dream, he decided to embark on a crusade of good. He wasted no time but set out in his Mercedes that very morning to see what needed to be done.

He had only just passed through the main gate of his mansion when he saw a beggar-man sitting on the ground, his hand stretched out imploringly. The rich man was very upset on seeing the beggar's wretched condition. He hesitated for a moment, but then ordered his chauffeur to step on the gas. He couldn't afford to stop to attend to one beggar-man, no matter how wretched his condition.

He travelled the length and breadth of the city. He discovered that the problems were vaster, and the needs greater, than he had imagined. As he returned home in the late evening his mind was overflowing with plans, schemes, and projects. The only problem was where to begin. Should he begin with a hospital, a school, a factory, or what?

As he came to the gate of his mansion he noticed that the beggar-man was still there, in the exact same position as in the morning. 'Just imagine, that poor man has been sitting there all day in the burning heat!' he said to himself. Once again a wave of pity passed over him, but once again he passed by.

That night he had another dream. Again he heard cries for help. Except this time they were coming, not from a multitude of people, but from one individual. That individual was the beggar-man he had seen at his gate. When he woke up next morning he knew exactly where to begin.

Mother Teresa says, 'I always say that love starts at home: family first, then your town or city. It's easy to love people who are far away, but not so easy to love those who live with us or who are next door to us. I don't agree with the big way of doing things – love needs to start with an individual. To love a person, you must make contact with that person, become close. You have to let people come in contact with the poor. When you do that you cross this enormous divide. It's no longer these "millions" of people, but somebody you've actually touched.'

She tells the following story: 'Once in Bombay there was a big conference on poverty. When I reached the place, right in front of the door where hundreds of people were talking about food and hunger, I found a dying man. I took him to our home for the dying. He died there. He died of hunger. And the people inside were talking about how in fifteen years we will have so much food, so much this, so much that – and that man died.

'I never look at the masses as my responsibility. I look at the individual. I can only love one person at a time. I can feed only one person at a time. I picked up one person. Maybe if I hadn't picked up that one person I wouldn't have picked up 42,000. The whole work is only a drop in the ocean. But if I didn't put that drop in, the ocean would be one drop less. Same thing for you. Same thing in your family.'

The rich man could not have been expected to save the world. But he could have helped the beggar-man at his gate.

ANOTHER STORY

A wandering monk came to a village. He was about to settle down under a tree for the night when a villager came running to him and said, 'Give me the precious stone.'

'What stone are you talking about?' asked the monk.

'Last night I had a dream that if I went to the outskirts of the village at dusk I would find a monk who would give me a precious stone that would make me rich forever.'

The monk rummaged in his sack, found a stone and took it out. 'This is probably the stone you're talking about,' he said, as he handed it to the villager. 'I found it in the forest a few days ago. You are welcome to it.'

The man took the stone and gazed at it in wonder. It was a diamond, the largest one he had ever seen. He took it home with him. But all night he tossed about in his bed, unable to sleep. Early next day he went back to the monk and said, 'During the night I've done a lot of thinking. You can have the diamond back. Instead, give me the kind of wealth that makes it possible for you to give this diamond away so easily.'

The richer a person's inner life is, the simpler becomes his outer life – the less he needs or wants.

PRAYER OF THE FAITHFUL

President: Let us pray to the Lord that he may help us to understand what real poverty and real riches are.

Response: Lord, hear our prayer.

Reader(s): For Christians: that they may not be indifferent to the needs of those around them. [Pause] Let us pray to the Lord.

For government leaders: that they may be tireless in their efforts to eliminate poverty. [Pause] Let us pray to the Lord.

For those who through unemployment, poverty, or sickness sit on the sidelines of life. [Pause] Let us pray to the Lord.

For grace to seek to make ourselves rich in compassion rather than in the things of this world. [Pause] Let us pray to the Lord.

For our own special needs. [Longer pause] Let us pray to the Lord.

President: Almighty and ever-living God, fill our hearts with your love. Give us the grace to rise above our selfishness, and keep us faithful to you and to one another. We ask this through Christ our Lord.

REFLECTION   **How wealth is judged**

A week ago the sycamore tree was loaded with gold.
However, instead of sitting back and enjoying it,
it began to give it away.
At first it was just a leaf here and a leaf there,
whenever the wind asked for a contribution.
But soon it was giving it away in fistfuls,
without being asked,
and without a thought for a wintry tomorrow.
Wealth is judged,
not by the amount that is accumulated,
but by the amount that is given away.
The only wealth that is worth having is the wealth of the heart.
To close one's heart is to begin to die;
to open it is to begin to live.

Twenty-seventh Sunday of the Year
STILL ONLY SERVANTS

INTRODUCTION AND CONFITEOR

To serve God is not a duty but a privilege. The most important quality to bring to that service is love. What sort of spirit do we being to our worship and service of God? [Pause]

Lord Jesus, you help us to give and not to count the cost. Lord, have mercy.

You help us to toil and not to seek for rest. Christ, have mercy.

You help us to seek no reward except that of knowing that we do your will. Lord, have mercy.

HEADINGS FOR READINGS

First Reading (Hab 1:2-3; 2:2-4). The prophet complains to God about the prevalence of injustice, and God responds by promising to save those who trust in him.

Second Reading (2 Tim 1:6-8, 13-14). Paul encourages Timothy to be faithful to his ministry and to witnessing to Christ.

Gospel (Lk 17:5-10). A little faith, provided it is authentic, can do great things. The disciples are urged to serve God without any claim on a reward.

SCRIPTURE NOTE

All three readings speak of faith. The First Reading is part of a dialogue between God and the prophet. Like others before him, Habakkuk is feeling the burden of office. He complains about the prevalence of injustice and God's failure to intervene. Then comes the divine response: in due time God will intervene to save those who trust in him. Meanwhile, the upright must remain steadfast in faith.

This brings us to the Gospel, where Jesus says that a grain of authentic faith can achieve great things. The saying about the uprooting of a tree is not to be taken in a literal sense. It is a vivid eastern mode of expression, which means that with faith what looks impossible can become possible.

The parable of the unprofitable servant ('slave') would have shocked Jesus' hearers. A slave had no claim to either wages or thanks from his master, irrespective of how well he might have served him. At the time of Jesus, Judaism was dominated by the notion of merit – God 'owed' salvation to humans in return for keeping the Law. Jesus rejects this, and emphasises God's sheer goodness. The disciples must humbly acknowledge that they are only servants.

HOMILY 1   **Growth in faith**

They are very fortunate people who are born into a religious faith, and who with the passage of the years find this faith increasingly strong and sustaining. To possess a confident faith is a tremendous blessing. Only faith can answer the most profound questions of life.

Without faith, there is no reason for anything and nothing is in its proper place. Life is unintelligible and unbearable without God. Faith gives meaning to life. Faith also gives vision. A life without vision is like a night without stars.

Faith adds the buoyancy of hope to life. We need hope as much as we need food. But we can't have hope without faith. And faith results in joy. Happy those who discover the joy of believing, the rapture of faith in God, the ecstasy of heeding the divine invitation and clasping God's outstretched hand.

But we mustn't expect faith to clear everything up. We live in a world where many desperately seek to know all the answers. Just because we believe doesn't mean we know everything. But we don't need to know all the answers. People don't have to understand a work of art to be inspired by it. Faith is trust, not certainty.

Rationalists approach God and religion as something that can be understood and explained; mystics approach God as something mysterious which can neither be understood nor explained but only experienced. Logic cannot tell us everything. However, faith doesn't contradict reason; it goes beyond it, it transcends it. Faith is a gift of God, but God does not force himself on anyone.

Faith is not a thing, but a relationship with God. The expression *to lose your faith*, as one might lose a key or a purse, is really rather silly. Faith is not a thing which one loses; we merely cease to shape our lives by it.

All of us should make our own the prayer of the apostles: 'Lord, increase our faith,' because it is not enough to keep the faith; we have to grow in it. Faith is not acquired fully grown at the start. Faith has to grow, and as it grows it changes. Faith does not remain stationary, no more than any of our relationships remain stationary.

Faith grows when exercised. Faith also grows through regular nourishment. Those beliefs that we don't nourish become less solid. How do we nourish the faith? By prayer and contact with the believing community.

Faith is the greatest power in the world. That is what Jesus meant when he said, 'If you have faith the size of a mustard seed you could say to this mulberry tree, "Be uprooted and planted in the sea," and it would obey you.' This is a striking way of saying that with faith what looks impossible becomes possible. It's not the size of it but the quality of it that matters. 'Those with a grain of faith never lose hope, because they believe in the ultimate triumph of truth' (Gandhi).

HOMILY 2   **The faith of our youth**

Maurice is an alcoholic. When a priest visited him he was living in the basement with his dog while his wife lived upstairs. They were legally divorced, and were waiting for the house to be sold in order to separate.

He had a rough life. Most of his troubles stemmed from his heavy drinking. He says he has his drinking under control now – but many alcoholics say that. Once in a fit of despair he put a gun in his mouth, but when he saw on his finger the Claddagh ring given him by his daughter, he couldn't pull the trigger.

'I still believe in God,' he said. Then with tears running down his face he continued, 'But I wish I had the faith I had when I was young.'

'What was so good about that?' the priest asked.

'When I was young I believed everything – the whole lot. I was so certain about everything. But I no longer have that kind of faith. Now I'm not sure what to believe. I question everything.' He paused then added sorrowfully, 'Maybe the wife and I will get together again. But I have lost the feeling I had for her.'

'You have suffered a lot, Maurice,' the priest said.

'You can say that again,' he replied.

'Did you have any feeling that God was with you during all those years you were drinking?' the priest asked.

'I did, except maybe when I was going to kill myself. I felt abandoned at that point.'

Here one can sense some of the loneliness and heartbreak that lie deep in every person whose faith has been lost. Yet Maurice's faith was not altogether gone. Some of the outward things had been shorn away. But he still had the core – the conviction that God existed and cared about him.

Yet he pined for the faith of his youth. Everything was simple then. Everything was clear, everything was certain. He didn't realise that the greatest changes that had occurred were in himself. An abyss separated him from the child he once was.

We cannot but feel sympathy for him. Many pine for the faith they had as children. And rightly so – it was something beautiful. The poet, Emily Dickinson, said:

> We start to learn that we believed but once, entirely –
> Belief, it does not fit so well when altered frequently.
> We blush, that heaven if we achieve it – event ineffable –
> We shall have shunned, until ashamed to own the miracle.

We all long to recapture the religious sense of the world we had as children. But we all have to leave youth behind, and with it a world of certainties. Childhood faith passes or at least changes. However, it is not God that changes but us. Nevertheless, to feel as Maurice felt doesn't mean that we have lost the faith. All it means is that we are struggling with it.

The idyllic faith of childhood cannot be held onto eternally. Jesus said we should enter the Kingdom like a child, but he didn't say we had to have the faith of a child. Ours has to be an adult faith, a faith that takes account of the complexities and ambiguities of life.

All of us can make our own the prayer of the apostles: 'Lord, increase our faith,' because it is not enough to keep the faith; we have to grow in it. Faith grows when exercised. Faith also grows through regular nourishment. How do we nourish the faith? By prayer and contact with the believing community.

HOMILY 3   **Serving God out of love**

There is a tendency among religious people to think that God owes them something. They imagine God as being like the typical employer. If we do the work, then in justice our employer owes us our wages. God owes us a reward in heaven provided we serve him faithfully on earth. This is a very understandable attitude. But it introduces a mercenary attitude into what is essentially supposed to be a love affair between God and us. Besides, it is at complete variance with the Gospel.

The stark truth is: we can never put God in the position where he is in debt to us. Jesus says that even when we have done all we are expected to do (and which of us would be so bold as to make that claim?), we still can't make any demands on God. At the time of Jesus, Judaism was dominated by the idea of merit. Jesus was hitting at that attitude.

The fundamental truth about Christianity is that it is a religion of grace and not of merit. Salvation cannot be earned. We can never put God in our debt. But we don't have to. God is our Father. We are his children. Children do not do the will of their father for the sake of rewards. They do it because they want to try to return his love for them.

It comes as a great relief to discover that we don't need to prove ourselves to God. We don't have to earn God's love. God loved us long before we could have done anything to deserve it. And he loves us even when we are sinners. Our task is to return God's love.

We don't keep the commandments so that God will love us; we keep the commandments because God loves us. The Good News might be summed up like this: A generous Lord wants his disciples to serve him out of love, not out of duty. Hence, faith is not enough; we need love too. While faith makes all things possible, love makes all things easy.

The most generous and heroic deeds in life are those which are performed, not in the line of duty or in the hope of monetary or other rewards, but out of pure love. Consider the following example.

It was late afternoon on a raw winter's day. Everybody was in a hurry to get home. Suddenly a cry arose: 'There's a man in the river!' People rushed to the wall and looked down into the muddy, uninviting water. Sure enough – there was a man down there trashing about in the dark water. His desperate cries for help reached the onlookers above the din of the traffic.

Then, with a screech of brakes, a car swung out of the line of traffic, and came to a halt close to the kerb. A young man jumped out, throwing off his coat and shoes as he did so. He got up on the wall, took a quick look down, and then dived into the murky waters. After a couple of unsuccessful dives he eventually grabbed the drowning man and hauled him to safety.

Out on the roadside a crowd gathered around the rescued man as they waited for an ambulance to come. Presently it arrived and took the man to hospital from where he was later released, none the worse for his ordeal. A reporter came by, and seeing the possibility of a story, began to fish for information. But, far from seeking the limelight or the plaudits of the people, the rescuer had vanished.

What God wants from us is that we should come to him as children come to their Father; he wants us to behave ourselves honourably, not out of hope of a reward, but out of love for him and zeal for his service.

Salvation is a gift, not a wage. A wage is a great thing, but it can't compare with the joy one experiences on receiving a gift.

PRAYER OF THE FAITHFUL

President: With confidence in God's love for us, let us bring our needs before him.

Response: Lord, hear our prayer.

Reader(s): For the pope and the bishops: that they may guide the Church in unity, love and peace. [Pause] Let us pray to the Lord.

For political leaders: that they may speak wisely and act justly. [Pause[Let us pray to the Lord.

For employers: that they may treat their employees justly. [Pause] Let us pray to the Lord.

For the unemployed: that the Lord may sustain their faith and hope. [Pause] Let us pray to the Lord.

For all gathered here: that the Lord may help us to serve him, not out of a sense of duty, but out of love. [Pause] Let us pray to the Lord.

For our own special needs. [Longer pause] Let us pray to the Lord.

President: Teach us, Good Lord, to serve you as you deserve: to give and not to count the cost; to fight and not to heed the wounds; to toil and not to seek for rest; to labour and not to ask for any reward save that of knowing that we do your will. We ask this through Christ our Lord.

REFLECTION   **Towards the beautiful gate**

I must be filled with joy if my feet are on the right road
and my face set towards the gate which is called beautiful,
though I may fall many times in the mire
and often in the mist go astray.
Far off, like a perfect pearl, one can see the City of God.
It is so wonderful that it seems as if
a child could reach it in a summer's day.
And so a child could.
But with me and such as me it is different.
One can realise a thing in a single moment,

but one loses it in the long hours that follow with leaden feet.
We think in terms of eternity,
but we move slowly through time.   *(Oscar Wilde)*

Twenty-eighth Sunday of the Year
THE TEN LEPERS

INTRODUCTION AND CONFITEOR

We are gathered to celebrate the Eucharist. The word *Eucharist* means 'thanksgiving'. In celebrating the Eucharist we are giving thanks to God for all the blessings he has conferred on us, especially through Jesus, his Son. Let us call to mind that we haven't always shown gratitude to God for his goodness to us, nor have we always shown gratitude to others for their goodness to us. [Pause]

Lord Jesus, you are slow to anger and rich in mercy. Lord, have mercy.

You do not treat us according to ours sins nor repay us according to our faults. Christ, have mercy.

Your love is everlasting upon those who revere you. Lord, have mercy.

HEADINGS FOR READINGS

First Reading (2 Kgs 5:14-17). On being cured of leprosy, Naaman comes to believe in the true God, and is lavish in his gratitude towards the prophet Elisha.

Second Reading (2 Tim 2:8-13). Paul tells Timothy that the work of preaching the Gospel will result in hardship, opposition and persecution.

Gospel (Lk 17:11-19). The story of ten people who were cured of leprosy by Jesus, and how only one came back to thank him.

SCRIPTURE NOTE

The First Reading tells how on being cured of leprosy Naaman acknowledges Yahweh as the supreme and only God. However, when he tries to express his gratitude to Elisha, the prophet refuses to accept it, because it would suggest that the cure was due to him rather than to God. As commander of the Syrian army, Naaman was a Gentile.

This story prepares us for the Gospel account of the cure of ten lepers by Jesus, and of how only one of them, a foreigner (a Samaritan), came back to thank him. The stranger puts the Jews to shame. His reaction anticipates the glad reception of the Good News by the Samaritans in Acts 8:1-25.

HOMILY 1   **Gratitude**

Thanks to the book *Schindler's Ark*, and the film, *Schindler's List*, the name Oskar Schindler became known to millions of people around the world. Schindler was a German industrialist. During World War II he saved over a thousand Polish Jews from the concentration camps. As the war ended the Germans pulled out of Poland, and the people awaited the arrival of the Russians. Just before the Russians arrived, Schindler too decided to flee westwards.

When his Jewish workers, now free, heard he was leaving they got together to see how they could express their gratitude to him. All that was to hand to make a gift was base metal. Then one of them suggested something better. He opened his mouth to show his gold bridgework.

'Take this,' he said. 'Were it not for Oskar, the SS would have had the stuff anyway. My teeth would be in a heap in some SS warehouse, along with the golden fangs of many others.'

At first the others resisted the man's offer but he insisted. So he had his bridgework extracted by a prisoner who had once been a dentist in Cracow. A jeweller among them melted the gold down and fashioned a ring out of it. On the inner circle of the ring they inscribed these words from the Talmud: 'The one who saves a single life, saves the entire world.'

It was an astonishing and deeply moving gesture of gratitude. That is one of the marvellous things about gratitude – it makes us want to give something back. 'Gratitude is the heart's memory' (French Proverb). But then someone might say that it was the least they could do since they owed their lives to Schindler. The ten lepers in the Gospel also owed their lives to Jesus; yet only one of them came back to thank him.

It's seems strange that the one who came back to give thanks was an outsider – a Samaritan. But isn't that how it it often is? The insider takes everything for granted, and is taken for granted too. The outsider, on the other hand, sees everything as a gift. We find the same thing in the First Reading. We see the foreigner, Naaman, coming back to thank Elisha for curing his leprosy.

We are better at demanding gratitude than at giving it. This indicates how selfish much of our giving can be. If anyone finds his brother ungrateful, it is not the other person's happiness he is seeking, but his own.

Jesus demanded gratitude, but not for himself. What he said was, 'Has no one come back to give praise to God except this foreigner.' From this it's clear that he wasn't thinking of himself. He was thinking of the lepers. It is a good and necessary thing for the recipient of a favour to be able to show gratitude.

It is very important for us to be able to express thanks. It's good for ourselves in the first place – it forces us to acknowledge the debt we owe to others. And of course it's good for the other person – it makes him/her feel appreciated. The person who does not give thanks for little, does not give thanks for much. Hence, the importance of being grateful for, and appreciating, the small favours done and services rendered every day.

As for expressing gratitude to God: God doesn't need our thanks, But we need to thank God. It reminds us that everything we have we owe to him. It's easy to be grateful to God for the good things that happen to us. But we must try to be grateful for all of our lives – the bad as well as the good, the sorrows and the joys, the failures and successes. This is no easy task. We can truly call ourselves grateful people only when we can say thanks for everything that has brought us to this moment. This kind of gratitude enables us to reclaim our whole past, and to see it as the concrete way in which God has led us to this moment.

When we look back over our lives, we see that the things that hurt us and the things which helped us cannot be separated from each other. We must try to see the guiding hand of a loving God in all that has brought us to where we are now.

HOMILY 2 **How could this happen?**

At the time of Jesus there was no cure for leprosy. Once a person contracted it, life became a living death. How then could it happen that nine of the lepers didn't come back to thank Jesus for their cure? We don't have to stretch our imaginations too much to imagine how it could happen. Let us suppose that it happened in our times.

The first was Miriam, wife of a shopkeeper. On returning home she found the house in a mess. It wasn't her husband's fault. He had a business to run. Going back was out of the question – for the moment at least.

The second was Aaron, a farmer. That summer had been a very bad one, and the entire harvest was in danger of being lost. The weather forecast was good. Time was precious. There would be plenty of rainy days when he could go back.

The third was Saul. When he got back home the family threw a big party for him. They wouldn't hear of he going anywhere. Hadn't he been away long enough? It was *they* who prevented him from going back.

Martha was the fourth. When she got home, her all-time favourite TV programme was on, something of which she had been starved during her isolation. She lost herself in the programme. She would go back tomorrow. But tomorrow never came.

The fifth was Daniel. Prior to his illness he had a very successful business. When he got home he saw that the business was very rundown. Going back was low in his priorities. Soon he forgot about it altogether.

Amos, the sixth, had no home to go to. He was feeling very bitter about his leprosy and about life in general. When he got back he collected some money that was owed to him, went on the town, and got drunk. Going back never entered his head.

Peter was the seventh. When he got back he had no job. Then he heard about an interview for a good job. He went for the interview. Going back was not on for the moment.

Anna was the eighth. There was a petrol shortage. She was actually on the way back when she saw a filling station open. She queued for three hours and got a fill-up. Then she went straight home. It would be a pity to waste petrol on a journey that wasn't really necessary.

Ninth came Joseph. When he got home he decided to sell his story to a newspaper. There was no time to lose. One of the others might get the same idea and beat him to it. Going back had no place in his plans.

Finally, there was Simon. He had several good reasons for not going back. One was especially compelling. He was a Samaritan, and the man who cured him was a Jew. It wouldn't be easy for a Samaritan to thank a Jew. But, being the kind of person he was, he brushed all these reasons aside, and went back to give thanks.

Excuses! Some plausible, some petty, some downright shabby. But in nine cases out of ten they were effective. They prevented those nine people from doing the one thing that cried out to heaven to be done.

'We write in the sand the benefits we receive, but the injuries we write on marble.' (Thomas More).

Nine of the lepers weren't able to express gratitude. What does this tell us? It seems to suggest that their cure was only skin-deep. Their leprosy was gone, but nothing else about them had changed. After their bitter experience, they returned to their old attitudes, habits, goals, and general shallowness of life. They had learned nothing from their pain. That was a real tragedy.

It's obvious that the Samaritan learned from his painful experience. He was a completely changed person afterwards, as was Namaan after his cure. The other nine lepers were cured in body only. Naaman and the Samaritan were cured physically and spiritually.

In good times we forget God, even though we may continue to pay lip-service to him. But then an illness brings us to our knees, and suddenly we are faced with our own poverty, weakness and mortality. However, if this brings us closer to God, and makes us more spiritual, it will prove to be a blessing in disguise. It seems that of the ten lepers only one of them was brought to closer to God through his illness and recovery.

HOMILY 3   Looking deeper

The story of the ten lepers has a very obvious lesson, namely, the importance of showing gratitude. But it has another lesson: finding God through pain. Pain can drive people away from God, or it can bring them close to God. Many converts are Good Friday converts – they enter the Kingdom through the gates of suffering. Naaman is a good example.

At one stage in his life he was on the crest of a wave. He had a prestigious job – commander-in-chief of the mighty Syrian army. He was highly regarded by his king. He had all the trappings of worldly success – wealth, power, fame. He had no need of God. Religion played no part in his life. He is typical of a some successful people today who seem to have no place for God in their lives.

However, when he was at the height of his power he contracted the dreaded disease of leprosy. All of a sudden his world began to disintegrate. One minute he was on top of the world. Next minute he was falling into the abyss.

Desperate for a cure, he swallowed his pride and sought help from the prophet Elisha in Israel, the little country he had plundered and despised. However, what he was looking for was a 'quick fix' so that he could go back and resume his old life exactly as before.

But he soon discovered that there was no such thing as a 'quick fix'; there was no quick and painless cure. So he had to learn to be humble and patient. He had to learn to take orders for a change. But it proved well worth his while because not only was he cured of his leprosy, but he was converted as well. He found the true God. So in the end he had reason to give thanks for his leprosy, because through it he received the gift of faith.

One wonders what the nine lepers derived from their terrible experience. Since they didn't thank God, it is unlikely that they derived any spiritual benefit from the experience.

Like Naaman before his illness, in good times we forget God, even though we may continue to pay lip-service to him. But then an illness or some such thing brings us to our knees, and we are suddenly face to face with our poverty, weakness and mortality. We realise how flimsy are the foundations on which we have built our hopes.

If this brings us closer to God, and makes us more spiritual, it will prove to be a blessing in disguise. It seems that of the ten lepers only one of them was brought to closer to God through his illness and recovery.

We don't always have control over what happens to us, but we do have control over how we react to what happens to us. For instance, two people are severely wounded in an accident. One chooses to live the experience in bitterness, and is destroyed by it. The other lives it in gratitude. He trusts that what happened, painful though it was, holds the possibility that good can come out of it. It's not a question of forgetting it, but of remembering it and integrating it into his life.

The willingness to give something back is a great sign of gratitude. When you are full of gratitude, there isn't room for bitterness or resentment. All happy people are grateful. Ungrateful people cannot be happy.

ANOTHER STORY

One day David gave alms to a poor man he met on the street. As he walked away he began to glow with self-satisfaction. But then a shadow passed over him – he remembered that the poor man hadn't thanked him. Later he related the incident to his rabbi. The rabbi listened patiently, then said, 'How did you feel when you gave the alms?'

'I felt very pleased with myself,' David replied.

'Wasn't that sufficient reward for you?'

'I still think he might have thanked me,' David persisted.

'Surely you don't want to be thanked for behaving as a religious man should? By the way, did *you* thank God?'

'For what?' asked David in surprise.

'For giving you an opportunity of being an instrument of his love towards a fellow human being,' came the reply.

PRAYER OF THE FAITHFUL

President: With gratitude in our hearts to God for all his past benefits, we bring our present needs before him now.

Response: Lord, graciously hear us.

Reader(s): For all believers: that they may see the guiding hand of a loving God in all the events of their lives. [Pause] Lord, hear us.

For all people: that they may be grateful for the gift of life, and show their gratitude by living good lives. [Pause] Lord, hear us.

For the sick and those who minister to them. [Pause] Lord, hear us.

For those who have been good to us and to whom we haven't shown sufficient gratitude. [Pause[Lord, hear us.

For our departed relatives and friends, to whom we owe so much. [Pause[Lord, hear us.

For our own special needs. [Longer pause] Lord, hear us.

President: God of love and mercy, you are the source of all we have and are. Grant that we may be grateful for the benefits you have given us, and show our gratitude by using them well. We ask this through Christ our Lord.

REFLECTION   **Gratitude**

Once there was a young man
who had never thought of donating blood.
But then his father got very ill and was hospitalised.
One day the son was sitting by his father's bedside
as he was getting a blood transfusion.
As he watched the blood flowing into his father's veins,
he suddenly realised that someone had donated

the blood that was now keeping his father alive.
Straightaway he made up his mind to become a donor,
and he was as good as his word.
Many are willing to avail of the generosity of others,
but few are willing to give something back.
This is why gratitude is so important.
It makes us want to give something back.

Twenty-ninth Sunday of the Year
PRAY WITHOUT CEASING

INTRODUCTION AND CONFITEOR

Prayer and faith are very closely connected. It's because we have faith
that we pray. At the same time prayer sustains our faith. We need to pray,
not just when we are in trouble, but at all times. Let us now turn to God,
in whom our hope lies. [Pause]

Lord Jesus, we lift up our eyes to you from whom our help comes.
Lord, have mercy.

You keep our feet from stumbling and our hearts from straying. Christ,
have mercy.

You guard our coming and going both now and for ever. Lord, have
mercy.

HEADINGS FOR READINGS

First Reading (Ex 17:8-13). The Israelites gain a victory over their enemies through the power of God which comes to them as a result of the
prayer of Moses.

Second Reading (2 Tim 3:14-4:2). Paul instructs Timothy to abide in the
sound doctrine which he has been taught since childhood, and to be zeal-
ous in preaching the message of Jesus.

Gospel (Lk 18:1-8). Jesus exhorts his disciples to pray continually and
never to grow discouraged.

SCRIPTURE NOTE

The First Reading tells of the first battle the Israelites fought after their
deliverance from Egypt. Their victory resulted, not from their own efforts alone, but from the power of God mediated through the intercession of Moses.

In the parable of the unjust judge (Gospel), Jesus exhorts his disciples
to pray continually and never to lose heart. The judge is approached by a

widow – she represents the powerless ones. It is presumed that she has right on her side. But the judge is not interested in the rights of a penniless widow. However, when she persists in her plea, he finally relents, but only to get rid of her.

The message is intended for the disciples who are faced with suffering and persecution. If an amoral judge can be moved by the persistent pleading of a widow, how much more will God see justice done for his faithful ones who cry out to him continually. The only question is: will they be found capable of confident and persevering prayer, or will they throw the towel in and abandon the faith, just because their prayer isn't answered immediately?

HOMILY 1   **The role of prayer**

No one can live a Christian life without prayer. But we have to understand what prayer is and what it does.

Three men were trapped in a dark cellar which had no doors or windows. How did they react to their predicament?

The first was a writer by the name of George. He had no faith. He just sat there cursing the darkness. 'There's nothing we can do,' he said despairingly. 'We might as well resign ourselves to our fate.'

The second was Peter, who was a very religious man. He prayed for a long time. When he had finished, he sat back and waited for a miracle.

The third man was a bricklayer by the name of Ivan. He was quite religious in his own way. But he was also a very practical man. He had a small chisel in his pocket. With the light of a match he found a small stone. Using this as a hammer he began to chip away at the wall.

The work was slow, monotonous and extremely tiring. He got dust in his eyes, and blisters on his hands. Neither of the other two showed any inclination to help him. George sat in one corner smoking. Peter sat in another corner praying. From time to time Ivan too prayed: 'Dear God, I believe that with your help we can make it out of here. So help us now.'

Finally, after hours of painful work, a big stone dislodged itself and light streamed in from next door. He began to shout for joy, praising and thanking God at the same time. His two companions helped him to widen the hole, and eventually all three crawled through and were free.

Here we see three different attitudes to prayer. For George it was a waste of time. Since he had no faith, his attitude was logical. If you don't believe in God, who can you pray to? For Peter, prayer was a substitute for action. So, once he had prayed, he sat back and waited for God to come to his rescue. A lot of our prayer is like that, especially our prayer on behalf of others. It's just words, an excuse for doing nothing.

Ivan believed in prayer, not however as a substitute for action, but as a spur to action. Having prayed, he immediately took whatever action he could. His prayer served the purpose of keeping up his courage and hope. It also gave him a sense of God's nearness, and an assurance that God had not abandoned him. He drew great strength from this.

If we look at the First Reading we will see Ivan's view of prayer in action. On their journey to the Promised Land the Israelites were set upon by the Amalekites. In their struggle they relied on the prayer of Moses, not as an excuse for doing nothing, but as a spur to action. And Jesus urges us in the Gospel to pray continually and never lose heart.

Prayer does make a difference. It sustains us. Those who pray never lose heart. When we turn our thoughts to God, we feel a new strength in our soul, in our entire being. 'Without divine assistance I cannot succeed; with it I cannot fail.' (Abraham Lincoln)

And faith and prayer are interconnected. St Augustine said, 'Faith pours out prayer, and the pouring out of prayer sustains and strengthens faith.' Prayer is the oil that keeps the lamp of faith burning. The fruit of prayer is faith. The fruit of faith is love. The fruit of love is service. And the fruit of service is peace.

HOMILY 2   **Praying with outstretched hands**

Jesus said to his disciples and says to us, 'Pray continually and never lose heart.' From our childhood days we were taught to join our hands when praying. Yet during the great prayers of the Mass the priest opens his hands and stretches them out. Both ways of praying are good and have their place. But what do the different gestures mean?

To join one's hands means that for a while we stop our normal activities and take time out to pray to God. This is more suited to private prayer. To pray with open hands is more suited to public prayer. To pray like this is to acknowledge that before God we are poor. Therefore we hold up our empty hands to God as a beggar holds out an empty bowl to passers-by. We are saying in effect, 'Lord, before you I am as poor as a beggar. I need you to fill my emptiness.'

The gesture of praying with open hands makes a powerful statement. It's a sermon in itself. The gesture is as old as the Bible. There's an example of it in the First Reading of today's Mass. We see Moses on a hilltop praying with extended hands for his people in their life-or-death battle with the Amalekites. When his hands dropped, the Amalekites prevailed. But when he kept them aloft to God, the Israelites prevailed. This is meant to illustrate the power of prayer. As long as the Jewish people put their faith in God, they moved forward. As soon as they forgot to look to God, they were forced to retreat.

Jesus urges us to keep on praying and not to lose heart. If we stop praying, we are likely to lose heart and give up. If we pray continually we will never lose heart. To pray means to put oneself and one's destiny in the hands of God. To pray means to rely on God's strength and not on our own. When we pray another kind of power becomes available to us.

The priest says the prayers of the Mass with outstretched hands. Like Moses, he is praying not just in his own name, but in the name of the worshipping community. Even if we don't pray like this ourselves, we can try to have the same attitude before God as this suggests – an attitude of humility and trust.

A prayer is answered, not when we get what we are asking for, but when we are granted a sense of God's nearness. The prayer of a sick person is answered, not by having his disease disappear, but by his gaining a sense of God's nearness, the assurance that his illness is not a punishment from God and that God has not abandoned him. Prayer may not change the world for us, but it can give us the courage to face it.

When we learn how to pray, we learn not just how to recite words, but how to open the heart. The practice that nourishes one most is quiet prayer of the heart. Just sitting very quietly and opening the heart and letting God in.

HOMILY 3   **Pray continually**

Jesus said to his disciples and says to us, 'Pray continually and never lose heart.' Some people do not see the value of regular prayer. They think it is enough to pray when and as they feel inspired to. For such as these the following story is told.

There was a small town which had all the municipal institutions: a bathhouse, a cemetery, a hospital, and a law court; as well as all sorts of crafts-people – tailors, dressmakers, shoemakers, carpenters, masons and so on. One trade, however, was lacking: there was no watchmaker.

Now as the years went by many of the clocks became so inaccurate that their owners just decided to let them run down, and ignored them altogether. There were others, however, who maintained that as long as the clocks ran, they should not be abandoned. So they wound their clocks day after day even though they knew they were not accurate.

One day the news spread through the town that a watchmaker had arrived, and everyone rushed to him with their clocks. But the only ones he could repair were the ones that had been kept running. The abandoned clocks had grown so full of rust that he could do nothing with them.

Why is prayer important? What does it do? Prayer clarifies our hope and our intentions. It helps us to discern between the important and the trivial. It helps us to discover our true aspirations, the pangs we ignore, the longings we forget. It is an act of self-purification.

Prayer teaches us what to aspire to. It helps to implant in us the ideals we ought to cherish. Purity of tongue may float about as an idea in our mind, but the idea becomes a concern, something to long for, a goal to be reached, when we pray, 'Lord, guard my tongue from evil and my lips from speaking guile.'

Prayer is no substitute for action. It is, rather, like a beam thrown from a flashlight before us into the darkness. It helps us to go forward, it encourages us to act.

Is not an escape from life but a journey into the heart of life. We learn to stand on our own feet before God and the world, and to accept full responsibility for our lives.

Its main purpose is to foster our relationship with God. This, and not our work, is the most important thing of all. This is the anchor of our spiritual lives. The spiritual life is not an extra. It is the life of the real self. It is not a matter of merely saying prayers.

Prayer is not a stratagem for occasional use, a refuge to resort to when things are bad. It is an established residence for the innermost self. Prayer is not asking things of God, but receiving what he wants to give us.

Prayer is its own reward. It enriches us. It enables us to live not only more spiritually, but more deeply, more fully, more authentically.

ANOTHER STORY

Once there was a shoemaker who set great value on daily prayer. His clients were poor people who owned only one pair of shoes. The shoemaker would take delivery of the shoes in the late evening, work on them all night and part of the morning, in order to have them ready so that their owners could go to work.

That left him with a problem: When should he say his morning prayers? Should he pray quickly first thing in the morning, and then go back to work? Or should he let the appointed hour of prayer go by and, every once in a while, raising his hammer from the shoes, utter a sigh: 'Woe unto me, I haven't prayed yet?'

We too face this dilemma of wholehearted regret or perfunctory fulfilment. Many of us regretfully refrain from habitual prayer, waiting for ideal conditions.

But perpetual refraining can easily grow into a habit. When the hour of prayer comes it seems as if our tongues are tied, our minds inert, and our inner vision dimmed. Hence, we do not pray. We do not refuse to pray; we abstain from it. Futile self-indulgence prevents us from immersing ourselves in the stillness that surrounds the world, the stillness that preceded our birth and which will follow our death.

Why do we not set apart an hour of living for devotion to God by surrendering to that stillness? We dwell on the edge of mystery and ignore it.

PRAYER OF THE FAITHFUL

President: Jesus urged us to pray without ceasing. So let us now pray to God for our own needs, and for the needs of the Church and world.

Response: Lord, hear our prayer.

Reader(s): For all believers: that they may never doubt God's presence with them in all their trials. [Pause] Let us pray to the Lord.

For the leaders of the human community: that God may give them strength and wisdom so that the nations may live in peace. [Pause] Let us pray to the Lord.

For the sick and those who care for them. [Pause] Let us pray to the Lord.

For those who are in trouble of any kind. [Pause] Let us pray to the Lord.

For grace to make room for prayer in our daily lives. [Pause] Let us pray to the Lord.

For our own special intentions. [Longer pause] Let us pray to the Lord.

President: Lord, grant that what we have said with our lips, we may believe in our hearts, and practise in our lives. We ask this through Christ our Lord.

REFLECTION   **Prayer**

I am neither a man of letters nor of science,
but I humbly claim to be a man of prayer.
It is prayer that has saved my life.
Without it I would have lost my reason long ago.
If I did not lose my peace of soul,
in the midst of my many trials,
it is because of the peace
hat came to me through prayer.
One can live several days without food,
but not without prayer.
Prayer is the key to each morning,
and the lock to each evening.
It is a sacred alliance between God and us.
Let everyone try this experience, and they will find
that daily prayer will add something new to their lives,
something which cannot be found elsewhere.   *(Mahatma Gandhi)*

Thirtieth Sunday of the Year
THE PHARISEE AND THE TAX-COLLECTOR

INTRODUCTION AND CONFITEOR

Jesus told a story about a Pharisee and a tax-collector who went into the Temple to pray. The Pharisee boasted that he was not like other people. By this he meant that he was not a sinner. Well, at the start of the Mass we confess that we *are* sinners. [Pause] Let us now confess our sins to the Lord, asking him to turn his face from our sins, but not from us.

I confess to almighty God …

HEADINGS FOR READINGS

First Reading (Sir 35:12-14.16-19). God shows no partiality for the rich and powerful, but listens to the humble prayer of the just and the lowly.

Second Reading (2 Tim 4:6-8.16-18). Paul, a prisoner in Rome, feels that his death is drawing near. But his confidence is unshaken and his hope of the 'crown of glory' is bright.

Gospel (Lk 18:9-14). The parable of the Pharisee and the tax-collector.

SCRIPTURE NOTE

Today's readings continue the theme of prayer. In a society where money and power are everything, the 'little people' don't have a chance. The First Reading states that God treats all people fairly. He shows no partiality to the rich and powerful. He listens to the humble prayer of the just and the lowly.

The parable of the Pharisee and the tax-collector makes the same point even more forcefully. The proud Pharisee is relying on his good works. Because of these he thinks that God owes him salvation. The tax-collector has nothing to rely on. He knows he's a sinner. So he throws himself on the mercy of God. His words are few, but the attitude of his heart makes him pleasing to God. His humble prayer wins him forgiveness.

The parable was aimed at those who prided themselves on being virtuous and despised everyone else. Although he was boastful, the Pharisee was not a hypocrite. His problem was that he had no concept of his need of God or grace or forgiveness.

HOMILY 1   **How not to pray**

Six people went into a church to pray. [Different voices could be used.]

The first (man) prayed like this: 'Thank you, Lord, that I have a good job. Mind you, I worked hard to get it and to keep it. I thank you that I've never had to draw the dole. Every penny I have I've earned by the sweat of my brow. I'm not like those others who sponge on society. They should all be put to work.'

The second (woman) prayed like this: 'Thank you, Lord, that my kids are well-behaved. I'm not saying that they're angels, but you won't find them going around wrecking telephone kiosks or terrifying old people. Nor will you hear them using bad language. Unlike those gurriers down the street, who are let run wild. These are the criminals of tomorrow.'

The third (woman) prayed like this: 'Thank you, Lord, that my marriage is working out. Jim and I have had our problems, but we've stuck together. Not like those others whose marriages are breaking up left, right and centre. The first sign of a problem and one or both are gone. They can't take the rough with smooth. It's society that will pay for their fickleness, when all those kids from broken homes are let loose on it.'

The fourth (man) prayed like this: 'Thank you, Lord, that I can take a drink and leave it at that. I'm not like those others who don't know when to stop. They live in the pub. Like your man next door who comes home footless every night. It's locked up the likes of him should be.'

The fifth (woman) prayed like this: 'Thank you, Lord, that I have been able to stick to the religion I was brought up in, unlike a lot of my neighbours. Maybe I'm a bit of a traditionalist. I don't go for Communion in the hand. I'm not worthy of touching the Host. When I see Mrs So-and-So coming up with her hand out, I feel like getting sick. You'd think by her holy attitude that she was the Blessed Virgin Mary herself.'

The sixth (man) didn't go inside the church at all, but said this prayer as he passed by: 'Lord, I thank you that I am not like that crowd who go in there every Sunday to worship you. They're nothing but a bunch of hypocrites. Inside there they give each other a handshake as a sign of peace, and I know for a fact that some of them aren't even talking to one another. At least I'm being honest. I know I'm no saint, but then I don't pretend to be one.'

The Pharisee in Jesus' story was not a scoundrel. In fact, he was an honest, faithful, family man, and a meticulous observer of the Law. He did even more than the Law required of him. It required only one fast a year (on the Day of Atonement), but he fasted twice a week! It required tithes of certain commodities, but he paid tithes on everything.

Where then did he go wrong? First of all in his attitude to God. He believed that he had run up a formidable credit-balance with God. Therefore, he had got God in his debt. Secondly, in his attitude to others. He despised others. He was a proud man without a trace of humility. And humility is the soil in which all other virtues flourish. In him we see arrogant self-reliance, complacency, and scorn of the sinner.

'There is no odour as bad as that which arises from tainted goodness.' (Thoreau)

He was full of himself. He didn't pray to God, but to himself. No less than six times in that short prayer he mentions 'I'. There is no room for God in one who is full of himself. 'If a man, after prayer, is proud or self-satisfied, he has prayed not to God, but to himself.' (Baal Shem Tov)

The prayer of the tax-collector is a model. He said simply, 'Lord, be merciful to me I am a sinner.' This is the most moving of all prayers, and one that God cannot fail to hear. In saying this, he was simply telling the truth. If we can say, 'I'm a sinner' with conviction and humility, we are very close to God. 'I'm old enough to know that I am no better than others.' (Carlo Carretto)

HOMILY 2   **Sins versus sinfulness**

The Pharisee was completely unaware of his own sinfulness. He didn't think he had any sins at all. He wasn't a sinner like the rest of humankind. No. He was different. Therefore, instead of examining his own conscience and confessing his own sins, he examined the conscience of others and confessed their sins – greed, injustice, adultery, and so on.

Yet he had sins. In fact, he had very serious sins. His chief sin was that of pride. But he was also vain and self-righteous, and he despised others. His sins were not so much bad deeds as bad attitudes. He had an attitude problem – as people say in America.

The tax-collector might well have confessed the sins of the Pharisee. But he didn't do so. He concentrated on himself, and left the sins of others between them and God. With radical honesty he laid bare his heart before God. He made no attempt to hide anything. He stood before God and, in all humility, said, 'Lord be merciful to me for I am a sinner.' As a result he went home at rights with God. 'The humble person's prayer pierces the clouds' (First Reading).

We can learn from both of them. Firstly from the Pharisee. In fact, there is a Pharisee lurking in each of us. Like him we may be very conscious of the sins of others but blind to our own. It's easy to get into the habit of confessing the sins of others. But this is dangerous because it prevents us from looking at our own sins. Besides, it's impossible to weigh the sins of others without putting our own finger on the scales.

And we can learn from the tax collector. He shows us how to confess our sins. Even though we may not be conscious of any specific sins, each of us can still say in all truth, 'I am a sinner.'

Many people approach the Sacrament of Reconciliation with a prepared list of sins. Most of the things that appear on that list are trivial matters and don't wary much from one Confession to the next. No attempt is made to get down to the roots of their relationship with God and other people. Too much emphasis is placed on the sins, not enough on the fact of being a sinner.

It would have been easy for the Tax-Collector to produce a list of sins. But he didn't do this; he did something better, and also harder. He said, 'I am a sinful man.'

We too must be prepared to stand before God as sinners, as much in need of God's mercy as the ground is in need of rain. What we have to face is not the fact that we commit sins, but that we are sinners. We are sinful, fallen people – that is the reality. Sin is not just an act or series of acts, but a condition in which we live. This is the great truth which the Tax-Collector grasped.

A great problem of our time is man's failure to know himself, to recognise evil and deal with it within himself. People in support groups say that the turning point for them in when they can name their weakness.

The Pharisee was full of himself, the centre of his own world. He had exalted himself. From that exalted position he looked down on others, some of whom he despised. The Tax-Collector, on the other hand, humbled himself before God. He placed his hope in the mercy of God. We would do well to do the same. God prefers the broken and contrite heart that knows its failures over the complacent and arrogant one that claims never to have sinned.

'Better a sinner who knows he's a sinner than a saint who knows he's a saint.' (Yiddish saying)

HOMILY 3   **Confessing one's own sins**

The prayer of the Pharisee went like this: 'I thank you, God, that I am not grasping, unjust, adulterous like the rest of mankind, and particularly that I am not like this Tax-Collector here. I fast twice a week; I pay tithes on all I get.'

The prayer of the Tax-Collector might well have gone like this: 'Lord, look at the Pharisee standing up there so that everybody can see him praying. He thinks he's better than everybody else. He despises people like me. See the long robes he's wearing so as to make himself feel holy and attract attention to himself.

'Everything he does is done, not to bring honour to you, but to win the esteem of others, and thus bring honour to himself. He makes sure to get the seats of honour at banquets and in the synagogue. He loves it when people salute him in the marketplace and call him "Rabbi".

'He gets all hot and bothered about silly little rules of his own making, while neglecting the things that really matter – the practice of justice and mercy. He's good at laying down the law for others. He ought to practise what he preaches. He lives off the contributions of widows.

'Ah, Lord, don't be taken in by him. It's all an act, it's all a show. He's not genuine. He may look clean on the outside, like a whitewashed tomb, but inside he's full of corruption. He's the biggest hypocrite on two feet.'

All this and more the Tax-Collector could have said. And the Lord might have added, 'I agree with every word you've said,' because the Lord himself said all these things about the Pharisees. But the Tax-Collector said nothing of the sort. Instead, he simply said, 'God, be merciful to me, a sinner.'

What the Pharisee did was confess the sins of others, while at the same time parading his own good deeds. The Tax-Collector did the exact opposite. He confessed his own sins, and left the sins of others between them and God. As a result the Tax-Collector went home at rights with God, whereas the Pharisee did not. We have Jesus' word for this.

It's easy to get into the habit of confessing the sins of others. But it's dangerous because it prevents us from looking at our own sins. Besides, it's impossible to weigh the sins of others without putting our own finger on the scales.

The successful are always tempted to regard their success as a sort of blessing from God or a reward for righteousness. This leads to judgements being made about the unsuccessful, which are both uncharitable and untrue.

We may have been brought up to believe that we had to be dressed up, both outwardly and inwardly, before daring to show our faces in 'His' church. But we have to come before God as we are. Because, as Francis of Assisi said: 'I am what I am before God. Nothing else. Nothing more. Nothing less.'

ANOTHER STORY

The Scottish biblical scholar, William Barclay, told the following story.

He was on a train journey from Scotland to England. As he was passing through the Yorkshire moors he spotted a little whitewashed cottage. Its radiant whiteness shone out against the drab moors. A few days later he passed that way again. Meanwhile snow had fallen and covered the ground. He came again to the little whitewashed cottage. But now its whiteness actually seemed drab against the virgin whiteness of the snow.

If we should be tempted to compare ourselves with others, let us compare ourselves only with Christ himself. When we lay our imperfect lives beside his sinless life, all we will be able to say is: 'Lord, be merciful to me, I am a sinner.'

PRAYER OF THE FAITHFUL

President: With humble but trustful hearts, let us pray to God for our own needs and the needs of the Church and the world.

Response: Lord, be merciful to me a sinner.

Reader(s): That our Churches may be places where sinners can experience the healing mercy of God. [Pause] Let us pray.

For all those in authority: that they may have the humility to acknowledge their mistakes, and the courage to correct them. [Pause] Let us pray.

For tax-collectors and all those who do unpopular but necessary jobs. [Pause] Let us pray.

For grace never to look down on others or belittle their dignity. [Pause] Let us pray.

For grace always to strive to come before God exactly as we are, with our virtues and sins, our failures and successes. [Pause] Let us pray.

For our own special needs. [Longer pause] Let us pray.

President: Lord, give us the humility not to hide our weakness, the wisdom to learn from our mistakes, and in facing life's difficulties, let us know that your grace will be sufficient for us. We make this prayer through Christ our Lord.

REFLECTION   **Sinners in church**

If the Pharisee had his way the Tax-Collector
would not have been allowed into the Temple at all.
Some people believe that sinners should never go to church.
They cry 'hypocrites' at those who do.
According to them only saints should be admitted to church.
But that would result in a very small church,
and would make as little sense as a repair shop
that accepted only sound things,
or a hospital that accepted only healthy people.
We go to church not because we are worthy,
but because we need to.
We are brave enough to admit our sinfulness,
but are willing to strive for something better.
We need the healing mercy of God,
as well as the support of the community,
if our efforts at self-improvement are to bear fruit.

Thirty-first Sunday of the Year
ZACCHAEUS

INTRODUCTION AND CONFITEOR

In the Gospel of today's Mass we see the Lord's compassion towards a sinner – the tax-collector, Zacchaeus. The Lord extends his compassion to us too, as we now call to mind our sins. [Pause]

Lord Jesus, you are kind and full of compassion. Lord, have mercy.

You are slow to anger and abounding in love. Christ, have mercy.

You support all who fall, and raise all who are bowed down. Lord, have mercy.

HEADINGS FOR READINGS

First Reading (Wis 11:22-12:2). God, who created the world out of love, overlooks people's sins so that they can repent.

Second Reading (2 Thess 1:11-2:2). Paul urges the Thessalonians to be worthy of their call, and assures them that the Second Coming of Christ has not yet taken place.

Gospel (Lk 19:1-10). We hear the story of the conversion of the rich tax-collector, Zacchaeus.

SCRIPTURE NOTE

The world and all it contains is like a grain of sand compared with the greatness of God. Yet God loves all that he has created, and overlooks people's sins so that they can repent (First Reading). The Gospel gives us an example of this in the way Jesus seeks out the tax-collector, Zacchaeus, and calls him to repentance.

At that time tax-collectors were put in the same category as thieves, murderers and prostitutes. Furthermore, because they worked for the Romans, they were regarded as traitors, and treated as outcasts. We can understand, then, how the good people of Jericho were offended when Jesus went to the house of Zacchaeus. But Jesus justified his action by saying that Zacchaeus too was a son of Abraham, and therefore entitled to the mercy of God as any other Israelite. And he declared that it was to seek out and save people like Zacchaeus that he had come.

Touched by the kindness of Jesus, Zacchaeus saw the error of his ways and resolved to change. In this episode we again see Luke's concern for the proper use of wealth – it should be distributed to the poor.

HOMILY 1   **Conversion of heart**

It's clear that Zacchaeus had heard a lot of good things about Jesus. But he wanted to see for himself. Firstly, he wanted to see what Jesus looked like. Secondly, and more importantly, he wanted to see what kind of person Jesus was.

A huge crowd of people showed up to see Jesus. In spite of all the attention and adulation, Jesus spotted Zacchaeus on the tree. It shows that Jesus was more interested in others than in himself. The first thing, then, that would have impressed Zacchaeus was the fact that Jesus noticed him. It's nice to be noticed.

But having noticed him, Jesus might have snubbed him. Had he done so he would have increased his popularity in that town. But Jesus did not snub him. He stopped under the tree and looked up at him. In this way he showed Zacchaeus that he was interested in him.

But there was better to come. He spoke to him. In deciding to speak to him he might have condemned him as a money-grasper and exploiter of the poor. But he didn't utter one word of condemnation – at least not in public. Instead, addressing him by his name, he called him down and said that he wanted to stay at his house. In so doing he made himself extremely unpopular with the townspeople. But Zacchaeus was delighted, and welcomed him with joy.

Zacchaeus had come in order to see what kind of man Jesus was. Well, by the end of the day he had got a lot more than he bargained for or hoped for. Instead of getting a mere passing glimpse of Jesus, he had a face-to-face, and a heart-to-heart encounter with him.

He not only discovered what Jesus looked like but also what his heart was like. And to know the heart of Jesus was to know the possibilities of his own heart too. Zacchaeus liked what he discovered about Jesus. And he also liked what he discovered about himself. He experienced 'the melting of the heart'. His heart came to life like a desert landscape after a rainfall.

Zacchaeus' conversion was immediate, visible and, we feel sure, permanent. It was not, however, just an intellectual conversion. He had a change of heart. From a Gospel viewpoint this is most important conversion of all. It is, perhaps, harder to achieve than an intellectual conversion, and is certainly more far-reaching in its consequences. Fear can't produce this kind of conversion. Only an encounter with love can.

The central issue for human beings in how we can have a change of heart and learn to love one another. There has to be a touching, a softening, a moving of the heart, which leads to an opening of the heart, and finally to a sharing of the heart's riches. A harsh approach causes the heart to close and harden. A kind approach, such as Jesus adopted with Zacchaeus, causes the heart to soften and open. Nothing but the heart can change the heart.

Treat a man as he is, and he will become worse; treat him as he ought to be, or as he aspires to be, and he will become better, because our aspirations are the most real part of us (Goethe).

Jesus saw that Zacchaeus' wrongdoing was not the whole of him, and that he had within him the possibility of goodness. Jesus' vision of Zacchaeus affected the way Zacchaeus saw himself. Goodness evokes goodness.

Zacchaeus' conversion was a conversion to goodness. All of us stand

[341]

in need of such a conversion. Each of us has the capacity that Zacchaeus had, though it may be hidden or unexpressed. Each of us stands in need of daily conversions from a closed heart to an open heart, from a heart of stone to a heart of flesh.

HOMILY 2   **Surprised by love**

In correcting people, the kind of approach we adopt is all-important. If we approach them only to confront them with their faults, in all probability we will achieve nothing. In fact, we are likely to make matters worse. They will close up, become resentful, and harden their hearts.

A prison governor has said that the only way to change people is through a relationship with them. You never improve people by avoiding them or rejecting them. A cold climate doesn't encourage growth.

If you snub a person, all you do is harden his heart. You have to find a way of touching a person's heart. All people, even the most seemingly cold-blooded, have a core of decency, and are capable of changing if their hearts are touched.

We have to approach people in such a way that we show them that we believe in them, that we have confidence in them. The result is that they drop their guard and open up. Once they open up anything can happen. We see this in case of Zacchaeus.

Jesus spotted Zacchaeus on the tree. Now Zacchaeus' lifestyle was in complete opposition to everything Jesus stood for. No doubt the people expected and hoped that Jesus would read the riot act to him. Had he done so he would have enhanced his popularity in the town.

But Jesus refused to read the Riot Act to Zacchaeus. Instead, he did something which made him immediately unpopular with the people. He asked Zacchaeus if he could dine in his house, and surprisingly Zacchaeus received him with joy. The people complained, 'He has gone to stay at a sinner's house.' They hated Zacchaeus. They didn't want to see him saved. They wanted to see him condemned and punished.

But Jesus didn't think like this. He saw that what Zacchaeus needed was not condemnation but salvation. There was no question of whether or not he deserved salvation. He needed it – that was enough for Jesus. By coming to his house, in the face of the angry disapproval of the townspeople, Jesus showed Zacchaeus that he cared about him. Had he avoided him or condemned him, the miracle would never have happened.

Zacchaeus experienced the love of Jesus. This must have been a wonderful experience for a man who up to this had experienced so much hate. It's marvellous to feel that somebody has confidence in us, that we are not judged or condemned, but loved. Zacchaeus' heart burst into life like a desert landscape after a rainfall.

To be loved in one's goodness is no big deal. It's no more than one deserves. But to be loved in one's badness – as Zacchaeus was – that's magic. He experienced the surprise of being loved. It led to the flowering of the best that was in him. His conversion was a conversion to goodness. To a greater or lesser degree, all of us need this kind of conversion.

HOMILY 3   **From spectator to participant**

Television is threatening to turn us all into spectators, onlookers, and bystanders. Suppose you are a nature lover. Now, you don't have to get your shoes dirty, or let the rain fall on you. You don't even have to leave your own sitting room, or even move from the fireside. Television provides you with a feast of sights and sounds. There is no risk, no pain, no trouble. Yet what a poor substitute this is for the real thing.

There are people who claim to love nature who seldom, if ever, have walked in the woods, across the fields, or along the shore. In other words, they are mere spectators. They are not really involved. To be involved is to give a part of oneself to it. But you get back far more than you give.

However, there is at least this to be said for the spectator – he or she is interested. And where there is interest, there is the possibility of a real involvement.

So it was with Zacchaeus. At the start of the story he was a mere spectator. He could see without being seen. He was just an onlooker. He felt comfortable in the position of observer but uncomfortable as the observed. But don't we all?

He didn't join the crowd. He climbed up among the branches of a sycamore tree. In more ways that one, he was out on a limb. He was marginalised, not by poverty, but by riches. His riches isolated him from his fellow townspeople who, by and large, were poor.

As an onlooker he was involved only passively. He was there on his own terms. There was a certain interest, but no risks, no commitment. When it was over he could go home, and if he so wished, forget about the whole thing.

But what happened? Jesus saw him and invited him to become a participant. Suddenly Zacchaeus was whisked from the touchline right into the centre of the action. He was like a spectator who goes to a football match, and suddenly the manager spots him, throws him a set of gear, and says, 'You're on!' And he finds himself playing.

The amazing thing is this. Not only did Zacchaeus respond positively, but he did so immediately and joyfully. There is joy in watching, but there is far more joy in participating. The consequences for him were enormous. It changed his life. The active living out of our Christian vocation will change our lives too.

Zacchaeus experienced a conversion – a conversion to goodness. To a greater or lesser degree, all of us need this kind of conversion.

PRAYER OF THE FAITHFUL

President: Let us pray for some of that open and generous love Jesus showed to Zacchaeus.

Response: Lord, hear us in your love.

Reader(s): For the Church: that like Christ it may see its primary mission as saving the lost. [Pause] Let us pray to the Lord.

For the leaders of governments: that they may carry out their responsibilities with wisdom and integrity. [Pause] Let us pray to the Lord.

For the conversion of the rich and the powerful. [Pause] Let us pray to the Lord.

For all the outcasts of society. [Pause] Let us pray to the Lord.

For our own special needs. [Longer pause] Let us pray to the Lord.

President: God of mercy and compassion, you never write off anyone. May this give us hope for our own lives, and serve as a model in our dealings with others. We ask this through Christ our Lord.

REFLECTION   **Change of heart**

It is only with the heart that we can repent rightly.
Repentance must involve a change of heart.
Anything less won't produce a new being.
It will be like decapitating weeds
while leaving their roots intact.
But if we change our hearts,
then we will change our lives too.
After his encounter with Jesus, Zacchaeus' heart
burst into life like a desert landscape after a rainfall.
Fear can't produce a conversion of heart;
only an encounter with love can.
Zacchaeus' conversion was a conversion to goodness.
All of us stand in daily need of such a conversion.
We need to move from a closed heart to an open heart,
from a heart of stone to a heart of flesh.

Thirty-second Sunday of the Year
TRAVELLING IN HOPE

INTRODUCTION AND CONFITEOR

The liturgy today is dominated with the assurance of an afterlife. It is a splendid hope. Life is not a journey to nowhere. It is a journey to the promised land of eternal life. This hope rests not on anything human, but on the word and power of God. [Pause]

Lord Jesus, you have gone ahead of us to prepare a place for us. Lord, have mercy.

You banish the darkness of our doubts with the light of faith. Christ, have mercy.

You bind us together as the new People of God, journeying in hope towards the promised land of eternal life. Lord, have mercy.

HEADINGS FOR READINGS

First Reading (2 Macc 7:1-2.9-14). This tells (in part) the story of the martyrdom of a mother and her seven sons. They drew their strength from their faith in the resurrection of the just.

Second Reading (2 Thess 2:16-3:5). Paul prays for the Thessalonians that they may remain steadfast in the pursuit of goodness.

Gospel (Lk 20:27-38). Jesus deals with a question posed by the Sadducees about the existence of an afterlife.

SCRIPTURE NOTE

The First Reading is taken from 2 Maccabees. A feature of this book is its confident teaching on the afterlife. Our reading tells (in part) the story of the martyrdom of a mother and her seven sons. This is an example of the resistance of the Jews against their conquerors. The woman and her sons drew their strength from faith in the resurrection of the just. And it is this latter idea which connects the reading with today's Gospel.

Jesus is drawn into the argument which went on between the Sadducees and the Pharisees regarding the resurrection. The Saducees did not believe in the resurrection; the Pharisees did. The Sadducee used the tactic of *reductio ad absurdum*.

Jesus used the insincere inquiry as an opportunity to deliver a genuine teaching. The first thing he did was to challenge the assumption that the afterlife is just a continuation of this life, with some extras thrown in. He made it clear that there is no comparison between this life and that of the resurrection.

Then he went on to use another argument to support belief in the resurrection of the dead. God is known as a God of the living. But he is also known as the God of Abraham, Isaac and Jacob. This means that the patriarchs must be still living.

As Christians our hope of resurrection is founded on the love God has shown us in Jesus (Second Reading). Nevertheless, the above readings will help to strengthen our faith as believers.

Eternal life

In different ways, all three readings of today's Mass deal with the theme of eternal life.

An old and infirm man was living in a shack on the edge of the forest. One winter's morning he got up to find only one meal of porridge left, the fireplace empty, and snow on the ground. He felt like asking God to take him to heaven there and then. However, he managed to summon up a little spirit, and went into the forest to collect firewood.

He collected a large bundle of sticks. Then he put a rope around it and tied a knot. However, when he tried to lift the bundle onto his shoulders, he found that he couldn't even move it. With that a wave of depression swept over him. He looked up to heaven and said, 'Lord, take me now. I've nothing left to live for.'

In an instant a strapping young man appeared at his side. The stranger introduced himself as the Angel of Death and said, 'You sent for me. Well, now that I'm here, what can I do for you?' Quick as a flash the old man replied, 'Hey son, would you ever give me a hand with this bundle of sticks.'

As we go on in life we become increasingly aware of how fleeting life is, and how precarious is our hold over it. In spite of ourselves we become familiar with the thought of death. But this need not be a negative or morbid thing. In fact, it can be a very positive thing. Thinking about death can result in a true love of life. When we are familiar with death, we accept each day as a gift. And when we accept life bit by bit like this, it becomes very precious.

By facing our mortality we are put in touch with that other life, eternal life, the seeds of which have been planted in our hearts and souls. Death is the passage to a new life, which (as Jesus says in the Gospel) utterly transcends the life we know now. This sounds beautiful, but that doesn't mean it's easy.

Our passage from this world is preceded by many other smaller passages. When we were born we made the passage from life in the womb to life outside the womb. When we went to school we made the passage from life in the family to life in the larger community. Those who have married have made the passage from a life with many options to a life committed to one person. Those who have retired have made a passage from a life of clearly defined work to a life without such work. Each of these passages results in a kind of death but also leads to new life. When we live these passages well, we are preparing ourselves for our final passage.

The thing that best helps us to confront the reality of death is our Christian faith. Faith enables us to face death with courage and hope, because we know we can overcome it in Christ. But the courage and faith of people such as the woman and her seven sons (First Reading) also serve as a powerful example to us who follow them in faith. The martyrs, by their witness to the Spirit, show that life is stronger than the forces of death.

'Proofs' based on the immortality of the soul are not very helpful. For the Christian, the real ground of immortality is fellowship with the risen Lord and with the living God. As Paul says, 'God has given us his love and, through his grace, inexhaustible comfort and such sure hope' (Second Reading).

God has made promises to us in Christ which cannot fail, promises which death cannot annul. Our hope of resurrection lies in the power and love of God. Death is not the enemy who puts an end to everything but the friend who takes us by the hand and leads us into the Kingdom of eternal love.

HOMILY 2   **The meaning of courage**

There are two kinds of courage. The first is loud, angry and assertive, and is associated with places such as the battlefield. The second is quiet, serene and unassertive. Nevertheless, it is utterly unflinching, and is impervious to the most alluring blandishments as well as to the direst threats.

We see an example of the second kind of courage in the mother and her seven sons. But there are examples closer to our own times. The following incident happened in a Jewish ghetto in eastern Europe during the Second World War.

The German authorities appointed a man by the name of Ephraim to the post of president of the Jewish Council. One day they asked Ephraim to submit a list to them of thirty people for slave labour. Ephraim went away and thought about it. Eventually he came back and presented a list to the German authorities. When they examined the list, instead of finding thirty names, they found one name written thirty times. That one name was Ephraim's own.

Ephraim knew that in doing what he did he was signing his own death warrant. Yet he refused to betray any of his brothers or sisters. Before courage such as this one feels poor.

We tend to think that fear and courage are mutually exclusive. But this is not so. Courage is not never being afraid. It is being afraid, and overcoming it, or carrying on in spite of it. Nelson Mandela says:

I learned the meaning of courage from my comrades in the struggle. Time and time again, I have seen men and women show a strength and a resilience that defies the imagination. I learned that courage was not the absence of fear, but the triumph over it. The brave man is not he who does not feel afraid, but he who conquers that fear.

The conviction that one is doing the right thing gives one enormous strength. We are acting out of the deepest goodness that is in us – out of the image of God within us.

Courage is such an important virtue because, without it, you can't practise any other virtue with constancy. However, what the world needs is not so much heroism but ordinary courage. We can see a great deal of this in the daily lives of a lot of people, when we think of the sufferings they bear, and the hardships they suffer. Courage is not so much about climbing mountains as accepting defeat without losing heart.

Each Sunday we end the Creed with these words: 'We look for the resurrection of the dead, and the life of the world to come.' Belief in an afterlife is one of the most important of our beliefs as Christians. Without it, our lives on earth are a journey to nowhere. With it, our lives on earth are a journey to the promised land of eternal life.

Hope is a vital part of life. What bread does for the body, hope does for the spirit. We spend a great deal of our lives waiting, hoping, and longing for one thing or another. But we know that this world can never fulfil our deepest hopes and longings. Only God can do that.

God has made us not for death but for eternal life. 'God so loved the world that he gave his only Son, so that everyone who believes in him may not perish but may have eternal life' (Jn 3:14-15).

The splendid prospect of eternal life should enable us to live out joyfully the mystery of our fragile human condition which sees us suspended between earth and heaven, between time and eternity, between nothingness and infinity.

HOMILY 3   **Witnessing to eternal life**

We could argue intellectually in favour of life hereafter. But it is those who have witnessed, not with words, but with deeds, and sometimes with their lives, who are the best argument of all. It is the martyrs, by their witness to the Spirit, who show that life is stronger than the forces of death. We think of the mother and her seven sons (First Reading). But there are examples closer to our day.

In May, 1992, the *Observer* newspaper carried the following story. Thirty Russian Orthodox nuns were imprisoned by Stalin in 1929 in the former monastery of the Solovetsky Islands on the northern coast of Russia. Like all inmates of the camps, the nuns were expected to work. But they steadfastly refused to do so, explaining that they could not agree 'to work for the agents of the Antichrist.'

The administration reacted with severity. Unless they were medically certified as unfit for work, those refusing to work were severely beaten and then sent to a punishment island from which no one came back alive.

However, the prison authorities seemed strangely reluctant to visit such punishment on the nuns. The chief of the camp's medical section was baffled by the nuns. In his eyes they were 'difficult prisoners', yet their behaviour was not what he had come to expect from 'difficult prisoners'. Instead of shouting and screaming, the nuns exhibited only simplicity, humility and gentleness.

Feeling sorry for them, he asked a doctor to declare the nuns unfit for work. The doctor, himself a prisoner, was deeply impressed by the nuns, who were calm and self-possessed, wearing habits that were worn but clean. Their faces conveyed an astonishing purity of spirit that evoked deep reverence.

The doctor tried to persuade the nuns to work, citing the example of other Christian prisoners. When the nuns remained unmoved, he said he would think up illnesses for them, and declare them unfit for work. 'Forgive us,' a nun interrupted, 'that is not true. We are healthy. We are able to work. But we will not work for the Antichrist.'

The doctor explained that they would be tortured rather than killed. 'God will help us endure torture too,' one of the nuns replied quietly. Years later the doctor wrote, 'Tears came to my eyes. I bowed to them in silence. I wanted to kiss their feet.'

Some time later the nuns did agree to make quilts for the camp sick bay, provided they were allowed to sing psalms together quietly while they worked. However, a priest arrived in the camp and told them that it was wrong of them to do any work for the 'agents of Antichrist.' So the nuns refused to work. The priest was taken out and shot. Before long the nuns met the same fate.

The nuns appeared to show no hesitation or doubt or uncertainty. But this doesn't mean that what they did came easy. Everybody loves life. They loved life too, but they did not cling to it at all costs. For them the real life was eternal life. Faith in eternal life enabled them to sacrifice their earthly lives for Christ.

Those nuns put their trust in God. So did the mother and her seven sons. We can do not better than imitate their trust in God. Paul says that we have a sure hope. This hope comes not from ourselves but from God. He is the God of the living. We are his children. He made us for life, here and hereafter. This splendid prospect enables us to treasure life without clinging to it. And it should spur us to live it rightly.

PRAYER OF THE FAITHFUL

President: God raised Jesus from the dead so that we might have a sure hope of an inheritance that will never fade. Let us pray to God as members of a hopeful people.

Response: Lord, hear our prayer.

Reader(s): For Christians: that the hope of eternal life implanted in their hearts at baptism may be fulfilled in the kingdom of heaven. [Pause] Let us pray to the Lord.

For the human family: that all its members may reach the goal God intended for them. [Pause] Let us pray to the Lord.

For those who mourn: that they may find comfort through their belief in eternal life. [Pause] Let us pray to the Lord.

For ourselves: that our lives may bear witness to the hope we carry in our hearts. [Pause] Let us pray to the Lord.

For our relatives and friends, and for all who have gone to their rest in the hope of rising again. [Pause] Let us pray to the Lord.

For our own special needs. [Longer pause] Let us pray to the Lord.

President: Almighty and ever-living God, may you support us all day long, till the shadows lengthen, and evening falls, and the busy world is hushed, and the fever of life is over, and our work is done; then in your mercy, Lord, grant us a safe lodging, a holy rest, and peace at the last. We ask this through Christ our Lord.

PRAYER/REFLECTION   **Returning to God**

We are born in exile and die there too.
As soon as we set sail on the great voyage of life,
we begin our return.
When we die,
we do not so much go to God as return to him.
Like homesick cranes that fly night and day
back to their mountain nests,
so let all our lives take their voyage to you, O Lord.
For you have made us for yourself,
and our hearts will never rest, until they rest in you.
Only those who have flown home to You have flown at all.

FINAL BLESSING

May God, who kindled in your hearts the hope of eternal life, guard this hope with his grace, and bring it to fulfilment in the kingdom of heaven.
May almighty God bless you ...

Thirty-third Sunday of the Year
WITNESSING TO CHRIST IN A WORLD OF CONFUSION

INTRODUCTION AND CONFITEOR

We live in a world which is full of confusion and unrest. In the midst of such a world we are expected to witness to Christ. To be good and faithful witnesses we need help from on high. Therefore, it is to God we now turn for the courage and strength we need. [Pause]

Lord Jesus, you strengthen us when we are weak. Lord, have mercy.
You give us courage when we are afraid. Christ, have mercy.
You give us hope when we fall into despair. Lord, have mercy.

HEADINGS FOR READINGS

First Reading (Mal 3:19-20). For evildoers, the Day of the Lord will be a day of judgement; but for the upright it will be a day of salvation.

Second Reading (2 Thess 3:7-12). As far as possible, all should try to earn the food they eat.

Gospel (Lk 21:5-19). We hear a prediction of the destruction of the temple, and are told of the situation of Christians in a time of trial.

SCRIPTURE NOTE

As the liturgical year draws to a close, the focus is on the end of the world and the Second Coming of Christ. The prophet Malachi (First Reading) says that for evildoers the Day of the Lord will be a day of judgement; but for the upright it will be a day of salvation. His stark message was meant to act as a warning to sinners and as an encouragement to the just.

The Second Reading also relates to the Second Coming. Some of the Thessalonians, believing that the *parousia* was imminent, saw no need to work. Presenting himself as an example, Paul tells them to go on living and working as normal, and not to be content to live off the community.

Luke talks about the *parousia* in close association with the destruction of Jerusalem and the Temple. The destruction of the Temple, which Jesus had predicted, had already occurred by the time Luke was writing. This would have been interpreted by some as a sign that the end of the world was starting. But Luke reminds them of the words of Jesus, in which he warned his disciples not to be deceived by rumours and apparent signs that the end was near.

The Gospel goes on to address the situation of Christians in a time of persecution. Persecution will be an opportunity to bear witness to the Gospel. The Lord himself will see to it that believers will triumph in the end, provided they remain steadfast.

HOMILY 1   **Faith can thrive in adversity**

Jesus didn't hold anything back from his disciples. He told them that things would be difficult. When he spoke about the world he was very realistic. He spoke about wars and revolutions, earthquakes, plagues and famines, persecution and imprisonment, betrayal, hatred and killings.

He told them that such happenings would provide them with an opportunity to bear witness to him and to the Gospel. It is in times of darkness that the light is needed. It is in times of falsehood that the truth is needed. It is in times of hatred that love is needed. It is in times of war that peace is needed. And it is in difficult times that Christian witness is needed.

By forewarning them Jesus was forearming them. He was saying: You'll need wisdom – don't be deceived. You'll need courage – don't be afraid. You'll need staying power and endurance – don't give up. He will see to it that they will triumph in the end, provided they remain steadfast.

Our times offer numerous opportunities to bear witness to Jesus and his Kingdom. The many tragedies and disasters that occur in our world could easily lead us to despair and convince us that we are the sad victims of circumstances. But this is not how Jesus looked on events. He called them opportunities.

Faith seems to thrive in adversity. Indeed, sometimes faith is born out of adversity. In this respect it resembles certain wild flowers: put them in a garden and they go to seed; but put them on a mountain-side and they bloom.

During the communist regime in Russia there was a ten-year-old girl whose whole family had been scattered to distant labour camps because of their belief in God. The girl was first taken to an orphanage. There, she refused to give up the crucifix her mother had hung around her neck before leaving. She tied a knot so that they could not take it from her during sleep. The struggle went on and on, but it was no good. She would not give up the cross.

She also refused to submit herself to retraining, to daily lessons in party propaganda. In the orphanage she was forced to live with children who were the very dregs of Russian society. Yet she refused to curse or steal. They never broke her. She ended up doing ten years in a labour camp.

In a world of so much social and political turmoil, people of faith will often be regarded as naive and ineffective and irrelevant. However, we must not be afraid of scepticism and cynicism, but trust that God will give us the strength to hold our ground.

What sustains us is the belief that ultimately good will triumph over evil. So, even in the midst of turmoil, joy can be ours, because we know that God is with us. That knowledge gives us strength to live through tragedy with our spirit unbroken.

Jesus spoke about the destruction of the Temple. This would have come as a shattering blow to any Jew. Our generation has seen enormous changes. It's not a building but a whole world that has passed away. The only thing that endures is God's faithfulness, The only thing that does not change is God's love for us.

Faith is not a way of wishing that things were different. No one is helped by denial. Faith gives us the strength to cope with reality as it is. God does not spare us pain, but rescues us from despair.

HOMILY 2   **Endurance**

Anne Frank was a teenage Jewish girl who lived in Amsterdam during the early years of World War II. When the Germans started rounding up all Jews, she and her family went into hiding. Seven people in all, they hid for two years in an attic. There they waited in daily fear of being discovered by the Nazis.

During that time Anne kept a diary, which her father found after the war ended. Translated into many languages, it has been read by millions of people. In it Anne expressed her thoughts and feelings with a maturity way beyond her years. In one remarkable passage she says:

It's twice as hard for us young people to hold our ground, in a time when all ideals are being shattered and destroyed, when people are showing their worst side, and do not know whether to believe in truth and right and God.

It's really a wonder that I haven't dropped all my ideals, because they seem so absurd and impossible to carry out. Yet I keep them, because in spite of everything I still believe that people are good at heart.

I see the world being turned into a wilderness, I hear the ever-approaching thunder, which will destroy us too, I can feel the sufferings of millions and yet, if I look up into the heavens, I think that it will all come right, that this cruelty too will end, and that peace and tranquillity will return again.

It's an amazing expression of faith and hope at a time of such upheaval. Anne never saw peace and tranquillity return. One day the dreaded knock came to the door. She and her family were taken to Belsen Concentration Camp where she died in 1944.

What is it that helps a person to endure? The rightness of one's cause gives one great strength. The example and support of others is also a great help. And then there is the best help of all, namely, faith. Faith gives one the conviction that goodness will triumph in the end, and that God will have the last say.

'A person with a grain of faith in God never loses hope, because he ever believes in the ultimate triumph of the truth.' (Gandhi)

In a world of so much social and political turmoil, people of faith will often be regarded as naive and ineffective and irrelevant. However, we must not be afraid of scepticism and cynicism, but trust that God will give us the strength to hold our ground.

Jesus said to his disciples, 'Do not be frightened.' One would not be human if one didn't feel fear when danger threatens. It's not fear but the

[353]

overcoming of fear that is the question. 'A person without fear is no hero; the person who overcomes fear is.' (Solzhenitsyn)

Jesus says: 'By your endurance you will gain your souls.'

Faith can only be proved in suffering and endurance. Jesus showed patience and endurance when he bore the cross. Endurance is something we all need. Endurance means to share in Christ's suffering. If we share in his suffering, we shall share in his glory.

HOMILY 3   **Sharing our powerlessness**

Jesus saw that Jerusalem was heading for destruction. He foresaw that the magnificent Temple would be reduced to a pile of rubble. To the ordinary Jew, it must have seemed impossible, even unthinkable. This was no ordinary building. The Temple symbolised the entire Jewish system of worship.

Jesus' prophecy came true to the letter. Jerusalem was destroyed by the Romans in the year 70 AD after a long siege. A million people were killed or died of starvation during the long siege. The Temple was burned to the ground.

Jesus dearly wanted to save Jerusalem, but was unable to do so. Once, with tears in his eyes, he said: 'Jerusalem, Jerusalem! I longed to gather your children to myself, as a hen gathers her chickens under her wings, but you refused.'

It's terrible to be at the bedside of a friend who is suffering or dying, and not be able to save him/her. We feel so inadequate. Often there is nothing we can say either. It's a comfort to know that Jesus shared our powerlessness. He felt like we do, and yet he didn't walk away. In cases like that, our only ministry is that of simple presence. Even though this is difficult, it is a precious and vital thing. Like Mary at the foot of the cross, we must stay with the suffering or dying person. A reassuring, supportive presence can mean the world to the sufferer.

Leonard Cheshire distinguished himself as a pilot during World War II. At the end of the war he left the RAF. He felt terrible about the war, and wanted to do something better with the rest of his life. Eventually he decided to dedicate his life to working for the disable. The first person to be sent to him was a man by the name of Arthur, who was dying of cancer. Cheshire felt totally inadequate, but decided to offer him the only thing he could, namely, companionship.

During the last months of Arthur's life a great bond developed between them. Arthur was in a lot of pain. The long nights were the loneliest time of all. When he got very ill, Cheshire put a mattress outside his bedroom door and slept there. He gave Arthur a little hand bell, which he could ring whenever he needed help.

The presence by his side of someone who cared deeply about him made the world of difference to Arthur, even though it did not take away his pain or hold back the advance of death. Though Arthur was a simple man he died with great dignity. A lapsed Catholic, during his last months he regained his faith, and acquired a serenity that made him an altogether different person from the one he had been up that time. Thanks to Arthur's example, Cheshire became a Catholic himself.

To know that there is someone there who cares, makes the world of difference to the sufferer. It saves him/her from the awful prospect of dying alone and abandoned.

No particular skills are needed for this kind of ministry. Just love. Those who truly love offer the sufferer incalculable strength, just by being there, by standing alongside. And in a world where selfishness is rampant, love is the best way of witnessing to Christ and to the Gospel.

PRAYER OF THE FAITHFUL

President: Let us pray that we may witness to Christ in a world marked by tragedy, violence and sorrow.

Response: Lord, hear our prayer.

Reader(s): For the followers of Christ: that they may not lose heart in times of trial and persecution. [Pause] Let us pray to the Lord.

For world leaders: that in spite of setbacks they may persevere in their efforts to bring about a just and peaceful world. [Pause] Let us pray to the Lord.

For those who are confused and lost, and who therefore are easy prey for false prophets. [Pause] Let us pray to the Lord.

For those who are terminally ill and for all those who care for them. [Pause] Let us pray to the Lord.

For grace that we may bear witness to Christ with lives of truth, honesty, and goodness. [Pause] Let us pray to the Lord.

For our own special needs. [Longer pause] Let us pray to the Lord.

President: God of love and mercy, in the midst of the uncertainties of this changing world, keep us secure in your love, and give us the peace this world cannot give. We ask this through Christ our Lord.

REFLECTION   **From failure up**

Can a man grow from the dead clod of failure
Some consoling flower
Something to wear as a buttonhole in Heaven?
Under the flat, flat grief of defeat maybe
Hope is a seed.
Maybe this is what he was born for, this hour
Of hopelessness

Maybe it is here he must search
In this hell of unfaith
Where no one has a purpose
Where the web of meaning is broken threads
And one man looks at another in fear.
O God, can a man find You when he lies with his face downwards
And his nose in the rubble that was his achievement?
Is the music playing behind the door of despair?
O God, give us purpose.
(From *The Complete Poems of Patrick Kavanagh*, 1984, Goldsmith Press).

Thirty-fourth Sunday of the Year
CHRIST THE KING

INTRODUCTION AND CONFITEOR

Today we honour Christ as our King. And we honour him best by helping to spread his Kingdom. Our sins are a blight on our service of Christ.
But Christ, who forgave the repentant thief, will forgive us too. Let us,
then, with confidence call to mind our need for forgiveness. [Pause]

Lord Jesus, you help us to spread your Kingdom by making peace
with others. Lord, have mercy.

You help us to spread your Kingdom by forgiving others. Christ, have
mercy.

Lord, you help us to spread your Kingdom by caring about others.
Lord, have mercy.

HEADINGS FOR READINGS

First Reading (2 Sam 5:1-3). e see how David became king of a united
country. His kingship prefigures the universal kingship of Christ.

Second Reading (Col 1:11-20). Christ is not only head of the Church but
Lord of all creation.

Gospel (Lk 23: 35-43). Christ reigned from the cross, and brought salvation to one of the thieves crucified with him.

SCRIPTURE NOTE

David had already been anointed King of Judah by his own people at
Hebron. Now we hear how the northern tribes also acknowledge him as
their king (First Reading). Thus David became king of a united country.
His kingship prefigured the universal kingship of Christ.

The Second Reading is essentially a liturgical hymn in praise of Christ.

The first part speaks of his role in creation; the second of his role in redemption. On this feast we acclaim Christ as head of the Church and ruler of the universe.

In the Gospel we see how the inscription over the cross, and all those who witnessed the crucifixion (the crowd, the rulers, the soldiers, and the thieves) unwittingly proclaim the true identity of Jesus. The irony is that the titles which are pronounced in mockery are true: Jesus is both Messiah and King.

HOMILY 1   **The thieves**

Let us consider the two thieves. First the unrepentant thief. He is a profoundly disturbing character. There was no sympathy, no pity, no humanity left in him. Even with death staring him in the face, he didn't show a trace of remorse.

Even Jesus couldn't reach him. No one can save the person who doesn't want to be saved. The sun can't shine behind closed curtains. God's forgiveness is there, but one has to have the disposition to receive it. 'He who is in a state of rebellion cannot receive grace.' (Oscar Wilde)

Now let us look at the repentant thief. Some may think that he got off very lightly. After a life of crime, he made a quick act of contrition, and went straight to heaven. At the very least, we would have expected him to do a stretch in purgatory.

Yet, when we think about it, what he did was a tremendous thing. Hanging there on the cross, he did a review of his life. And when he looked back what did he see? He saw a heap of rubble. He had wasted his life. A wasted opportunity is one thing. But a wasted life!

He might have made excuses or blamed others – his upbringing, his environment, his companions … But he didn't. In effect, what he said was: 'I am guilty. I am getting what I deserve.' He took full responsibility for the person he had become.

What a refreshing attitude. Today there is a disturbing tendency to take responsibility away from the individual. It is common to blame someone else. According to psychiatrists, our sins aren't really sins at all, but accidents set in motion by forces beyond our control.

To do what the thief did is never easy. Pride makes a person try to salvage something. And to do it in the atmosphere which prevailed on Calvary was greater still, given the jeering of the religious leaders, and the mocking of the soldiers and his comrade. Furthermore, it was now too late to do anything about it, too late to clear away the rubble and start to build again.

Still, his act of repentance, great though it was, would have availed him nothing if there was no one there who could help him. But Jesus, the friend of sinners, was there. The thief's clean and humble confession went straight to the heart of Jesus. It won for the thief, not only forgiveness, but heaven itself.

The good thief gives hope to us all, but especially to those who come to the end of life and have nothing that they can feel good about, nothing that they can be proud of in their lives. Even at the eleventh hour there exists the possibility of letting the sunlight in. As long as we breathe there is no final verdict on our lives. And that final verdict is up to God.

HOMILY 2   **Stumbling block or stepping stone**

Once, two travellers were going through a forest when night came upon them. In a matter of minutes, the narrow path which they had been following became invisible. In the darkness terror lurked everywhere. Then, to make matters worse, a violent thunderstorm broke over the forest. Terrifying flashes of lightning were followed by loud peals of thunder which shook the ground under their feet. Torrents of rain poured down on them. The trees swayed dangerously.

The first man looked on the storm as a calamity. Every time there was a flash of lightning, he looked up at the sky and cursed. The result was that he strayed from the path and got lost in the forest. The second man, however, looked on the storm as a blessing in disguise. Each flash of lightning lit up a little bit of the path ahead of him, and thus he was able to take a step forward. By keeping his head down, he succeeded in staying on the path. And so, a step at a time, he made his way out of the forest.

Sometimes that's the way it is in life: there is just enough light to be able to take the next step; just enough strength to do the present task.

The thunderstorm was the exact same for both travellers. Yet for one it proved to be a stumbling block, while for the other it proved to be a stepping stone.

The travellers remind us of the two thieves in the Gospel story. Both of them were caught up in a terrible darkness. First of all there was the darkness of their own lives of crime. Then there was the terrible darkness that descended on Calvary at the crucifixion of Jesus.

One of them cursed the darkness. The other saw a gleam of light through it. That light came from the presence of Jesus, Jesus the friend of sinners, who came to seek out and to save the lost. The thief's clean and humble confession went straight to the heart of Jesus. It won for the thief, not only forgiveness, but heaven itself.

In the end the only one who knows and understands us fully is God. He is the only biographer in whose accuracy we can absolutely trust because he alone sees what's in the heart. He sees our wounds and sorrows, our scars and handicaps, our hopes and longings. Jesus looked at the thief, and seeing the sad tatters of his life, was moved with compassion for him.

The good thief gives hope to us all, but especially to those who come to the end of life and have nothing to show but the works of darkness. Even at the eleventh hour there exists the possibility of letting the sunlight in. Through his sheer goodness, Jesus turns our darkness into light.

Salvation is always a gift from God. He gives it most freely to those who (like the good thief) know they are poor, and who ask for it with empty hands and expectant hearts.

OMILY 3   **Goodness evokes goodness**

Late one night in Dublin a nurse was hurrying along the quays to catch a bus when she saw a young man lying on the pavement ahead of her. He seemed to be sick or injured. She stopped to see if she could help him. But as she bent over him, he jumped up and grabbed hold of her handbag. She refused to let go. A struggle ensued. At some point their eyes met. Suddenly the young man let go and said, 'Oh, you're Nurse O'Reilly!'

They started to chat. It emerged that some time prior to this he had been in hospital with a broken leg, and Nurse O'Reilly had been very kind to him. He asked her where she was going. She told him that she was going to catch a certain bus. He walked her to the bus stop and waited until the bus arrived. Then apologising for what had happened, he bade her good-bye.

This is a true story. What does it teach us? Perhaps the main lesson is: One is never completely lost to evil as long as one can recognise goodness and respond to it.

Sometimes just to see the goodness radiating from another can be all one needs in order to rediscover it in oneself. A good memory saves certain characters in crucial moments. Empathy is what calls a human being back from the darkness.

Had it been any other woman coming along the quay that night, the young man would not have acted as he did. He would have robbed her, and felt no remorse in doing so. But because it was someone who he knew from personal experience was a good person, he could not find it in him to treat her badly. Her goodness made him see the evil he was doing. What's even more important: it made him aware of his own capacity for goodness. It evoked what little goodness was still alive in him.

This story reminds us a little of the encounter between Jesus and the thieves on Calvary. One of those thieves was so lost to the darkness of evil that he didn't want the light. The other recognised the light of Jesus' goodness, and responded to it.

The good thief recognised that Jesus was innocent. And what's more, he spoke up for him before his companion. He was the only one to bear witness to the innocence of Jesus. The goodness of Jesus made him see the wretchedness of his own life, but it also awakened his own lost goodness. He turned to Jesus, realising that he was the only one who could help him at this late moment in his life. And Jesus did not disappoint him.

Jesus is indeed a king, but a strange kind of king. He came not to conquer but to convert, not to dominate but to liberate, not to rule but to serve. He died as a criminal, yet reigned from the cross. He responded to the worst with what was best in him. Why didn't he hit back at his executioners? The poet, Seamus Heaney, talks about 'the power of power not exercised.'

All we can do is repeat what St Paul said: 'Thanks be to God, who has taken us out of the power of darkness, and transferred us to the kingdom of his beloved Son; in whom we gain our freedom, and the forgiveness of our sins.'

ANOTHER APPROACH

The story of what happened to the repentant thief on Calvary raises a very important question: Does one die the way one has lived? And the answer seems to be: Not necessarily. There have been people who have lived through a life of hell who have had a luminous death. Divine grace has nothing to do with merit.

A story

Mother Teresa told how one day in Calcutta she picked a man out of the gutter and brought him to the home for the dying. Before he died he said to her, 'I have lived like an animal but I'm dying like an angel, loved and cared for.' Mother Teresa remarked on the greatness of a man who could speak like that and who could die without blaming anyone or cursing anyone. She felt privileged to have been able to help him to live out his last hours feeling loved and cherished.

An illustration

The most beautiful sunsets are not those that occur when the sky is cloudless, but those that occur when there are some clouds in the sky. The clouds reflect the light of the setting sun and scatter it all across the sky, sometimes in a stunning variety of colours.

It was an August day in America. A strange day it was. During the morning there was thunder and lightning, and short bouts of heavy rain. During the afternoon it got hot and sticky. The evening was murky and miserable. Yet just when the curtain was about to come down on a wretched day, something beautiful occurred. There came one of the most beautiful sunsets one could wish to see. And so, that ugly August day ended in beauty.

It reminds us a little of what happened to the good thief on Calvary. The curtain was going down on his murky life of crime. Everything was dark and hopeless. But then a wonderful thing happened. Something inspired him to speak up for Jesus – the only one to do so on Calvary. Then he turned to Jesus and said, 'Jesus, remember me when you come into your kingdom.' And Jesus said, 'This day you will be with me in paradise.'

Suddenly the sky of his life was resplendent with beauty. It was Jesus who made the difference. Jesus transformed that dark and wretched scene by the light of his goodness. Whereas Zacchaeus was surprised by love, the thief was surprised by mercy.

The good thief had lived a bad life, yet thanks to his encounter with Jesus, he found love and peace and hope at the end. His story teaches us that there is no such a thing as too late. Christ the King can make even the darkest ending bright with hope. He can turn a desert into a garden, and dross into gold.

PRAYER OF THE FAITHFUL

President: Let us pray to our heavenly Father who has delivered us from the dominion of darkness and transferred us to the Kingdom of his beloved Son.

Response: May your Kingdom come.

Reader(s): For the Church: that its members may be messengers of Christ's love to the world. [Pause] Let us pray to the Lord.

For our political leaders: that they strive to build a just and peaceful society. [Pause] Let us pray to the Lord.

For those who do not acknowledge Christ as their Saviour and King: that they may discover him in his followers. [Pause] Let us pray to the Lord.

For those who are embarked on a life of crime. [Pause] Let us pray to the Lord.

For the abolition of the death penalty. [Pause] Let us pray to the Lord.

For grace that we may not be afraid to profess our faith in Christ before an indifferent and sometimes hostile world. [Pause] Let us pray to the Lord

For our own special needs. [Longer pause] Let us pray to the Lord.

President: God of power and love, may we do with loving hearts what you ask of us and come to share the life you promise in the Kingdom of your Son, who lives and reigns with you and the Holy Spirit, one God, for ever and ever.

REFLECTION   **The victory of love**

On the cross Jesus endured insults and mockery.
Yet his heart remained open, even to his enemies.

He absorbed all the violence, transformed it,
and returned it as love and forgiveness.
One's pain can so easily turn into rage,
so that one wants only to lash out blindly
at whoever happens to be within range.
From the depths of his own pain,
Jesus reached out to comfort the thief.
Some people are like sugar cane:
even when crushed in the mill, what they yield is sweetness.
Jesus stretches our capacity for compassion.
He challenges our idea of love.
Each of us has a great capacity for love.
The pity is that it often goes unused.
By our love people will know that we
are followers of Christ the King.

SOLEMNITIES

Jesus' Farewell to His Mother

PATRICK PYE

St Patrick's Day
17 MARCH

INTRODUCTION AND CONFITEOR

St Patrick brought us a wonderful gift - the gift of faith. St Patrick's faith was very much centred on Christ, and rightly so. Let us turn to the Lord now, asking him to strengthen the bonds we have with him and with one another because of our faith. [Pause]

Lord Jesus, you are the vine, we are the branches. Lord, have mercy.
You unite us to yourself. Christ, have mercy.
You make our lives fruitful. Lord, have mercy.

HEADINGS FOR READINGS

First Reading (Jer 1:4-9). This tells of the call of the prophet Jeremiah. Patrick had a lot in common with Jeremiah.

Second Reading (Acts 13:46-49). Paul decides to preach the Gospel to the Gentiles who receive it with enthusiasm. Patrick's preaching to the Irish met with a similar reception.

Gospel (Lk 10:1-12.17-20). The sending of Patrick to preach the Gospel to the Irish has its origin in Christ's sending out of seventy-two disciples to preach the Gospel to their contemporaries.

HOMILY   **New challenges for the faith**

They are very fortunate people who are born into a religious faith, and who, with the passage of the years, find this faith increasingly strong and sustaining. To possess a confident faith is a tremendous blessing.

But to possess such a faith is becoming more difficult in modern Ireland. In the past the climate was conducive to faith. The culture was basically Christian, and believers felt supported by that culture. It was as if the wind was at their backs. But this is no longer the case. Ireland is a changed place. We now live in a society that is largely secular. And with the steady influx of immigrants, Ireland is on the way to becoming a multicultural and a multi-racial society.

Furthermore, Ireland is now a prosperous country. At long last its citizens are able to find employment at home. In fact, we have the phenomenon of outsiders coming here in the hope of beginning a new life. There is much to be happy about in the new Ireland.

But many fear that in our new-found prosperity we are in danger of losing values we once treasured. In particular, we are in danger of abandoning the Christian inheritance that meant so much to us in the past.

All of these changes present great challenges for the Church. Ireland has always sought to bring the faith to other countries. The need now is to witness to Christianity within Ireland itself. The first thing is to keep the faith. But that is not enough. We have to grow in the faith. Faith grows when exercised and through regular nourishment. How do we nourish the faith? By prayer and contact with the believing community. The common faith of the community strengthens the faith of each individual.

At a time when many are abandoning the faith, it is all the more important that there are those who remain faithful so that Christianity may continue to be a leaven in Irish society. The need is for people who believe out of personal conviction.

The role of Christians is to bear witness to love in the midst of indifference, to tolerance in the midst of prejudice, to spirituality in the midst of rampant materialism, to light in the midst of darkness, and to hope in the midst of upheaval and death.

In preaching the Gospel to the Irish, St Patrick encountered much opposition and many dangers. Yet he remained faithful. What gave him strength was the conviction that God was with him. He said: 'I give thanks to God who kept me faithful.'

Patrick's life of fidelity is an inspiration to us. He shows us where our strength lies. It lies in the Lord. But we also need to confirm one another. Our presence at the Sunday Eucharist can make both of these things happen. It is easier to be faithful when one is a member of a supportive community.

The faith Patrick preached was positive and life-giving. It was also a faith that inspired sacrifice and service of others in those who embraced it. Genuine faith is always like that. It expands the possibilities of human love and courage.

Faith is the most important element in life. Only faith can answer the most profound questions of life. Let us pray that the lamp of faith Patrick lit may continue to illuminate this island, and that from here its light may go out like a beacon to make the world a brighter place.

PRAYER OF THE FAITHFUL

President: God showed his love for us by sending his servant Patrick to bring the faith to us. Let us pray that we may treasure the faith and experience joy in living it.

Response: Lord, graciously hear us.

Reader(s): For all Christians: that the faith they profess with their lips may bear fruit in their lives. [Pause]

For our political and civil leaders: that under God's guidance they may speak wisely and act justly. [Pause] Lord, hear us.

For Irish society: that it may guard against selfishness and materialism, and maintain generosity and hospitality towards the stranger. [Pause] Lord, hear us.

For peace and reconciliation in our country. [Pause] Lord, hear us.

For the spiritual and temporal well-being of our exiles. [Pause] Lord, hear us.

For our missionaries and aid-workers: that God may sustain them in their generosity. [Pause]

For all those who passed on the faith to us, and who are now deceased: that God may reward their faithfulness. [Pause] Let us pray to the Lord.

President: God of power and love, grant us in all our tasks your help, in all our doubts your guidance, in all our weaknesses your strength, in all our sorrows your consolation, and in all our dangers your protection. We ask this through Christ our Lord.

REFLECTION   **Beatitudes**

Blessed is the tree which puts down deep roots
– it shows us what we must do to withstand the storm.
Blessed is the seed which falls on good soil
and so produces a rich harvest
– it shows us what happens when we hear the word of God and act
  on it.
Blessed are the flowers of the field
– their beauty bears witness to God's prodigal artistry.
Blessed are the ubiquitous sparrows
– their carefree attitude to life gives us a lesson in trust in Providence.
Blessed is the sun which bestows its light and warmth on bad people
  as well as good, and the rain which falls without favour on all
  fields
– in them we see a reflection of God's indiscriminate love for his
  children.

The Assumption of the Blessed Virgin Mary
15 AUGUST

INTRODUCTION AND CONFITEOR

Today the Church honours the humble maid of Nazareth through whom the world received its Saviour. We rejoice that she shares in the glory of her Son in heaven. From heaven she watches over us. Let us now turn to God who, as Mary said, is rich in love and mercy. [Pause]

Lord Jesus, your mercy reaches from age to age. Lord, have mercy.
You fill the humble with good things. Christ, have mercy.
You raise up the lowly who trust in you. Lord, have mercy.

Vigil Mass

First Reading (1 Chron 15:3-4.15-16; 16:1-2). This shows the reverence with which the ark of the old covenant was regarded. Mary is seen as the ark of the new covenant.

Second Reading (I Cor 15:54-57). This celebrates Christ's victory over death, a victory in which Mary shares fully.

Gospel (Lk 11:27-28). Mary is blessed, not simply because she is the mother of Jesus, but because she heard the word of God and obeyed it.

Day Mass

First Reading (Rev 11:19;12:1-6.10). This describes the battle between God and evil, with the ultimate triumph of God. Mary and her Child were at the heart of that battle.

Second Reading (1 Cor 15:20-26). Christ is the new Adam who undoes the harm done by the old Adam. (The Church sees Mary as the new Eve who undoes the harm done by the old Eve.)

Gospel (Lk 1:39-56). Mary visits Elizabeth, and sings a hymn of praise to God for his goodness to her and to his chosen people.

SCRIPTURE NOTE

This note refers only to the reading from Revelations. The Book of Revelation describes the ultimate battle between God and evil, represented here by the dragon (the serpent of Genesis). The woman represents the Church, and the child represents Christ (the Messiah). Like the woman in the vision, the Church was undergoing suffering and persecution.

The dragon confronts the woman to devour her child. But the child is taken up to God – a reference to the ascension of Jesus. Jesus defeated the dragon and was exalted to God's right hand. The woman (the Church) flees to the desert to escape the persecution. There she is nourished by God, just as the Israelites of old. The final verse praises the triumph of God and Christ.

The reading was meant to encourage the early Christians by assuring them that God would finally triumph. It should assure us in the same way. Even though the figure of the woman in the first place represents the Church, it can also be seen as representing Mary. As the mother of Jesus, she was at the heart of the battle between God and the powers of evil. Therefore, it is entirely fitting that (through her assumption) she should share in the spoils of victory.

HOMILY 1   **Scripture Readings**

This homily is a reflection on the readings for the Day Mass.

First Reading: The Book of Revelation describes the ultimate battle between God and evil, represented here by the dragon (the serpent of Genesis). The woman represents the Church, and the child represents Christ (the Messiah). Like the woman in the vision, the Church was undergoing suffering and persecution. The final verse praises the triumph of God and Christ.

As the mother of the Saviour, Mary was at the heart of the battle between God and the powers of evil, which the reading from Revelation talks about. Therefore, it is entirely fitting that (through her assumption) she should share in the spoils of victory.

The reading from Revelation was meant to encourage the early Christians who were undergoing suffering and persecution. It was meant to assure them that God would finally triumph. It should also encourage us. God took special care of Mary. God will take care of us too. He won't save us from encountering evil, but will help us to overcome it.

Second Reading: Jesus is the new Adam, who, through his obedience, restored to us the gifts lost by the disobedience of the first Adam. The Church sees Mary as the new Eve who through her obedience to God, undoes the harm done by the disobedience of the first Eve.

At the annunciation Mary said, 'It's not what I want, but what God wants that matters. Let what God wants be done to me.' She accepted the task God gave her. Even though she didn't understand all the implications of it, she trusted that God would give her the help she needed.

Today many people seek fulfilment and happiness through 'doing their own thing'. They believe that happiness lies in having no commitments, no one to answer to. Mary is a great example for us, because life imposes a lot of duties on us – duties to ourselves, to others, and to God. Those who accept duty as Mary did, may not find happiness and fulfilment in the eyes of the world, but they certainly will find it in eyes of God. And deep down they will know it.

Gospel: After the Annunciation, Mary might have gone off and concentrated on herself. Instead, she went with haste to visit her cousin, Elizabeth, who also was expecting a child. Mary's visit meant a great deal to Elizabeth. But Mary too benefited from it. And that happens in every visitation. When we pay a visit to someone, we see ourselves as doing good to that person. And that is true. But we too benefit, if only by seeing how others cope with difficult situations.

Elizabeth spoke some lovely words of affirmation to Mary: 'Blessed is she who believed that the promise made to her by the Lord would be fulfilled.' The theme of the blessedness of those who believe is the central theme of the Gospel.

However, it is not simply a matter of believing, but of believing and acting on that belief. Mary is blessed, not simply because she believed, but because she acted on it. For her religion was not a matter of mere sentimentality. It was something to be converted into deeds.

Faith doesn't always make things easy. The opposite is more likely to be the case. It's because we have faith that we refuse to give up. Faith impels us to struggle on, often with no guarantee of a happy outcome. A person with faith never gives up.

Mary was the first and most perfect disciple of Jesus. This is why the Church proposes her as a model for us and why we honour her today. We too will be blessed if, like Mary, we hear the word of God and act on it.

HOMILY 2   **The battle against evil**

The Book of Revelation describes the ultimate battle between God and evil. The dragon represents the power of evil (the serpent of Genesis). The woman primarily represents the Church, and the child represents Christ (the Messiah).

The woman is in the throes of childbirth, a common image for the coming of a new age. The dragon approaches the woman with a view to devouring her child. But the child is taken up to God – a reference to the ascension of Jesus. Jesus defeated the dragon and was exalted to God's right hand. Meanwhile, the woman (the Church) flees to the desert, where she is nourished by God just like the Israelites of old. The final verse praises the triumph of God and Christ.

When this text was written, like the woman in the vision, the Church was undergoing suffering and persecution, and fled to the desert to escape. The reading was meant to encourage the early Christians by assuring them that God would finally triumph. It should encourage us also.

Even though 'the woman' primarily stands for the Church, it has always been linked to Mary. As the mother of the Messiah, she was at the heart of the battle between God and the powers of evil. Therefore, it is entirely fitting that (through her assumption) she should share in the victory of her son.

The image contained in the Apocalypse is not a pretty one. In truth, the idea of a ten-headed dragon waiting for the woman to give birth so as to devour her child is nothing short of horrific. We have to remember that the scene depicted here is highly symbolic. It enacts the drama foreshadowed in Genesis where enmity was placed between the Serpent and the Woman. The woman was involved in the struggle with the power of evil, symbolised by the dragon. But by the power of God the woman was victorious.

Most of our Marian statues portray Mary as a sweet little school girl, who seems untouched by the evil of the world, a far cry from the woman who faced the dragon and was victorious. Yet the latter image represents an important truth about Mary. Mary did face the dragon. She experienced the pangs of childbirth. No sooner had she given birth than she had to flee into Egypt because the tyrant, Herod, wanted to kill her child. Her soul was pierced with sorrow on Calvary as she saw life draining away from her Son. This is the story of Mary told in the Scriptures.

Just as Christ is the second Adam, so Mary is seen as the second Eve. But unlike the first Eve, she is obedient to God. Therefore, she is a beacon of hope for us because she escaped the clutches of the dragon and has been taken up into heaven. From there she helps us in our struggle against evil. Her victory gives us hope. Her intercession gives us confidence. Her example gives us courage and strengthen to continue the struggle.

There is a lot of pain, anguish, injustice, and violence in the world. All of us are touched by it. And we also have to struggle against sin. Then there is the last great evil which has to be overcome, namely, death.

Like Jesus, Mary absorbed all the violence, transformed it, and returned it as love and forgiveness. This is the victory of love over all the powers of destruction. There was nothing but love in her. It helps to think about that when we are going through hard times.

HOMILY 3   **Sharing in her Son's Glory**

In this feast we are celebrating Mary's assumption into heaven, where she shares fully in the glory attained by Jesus her Son at the right hand of the Father. All Mary's greatness comes from her relationship with Jesus. We cannot understand her or appreciate her role in the Church without keeping this in the forefront of our minds.

There is a story about a woman who was very interested in paintings. Adrienne was her name. One day in a small rural antique shop she came upon a small painting which she believed was a self-portrait by one of the great masters. Naturally, she was very excited at her discovery. Little did she know how much trouble it would bring her.

Having brought the painting home, she set about cleaning it. As she worked on it, she became more and more convinced that it was indeed an original, though naturally she had her moments of doubt.

Thinking that the nation's museums would be very interested to know about her discovery, she sent photos of the picture to the country's most distinguished authorities on art. Much to her surprise they weren't interested. Most of the experts didn't even bother to go to see the picture when it was displayed in a public gallery. The director of the National Gallery declared authoritively that it definitely was not an original.

But Adrienne didn't give up. She just tried harder. She had the picture X-rayed in a police laboratory, and under infra-red examination the master's initials came to light under the top layers of paint. She immediately sent off her findings to one of the experts. He displayed a polite interest but stuck to his former view that it was not an original.

Next she delved into history and unearthed more evidence which more or less proved beyond doubt that she was right. Eventually a celebration was held at the Academy of Arts to honour her. Without her efforts, perseverance and conviction the painting would never have come to light.

Jesus is a self-portrait of God. But it was through Mary that he came to birth among us. She cared for him during all the years he remained in the shadows, unknown and unrecognised. And when at last he emerged from those shadows and came out into public view, he did not meet with universal acclaim. Indeed, the religious establishment refused to believe in him. But Mary continued to believe in him and stood by him to the end.

God raised him from the dead, vindicating him, and putting his stamp of approval on all that he has stood for and lived for. Jesus was raised up to glory at God's right hand. Is it not right then that Mary should share in the spoils of his victory? That is exactly what we are celebrating today - the glorification of Mary, the humble maid of Nazareth.

Each of us is made in the image of God. As she did at Cana, Mary continues to intercede on our behalf. She helps us in our struggle to believe in our human and divine dignity, and to live a life that befits that dignity. And with her help, and the grace of God, we can hope to share in her glory and the glory of her Son in heaven.

PRAYER OF THE FAITHFUL

President: God has done great things for us in Christ his Son. Let us bring our needs before him with great trust and confidence.

Response: Lord, graciously hear us.

Reader(s): That all who believe in Jesus may grow in faith through the prayers of Mary. [Pause] Lord, hear us.

That all in positions of authority may seek to serve as Mary served. [Pause] Lord, hear us.

That all mothers may experience the power of Mary's intercession. [Pause] Lord, hear us.

That like Mary, we may hear the word of God and do it. [Pause] Lord, hear us.

That our own special needs may win God's favour. [Longer pause] Lord, hear us.

President: Lord, you looked on the lowliness of Mary, and raised her up in glory. Raise us up also to share with her in the fullness of that redemption won for us by your Son. We ask this through the same Christ, our Lord.

AFTER COMMUNION

Mary sang her song, the song of the poor and lowly who put their trust in God. We ought to be able to make our own Mary's great song. Let us recite it together: *recite the* Magnificat *with the congregation.*

Life's journey

For each of us life is a journey.
Birth is the beginning of this journey,
and death is not the end but the destination.
It is a journey that takes us from youth to age,
from innocence to awareness,
from foolishness to wisdom,
from weakness to strength and often back again,
from loneliness to friendship,
from pain to compassion,
from fear to faith,
from defeat to victory and from victory to defeat,
until, looking backward or ahead,
we see that victory does not lie at some high point along the way,
but in having made the journey, stage by stage.

(Adapted from an old Hebrew prayer).

Feast of All Saints

1 NOVEMBER

INTRODUCTION AND CONFITEOR

On this, the feast of All Saints, we honour in a special way the 'little' saints, that is, those who will never be officially canonised. Let us reflect for a moment on the fact that each of us is called to holiness. [Pause]

Lord Jesus, you call us to be poor in spirit and pure of heart. Lord, have mercy.

You call us to be gentle and merciful in our dealings with others. Christ, have mercy.

You call us to hunger and thirst after goodness and right living. Lord, have mercy.

HEADINGS FOR READINGS

First Reading (Rev 7:2-4.9-14). Here we have a vision of the victorious followers of Christ rejoicing in his presence in the heavenly Kingdom.

Second Reading (1 Jn 3:1-3). In his love for us God has made us his children, destined one day to see him as he is. We should live a life consistent with this great hope.

Gospel (Mt 5:1-12). Here Jesus talks about the qualities he wishes to see in his disciples, qualities that are exemplified in the lives of the saints.

HOMILY 1   **Becoming real**

There is a story about a little boy who got a present of a rabbit for Christmas. Not a real rabbit, but a stuffed one made of beautiful velvet. There wasn't a crease or wrinkle, a spot or a stain on the rabbit's shiny skin. The little boy was delighted when he found him in his stocking on Christmas morning. However, by the end of the day the rabbit had been cast aside.

For a long time the rabbit lived in a cupboard full of all kinds of toys. Some of these seemed far superior to him, especially the mechanical ones, who acted as if they were real. The rabbit felt lost and inadequate among all those fancy toys. The only one who was kind to him was the Skin Horse.

The wise old horse wasn't impressed by the mechanical toys. He saw how they were full of noise as long as the mainsprings lasted, but as soon as the springs gave way, they became utterly useless. The little rabbit then realised that they weren't real after all. But he still longed to be real. One day he asked the horse, 'What does it mean to be real?'

'Real isn't how you are made,' the horse replied. 'Real is something that happens to you. When someone loves you for a long time, not just for the use he gets out of you, but for yourself, then you become real.'

'Does it hurt to become real?' asked the rabbit.

'Sometimes it does, but it's a small price for becoming real.'

'Does it happen all at once or bit by bit?'

'It happens bit by bit. That's why it doesn't often happen to people who break easily. Generally, by the time you are real, most of your hair will have fallen out, your eyes will have grown dim, and your skin will be full of wrinkles. But these things don't matter, because when you become real you acquire another kind of beauty.'

On hearing this the rabbit longed even more ardently to become real. But the idea of growing worn and shabby made him sad. He only wished he could become real without any unpleasant things happening to him.

One night when the boy was going to sleep, his mother couldn't find his teddy bear so she gave him the rabbit instead. From that night on the boy kept the rabbit in his bed. At first the rabbit was very uncomfortable. But in time he grew to love it, especially when the boy was nice to him and talked to him before falling asleep. Time went by and he was very happy, so happy that he never noticed that his lovely velvet fur was growing shabbier, his tail was coming unsewn, and his bright eyes were full of scratches.

One night, unable to find the rabbit, the boy refused to go to sleep. His mother scolded him saying: 'But he's only a toy!' But he replied: 'He isn't just a toy. To me he is real.' On hearing this the little rabbit became very happy, for he knew that what the horse had said had come true at last. He was a toy no longer. He was real. The boy himself had said so. That night

[373]

he was almost too happy to sleep. When he did eventually fall asleep his dreams were sweeter than usual.

To become a saint is to become real. It means that the real person, which is often hidden under layers of foolishness and pretence, gradually emerges. The hidden goodness that God has placed in us is given expression. And it all starts with the realisation that God loves us just as we are.

The saints were people who believed the Good News of God's unconditional love, and who began to return his love, and found their lives changed, not overnight, but through a gradual process of growth which didn't rule out failures. In some cases it took a long time. A lot of corners had to be knocked off before they became real. We all want things to happen quickly, and without having to work for it. But it cannot be.

As this was happening to them, the saints discovered a tremendous joy and freedom. There can be no joy for us as long as the things we do are different from the things we believe in. And there is no freedom for us outside the will of God. When we do the will of God things hum sweetly. We become like an instrument that is being played properly.

HOMILY 2   **Saints are converted sinners**

Many people have a false idea of what a saint is. They think saints are people who never committed a sin in their entire lives; people who were always shining with virtue. But this is a fallacy. It implies that the saints were saints from the cradle onwards, that they were born saints.

The saints were made of the same human material as us, the same flawed material that might have become something else. They faced the same temptations as we do. They did not have things easier than us. They just struggled harder. The saint who resists temptation knows more about its power than the sinner who submits at the very onset of temptation. Saints become saints through the choices they make.

Every saint underwent a conversion. We see this in the lives of some of the greatest names in the Church's register of saints: Francis of Assisi, Ignatius of Loyola, Augustine of Hippo, Paul of Tarsus … Each of these at a certain moment in their lives heard and obeyed the words of Christ: 'Repent and believe the Good News.'

All the saints were converted from darkness to light, from selfishness to generosity, from sin to virtue. A conversion is not something that can be achieved overnight. Rather, it is the result of a long and painful struggle. This is why the saints, even the 'little' ones, are such a challenge to us. We cannot think about them without experiencing a call to conversion – a call to rethink our basic attitudes to life, to redefine our goals, to confront our sinfulness, and to throw ourselves open to God's love and mercy. The saints show us what we could be if we were willing to take the risk of total surrender to the love of God.

The saints serve as models for us precisely because they were sinners like the rest of us. But they were not overwhelmed by their sins or crippled by feelings of guilt and shame. They rejoiced in God's forgiveness, and with the help of his grace, succeeded in putting their sins behind them.

Today, few people relate to the plastic saints of perfectionism. We have to respect the dark side of human nature. To deny it is to drive it underground where it works hiddenly. Today we extol people who have tried to live fully rather than those who have withdrawn from life.

Today's feast is a celebration of the capabilities of human beings, of what God's grace has been able to achieved when human cooperation was forthcoming. It is good to be reminded that human beings have such a side especially in these days when it seems that only the most brutish side of humans is displayed in the newspapers and on television.

Holiness has been defined as loveliness of spirit. In each saint we get a glimpse of the mystery of our journey, our failings, and the need of grace and unconditional love.

HOMILY 3   **Hidden pillars of the universe**

There is a charming Jewish legend which says that the continued existence of the universe depends on the presence of thirty-six just people. No one knows who these are. They themselves do not know who they are. They are thought of as being uneducated and insignificant people, who perform humble tasks, and therefore pass unnoticed among their contemporaries. They will generally be found restoring the world to sanity by exaggerating whatever the world neglects. These thirty-six anonymous saints are the hidden pillars which uphold the universe. Without even one of them the universe would collapse.

Notice that the story talks about thirty-six *just* people, not thirty-six *holy* people. But, in biblical terms, to be called a just person is the greatest tribute that could be paid to anyone. It would be the equivalent of calling someone 'a walking saint' today.

What does it mean to be a just person? The just person is someone without falseness or deceit. The just person is honest, faithful, and reliable. The just person shuns evil and does good. The just person makes the Law of God the guiding force of his/her life. The biblical concept of holiness was summed up like this by the prophet Micah: 'This is what Yahweh asks of you, only this: That you act justly, love tenderly and walk humbly with your God' (6:8). Here is no sugary holiness. Here is a worldly holiness that modern people can relate to. People are made holy by doing what is right.

And Jesus summed it up in the beatitudes. The things the beatitudes stand for are very beautiful and very precious – things such as peace, goodness, joy, love, gentleness, compassion, mercy, integrity … The beatitudes are the badges of a true disciple of Christ. They are the marks of a child of God. They make us rich in the sight of God.

If we met a saint in all probability we wouldn't be able to detect any outward signs of holiness. The real saints are hidden, and therefore go unnoticed. At the same time tradition allows that there may be certain moments when we get a sense of having encountered or glimpsed one of these just people. Such an encounter, or even just the possibility of it, can redeem a dark situation.

There are on earth those whose integrity, kindness, and generosity make up for the greed and selfishness of others. The Church instituted this feast to recognise these and to celebrate their goodness. The lives of many people are littered with great sacrifices and acts of quiet heroism. Even the little saints cause the vision of a higher and a purer life to rise up before us. They enlarge our understanding of courage and love. When we look at them, we see human beings at their brightest and best.

A pioneer pilot said: Sometimes the storms and the fog will get you down. But think of all those who have been through it before you, and just tell yourself: 'They did it, so it can be done again.'

As well as inspiring us, the saints also help us. We feel their strength supporting us, and their standards and values are pointing in the direction we are to go. This great company of witnesses spurs us on to victory, to share their prize of everlasting glory.

ANOTHER STORY

The man had often passed the pond but never stopped until one day a beautiful water lily caught his eye. It lay on the surface, kept afloat by its large round leaves. Each of its petals was perfectly shaped. The petals were yellow at the outer edges, and deep orange towards the centre.

Since the pond was transparent, he was able to follow the lily's rope-like stem to were it disappeared into the mud at the bottom of the pond. It was then that it struck him. How come a creature of such rare beauty sprang from such murky origins?

But when he gazed into those muddy depths, he saw it wasn't all mud down there. He saw sand and stones down there. Still, it was a most unpromising cradle. Yet, under the gentle coaxing of the sun, the lily emerged from that cradle clean and fresh and fragrant.

That lily could be as an image of what a saint is. The saints spring from the same origins as ourselves. That is why they can serve as models for us. In the depths of the human heart there is mud – mud that has been part of us since the day of our conception. To what depths of evil people can sink. However, deep within us there is also good soil, clean sand, and solid rock.

The saints show us what human beings are capable of. They show us that good is more natural to us than evil. It is good to be reminded that human beings have such a potential. Holiness has been defined as loveliness of spirit.

PRAYER OF THE FAITHFUL

President: With the example of the saints to inspire us, let us pray for the things that will make us pleasing in the sight of God.

Response: Lord, hear us in your love.

Reader(s): For all Christians: that they may hunger after goodness and holiness of life. [Pause] We pray in faith.

For all holders of office: that they may be gentle and caring in the exercise of their authority. [Pause] We pray in faith.

For Christians who suffer for their faith, and for all who suffer in the cause of right and truth. [Pause] We pray in faith.

For those who are working for justice and peace. [Pause] We pray in faith.

For grace to see holiness as a call to live up to our dignity as children of God and followers of Christ. [Pause] We pray in faith.

For our own special needs. [Longer pause] We pray in faith.

President: Father, give us a love for what you command, and a longing for what you promise, so that amidst the changes of this world our hearts may be set on the world of lasting joy. We ask this through Christ our Lord.

REFLECTION   **Holding up a mirror**

There are people who have a steady flame
shining from deep inside them.
This flame is not extinguished
when others criticise or ignore them,
for it is not dependent on what others think of them;
it is what they think of themselves with a quiet certainty.
Each of us can behave in either of two ways:
we can behave like a sinner or a saint.
We help people more by giving them
a favourable image of themselves
than by constantly harping on their faults.
The saints hold up a mirror before us.
In this mirror we get a most favourable image of ourselves.
We see what we are capable of.
All we need is the will to walk
in the light of what we have seen.

The Immaculate Conception

8 DECEMBER

INTRODUCTION AND CONFITEOR

St Paul says, 'God has chosen us in Christ to be holy and spotless, and to live through love in his presence' (Second Reading). Today we celebrate the holiness of Mary. Right from the first moment of her existence she lived in the light. On the other hand, our souls are darkened by original sin and by personal sin. Let us call to mind the sins which darken our lives. [Pause]

Mary, our Mother, will intercede for us as we confess our sins and ask forgiveness of God and one another.

I confess to almighty God ...

HEADINGS FOR READINGS

First Reading (Gen 3:9-15.20). We look at the origin and consequences of sin, and at God's promise of salvation.

Second Reading (Eph 1:3-6.11-12). In Christ, God has adopted us as his children, and called us to holiness.

Gospel (Lk 1:26-38). In the story of the Annunciation, we see Mary's obedience to God, which opens the way for the coming of the Saviour.

SCRIPTURE NOTE

The First Reading tells the story of the origin and consequences of sin. Sin is essentially disobedience to God. The reading ends with God's promise of salvation. As we know, Mary had a major role to play in that salvation. That is why this reading is chosen for today's feast.

The Second Reading is a hymn of praise to God for the blessings he has given us in Christ. God has chosen us to live in holiness. Today we are celebrating the radical holiness of Mary.

In the story of the Annunciation (Gospel), we see how through her obedience to God Mary cancels the disobedience of Eve, thus opening the way for the coming of the Saviour. For her (and for us) holiness consists in doing the word of God.

HOMILY 1   **Mary, model of faith**

The theme of the blessedness and happiness of those who believe runs right through the Bible. It is the central theme of the Gospel. The chief purpose of Jesus' preaching was to elicit faith in people. Wonderful things happen for those who believe.

Abraham is the Old Testament model of the pilgrimage of faith. At the word of God he left home, family, country, and set out for a land he had never seen. The only compass he had was faith in God's promise. God blessed him and rewarded his faith by making him the father of a great people.

Mary is the New Testament model of faith. At the Annunciation she said 'Yes' to what God was asking of her. That 'yes' involved a leap of faith. She didn't know the implications of what she was agreeing to? She had no idea that at the birth of her son every door would be closed in her face. That shortly after his birth she would be a refugee in a foreign country. That some thirty-three years later she would see him executed as a criminal. Many times during her life she had to confirm that original Yes.

Mary's faith never wavered. Yet she wasn't afraid to ask questions. Faith is not blind. It is beyond reason but not against it. When she didn't understand something, she pondered in her heart until she did. Mary was the first person to receive the gift of faith in Jesus. Elizabeth declared her 'blessed'. And the cause of her blessedness was her faith: 'Blessed is she who believed that the promise made her by the Lord would be fulfilled.'

Faith fills our lives to the brim with things without which our lives would have no meaning. Still, to have faith is not to have all the answers. It doesn't mean all the work is done for us. The opposite would be nearer the truth.

Faith commits us to a life of searching. But at the end of the day, we have to bow to the mystery. We have to let God be God. .

And faith doesn't necessarily make life easy. It is not a magic wand. In fact, the opposite is more likely to be the case. It is because we have faith that we refuse to give up. Faith impels us to persevere, to struggle on.

However, biblical faith is not simply a matter of believing, but of believing and acting on that belief. It is a question of hearing the word and doing it – taking risks on it, and making sacrifices because of it.

Here Mary sets a great example. She is blessed because she not only believed but also acted on that belief: 'Let it be done to me according to thy word.' She was the first and most perfect disciple of Jesus. This is why the Church proposes her as a model for us.

Today we are celebrating the radical holiness of Mary. For her holiness consisted in hearing the word of God and doing it. We too will become holy if, like Mary, we hear the word of God and act on it.

HOMILY 2   **Glimpses**

In a novel we may be given only glimpses of a particular character. However, from these glimpses it may be possible to deduce quite a lot about the character in question. These glimpses are not there by chance. They have been deliberately put there by the author. And just because we only get glimpses of some character, doesn't necessarily mean the character is only a minor one and has only a minor role to play in the story.

Mary puts in only the occasional appearance in the Gospel story. But since these appearances are not chance ones, but have been deliberately put there by the evangelists, we can glean a lot from them. If we take them collectively we can build up a picture of the kind of person Mary was. And even though the resulting picture lacks detail, the core, the essence, is certainly there.

What we have in the New Testament is not a biography of Mary so much as an already well developed theology. But do we build a large building on a very narrow foundation? No. The little that is said about her is highly significant, not just scanty tit-bits of biography.

When we look at when those appearances occur, we notice that they are at crucial moments in the story. She appears at the start of it: it is she who conceives and gives birth to Jesus, and she is present at the beginning of his ministry (the wedding at Cana). And she is there at the end of it: she is present on Calvary, and at the launching of the Church at Pentecost. From this we can conclude that Mary had a central role to play in our salvation.

And from those glimpses, what can we conclude about the character of Mary? We can conclude that Mary was a loving and caring person. Every time we meet her in the Gospels we see the same thing. We see someone who was concerned about other people. Not only did the light of God's love illuminate her own life, but it shone out through her and illuminated the lives of all those around her.

When we say that Mary was conceived without original sin, what are we saying? We are saying that she was as holy as it is possible for a redeemed creature to be. But there can be no Christian holiness without love. Piety is no substitute for goodness. Perhaps there can be goodness without holiness. But there is no holiness without goodness. All of us have the capacity for goodness. In the final analysis, love is what matters. A loving person is a holy person.

HOMILY 3   **Mary's receptivity**

At a time of water shortage in her village, a woman went looking for a vessel with which to draw water from a distant well. But the first vessel she found was full of milk. The second was full of oil. The third was full of grain, and so it went. However, she eventually found an empty one. She cleaned it out, took it to the well, and returned with a bucket of clear, cool water which she willingly shared with all her neighbours.

In effect, the only vessel that was available to that woman was the empty one. The usefulness of a vessel lies in it hollowness or emptiness, that is, in its capacity to receive, to hold and to carry.

Mary's greatness consisted in her availability to God. Many are not available to God; they are too full of their own plans. No doubt, Mary too had her own plans for her life. Hence, she might have said to the angel, 'Sorry, but I have my own plans.' But what she said was, 'It's not what I want, but what God wants that matters. Let what God wants be done to me.'

Mary made a complete gift of herself to God, and accepted the task he gave her. Even though she didn't understand all the implications of it, she trusted that God would give her all the help she needed.

Some feminists tend to see Mary as too passive, not sufficiently belligerent and self-assertive. But Mary was receptive. That doesn't mean that she was completely passive in God's hands. After all, God didn't order her to become the mother of Jesus; God asked for her consent. In other words, she was a free agent. She didn't have to say 'yes'. She could have said 'no'.

Mary was not a weak woman. She was a strong woman. Strength is not the same as power. One could enjoy great power and yet be very weak. And one might have no power at all and yet be very strong. Like most mothers, Mary had great powers of endurance, and seemed always capable of renewing herself, no matter what misfortune hit her.

She knew what oppression was when she couldn't find a room in which to give birth to Jesus. She lived as a refugee in a strange land. She knew the pain of having a child who doesn't follow the accepted path. She knew the loneliness of the widow, and the agony of seeing her only son executed as a criminal.

Mary is truly a woman of our time. Women everywhere will find plenty that they can identify with in her life. She is the friend of all the poor and oppressed women of our times. She gives hope to those who struggle for justice, and challenges us all to live a simpler life, a life of unconditional trust in God.

Mary keeps the vocation of holiness before us, and serves as a model for us. She attained to holiness by obedience to God. She is blessed, not simply because she was the mother of Jesus, but because she heard the word of God and did it.

PRAYER OF THE FAITHFUL

President: As we honour the greatness of Mary, let us ask God to help us to imitate her holiness.

Response: Lord, hear us in your love.

Reader(s): That all Christians may experience the love of Mary, and draw inspiration from her obedience to God. [Pause] Let us pray in faith.

That in a world darkened by greed and selfishness all who hold public office may set an example of service. [Pause] Let us pray in faith.

That society and the Church may give women their rightful place and role. [Pause] Let us pray in faith.

That, like Mary, we may be concerned about the needs of those around us. [Pause] Let us pray in faith.

That our own special needs may reeive God's blessing. [Longer pause] Let us pray in faith.

President: Father, in your gentle mercy, guide our wayward hearts, for we know that, left to ourselves, we cannot do your will. We ask this through Christ our Lord.

REFLECTION   **Anchored in God**

We all need anchors in our lives
by way of true values and enduring truths.
But we need anchors other than principles.
We need relationships with other people.
People who have never known a close relationship
with another human being are anchorless.
They are at the mercy of the cold winds
of anguish and loneliness.
But the best anchor of all is the anchor of faith.
It means we have truths to believe in
and a Person to relate to, namely, God.
We can make our own the beautiful words of Mary:
'My soul proclaims the greatness of the Lord,
and my spirit rejoices in God my Saviour.
The Almighty has done great things for me.
Holy is his name.'